UNTOUCHABLE PASTS

SUNY Series in Hindu Studies
Wendy Doniger, editor

UNTOUCHABLE PASTS

Religion, Identity, and Power
among a Central Indian Community,
1780-1950

Saurabh Dube

State University of New York Press

Cover Photo: Satnami mother and daughter, circa 1898. Source: J. J. Lohr, *Bilder aus Chhattisgarh und den Central Provinzen Ostindiens* (1899).

Published by
State University of New York Press, Albany

© 1998 State University of New York

For information, address State University of New York Press
State University Plaza, Albany, NY 12246

Production by Dana Foote
Marketing by Nancy Farrell

Library of Congress Cataloging-in-Publication Data

Dube, Saurabh.
Untouchable pasts : religion, identity, and power among a central Indian community, 1780–1950 / Saurabh Dube.
p.   cm. — (SUNY series in Hindu studies)
Includes bibliographical references and index.
ISBN 0–7914–3687–X (alk. paper). — ISBN 0–7914–3688-8 (pbk. : alk. paper)
1. Satnāmīs—India—Chattīsagaṛh—History.   2. Chattīsagaṛh (India)—Social conditions.   3. Chattīsagaṛh (India)—Economic conditions.   4. Chattīsagaṛh (India)—Religious life and customs.
I. Title.   II. Series
DS432.S359D834   1998
954'.3—dc21   97–49929
CIP

10 9 8 7 6 5 4 3 2 1

S. C. Dube (1922–1996),
Anthropologist and Parent

Vespasia stood up and walked over toward the window. "I thought it was the question as to whether some men have the right to make mock of other men's gods, because they believe them to be either vicious or absurd—or simply irrelevant."

"One has the right to question them," Charlotte said with irritation. "One must, or there will be no progress of ideas, no reforming. The most senseless ideologies could be taught, and if we cannot challenge them, how are we to know whether they are good or evil? How can we test our ideas except by thinking—and talking."

"We cannot," Vespasia replied. "But there are many ways of doing it. And we must take responsibility for what we destroy, as well as for what we create."

—Ann Perry, *Highgate Rise: A Victorian Mystery Featuring Charlotte and Inspector Thomas Pitt*

CONTENTS

PREFACE

In March 1996, while doing field work on the evangelical encounter in central India, I traced the pathways of an indigenous catechist who had preached Christ in southwestern Chhattisgarh at the beginning of this century. Through a part of this journey, I carried the ashes of my father. S. C. Dube had begun his vocation as an anthropologist by conducting field work among an adivasi group in the region in the 1940s. Mapping the ragged routes traversed by a native soldier of Christ, I immersed my father's ashes in the Mahanadi, a river sacred to the adivasi peoples of the region. An imaginary cartography of everyday encounters of the past was conjoined with the consigning of an ethnographer's remains to the ebb and flow of time. The personal and the professional, the autobiographical and the anthropological, ethnography and time, history and the here and now, the preface and the book, never separate, actually bind each other in many different ways, a reminder also of the sometimes ironic but always evocative interplay between beginnings and ends. S. C. Dube had first encouraged me to work on the Satnamis of Chhattisgarh. This book is dedicated to him.

Rather more than an Indian history, *Untouchable Pasts* is an ethnographic history that works with South Asian materials, articulating a wider set of concerns. My effort in this book is to elaborate a third space beyond two dominant, competing conceptions. On the one hand, we need to question authoritative Eurocentric imaginings, to interrogate the aggressive self-representations of post-Enlightement traditions and Western modernities. After all, violence is not merely physical—epistemic violence is very much a part of our here and now, defining the murky worlds we inhabit. On the other hand, we also need to guard against adopting and reproducing the several facile strains of anti-Enlightenment rhetoric that are on offer today. To reify and romanticize traditions or communities is not only to construct a new nativism—it is also to mock the subjects we study, to pillory the peoples who form the basis of our interventions.

    The problem has deep roots. For very long now, mired as we have been in colonial, postcolonial, and Western modernities, our thinking has been governed by a crucial set of oppositions and antinomies. We have been conditioned in the academy and outside to separate dynamic and complex Western societies with history and modernity, on the one hand, and simple and sacral non-Western communities rooted in myth, ritual, and tradition, on the other. This mode of thinking is actually rather more persuasive and insidious than one (often wishfully) imagines: it extends from conservative think tanks, to left ideologues, to liberal thinkers, to radical NGOs, to contemporary primitivist and New Age alternatives. If one side celebrates modernity and Western reason, the other glorifies tradition and non-Western community. (Note that the different imaginings at work here render their chosen objects of desire in the capital case and in the singular, so that figuratively we are dealing with Modernity and Reason, Tradition and Community.) There is a single underlying logic: the two sides often mirror each other.

Here bloated images of a single modernity suppress envisionings of the several chequered and contradictory modernities that have defined our pasts and that continue to be a palpable presence; and reifications of tradition have little place for the ways in which traditions are continuously constructed (sometimes overnight), variously contested, and differentially elaborated in, through, and over time. These renderings also often overlook that traditions and modernities are products of the joint energies of superordinate and subordinate groups, creations of the pooled resources of the colonizers and colonized. But this is not all. The binary division between tradition and modernity both generates and is sustained by a series of other homologous oppositions that I have alluded to earlier, oppositions between myth and history, ritual and rationality, emotion and reason, magic and the modern, and indeed between those two fetishized concept metaphors of community and state.

It is important to think through these oppositions. An intervention in the politics of the past, the exercise may also hold suggestions for a politics of the possible. To return to the opposition between state and community, we must try to understand the various ways in which symbols of state(s) can often be drawn upon by communities to order legalities and construct pathologies. To lyrically portray communities and traditions as outside the realms of disciplinary imaginings and state power has its many charms, including as a (romantic, therefore powerful) challenge to statist imaginings. Yet, it obscures the many implications of reworkings of disciplinary imaginings and state power in the constitution of communities and the making of traditions. At the same time, we must guard against fetishizing the state as a mere panoply of institutions and policies, a concrete locus of abstract power. Rather, states also need to be explored as varieties of imaginings. In other words, states (and nations) are also states of mind as it were, the ways in which signs of nation and symbols of state are culturally reworked and imaginatively rendered by peoples and communities in their meaningful practice, constructions of creative cartographies defining spaces in time and places in history. To recognize this is to exceed, rather than to reify and fetishize, the ways in which states represent themselves, and to better understand the strategies of domination and the hegemonic sway of nations. Finally, to end this brief interrogation of overarching oppositions that hold sway in the academy in Western and non-Western contexts, I suggest that there is much to be gained by stepping outside the boundaries of binaries between magic and the modern and between reason and emotion. For by doing so we consciously confront the spectacular and the silent magic of modernities—consider the many enchantments of the dance of commodities in a supermarket or on a high street—and the various ways in which emotions form modes of reasoning within embedded practice, including the grounding of social practices in various constructions of personhood, the frames of reference and contexts of meaning through which they are apprehended and elaborated. Having learned much from studies with various analytical concerns but a mutual critical sensibility, studies that range across numerous cultures in different continents, *Untouchable Pasts* takes a small step in dismantling some of the grand oppositions that articulate traditions and modernities.

There is another sense too in which *Untouchable Pasts* is an ethnographic history that works with South Asian materials. Recently, a sensitive ethnographic account of the gendered watching of television soap operas in New Delhi, suggested that its author had decided to study the media in urban India because of her larger dissatisfaction with the body of anthropological knowledge on South Asia, a corpus that tends to organize itself around marks of radical otherness such as caste in village India. Yet, the problem is perhaps less with what is studied, and rather more with how we cast our enquiries, the ways in which we write. Recognizing that ethnographic and historical accounts of South Asia, through their language and concepts, can construct analytical terrains that are separate unto themselves, I have tried to write *Untouchable Pasts* in a manner that issues of caste and untouchability, sect and kinship, myths and pasts are rendered here as part of a wider dynamic between religion and power, gender and community, writing and the constitution of traditions, ritual and the making of modernities, and orality and the construction of histories.

Untouchable Pasts was written in Cambridge, Shimla, and Mexico City, and I would like to thank Churchill College, the Indian Institute of Advanced Study, and El Colegio de Mexico for being such splendid places in which to work. The archival research and field work on which this book is based have been spread somewhat further. In archives, repositories, and libraries, for their help and advice I thank: Dr. Lionel Carter of the Centre of South Asian Studies, Cambridge; Dr. Lowell Zuck of the Eden Archives, St. Louis; and the staff of the District and Sessions Court Record Room, Raipur; the

Preface

Madhya Pradesh Secretariat Record Room, Bhopal; the Madhya Pradesh State Archives, Bhopal; the Madhya Pradesh Record Office, Nagpur; the Nehru Memorial Museum and Library, New Delhi; the India Office Library and Records, London; the National Archives of India, New Delhi; the Bilaspur Collectorate Record Room, Bilaspur; the Library of the Royal Asiatic Society, London; the University Library, Cambridge; the Divinity School Library, Harvard; and the Sunderlal Sharma Library, Raipur. In the field, Shambhu, Sitaram, and Uttara were friends who helped in different ways. In various villages, several Satnamis (and members of other castes) welcomed, ridiculed, and (sometimes) abused me: it was their hospitality that was always overwhelming. The archival and field work in India, England, and the United States was made possible by financial support from the Association of Commonwealth Universities, London, and from the Smuts Memorial Fund, the Worts Travelling Scholar's Fund, the Bethune-Baker Fund, the Lightfoot Grant, the Cambridge Historical Society, the Maitland Memorial Fund, and Churchill College, all at Cambridge. A research award (Gr. 5603) from the Wenner Gren Foundation for Anthropological Research, New York, for a project on the evangelical encounter in central India also made possible further clarifications in the archive and the field in the United States and Chhattisgarh in 1993, 1994, and 1996.

I am grateful to the following holders of copyright for permission to reprint parts of my previously published pieces in this book: Oxford University Press for "Myths, symbols and community: Satnampanth of Chhattisgarh," in Partha Chatterjee and Gyan Pandey (eds.), *Subaltern Studies VII: Writings on South Asian History and Society* (Delhi: OUP, 1992), 121–56; the Indian Institute of Advanced Study for "Caste and sect in village life: Satnamis of Chhattisgarh 1900–1950," *Occasional Paper 5, Socio-Religious Movements and Cultural Networks in Indian Civilization* (Shimla: IIAS, 1993); the Indian Economic and Social History Association for "Idioms of authority and engendered agendas: The Satnami Mahasabha, Chhattisgarh, 1925–50," *The Indian Economic and Social History Review*, 30 (1993), 383–411; and *Modern Asian Studies*, Cambridge University Press for "Paternalism and freedom: The evangelical encounter in colonial Chhattisgarh, central India," *Modern Asian Studies*, 29 (1995), 171–201.

Untouchable Pasts owes much to the interaction, in different places, with scholars associated with *Subaltern Studies*: Shahid Amin, David Arnold, Gautam Bhadra, Dipesh Chakrabarty, Partha Chatterjee, Ranajit Guha, David Hardiman, Gyan Pandey, Sumit Sarkar, and Ajay Skaria. The work acquired shape in different contexts, various arenas, and there are many who influenced this process in several, important ways. In Cambridge: Crispin Bates (who was around in Bhopal too), Chris Bayly, Susan Bayly, Gordon Johnson, David Ludden, Javed Majeed, Rosalind O'Hanlon, T. N.

Pandey, and Chris Pinney. In Delhi: David Baker, G. Balachandran, Robi Chatterjee, Veena Das, Nick Dirks (though our meeting in Calcutta was longer), P. S. Dwivedi, Ravindran Gopinath, Ram Guha (whose meticulous reading of an early version of the manuscript helped me enormously), Sumit Guha, Ravinder Kumar, Ashis Nandy, M. N. Pannini, Rowena Robinson, Satish Saberwal, Tanika Sarkar, Minnie Sinha, and Sanjay Subrahmanyam. In Shimla: Javed Alam, J. S. Grewal, Mrinal Miri, D. R. Nagaraj, and Chetan Singh. In Chicago and New York: Talal Asad, Bernard Cohn, John Comaroff, Joan Mencher, and Milind Wakankar. In Mexico: Andres Lira, Jose Rabasa, and V. Y. Mudimbe. Two anonymous readers for the State University of New York Press have greatly aided the project with their sensitive comments, and I am not sure if I would like to exorcize the memory of "Reader A" and "Reader B" from our everyday arrangements. I also thank the many other people whose contributions have not been formally acknowledged here, particularly the participants in talks and conferences in Bogota, Calcutta, Cambridge, Chicago, Delhi, Havana, Heidelberg, Lisbon, London, Madison (Wisconsin), Mexico City, New York, Santa Cruz, Shimla, and Viña del Mar (Chile) where parts of this work have been presented, and the students in my seminars at El Colegio de Mexico. Finally, Mukul Dube first saw to it that I read History, Gitasree and S. P. Banerjee have cheerfully coped with a son-in-law who has little more than his writings to offer them, and several friends have made life better. These include: Marigold Acland, Flora Botton (who has also kept us supplied with the complete works of Tony Hillerman and Sara Paretsky, among other fine authors of murder and detection), Pilar Camacho, Charu Chakravarty, Maina Chawla, Elisabetta Corsi and Guido de Biase, Dermot Dix and Chandana Mathur, Papiya Ghosh, Shirish Jain, Martand Khosla (and Kalpana Sahni and Romi Khosla too), Patricio Nelson, Paritosh Kumar, Mihir Pandey, Nalin Pant and Lekha Nair, Sheela and Bhisham Sahni, Amit and Anshu Tandon, and Bhavani and Venkat.

At the end, I move even closer home, where the (largely fictional) domains of the private and the public were straddled. David Lorenzen nurtured this project in its later life, particularly when I thought all was lost. S. C. Dube and Leela Dube told me not to be silly when flights of fancy overtook me, and directed me back to ethnography and history, both of them also undertaking field work to bolster my fledgling efforts. Ishita Banerjee Dube has defined so much of the art of the possible, from translating sources from the German, to coping with (my) lamentable lapses, to keeping the world in place.

Mexico City,
25 February 1997

ABBREVIATIONS

AD	Agriculture Department
ARM	Annual Reports of Missionaries
BRP	Baba Ramchandra Papers
CI	Commerce and Industry
CPG	Central Provinces Government
CPPBECR	*Central Provinces Provincial Banking Enquiry Committee Report*
DDM	*Der Deutsche Missionsfreund*
EAL	Eden Archives and Library, Webster Groves, Missouri
FS	Folder on Satnamis
GAD	General Administration Department
IOL	India Office Library, London
JASB	*Journal of the Asiatic Society of Bengal*
LRS	*Report on the Land Revenue Settlement*
MPDP	M. P. Davis Papers, Webster Groves, Missouri
MPRO	Madhya Pradesh Record Office, Nagpur
MPSRR	Madhya Pradesh Secretariat Record Room, Bhopal
NAI	National Archives of India, New Delhi
NMML	Nehru Memorial Museum and Library, New Delhi
NRSR	Nagpur Residency and Secretariat Records
PW	Prosecution Witness
QRM	Quarterly Reports of Missionaries
SSD	Survey and Settlement Department

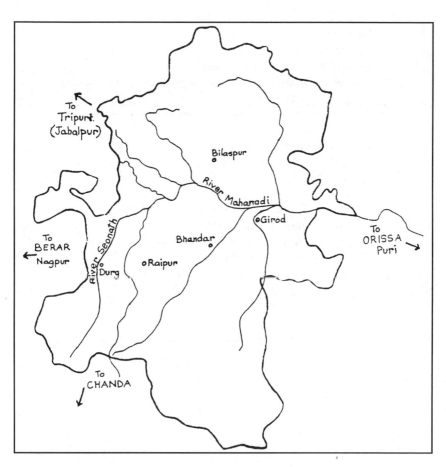

Map of Chhattisgarh: Main Towns and Satnami Centers

CHAPTER ONE

Introduction

In the early nineteenth century, around 1820, a farm servant named Ghasidas initiated a new sect primarily among the Chamars (traditionally, leather workers) of Chhattisgarh, a large linguistic and cultural region in central India. Ghasidas was born into a family of Chamar farm servants in the late eighteenth century, possibly in the 1770s, in Girod in the northeast of Raipur district. The Chamars constituted a significant proportion—a little less than one sixth—of the population of Chhattisgarh. The members of the untouchable group either worked on their own land or were sharecroppers and farm servants; but the ritual association of the community with hides, leather, and carrion meant that collectively it carried the stigma of the death pollution of the sacred cow. The close connections between divine, social, and ritual hierarchies located the Chamars at the margins of the caste order, and excluded them from Hindu temples. Ghasidas is believed to have thrown the idols of the gods and goddesses of the Hindu pantheon onto a rubbish heap. The rejection of these deities and the authority of Brahman specialists of the sacred, of temples and the Hindu *puja* (worship) offered in them was accompanied by the call to believe only in a formless god, *satnam* (true name). The new sect was called Satnampanth and its members, Satnamis.

There were to be no distinctions of caste between Chamars and a few hundred members of other castes within Satnampanth. The Satnamis had to abstain from meat, liquor, tobacco, certain vegetables—tomatoes, chilies, aubergines—and red pulses. They were prohibited the use of cows, as opposed to bullocks, in any of their agricultural operations and from ploughing after the midday meal. With Ghasidas began a guru *parampara* (tradition), which was hereditary. By the middle of the nineteenth century the Satnamis had fashioned an organizational hierarchy and developed a stock of myths, rituals, and practices that were associated in the main with the gurus and challenged the tenor of ritual power, upper-caste domination, and colonial authority in the region. Over the next hundred years the Satnamis coped within transformations in the agrarian social structure and the changing relations of power in the region, negotiated different efforts to regulate the internally differentiated community, and drew upon symbols of authority to question and contest their subordination. The community, which has combined the features of a caste and a sect, continues to be a significant presence in Chhattisgarh.

Analytical Overtures

This book constructs a history of the Satnamis, but it does not present the past as a mere unfolding of a chronologically sequential set of events. My story of Satnami endeavors, encounters, and experiences, with its inevitable subplots, is an interpretive exercise, an exercise in which the perspectives of history and anthropology are each inseparably bound to the other, where archival and nonofficial sources are read in an ethnographic mode and field work is cast as an engagement with the historical imagination. The account addresses a clutch of theoretical issues, a range of key and inextricably bound relationships between sect and caste, religion and power, myth and history, orality and writing, gender and order, community and hegemony, reform and authority, and resistance and domination. The arguments are woven into the larger tale, involving a dialogue between history and ethnography and an interplay of archival and field work.

Indeed, the book attempts to bring together the perspectives and possibilities defined by three overlapping but distinct theoretical developments that have all been elaborated in recent years: first, novel renderings of anthropologies and ethnographies of the historical imagination; second, critical constructions of histories from below, particularly by the collective *Subaltern Studies* endeavor; and, finally, a conceptual emphasis on the "everyday" as an arena for the production, negotiation, transaction, and contestation of meanings, often in a "local" and quotidian key, within wider networks and relationships of power.[1] By casting these analytical tendencies in an implicit critical dialogue with one another, my account works toward questioning some of those overarching oppositions—for example, between ritual and rationality, myth and history, tradition and modernity, and community and state—that have formed the conceptual core of several of our inherited traditions of social and political theory within the academy in both Western and non-Western contexts. Far from the fashioning of a new nativism, the challenge to such grand oppositions—and the teleologies and determinations they engender—is actually a mode of resisting conceptual schemes that obfuscate the many imaginative pathways of human practice. There are many ragged but meaningful bridle paths of the past, and this book highlights the distinct perspectives and the practice (but also the problems and the predicaments) of ethnographic history, an interpretive endeavor that still remains a somewhat fledgling enterprise in the South Asian context.[2]

A key emphasis in this endeavor, it seems to me, consists of writing against the grain of those *ur* blueprints of history and meaning, often (but by no means solely) derived from Eurocentric imaginings, which specify the trajectories of the past and the present across cultures by orchestrating particular historical and ethnographic cases, cases that are in turn cast as irremediably narrow illustrative material whose entire purpose is to fit into and elaborate a predetermined larger pattern, grist to the mill of overarching theoretical frameworks. Moreover, an abiding irony reigns here, for even those "alternative" writings which range themselves against teleologies and "foundational" histories are not entirely immune to the seductive charms of a motor of grand theory running specific historical and ethnographic cases, and critiques of Eurocentric imaginings often run the danger of reproducing the givenness of categories derived from the very frameworks they set out to question.[3] Clearly, this is not a plea for the eschewing of theory. Rather, it is a call against the rendering of theory in the capital case that only paves the way for its further aggrandizement. A sustained mutual dialogue and the play of concept (and categories) with evidence (and the empirical), where the domain of facts and information is simultaneously bound to the less conscious realm of popular imaginations, theory needs to be interwoven into narrative as a critical interpretive act, a crucial aspect of the telling power of tales, in elaborations of ethnographic histories.

This brings up the question of the place of the "particular" in our ethnographies, histories, and ethnographic histories. Here, let me rehearse a passage by Michel de Certeau that evokes this issue, a statement whose wide resonances run throughout my work.

> For what I really wish to work out is a *science of singularity*, that is to say, a science of the relationship that links everyday pursuits to particular circumstances. And only in the *local* network of labor and recreation can one grasp how, within a grid of socio-economic constraints, these pursuits unfailingly estab-

lish relational tactics (a struggle for life), artistic creations (an aesthetic), and autonomous initiatives (an ethic). The characteristically subtle logic of these "ordinary" activities comes to light only in the details.[4]

In this book on the Satnamis, a critical reading of the "singularity" and the "details" of a particular historical and ethnographic case and the wider analytical implications and theoretical import of the study are not artificially separated one from the other. Rather, they are rendered as inseparable domains, which mutually fashion each other. This Introduction does not cast matters on a resolutely grand theoretical scale, characteristic of writings that turn theory into a touchstone of truth, but takes the path followed by the rest of the book.

Meanings and Margins of Hinduism

For long years now the very categories of "Hinduism" and "Hindu" have been variously debated, dissected, and defended by students of religion(s), historians, and anthropologists.[5] More recently, scholars of different persuasions from one another have taken up matters of philology, etymology, and taxonomy to argue that the category of Hinduism, and to a greater or lesser extent the realities it encodes, is a nineteenth-century creation of colonial imaginings.[6] As for the term *Hindu*, although of a much older vintage than *Hinduism*, it had originally an ethnogeographical reference (the people of the lands around and beyond the river Indus) that was retained in the form in which it entered the English language in the seventeenth century, and it was only gradually that Hindu came to mean someone who was indigenous to India but was not a Muslim (or a Christian).[7] *Hindu* as a term, the argument proceeds further, also seems to have been barely used by the people whose religious affiliation it purported to describe, since the very homogeneity of the category ran counter to the fabric of the "interpenetration and overlapping of communal identities," characteristic of the "highly localized" nature of religious formations in India, that continued well into the nineteenth century.[8] Thus, it was only in the nineteenth century that the categories of Hinduism and Hindu, in conjunction with each other, came to clearly specify an Indian's religious affiliation, and this involved a twin birth but a single conception, a conception that was largely Christian but far from immaculate because of its colonial implications. Indeed, the picture was complete when the English-educated, often middle-class, social reformers and nationalists in nineteenth-century India responded to such Western appraisals of Indian religions by undertaking a series of different steps toward constructing their vision and practice of Hindu and Hinduism, blueprints that often tended to fashion homogeneous meanings and to reproduce the significance of colonial categories in their very articulation of difference from the West.[9] (Significantly, these blueprints came to be elaborated alongside the measures constructed by the imperial government with regard to religious communities.)

On the other side, historians, anthropologists, and scholars of religion have emphasized (in both implicit and explicit ways) that, philological and etymological issues notwithstanding, far too much is "currently [being] made of the colonial construction of caste and religious categories and too little of the precolonial basis for these categories, on which the colonial state had its impact."[10] In brief, precolonial India was not devoid of supralocal identities, and these historically constructed identities, from the twelfth century onward, involved different renderings of a Hindu "self" and various constructions of a Muslim "other" in wider contexts of processes of state formation, the development of a royal cult of the god-king Ram as a political theology, and the fashioning of discursive, linguistic, and popular-devotional communities in several significant parts of the subcontinent.[11]

Taken together, these emphases suggest both the need to question the givenness of the categories of Hindu and Hinduism and the necessity to explore the ways in which the relationships and arrangements that came to be named and ordered by these categories had a basis in precolonial India. Yet the very design of this debate also involves a somewhat single preoccupation with the "origins" of categories, and a casting of the definitions of Hindu and Hinduism rather exclusively in relation to other religions. One of the ways of going beyond the terms of the debate at hand is to explore the diversities, differences, and discontinuities in the production of the many meanings of Hinduism, the construction of multiple Hindu identities as a negotiated and contested resource, particularly by groups and communities who stood on the margins of these religious categories.

Indeed, it is these margins, rendered here as a history of the Satnamis, that provide an important filter to examine the constitution of the meanings of Hinduism and the articulations of Hindu identities—fashionings and elaborations not merely of these words themselves, but of the wider structure of the lived beliefs and practices to which they refer—over the nineteenth and twentieth centuries. For when I write of Hindu and Hinduism in these pages, I allude to patterns and arrangements of lived religious meanings and practices, the everyday transactions of the different members and groups within the sacred universe of an Indic religion, where the social, ritual, and cosmic domains have been integrally bound one to the other. Indeed, a crucial aspect of these transactions of meanings and practices concerns the several elaborations, negotiations, and contestations of the intermeshing of divine, ritual, and social hierarchies, which have been cen-

tral to Hinduism.[12] I need to add here that mine is not a call for the jettison-
ing of sacred texts in constructing our understanding of Hindu religion,
rather it is an argument for exploring the practices that underlie the construction, dissemination, apprehension, and appropriation of these texts,
an emphasis that reveals processes of the canonization and of the radical
reworkings of textual traditions by historically and politically situated interpretive communities within Hinduism. To be sure, this is neither a fool-
proof nor an exclusive definition of the categories in question, but in highlighting the issues of what Fuller has called "hierarchical inequality" and the
"partial continuity between humanity and divinity"—both matters inflected
by power—it foregrounds two interconnected aspects that are central to
lived Hinduism.[13] In a related move, my emphasis on practices, processes,
and power in our historical and ethnographic understanding of Hinduism
allows us to treat it as a religion that has been variously constructed and
contested in, through, and over time. Finally, my endorsement of the perspectives of margins, a history of an untouchable community, in discussing
the historically constituted meanings of Hinduism and Hindu identities
permits us to explore these issues as part of a wider dynamic between religion and power.

　　Clearly, religion is not treated here as a hermetically sealed-off domain of the sacred, a static repository of timeless traditions. Instead, it is
understood as an inherently historical set of signifying beliefs and practices
whose meaningful constructions—and active refiguring of perceptions—of
the social world are at once tied to processes of domination and to strategies
of resistance to authority. It follows that the processual character and the
simultaneously symbolic and substantive nature of religion are closely
linked to wider transformations in culture and society. Power in turn extends far beyond the exercise of authority grounded solely in control over
political and economic resources to include manifest and diffuse processes
of domination, hegemony, and control—cultural schemes, disciplinary re-
gimes, and discursive practices—which inform everyday social relationships
structured by the interlocking of different principles of social division. Now,
if these inclusive working definitions set the stage for a discussion of the
complex dynamic between religion and power among the Satnamis, there
are important issues at stake here. This dynamic reveals the negotiated and
interrogated, reworked and contested meanings of Hinduism and Hindu
identities—powerful resources in the subterranean and self-conscious simu-
lations of Satnami strategies and struggles—over the nineteenth and twentieth centuries. To take but two examples here. We explore issues of the formation and elaboration of Satnampanth, a subaltern religious endeavor
that fashioned its distinct identity by questioning the ritual power embedded within caste and by constructing "otherness" within the Hindu social

order in the nineteenth century. Equally, a little later in the account, we also discuss novel renderings of Hindu identities by the Satnamis under the regime of caste associations, within the wider context of culturally constituted understandings of Hinduism by nationalists and social reformers, understandings that were elaborated alongside measures constructed by the colonial government in relation to religious communities between the 1920s and 1940s. Indeed, the perspectives drawn from untouchable pasts, the meanings gleaned from margins, raise several important questions for central themes in South Asian history and ethnography. It is to these critical issues and key problems that I now turn.

Formative Issues: Rethinking Sect, Caste, Power, Contest

The formation of Satnampanth was informed by the wider context of Maratha rule (1742–1854) in Chhattisgarh, and my analysis of the early making of this religious endeavor locates it within the broader processes of state formation and revenue practices in the region. In fact, my arguments here constitute a part of a larger analytical endeavor, an attempt to attend to the changes and continuities in the domain of political economy while elaborating the fluid but constant interplay between cultural schemes, social relationships, religious meanings, and ritual power. Turning to the issue at hand, during the past few years nuanced historical accounts of economic and social institutions and processes in Maratha polities have revised our understanding of the eighteenth and early nineteenth centuries in India. The somewhat crude sketch of Maratha rule as a predatory empire of the saddle has been replaced by a more finely drawn picture that shows significant continuities between the Mughals and the Marathas, an expansion in cultivation in Maratha territories, and the crucial place of local expectations and resistance in the shaping of Maratha administration.[14] Chhattisgarh as a frontier province within the Maratha dominions shared features of this wider picture. The region also had its own peculiarities. The administrative measures of British superintendents—who governed Chhattisgarh between 1818 and 1830 when the Bhonsle raja Raghoji III was a minor—compounded these complexities. Satnampanth was a response to cultural and economic processes that had a contradictory dimension for the Chamars in the region. These processes allowed members of the group to establish their own villages and thereby to negotiate and partly escape the authority of upper-caste officials. But they also led to an increasing subordination and further marginalization of other Chamars in villages dominated by higher castes in the face of a growing rigidity of the norms of purity and pollution in the late eighteenth and early nineteenth centuries. My account of the formation of Satnampanth, while providing a filter to examine wider arguments about processes of continuity and change in the period at the frontier of Maratha polity and the East India Company's dominions, highlights the centrality of conflict and innovation in the arena of popular religious practices. It explores the symbolic construction of a subordinate religious initiative that carved for itself a distinct religious identity in relation to the ritual power of the social and divine hierarchies within the caste order in Chhattisgarh, an endeavor that worked toward reconstituting the ascribed untouchable status of Chamars by incorporating them as Satnamis.

Sect and caste generally tend to be conceived of as binary categories, a legacy of Louis Dumont's theory of asceticism in Hindu society that rests on a set of homologous oppositions between caste and sect, Brahman and renouncer, man-in-the-world and individual-outside-the-world, and householder and ascetic.[15] This influential model, based upon a Brahman householder's construction of renunciation and asceticism, ignores the fact that sects do not necessarily recognize the householder/renouncer opposition and adopt different approaches—from total rejection to varying forms of acceptance—toward rules of caste.[16] Now, these differences cannot be explained away through Dumont's physiological analogies of Brahmans "absorbing" renouncers and sects "degenerating" into castes.[17] Both, Richard Burghart's short but elegant formulation of the perspective of a set of nonhouseholding ascetics, the Ramanandis of Janakpur, who believed in caste rules of commensality within the sect, and Peter Van der Veer's detailed and sensitive account of the processes of "sedentarization," accompanied by a strong emphasis on the social origins of the ascetic, among the "open category" of renouncers of the Ramanandi monastic order of Ayodhya, provide a case in point here.[18] Indeed, Dumont's conception of caste and sect, householder and renouncer, ignores the perspectives of the ascetic and the non-twice-born caste.

Against the grain of Dumont's overarching oppositions, the career of Satnampanth, a sectarian formation that has elaborated the perspectives of a non-twice-born caste, underscores the importance of recognizing the diverse articulations and permeable boundaries of caste and sect, householder and ascetic in South Asian religious traditions. From the moment of its inception, at each step, Satnampanth has been governed by a logic avowedly committed to reconstituting the overwhelmingly untouchable caste status of its exclusively householder members. This has involved the forging of a particular set of relationships between principles of sect and caste within the subaltern religious endeavor. Thus, the symbolic constitution of Satnampanth as a sect in the first half of the nineteenth century involved both reworkings of the beliefs, symbols, and practices of popular sectarian traditions such as Kabirpanth that had posed alternatives to the hierarchies of caste and the appropriation of a set of focal signs from the ritual hierarchy of purity and pollution embedded within the caste order. At work here were two simultaneous movements: a rejection of Hindu gods and goddesses and of the *purohit* and *puja* within temples, involving an interrogation of the close connections between divine, ritual, and social hierarchies; and the creation of Satnampanth as a pure body through its accent on the appropriation of signs of ritual purity, which removed the impurities of the bodies of its members. It is hardly surprising that these seemingly contradictory moves worked together to question the ritual subordination of Satnamis, since the twin articulations were governed by a single logic that was made up of a fusion of the codes of caste and sect. As we shall see, to be and to become a member of Satnampanth involved both the initiation into a sect and the incorporation within a caste. Over the second half of the nineteenth century, the elaboration of an organizational hierarchy within Satnampanth, with the guru at its head, further clarified this pattern. Indeed, the fashioning of the figure of the Satnami guru constructed new meanings of asceticism: the guru, ever the householder, came to combine within himself the truth and purity of *satnam*—through a rejection of the integrally bound hierarchies closely connected to the Hindu pantheon and the creation of Satnampanth as a pure body—together with the attributes of a *raja admi* (kingly person)—derived from schemes of ritually fashioned kingship within the caste order—to become the living symbol of worship within the Satnami community. The guru and the Satnami organizational hierarchy enforced the norms and practices, an amalgamation of the principles of sect and caste, that maintained the boundaries of Satnampanth. All this provides a forceful reminder to reconsider the relationships between caste and sect, householder and ascetic, developed by Dumont and later deemed a dominant design in the scholarship on South Asia. At the same time, these principles governing the forms of organization, norms, and practices within Satnampanth also set limits to the group's challenge to caste society: Satnampanth not only rejected and reworked, but it also reproduced the significance of meanings embedded within the ritual hierarchy of purity and pollution and ritually fashioned kingship.

This brings to the fore questions of the wider interplay between religion and power in caste society in South Asia. Louis Dumont has argued that the ritual hierarchy of purity and pollution is the overarching organizing principle, the underlying structural logic, of caste within the Hindu social order.[19] In recent years, we have had forceful critiques of Dumont's exclusive preoccupation with a normative order presided over by the Brahman and defined by purity and pollution. The emphasis on "the complex and conjectural foundations of hierarchical relations" and the "several contextually shifting relations of intercaste relationships apparent in everyday village social life" has focused on the ideological, religious, and cultural character of kingship and the dominant caste.[20] Actually, the debate underscores the issue of power in the caste order. The influential work of Dumont encompasses power within the ritual hierarchy of purity and pollution, and renders it epiphenomenal.[21] The writings of Nicholas Dirks, Gloria Raheja, and Declan Quigley in turn open up possibilities for discussions of the intermeshing of caste structure, ritual form, and cultural attributes of dominance, but tend to locate power, almost exclusively, in constructs of ritually and culturally constituted kingship and dominant caste. In the end, these positions—an exclusive emphasis on the hierarchical concerns of purity and pollution, which brackets power from religion; and an embedding of caste within the political context of a culturally central, ritually fashioned kingship and dominant caste—seem to be mirror images.[22]

A history of the Satnamis constructed in the ethnographic grain suggests a different perspective on the nature of power in caste society in South Asia. The low ritual status of the group and its exclusion from the web of relationships defined by service castes—including the barber, the washerman, the grazier—in village life underscores that the ritual hierarchy of purity and pollution and the principles of a ritually central kingship and dominant caste were not separate and opposed principles but rather the two constituted intertwined cultural schemes, both charged with meanings grounded in relationships of power within the caste order. These distinct but overlapping schemes of ritual power worked together and reinforced each other in the definition of the subordination of the Satnamis and other untouchable communities. The formal establishment of colonial rule in Chhattisgarh in 1854 compounded these patterns of authority—a process, I would venture to suggest, also enacted with somewhat different emphases, over slightly altered time frames, in other parts of India. In the nineteenth and twentieth centuries, the idioms and practices of governance of the colonial order were critical in structuring the forms of dominance and power within caste society in South Asia. This was not a mere matter of the articulation of caste "movements" and identities, often (but by no means only) in the domain of institutionalized politics defined by the colonial administration. At work here were rather more complex and diffuse processes involving novel elaborations of hierachies of power and fresh renderings of rituals of dominance, which drew upon aspects of colonial governance, in the constitution of caste in village relationships and local arenas.

Now this issue too has generally tended to be ignored by the main protagonists in the debate about the nature of power in the caste order, which is possibly in keeping with their emphasis on constructing a synthetic theory of caste in order to reveal the *internal* logic of the Hindu social order. Of the different arguments rehearsed above, only Nicholas Dirks directly addresses the question of the links between caste and colonialism to argue that under colonial rule the embedding of caste in kingship lost its essential moorings in power, a characteristic of precolonial India. What was left in its place was a panoply of royal ritual devoid of power, a "hollow crown."[23] As a result, the masterful ethnohistory of a "little kingdom" produced by Nicholas Dirks accords little importance to the reworkings of colonial governance in local arenas, and his argument moves in a rather different direction from my focus on the symbols, metaphors, and practices of colonial rule as reinforcing and constituting the forms of power in the caste order. Indeed, Satnami oral narratives about village life in the colonial period elaborate how the constitution of authority within caste society, ordered by the metaphor of *gaonthia zamana* (the era of landlords), involved an intermeshing of the closely bound axes of dominance of the ritual hierarchy of purity and pollution and ritually fashioned kingship with the forms of power derived from the colonial order. Once again, historical margins reveal the need to rethink central theories of the relationship between caste and power in South Asia.

And what of arguments extending Dumont's position about a cultural consensus centering on purity and pollution within the Hindu social order to untouchable castes? I shall focus here on the most detailed account, Michael Moffatt's study of the untouchables of Endavur in Tamil Nadu, south India. Moffatt argues that the untouchables, a "discrete set of low castes," who are excluded for reasons of their extreme collective impurity from particular relations with higher human and divine beings, are also included in other relations with the same higher beings. The untouchables, in contexts of inclusion, complement higher beings by playing their appropriate low roles that are necessary for the maintenance of the human and divine order. Moreover, the consensus extends to situations of exclusion: the untouchables replicate and recreate among themselves the set of ranked relations of which they do not form a part.[24] My account shares Moffatt's concern to situate the untouchable castes within the broader set of cultural continuities in the caste system. However, it also highlights aspects of the pasts of the Satnamis that question the universal cast and the rigid form of the overarching oppositions underlying Moffatt's tidy picture of the principles governing untouchable communities.

To begin with, the Satnamis refused the "complementarity" of their position as lowly untouchables. As we have noted, the former Chamars, regrouped as members of Satnampanth, stopped accepting substances of death pollution of a higher being (the cow) from upper castes, and they also rejected the gods and goddesses of the Hindu pantheon and the close connection between divine and social hierarchies, all of which had defined the low ritual status of the group within caste society. Yet such redrawings of the boundaries of Satnampanth also reworked—not, as Moffatt would have it, merely "replicated"—the symbols and practices of the cultural schemes of the caste order. Now these acts of refashioning on the part of the Satnamis followed varied paths. The group drew upon the ritual hierarchy of purity and pollution in ways that may seem—at certain points, and in some readings—to be consonant with the logical patterns of replication established by Moffatt: but these acts of appropriation were conjoined with novel fashionings of the cultural and ritual attributes of kingship, a distinct scheme of authority within the caste order, and with fresh renderings of elements of popular traditions, traditions tied in turn to contestations of the interlocking hierarchies of caste. These reworked signs, drawn from different traditions but now situated next to each other within the matrix of Satnampanth, pressed new associations and critical meanings, and together they interrogated and challenged the low ritual status of the Satnamis.

Of course, it can be argued that the Satnamis—and indeed other related examples—provide an exception which in fact proves the general rule of Moffatt's arguments concerning the principles that govern untouchable communities. But this would be to ignore at least two critical analytical issues, quite apart from the sheer weight of empirical evidence about untouchable groups that militates against Moffatt's scheme.[25] First, in our analyses of social practice, as Bakhtin has argued in relation to linguistic and discursive performance, "the task of understanding does not basically amount to recognizing the form used, but rather to understanding it in a particular, concrete context, to understanding its meaning in a particular utterance, i.e., it amounts to understanding its novelty and not to recognizing its identity."[26] Second, these processes of the production of meanings occur within cultural fields defined by relationships of power, and the meanings constituted within social practices variously elaborate, negotiate, and subvert cultural *forms* that are tied in different ways to schemes of dominance and authority.[27] These twin perspectives clarify that Moffatt's model dwells on the identities of forms of ranked relations within the caste order that extend to the untouchable castes, but it accords little importance to the production of meanings involved in the appropriation and reappropriation of these forms by different castes, in this case by the untouchables of Endavur. A second general problem follows from the first. Moffatt's sharp distinction between "consensus" and "disjunction" also stands in the way of analyses of the construction of nuanced meanings of consensus and of elaborations of the disjunctive aspects of replication within the hierarchies of caste, the more so because his account, following Dumont, ignores the principles of power that are structured into the cultural schemes of caste society.

The Satnamis negotiated and contested these relations of power through a variety of cultural and ritual means in the nineteenth and twenti-

eth centuries, and my analyses here seek to overcome what Sherry Ortner
has identified as the "problem[s] of ethnographic refusal"—the severe lack
of an ethnographic perspective—in the recent spate of studies of "resistance."[28] We have seen that the creation of Satnampanth initiated the challenge to ritual power within caste society in Chhattisgarh. In the last four
decades of the nineteenth century, the Satnamis responded to their expropriation and exploitation under the new system of proprietary rights and
malguzari (village proprietor) settlement, established by the colonial regime
in the 1860s, with various strategies: they deserted villages, continued with
the practice of *lakhabata*—the periodic redistribution of land—in Satnami
villages, and their solidarity was evident in the challenge to upper-caste
malguzars over the issues of rent and loss of land in the 1890s. The enduring
and persistent contestatory practices of the Satnamis were rooted in the
domain of the familiar and the everyday. The organizational hierarchy of
Satnampanth, presided over by the guru who combined the twin, inextricably bound characteristics of the raja and the embodiment of the truth of
satnam served as an alternative ritual and symbolic power center to dominant groups and their network of relationships with service castes. Over the
nineteenth century, the group also fashioned modes of worship that combined an accommodation of the beliefs and festivals shared by the village
with the creation of new divinities, which challenged the tenor of upper-
caste Hinduism. The Satnamis developed a repertoire of myths, a part of
their oral tradition, which centered on the gurus. The myths drew upon and
questioned the relations of power constituted by the ritual hierarchy of purity and pollution, the cultural construct of kingship and dominant caste,
and colonial authority within Chhattisgarh. Finally, in the midst of efforts
(aided by upper-caste benefactors) to recast the identity of the Satnamis
along the lines of recently constructed authoritative blueprints of Hinduism
in the 1920s and 1930s, the group fashioned distinctive uses for the key
emphases of the Hinduisms that were on offer, and its reworkings of Hindu
identities were accompanied by a challenge to the upper castes. The
Satnami criticism of domination, with its accent on the refiguring of the
perceptions of the social world through ritual forms and mythic meanings,
reveals the challenge to authority in a religious idiom, between the violent
drama of rebellion and ordinary acts of daily subterfuge.[29]

Reworked Resources: Myths, Orality, Writing, Histories

The myths of Satnampanth, marked by a high degree of symbolic elaboration, were a part of the ongoing oral traditions of the community. They
suggest the need to explore the relationship between myth and representa-

tions of the past. Now the counterposing of history and myth as opposing categories reinforces the distinction between societies with a dynamic past and other people with unchanging mythic orders.[30] Indeed, this distinction is itself a part of a wider set of overarching oppositions—homologous to each other but articulated in various and often selective ways—between modernity and magicality, rationality and ritual, West and East, reason and emotion, and culture and nature. I repeat this truism because these oppositions and the meanings they engender are not mere specters from the past, now exorcised by a radical ethnographic will. They remain a persistent and palpable presence, a part of our here and now, within and outside the academy, in Western and non-Western contexts, their insidious influence exercising its enchantments over a wide spectrum of political and intellectual opinion from conservative think tanks, to mainstream liberals, to left ideologues, to strains of postcolonial radical and primitivist alternatives.

Clearly, we need to rethink these oppositions, and I take a small step in this direction here. First, myth can be a form of the ordering of historical consciousness and can embody specific cultural conceptions of the past. Moreover, the stratification of myth and ritual in temporally layered religious cults and movements underscores the importance of attending to the internal order and the structure of meanings of myths and rituals to elucidate the development of a mythic tradition.[31] My reading of Satnami myths combines these emphases and concerns. The myths ordered the past of Satnampanth. The Satnami gurus underwent trials, overcame obstacles, and negotiated and displaced figures of authority to define the boundary and orchestrate the symbolic construction of Satnampanth. The retelling of the myths in the performance of oral traditions reaffirmed the identity of the Satnamis as a bounded group, a community. Satnami myths allow us to trace, at once, the group's cultural conception of its past, and the creation of a new mythic tradition.

The Satnamis' telling of stories from their past, without the devices of literacy, invited those who stood outside the community—with manifest interests in the group—to intervene with written histories. It is, of course, difficult to sustain a view that writing and orality are entirely exclusive forms that exist independent of each other. The two forms constitute overlapping but distinct discursive modes, each with its own devices and ways of ordering the world.[32] This book explores the complex cultural encounter between orality and writing embedded in the Satnami past. The writing down of Satnami myths by Baba Ramchandra, an upper-caste outsider and former peasant leader of the radical Kisan Sabha movement of 1918–1920 in the Awadh countryside in north India, in a curious manuscript called *Ghasidasji ki Vanshavali* (the genealogy of Ghasidas) in the 1920s remained bound within the logic of orality. Even as Ramchandra sought to frame a continuously performed oral tradition in writing in the *Vanshavali*, the devices of literacy could not compromise the internal order of myth, and the written text actually derived its meaning from oral and mythic categories. Moreover, the writing of such outsiders came to define the contours of Satnami initiatives, and a key effort to reform and control the community and to redefine Satnami identity in the 1920s was conducted in an idiom of law and authority that was embedded within writing. The critical place of writing as an instrument of domination, in fact, meant that the Satnamis both contested and appropriated its symbolic and substantive power. Finally, the Satnami encounter with evangelical missionaries, which began in 1868, was marked by an interplay and interpenetration of oral narratives and written texts that produced a reordered past of Satnampanth. The Satnami converts to Christianity reworked their oral traditions and the "truth" learned from their evangelical benefactors to forge connections between Ghasidas and the gurus and Christ and the missionaries; the missionaries in turn seized upon these oral traditions to fashion alternative histories, contending pasts. The two processes fed each other. In the 1930s the pooled resources of orality and writing, of the converts and missionaries, resulted in an "authoritative" account of Satnampanth, an account that tried to link the Panth to the inexorable logic of the "truth" of Christ and formed a missionary's last bid to secure a metamorphosis of the Satnamis through their "witnessing" of the Savior. The short text, written by the missionary M. M. Paul, simultaneously took up the forms and idioms of popular religious discourse and followed modes of inscription that lent fixity to its allusions and tenor. This endeavor once again underscored the retention, subversion, and fashioning of meanings that lay at the heart of the relationship between orality and writing.

These processes involving the constitution of truths and the making of histories were a part of larger efforts to regulate the community and redefine its identity. The missionary M. M. Paul's narrative, which sought to string together speech and scripture, had its rivals. In the late 1920s Baba Ramchandra toyed with and then abandoned the myths he had so assiduously inscribed only a little earlier in the manuscript *Ghasidasji ki Vanshavali*. Instead, his *Satnam Sagar* staged an elaborate textual drama replete with the mysteries of classical cosmology, Brahmanical beliefs, and Vedantic vision. Its main protagonists were Hindu gods, goddesses, saints, and warriors, who now populated an esoteric and reified textual universe. The Satnami gurus put in a cameo appearance. The redemption of the Satnamis lay in following the path of the Vedas. Only a few years later, the Shri Path Pradarshak Sabha, a Satnami initiative to reform the community and to persuade the provincial administration to enter the group as Hindus rather than Harijans in official records, mapped a genealogy that reworked the origins of the group. It drew upon the laws of Manu, that ancient codifier of caste, only to turn them upon their head, and also worked on other popular and esoteric, oral and textual traditions to construct a novel past of the Satnamis. These contending accounts, premised upon a recognition of the significance of their past for the members of the community, seized upon history as a negotiable and reworkable resource in their bid to transform the Satnamis.

Colonial Modernities and Evangelical Encounters

Far too frequently, historical accounts, drawing upon classical social and political theory, set up an overriding opposition between state and community. This problem characterizes a great deal of the influential new scholarship on modern Indian social history, a difficulty, as we shall see, that extends from the earlier constructions of the pasts of subordinate groups in *Subaltern Studies* to the more recent shift within this series toward discussions of the dynamics of power and the discursive agendas—or, to put the matter (only) slightly differently, an interrogation of the histories—of the state and the nation in South Asia.[33] Here, even those exercises that actually discuss the fashionings of a colonial modernity in India often retain the givenness of a binary divide between state and community in their elaboration of the play of difference in the articulation of civil society with the colonial state.[34] Now this opposition between state and community tends to ignore the different ways in which the symbols and metaphors of the state and governance are drawn upon and imbricate themselves in the construction of communities, particularly in their fashionings of notions of order, legalities, and identities. Let me clarify that this is no mere trendy poltergeist of Foucault's illuminating but spooky rendering of "governmentality," although I cannot deny having learned something from the category in an idiosyncratic manner.[35] At stake here rather is the crucial importance of a working recognition, at once a theoretical need and an empirical necessity, of the interplay and interpenetration between symbols of state and forms of communities in the making of colonial modernities.

Illiteracy among the Satnamis, we have noted, provided political opportunities for mediations of change by those empowered by writing. These players often engaged with the provincial government, and the symbols, metaphors, and practices of colonial rule came to lie at the heart of efforts to remap Satnami identity and to reform the community. In the early 1920s, a set of influential members of Satnampanth got together with Sunderlal Sharma, a local upper-caste Hindu reformer, and G. A. Gavai, a leader of the depressed classes, to set up an organization called the Satnami

Mahasabha. The Mahasabha was an effort to reform the Satnamis and to participate in the emergent organizational and constitutional politics within the region and in the Central Provinces. The interventions of outsiders were critical in the making of the initiatives sponsored by the organization. G. A. Gavai drafted a petition from the Satnami Mahasabha to the governor of Central Provinces that appropriated the demands of the Satnamis to the concerns and the vocabulary of the depressed classes, a provincial political constituency. The petition won its key demand—the government duly recognized the reconstitution of Chamars as Satnamis within Satnampanth and inscribed this on official papers—and has since come to be celebrated by the group as a charter of victory. But it also introduced tensions within the Satnami organizational endeavor. The reworking of Satnami identity in a language whose grammatical rules were defined by caste associations and the provincial government stood in an uneasy relationship with a reiteration of the beliefs and traditions of Satnampanth within the Mahasabha. Such simultaneous, often contradictory, movements continued to be played out in several other ways in the activities of this Satnami endeavor. Between 1926 and 1930, Baba Ramchandra—the chronicler of Satnami myths and Brahmanical pasts, whom we had encountered a little earlier—took the lead in shaping the Satnami Mahasabha. Under his leadership, the Mahasabha drew upon the signs and resources of the language of the law of colonial administration and situated them alongside the symbols and forms of authority within Satnampanth to fashion new religious legalities under the wider rubric of the "true law of Ghasidas," and the project of the reform of the Satnamis came to be cast in an idiom of order and command. The community in turn worked within the interstices of these relations of power, of intervention and appropriation, to fashion its vision and practice. Thus, the Satnami leaders of the Mahasabha acquired those figures of speech that enabled them to engage with the political institutions and processes defined by colonial administration, the reworked categories of colonial law and administrative organization became enduring features of these leaders' drive to discipline and control the community, and the group itself came to recognize the centrality of the new idioms of legality, authority, and governance within the community.

Clearly, the community here was not a homeostatic centerpiece of timeless tradition—or a terribly impoverished part of the "there and then" of a corrupt modernity—locked in mortal combat with an essentially alien colonial state. It follows that colonial modernity too had a chequered career, configured by the joint energies of the colonizers and the colonized. Indeed, the symbols and practices of imperial rule offered a pool of resources that were deployed in selective, diverse, and even conflicting ways by the Satnamis to redefine identities, construct traditions, fashion legalities, and define pathologies within the community, and to thus participate in the construction of a colonial modernity.

This pattern of appropriations and ambiguities extended to the cultural encounter between the Satnamis and evangelical missionaries. The evangelical encounter was located at a critical intersection of meaning and power: the engagement of the mission project with colonial cultures of rule; and the interface of Protestant theology, evangelical beliefs, and the practices of missionaries with the principles of caste and sect and the institutions and dynamics of village life.[36] The missionaries and the members of indigenous congregations were protagonists and players in dramas of differential perceptions and contradictory practices.

In 1868 the missionaries began a bid to transform the Satnamis that was to last a hundred years. The community did not see its destiny in Christ and proved elusive. The project of conversions among the group grew sluggishly, principally through ties of kinship. The Satnami converts carved out strategies of subsistence and fashioned their understanding of Christianity within the paternalist structure of the missionary enterprise. The missionaries in turn participated—as active agents and hapless victims—in the creation of an indigenous Christianity. The combined efforts of the missionaries and the leaders of the converts' communities led to the setting up of regulations that retained and modified the rules of Satnampanth and institutions of village life. The communities of Satnami converts to Christianity received these regulations through the filters of local cultures, persisted with earlier kinship practices, and reworked the Satnami oral traditions. The mission project's initiation of a set of key practices revolving around buildings, writing and the printed word, and clothing to civilize the converts also had unintended consequences: these signs and arts of civilization were imbricated in the reinforcement of the power of missionaries; and the converts fashioned their own uses for these cultural artifacts, including as instruments to question missionary authority. Once again, the project of modernity ushered in by the missionaries was shaped by the shared past of the evangelical entanglement.

Differentiating Community: Autonomy, Authority, Gender

It is a truism that the Satnamis functioned within relationships of domination, subordination, and resistance. Now the *Subaltern Studies* endeavor has made a powerful case for the recognition of the autonomy and agency of subordinate groups in the making of history, mainly through the substantive contributions made by the series to South Asian historiography, contributions that have developed an already well-established trend in the wider writing of histories from below.[37] This emphasis has provided a valuable corrective to the tendency to appropriate the pasts of subordinate groups to overarching teleological schemes, although not all renderings of autonomy in the accounts constructed within *Subaltern Studies* have always entirely escaped the seductive charms of other teleologies.[38] At the same time, a preoccupation with autonomy tends to obscure the complex interdependence and interpenetration of agency, contestations, and domination and veers toward conceiving of subordinate groups and communities as homogeneous entities.[39] The Satnamis, at each step, functioned with schemes of symbolic representation that were charged with meanings grounded in hierarchy, authority, and power. These symbolic schemes circumscribed and limited Satnami practice, *and* the group followed evocative paths that drew upon the symbols of authority to cope with, negotiate, and challenge its subordination. This also meant that there was a reproduction of forms of domination within the internally differentiated community.

The differentials of property, office, and gender structured patterns of authority among the Satnamis. The power conferred by property was, in fact, intertwined with the propriety of office: Satnami *malguzars*, bound to the gurus' family through ties of kinship, occupied important positions within the organizational hierarchy of Satnampanth. The members of the gurus' family and the organizational hierarchy of Satnampanth sought out and settled disputes, established and enforced norms, and defined and punished transgressions to discipline and regulate the community. The mechanisms that questioned the subordination of Satnamis by dominant castes were also implicated in the exercise of control within the community. This became particularly clear—for instance, in the activities of the Satnami Mahasabha—when the authoritarian impulse of upper-caste interventions found a niche in the structures of authority within Satnampanth.

Gender played a critical role in the ordering and interplay of meaning and power among the Satnamis. Here some of the vast and impressive body of writing on gender in South Asia (and beyond) provides important insights for an implicit integration of questions of gender with other significant analytical issues and domains in history and anthropology.[40] The ideology and practice of kinship among the Satnamis valued the labor of women—even as they were denied entitlements to inheritance and firm rights in their natal and affinal homes—and afforded them a degree of flexibility in forming relationships of secondary marriages. This meant that Satnami women could strike bargains in gendered fields governed by patrilineal and patrivirilocal principles. At the same time, the high incidence of secondary marriages in the community combined with its low ritual status led upper-caste men with land and authority to turn their perceptions of the promiscuity and marginality of Satnami women into powerful instruments of sexual exploitation. The upper-caste construction of the sexual laxity of Satnami women also had other roots. The ambiguities and tensions of gender extended to the rituals and myths of the group. This is particularly true of *jhanjeri chauka*, a ritual centering on fertility and the reproduction of the group, which was conducted after a Satnami woman did not bear a child even after long years of marriage and cohabitation with one or several men. In the ritual, enacted during the night in circumstances consistently described as dark and dangerous, all too resonant with liminality, the Satnami woman, in the aspect of a primal goddess, would choose the men of the community with whom she would have intercourse one after the other. Now, if *jhanjeri chauka* poses extremely difficult problems of interpretation, foregrounding issues of voyeurism that may well be inherent in ethnography, there are nonetheless at least two of its emphases that stand out, emphases that simultaneously elaborate two sides of wider cultural perceptions of women's double-edged sexuality. The ritual implicitly underscored men's responsibility for woman's "barrenness" to provide an important twist to the dominant conception of the respective roles of women and men in biological reproduction in patrilineal South Asia, but it also turned the Satnami woman's body into a site for the reinforcement of the solidarity of the men within the community and rendered her sexuality into an instrument for the reproduction of the group and its boundaries. Moreover, although the evidence on this issue is thin, Satnami women were sexually exploited by members of the organizational hierarchy of Satnampanth, which suggests that within the community ritual power was tied to sexual access to women's bodies. Finally, the principles of feminine sexuality governed the construction of women in Satnami myths, and the unbridled and untamed desire of wives of the gurus evoked disruption and disorder within Satnampanth.

It is hardly surprising that the evangelical missionaries in Chhattisgarh saw Satnami practices as an instance of the moral murk and sloth of the heathen world and sought to stamp out adultery and impose marriage as a sacred contract between individuals. If the Satnami converts flouted missionary authority and continued to form the "adulterous" relationships of secondary marriages legitimated by the principles of Satnampanth, they also drew upon missionary injunctions against adultery and reworked the rules of caste and sect to turn the honor of women into an evocative metaphor for order within the community and a symbol that constituted its boundary. The converts defied missionary logic in fashioning their understanding of marriage and sexual transgression. Similarly, an important initiative within the Satnami Mahasabha's effort to reform the community and redefine its identity also centered on a reordering of family, conjugal relations, and gender within the Satnami household. The play upon monogamy and the creed of woman's fidelity to the husband was a part of the larger endeavor of the domestication of reform: the drive to control and dominate the diffuse domains of sexuality, nurture, production, and exchange in order to effectively exercise political and ritual power. Here too members of the community selectively appropriated and then waylaid these ambitious (en)gendered agendas. My account, instead of segregating gender, seeks to weave the category into the fabric of the Satnami past.

Beyond Caste Movements

For many years now we have had detailed accounts of caste associations and movements in the late nineteenth and early twentieth centuries in India. It is possible to distinguish three broad historiographical positions here. The first set of arguments suggested that in the articulation of caste and the political process, caste, the "natural association of traditional India," became a carrier of modernity in the realm of new institutionalized politics.[41] The second set held that caste associations came into being because of the development of communications—the growth of the press, railway networks, and towns as economic, educational, and administrative centers— and colonial administration. These processes involved self-interested patrons who conjured ideologies of caste unity and were essentially the "products of political opportunity."[42] Finally, studies of non-Brahman movements and initiatives of untouchable groups have revealed the limitations of these interpretations. The non-Brahman and untouchable initiatives played out the tensions and rivalries within indigenous society: religion was a mode of coping with, challenging, and, within limits, transforming an oppressive social order. The articulation of these initiatives and the forging of low-caste identities did not merely involve manipulation from above but engaged in a complex dialogue with the symbols, loyalties, and identities within popular traditions and local cultures.[43] Now, this history of an untouchable community shares the attention to the wide-ranging making of ideologies and the significance accorded to power and its contestations in the work on low-caste initiatives that challenged Brahmans and the caste hierarchy. Yet it also has different emphases from the existing literature on caste movements.

In writing about the Satnamis, I steer clear of framing the group's endeavors, encounters, and experiences as a "movement." An uncritical use of this category, even as a heuristic device, often carries dominant connotations of a preordained trajectory, a definite direction, and a determinate destination. Movements stand and fall by these yardsticks and those milestones, and the category lends fixity to fluidity and often forecloses the possibility of a recognition of the openendedness that may have inhered in the past, particularly in the case at hand. This first general point brings up a second specific issue. Most studies of caste initiatives have tended to focus on the organization and leadership of movements, which in turn have left behind sets of well-defined written materials. This book bases itself on a variety of both written sources and oral testimonies to address a wide range of often-ignored critical questions over a much longer period than most studies of caste initiatives have tried to consider, and to thereby overcome the constraints imposed by the somewhat narrow dimensions of narratives of caste movements.[44] Finally, it follows that my account suggests the need to address a clutch of issues that have been incorporated in the writings on caste initiatives at best in fledgling ways: the crucial place of the play of idioms of authority (tied in turn to relationships of power within communities), agendas of gender, the making of colonial modernities, and the refraction of dominant interventions through the grid of local categories in the articulation of caste initiatives in the nineteenth and twentieth centuries. In brief, to render the pasts of the Satnamis as a movement can detract from the task of constructing a history that seeks to unravel the finely textured and the roughly hewn fabric of the thoughts and practices of the group and to evoke the brilliant and the murky passions and energies of Satnami men and women over time.[45]

How Does the Garden Grow?

Having brought to a close the discussion of the different themes and strands that run through the book, here is a skeletal outline of the arrangement of its material and arguments, of the unfolding of the narrative. Chapter 2 discusses the making of Satnampanth in the wider context of processes of continuity and change and the administrative measures initiated by the Marathas and British superintendents in the late eighteenth and the first half of the nineteenth centuries in Chhattisgarh. It highlights the critical place of innovation, the interpenetration of meanings, and resistance in the construction of the initiative of a subordinate group and in the domain of popular religious practices in the period. Chapter 3 locates the Satnamis within an altered agrarian structure defined by a new set of proprietary rights under colonial rule, explores the Satnami response and resistance to strategies forged by upper-caste landlords, traces the development of Satnampanth—by focusing on the place of the guru in the community, the elaboration of the organizational hierarchy of the sect, and the fashioning of the rituals, beliefs, divinities, and practices of the group—and discusses the evangelical encounter, between 1850 and 1900. Chapter 4 profiles the Satnamis within processes in the agrarian economy and village life in

Chhattisgarh in the first half of the twentieth century. It discusses the forms of discrimination faced by the group—which involved an intermeshing of the principles of power structured into the cultural schemes of caste society with the symbols and practices of the colonial order—and explores the ordering of gender among the Satnamis by taking up questions of ritual, sexual exploitation, and kinship.

This discussion allows us to take up further interconnected issues. Chapter 5 examines Satnami myths that reveal the way the group ordered its past and underscore the symbolic construction of Satnampanth. The myths drew upon and questioned relationships of power within the region. But they also remapped cultural constructions of the intimate connections between feminine sexuality and male order. Chapter 6 focuses on the Satnami Mahasabha. Its efforts at the redefinition of the identity of the group were cast in an idiom and vocabulary of law and authority; the drive to reform the Satnamis brought into play an attempt to reorder conjugal relationships, gender, and the household within the community; dominant interventions were refracted through the filter of local categories; and the initiative negotiated the challenge of its rivals for the allegiance of the Satnamis in diverse ways. Chapter 7 discusses the construction of contending histories of Satnampanth that used the past of the group as malleable material to constitute novel truths. In the late 1920s Baba Ramchandra gave the community an official and canonical history that turned the Satnami gurus into bit players in an essentially Brahmanical drama. In the middle of the 1930s the Shri Path Pradarshak Sabha rehearsed and staged a novel drama centering on the origins of the group. At about the same time, the long history of the interface between orality and writing and the interplay of Satnami myths, convert tales, and missionary accounts resulted in the missionary M. M. Paul's authoritative inscription of a new and reordered past of Satnampanth. The making of these histories was a part of attempts to reform and regulate, transform and metamorphose the Satnamis, and also underscored the centrality of their past for the members of the community. The Conclusion draws out some of the wider implications of the account which stands at the intersection of history and anthropology.

CHAPTER TWO

The Making of Satnampanth, 1780–1850

The formation of Satnampanth in the early nineteenth century helped to forge a new identity for the Chamars of Chhattisgarh. The late eighteenth and early nineteenth centuries were a period of change in the region. Cultivation expanded, the revenue demand of the state increased, and a Brahman-dominated bureaucracy replaced older structures of authority. The various administrative measures of the Marathas and British superintendents who governed the region in this period had contradictory economic and cultural consequences for the Chamars of Chhattisgarh. If certain members of the group established their own villages and successfully resisted the authority of upper-caste officials, other Chamars were pushed to the margins of village society and faced a growing rigidity of the norms of purity and pollution in the region. In this wider context Ghasidas, a farm servant, initiated Satnampanth. The sectarian endeavor at once drew upon popular traditions and the ritual hierarchy of purity and pollution, rejected the divine and social hierarchies that centered on the Hindu pantheon, and repositioned old signs in a new matrix. It questioned and challenged the ascribed status of Chamars as low untouchables who were tainted with the stigma of the death pollution of the sacred cow. The Chamars who joined the sect were cleansed of their impurity and marks of ritual subordination and reconstituted as Satnamis. At the same time, in the new sect the rejection of distinctions of caste among its Chamar and—

only a few hundred—Teli, Rawat, and higher-caste members was accompanied by prohibitions governing transactions with other castes. The main features of Satnampanth were sketched by the middle of the nineteenth century.[1]

Marathas, British Superintendents, and Chamars in Chhattisgarh

The large geographical and linguistic region of Chhattisgarh lies in southeastern Madhya Pradesh. It is popularly held that the region is so named because it once had *chhattis* (thirty-six) *garh* (forts), although another suggestion has it that Chhattisgarh is a corruption of Chedisgarh, the forts of the lord of Chedi.[2] Etymological issues aside, what is clear is that the term has been widely used only over the past two centuries. In basic topographic terms, the region is made up, on the one hand, of the large and fertile rice-producing Chhattisgarh plain measuring about 10,000 square miles, watered in the main by the Mahanadi, the Son, and the Seonath rivers, and on the other, of hilly tracts covered by forests.[3] The region remained relatively isolated until the nineteenth century. It is bound in the north by the Maikal range and merges into the forest hill areas of Bastar in the south. In the east the hilly (and until recently, heavily forested) areas separate Chhattisgarh from the old feudatory states of Orissa. The Satpura range marks off the region from the Wainganga valley in the west. The limited trade of Chhattisgarh—where imports far exceeded exports—passed through Mandla in the north, along the Mahanadi, through Cuttack to the east coast, and *banjaras* (pack traders) linked the region with Nagpur in the west and Bastar and Kanker in the south.[4]

Chhattisgarh has constituted a well-defined social field. The people here share linguistic ties. Chhattisgarhi, the vernacular of the region, is a dialect of the language group called Eastern Hindi.[5] It has also picked up elements of Sawari, Marathi, Oriya, and Telugu. The social composition of the population of Chhattisgarh plain consists of Hindu castes that include Brahmans, Rajputs, Kurmis, Rawats, Telis, Gandas, Chamars, Ghasias, and Mehtars, and tribal groups such as Gonds, Binjhwars, and Bhainas. Over several centuries different social groups migrated to Chhattisgarh, interacted with other castes and tribal communities within the confines of a relatively isolated region, and acquired distinctive characteristics. This involved the development of specific regional cultural attributes, including verbal and nonverbal folklore traditions and social institutions such as ritualized friendships, which often cut across social divisions.[6] It also meant that different castes worked in agriculture and, often, retained only a nominal association with their ascribed caste occupation.[7]

An account of the dim and distant antiquities of Chhattisgarh has little place here, but a brief discussion of the early political structure of the region will facilitate our understanding of the patterns and processes of the late eighteenth and early nineteenth centuries that informed the making of Satnampanth. Until about 1000 C.E. the region, known as Dakshin (south) Kosala, was held by a succession of dynasties, including the Imperial Guptas in the fourth century C.E. At the same time, C. U. Wills has argued that throughout this period the internal political order of the region was characterized by a hierarchical political structure based on tribal clans, which controlled their own small kingdoms.[8] A chief had direct control over only a part of his immediate territory and the rest of the kingdom was controlled by members of the clan.[9] In about 1000 C.E. the region was conquered by the Kalachuris, who belonged to the Haihaya dynasty. The Kalachuris of Dakshin Kosala had their capital at Ratanpur. In the second half of the fourteenth century, the Kalachuris divided into two branches: the older branch continued to rule at Ratanpur, and the younger branch ruled a separate principality with its capital at Raipur. The Kalachuris, Wills argued, accepted local practices and constructed territorial units that retained a number of the structural features of earlier institutions. The two kingdoms were each subdivided into eighteen districts known as *garhs*, or forts, which were under the charge of *thakurs* or *diwans*, who owed allegiance to the Rajput king. The *garh* was also known as a *chaurasi* (eighty-four) because it was meant to be made up of eighty-four villages. The *garhs* in turn were made up of smaller units called *taluks*. The *taluk*, which was supposed to contain twelve villages and was also known as a *barhon* (twelve), was held by a *dao* or *barhainya* whose authority within the unit closely resembled that of the *diwan* within the *taluk*. The village was held by a *gaonthia* or headman.[10] This "symmetrical arrangement" was not at "any one time exemplified in full detail," but the development of the political system of Chhattisgarh within the confines of a relatively secluded and land-locked region did underlie its particular characteristics marked by a decentralization of authority.[11] Even as the Kalachuris replaced some of the tribal chiefs with north Indian Brahmans, the immigrants localized with subcastes of Chhattisgarhi Brahmans, and the titles Barhainya and Bargainya gradually came to denote a specific group of Brahmans in Chhattisgarh.[12]

In the middle of the eighteenth century Maratha armies passed through Chhattisgarh on their way to attack the Orissa kingdoms in eastern India. The Haihayavanshi kingdom fell to the Maratha general Bhaskar Pant in 1742. The ruler of Ratanpur was, however, allowed to continue under the suzerainty of the Marathas. After one and a half decades of court intrigues and alliances between members of the Haihayavanshi family and the Marathas, Chhattisgarh came under the direct rule of the Bhonsle rajas.

Bimbaji, the youngest son of Bhonsle raja Raghoji I, ruled the region from 1758 to 1787.[13] Now Bimbaji, although nominally subordinate to the raja of Nagpur, was independent for all practical purposes. He had a separate army and a court with ministers at Ratanpur. From 1787 to 1818 Maratha rule in Chhattisgarh was carried on through *subahdars* (governors).[14]

The Introduction has noted that studies of the Marathas over the past two decades have significantly altered the old understanding (with colonial legacies) of Maratha polity as a predatory empire of the saddle, featuring relentless raids on horseback and an unremitted looting of conquered lands, a portrait of chaos and anarchy, devastation and doom. The picture that has emerged is one of significant continuities between the Mughals and the Marathas, a complex and sophisticated system of revenue contracts and collection, an expansion in agricultural production particularly in the Maratha heartland, the use of coercion for tax collection not as a norm but as a strategy that was deployed selectively, and, finally, the important role of local expectations and resistance in the shaping of Maratha administration.[15] Maratha rule in Chhattisgarh confirms aspects of this picture, but the region also had its own peculiarities. Taken together, this pattern of continuities and differences of the Maratha regime in the region defined critical aspects of the wider context to the formation of Satnampanth. Clearly, we need to discuss these processes, the more so because a demonology of Maratha rule in Chhattisgarh characterizes the existing writings on the subject.

The Maratha domination of Chhattisgarh from the mideighteenth century introduced a number of changes in the political and social order of the region. The Haihayavanshi dynasty was firmly rooted in Chhattisgarh and had ruled over a loosely knit political unit. The Bhonsle, on the other hand, ruled from Nagpur. Chhattisgarh, as a part of a larger polity, was affected by court intrigues and the struggle for power in Nagpur, by the making and breaking of alliances, and by the dynamics of the Maratha confederacy. Moreover, the Marathas created political systems that simultaneously developed and extended constructs of Hindu kingship and made use of many of the administrative methods of the Mughals. The Bhonsle introduced a relatively centralized system of administration in Chhattisgarh. The hereditary position of the *diwans* was abolished. They were replaced by *kamavisdars* who were nonhereditary officials at the level of the administrative unit of the *pargana*, which was at once modeled on the *pargana* under Peshwa—and by extension Mughal—rule and constructed on the edifice of the *chaurasi* of Haihayavanshi rule.[16] The *kamavisdars*, who were paid "partly by acknowledged salaries and partly by perquisites," were followed by *patels*, whose position came to be hereditary, in the administrative hierarchy.[17] The *patels*, generally "needy Brahmins, Marathas and other upper castes," replaced a number of the *barhon* chiefs (the *barhainyas*). These *patels* received 16 percent of the revenue they collected for the government as payment and also claimed other perquisites.[18] The *pargana*, the effective administrative unit under Maratha rule was divided into villages under the charge of the *gaonthia*—generally an influential man of substance. The *patels* acted as the *gaonthias* in their own villages.[19] Thus, the administrative structure established by the Marathas was fashioned out of preexistent models.

Bhonsle polity had an endemic tendency to run short of resources, therefore to satisfy their monetary needs they followed a policy of territorial expansion and drew high levels of revenue from the conquered regions.[20] While certain tribal rulers continued to resist Maratha presence through armed raids on villages as late as the early nineteenth century, in large parts of the region—not unlike the *pargana* areas of Khandesh and Malwa—Maratha administration moved quickly from looting to a more orderly revenue system.[21] After 1790 the Bhonsle adopted the organizational means of revenue farming in Chhattisgarh.[22]

Captain J. C. Blunt described this practice in a narrative of a journey undertaken in 1794.

> The Subah of Chhattisgarh with its dependencies was at this time rented by the Berar government to Ital Pandit for a specific sum which was payable annually in Nagpur; and who in consideration of the rank of Subahdar and his appointment likewise paid considerable sum—upon further enquiry as to the means by which the Subahdar managed the country I was informed that he farmed different portions of it to his tenants for a constant period and for specific sums nearly upon the same terms as the whole was rented to him. The revenue is collected by his tenantry. . . . I was next led to enquire what method was adopted by the tenantry in collecting the revenue from the peasants. They informed me that it invariably consisted in taxing the ploughs and was always delivered in the produce of the lands.[23]

There are problems in the categories used by Blunt: but his narrative directs us toward an understanding of the revenue practices under Maratha *subahdars* in Chhattisgarh.

The total revenue demand for Chhattisgarh was fixed according to instructions from Nagpur, where the *subahdar* was meant to pay a certain sum annually to the Bhonsle capital. The *subahdar* took into consideration the collection of the previous year and divided the amount between the *parganas*. The *pargana* assessment, in turn, was apportioned between villages. The *patels* settled the assessment with the government for a group of villages and were responsible for its payment. To this end, they supplied the cultivators with seeds and cattle (particularly if the *gaonthia* of the village was unable to do this), and made loans of money and grain to *gaonthias* and cultivators, which could be repaid in grain. The distribution of the village assessment was settled by the *gaonthia* and the cultivators. The revenue was collected in three equal installments: the first two installments, collected around September and December, were generally based on the previous year's assessment—although even here the *kamavisdars* could ask the *patels* and *gaonthias* to collect more than in the past year—and the third installment, based on the revised revenue demand fixed by the *subahdar*, had to be paid in March of the following year. Given these rigors, if a *gaonthia* did not accept the arrangement, the village changed hands and a new *gaonthia* was appointed at the time of the payment of the third installment.[24] All this suggests that the edifice of revenue administration at the level of the *subahdar*, the *kamavisdar*, and the *patel* was geared toward maximizing the collection of revenue.

Yet it would be hasty to assume that the system was entirely arbitrary and marked by a purely coercive drive toward extortion of revenue. Andre Wink has shown that revenue farming under the Marathas was "the means to obtain settled revenue from unsettled territory," an organizational form of agrarian restoration at the frontier of agriculture and wasteland.[25] Indeed, in a frontier province like Chhattisgarh revenue farming led to an expansion of cultivation and to the agricultural improvement of land.[26] Moreover, at the time of the payment of the first revenue installment, the *gaonthias* made representations about lands that had fallen out of cultivation, about bad seasons, and about loss of cultivators and cattle, representations that were then considered by "attentive" *kamavisdars*. The *subahdar* in turn heard and investigated the complaints of the cultivators against *gaonthias* and *patels* during his annual tour through the province at the time of the collection of the third revenue installment.[27] Finally, evidence from other regions ruled by the Marathas suggests that the transition from "looting" to a sophisticated cash-based system in a short period of time had rested not only on the Maratha gain of Mughal rights to these areas but also upon their understanding and fulfillment of the expectations of villages.[28] The Bhonsle attempts to prepare rudimentary village papers in Chhattisgarh indicate that they too made efforts in this direction and tried not to override expectations within a village, particularly those of its elite.[29] Of course, local officials could make extra demands and resort to coercion, and in periods of absence of detailed control by the *subahdar* the revenue collections could be extremely high. The peasant response here took the form of resistance through desertion of villages, the strategy of "flight" or "avoidance protest," which was not in the long-term interest of Maratha administration, particularly since it was labor rather than land that was scarce in Chhattisgarh. On the whole, the system of revenue farming run by the

Bhonsle in Chhattisgarh did not necessarily ride roughshod over the expectations and practices of villages.

How did the revenue system operate at the level of the village? In Chhattisgarh the mode of revenue assessment was based on the *nagar* or the plough. A "plough" of land was an elastic measure. Its actual extent varied in different tracts, but it was intended to represent the area one plough and four oxen could cultivate. The village land and the share of the village revenue was divided among the well-established cultivators according to the number of ploughs of land for which each of them was responsible. This left out the farm servants and other members of the village community who held land broken up from waste outside the main cultivated area and paid rent in cash or kind. The *gaonthia*, an influential cultivator who was responsible for the collection of the village revenue, held one plough of land free of revenue for every eight ploughs of land that paid revenue. He also received remuneration for village expenses of one plough of land in sixteen.[30] Under Maratha rule, the *gaonthias* were generally keen to bring more land under the plough since, on the one hand, it increased their revenue-free holdings and, on the other, it helped them to cope with the revenue demand of Maratha administration. This fresh land could be brought under cultivation by attracting new settlers.

The *gaonthias* were aided in this process by the institution of *lakhabata*, or the periodic redistribution of land. Agnew first referred to the practice of redistribution of land by *gaonthias* and cultivators as a characteristic of the revenue administration under the Marathas in Chhattisgarh.[31] Later administrators emphasized the "tribal" and "egalitarian" features of the institution, and argued that it was a relic of pre-Maratha times.[32] Given the thinness of (official and oral) evidence about *lakhabata*, we cannot be certain about the roots of the institution or indeed about many of the details of the way the system actually worked. Yet, certain broad features of *lakhabata* stand out. Chhattisgarh is marked by considerable diversity of soils. The variety of lands within a village used to be constituted into equally valued plots: the *gaonthia* had a certain share in each of these blocks and the rest was distributed among the other cultivators within the village. The institution of *lakhabata* meant that blocks of land within the village were periodically redistributed to ensure that members of the village got a share of both poor and good land. It was carried out to accommodate new settlers. The practice also came into play when a village changed hands and a new *gaonthia* entered the fray, which was not uncommon under *subah* administration.[33] The practice of *lakhabata* made for an expansion in cultivation during Maratha administration. However, the institution also had a contradictory dimension since it meant that well-off cultivators could claim the lands of "poor and cattleless" cultivators, which included a large number of Chamars.[34]

What was the situation of Chamars within the agrarian hierarchy and the revenue system under Maratha administration? The evidence is extremely fragmentary. In 1820 Agnew reported that Chamars accounted for 12,306 of the total 100,603 families (households?) in the *khalsa* of Chhattisgarh.[35] He did not, however, specify the occupations of Chamars (or of any of the other castes) and their location within the agrarian hierarchy. Instead, Agnew provided a rough estimate—without indicating the basis on which he had arrived at the figures—that out of the total of 100,603 families 33,177 were cultivators, 53,180 were traders, merchants, and servants, and 14,246 were unemployed.[36] At the same time, his survey indicated the existence of Chamar *gaonthias*, and later colonial administrators emphasized that the Chamars of Chhattisgarh primarily worked on land.[37]

We have noted that the period of Maratha rule witnessed an expansion of cultivation in Chhattisgarh. In a land-surplus situation, the Chamars had the option of clearing the jungle and settling land. According to an oral tradition Kosa, a village in present-day Durg district populated primarily by Satnamis, was founded around the end of the eighteenth century by a Chamar.[38] Evidence on the pattern of settlement of castes from the second half of the nineteenth century indicates the existence of *ekjati* (single-caste) villages made up primarily of Chamars (who had now become Satnamis) with their own *gaonthias*.[39] What proportion of Chamars lived in these *ekjati* villages? There is little reliable evidence to provide a firm estimate. However, it is clear that the Chamars also lived in villages populated by other castes in a separate *para* (neighborhood). The settling of new villages required ploughs, cattle, and seeds, which often had to be borrowed from upper-caste *patels*. This made it difficult for all Chamars to set out and establish their own villages. In the late eighteenth and early nineteenth centuries, a large number of Chamar cultivators (who carried out agricultural operations by hiring cattle from more substantial members of the village community) and farm servants (who received one-fourth of the produce as their share) lived in villages inhabited by different castes, and they did not migrate to the single-caste Chamar villages.[40]

Was there an increase in the dependence and subordination of Chamars in this period? It is possible to discern two simultaneous movements. In a region where imports were consistently higher than exports and the spread of money economy uneven, a cash-based revenue system meant that problems of money supply, particularly in periods of warfare and turmoil, could lead to an increased dependence of Chamar cultivators and *gaonthias* on higher-caste *patels*, who also made loans of grain and money.[41] On the other hand, the lack of skilled labor in Chhattisgarh and the desire of Bhonsle administration to enhance cash revenue meant that Chamar ploughmen and agricultural laborers retained an element of bargaining power through the strategy of migration. Chamars, along with other day laborers and ploughmen, adopted the desertion of villages as a mode of resisting officeholders, landlords, and rich peasants. Entire villages were deserted during the period of *subahdar* rule.[42] In the 1850s British commentators were still lamenting the "migratory nature" of the people of Chhattisgarh.[43] We should not underestimate the difficulties involved in the strategy of flight since there was an element of uncertainty built into the tactic, but it offered poor ploughmen and farm servants a feasible way to resist and retain their bargaining power. Moreover, the results of *lakhabata* for Chamar cultivators were not uniform: in certain fertile areas their lands could be appropriated by *gaonthias* and substantial cultivators, and in other parts *lakhabata* led Chamars to meeting the revenue demand of the state and participating in the expansion of cultivation.[44] Did poor cultivators have any option other than the desertion of villages? We have noted that the *subahdar* was meant to hear the complaints of cultivators against *patels* and *gaonthias*, but the caste character of Maratha administration was weighted against Chamars and other low castes.

Bhonsle rule in Chhattisgarh was modeled on the structure of the Peshwas at Poona. Fukuzawa has demonstrated that the role of the Peshwas had included the enforcement of religious hierarchies and they had acted as the executors of Brahman religious authorities in disputes over ritual matters and in caste relationships.[45] The pattern tended to be replicated in Chhattisgarh. Maratha rule in the region was accompanied by the arrival of orthodox upper castes. The *kamavisdars* were Brahmans. The *barhon* chiefs were replaced by *patels* who were, once again, Brahmans from Maharashtra and other "high castes."[46] Maharashtrian Brahmans considered the Chhattisgarhis lower in purity and status.[47] The administrative practices of the Marathas were based upon Brahmanical values, and it was thus that they undertook steps toward the protection of cows in Chhattisgarh.[48] Agnew also commented on the pattern of unequal punishment for upper castes and lower castes under the Marathas: Brahmans and a few other castes were exempt from the penalty of death and from certain taxes, including the *pandhri* (house tax levied on nonagriculturists); the Chamars clearly did not figure in the list of castes who received lighter punishment.[49] Did this growing rigidity of Brahmanical concerns of purity and pollution under Maratha rule also lead to a greater reinforcement of the restrictions on the Chamars in the use of particular clothes, ornaments, and modes of transport? Did the Chamars now face a growth in prohibitions governing the use of ponds and tanks and access to resources such as trees and fallow lands in the domain of village life because of their ascribed low ritual status? We have little evidence, but this may well have been the case. Clearly, the difficulties of the group were compounded by the fact that the upper-caste *patels*, who supplied the cultivators with loans of grain and money, were important figures in the system of civil justice as the *gaonthias* of their villages. These *patels* also tended to exercise detailed authority over a group of villages, and could often influence Brahman *kamavisdars*.[50]

What can we make of the situation of Chamars under Bhonsle rule, particularly in the first two decades of the nineteenth century? Members of the caste had established Chamar villages with their own *gaonthias*. At the same time, other Chamars continued to remain sharecroppers, agricultural laborers, and poor ploughmen. Even Chamar *gaonthias* and substantial cultivators had to cope with the largely Brahman and upper-caste *patels*. *Lakhabata* both worked to the benefit of some Chamar cultivators and pushed others to the margins of village society. Migration and the desertion of villages provided members of the group with a mode to cope with, resist, and retain their bargaining power in relation to *patels* and influential *gaonthias*. At the same time, apart from the forms of discrimination that were structured into the specific caste character of Bhonsle administration, survival was particularly difficult during periods of warfare and at other times that witnessed a large increase in the revenue demand of the state. The depredations of the Pindaris in the early nineteenth century, for example, fitted the bill, and in the period between 1806 and 1817, the Pindaris under their leader Chitu devastated and plundered large parts of territories in Chhattisgarh. Likewise, in the course of the last eighteen years of *subahdar* rule the revenue assessment increased more than three times from Rs.1,63,000 to Rs.3,83,000.[51] If certain processes aided the Chamars, there was also a great deal working against the group.

In 1817, after the Bhonsle defeat in the battle of Sitabaldi, the administration of Chhattisgarh passed into the hands of the British. The Bhonsle had become a subsidiary ally of the company in 1815.[52] In the period between 1818 and 1830, when the Bhonsle king was a minor, the administration of Chhattisgarh was carried out by British superintendents. Major Vans Agnew, the most enterprising of these superintendents, undertook a series of significant measures during his tenure from 1818 to 1825. These measures increased the powers of the *gaonthia* and the village *panchayat*: the powers of the *patel* were restricted; Agnew sought to establish direct links with and supported the *gaonthias*; and the village *panchayats* were revived through official support to these institutions.[53] Thus, at the level of the village, the locus of power shifted from the *patel* to the *gaonthia* and the *panchayat*. These changes were further intertwined with the superintendents' enforcements and changes in the administration of law. Agnew made a bid to rationalize civil and criminal judicial administration. The system was streamlined so that treason, crimes against the state, murders, and major thefts were detected through the agency of the *gaonthia* and *kamavisdar* and reported to the superintendent. The *gaonthias* and *kamavisdars* were given powers of "judicial superintendence"—to be exercised in accordance with custom and local usage—over their villages and *parganas*, respectively.[54] Now these processes involving shifts in the configurations of power in local arenas could aid Chamar *gaonthias* against Brahman and Maratha *patels*. But the changes also meant that upper-caste *gaonthias* and *kamavisdars* could play upon British misunderstanding of customary legal forms to entrench themselves in power, which worked to the disadvantage of Chamars.

The period also witnessed two simultaneous processes in the field of revenue administration and practices. The British modified the Maratha revenue system by abolishing supplementary revenue demands and the revenue officials' unauthorized perquisites, by fixing the times for the payment of revenue installments at periods that suited the cultivators and by granting receipts to the cultivators for payments made to *gaonthias*. However, there were no radical changes in the method of assessment and there were important continuities in revenue practices. The colonial goal of a progressively rising land revenue, evident under the administration of the superintendents, could contradict the hopes of an improvement of the peasantry. *Lakhabata* too worked against the poor Chamar and other low-caste ploughmen. Sinclair, a settlement officer, commented on the functioning of the institution between 1820 and 1854.

> The cultivators as a rule never demurred; they, in fact, looked upon this partition or *bata* as a means of protection from the landlords' extra demands on the steps of the increased government demand. They knew that a certain sum must be paid and from their pockets and, therefore, the best policy was to turn out the poor and cattleless Raiyats and apportion their lands pro ratio among the better classes.[55]

The Chhattisgarhi cultivators, including Chamars, still resisted these developments through the desertion of villages. The increased emphasis on settled agriculture as a mark of rural stability, however, meant that the tactic perhaps did not always work well as a bargaining strategy since now the cultivators courted the danger of being cast as unruly elements. Once again, the Chamars gained in certain fields but lost out in other arenas.

The period from the late eighteenth century to the midnineteenth century was attended by fairly rapid changes in the center of authority. We have seen that the Maratha *subahdars* who had assumed charge of Chhattisgarh from the 1780s were followed by British superintendents within three decades. In both cases, the change in central authority was emphasized by the new administrative measures introduced by these Maratha and British officials. Once more, after Raghoji III came of age in June 1830, the administration reverted to the Bhonsle raja, and Chhattisgarh was governed by Maratha *subahdars* till 1854. Although the Marathas did not tamper with the new and modified scheme of administration inaugurated by the British superintendents, their assumption of rule between 1830 and 1854 nonetheless formed part of a wider pattern. Indeed, the displacements in central authority between the late eighteenth and midnineteenth centuries served to highlight the stress of the period and the strain of the time centered on processes of social change, which often pulled in contrary directions. This wider context—its threads will be picked up again very shortly—informed the construction of Satnampanth in Chhattisgarh in the early nineteenth century.

Popular Traditions, Hegemonic Hierarchies, and the Construction of Satnampanth

Satnam as a sign and symbol of the sacred had been the centerpiece of sects in north India long before it was seized upon by the Chamars of Chhattisgarh. The Satnamis first find mention as a small sect that rebelled against Aurangzeb in the fifteenth year of his reign (1672 C.E.). It was founded by Birbhan in 1657 in Narnaul, eastern Punjab.[56] A seventeenth-century chronicler described the group as mendicants, also known as Mundiyas, consisting of between four and five thousand householders in the Mughal *parganas* of Narnaul and Mewat.

> Although these Mundiyas dress like mendicants yet their livelihood and profession is usually agriculture and trade in the manner of small merchants with small capital. Living according to the ways of their own community they aspire to reach the status of a good name (*nek-nam*) which is the meaning of the word Satnam. But if anyone should want to impose tyranny and oppression upon them as a display of courage and authority, they will not tolerate it; and most of them bear arms and weapons.[57]

The group's lack of submission to the authorities then was apparent long before the actual revolt against the Mughal emperor which in turn began as a "rural affray."[58] The popular character of the rebellion was clear, "It is cause for wonder that a gang of bloody, miserable rebels . . . carpenters, sweepers, tanners, and other ignoble beings, braggarts and fools of all descriptions, should become so puffed up with vain-glory as to cast themselves headlong into the pit of self-destruction."[59] A "millenarian" aspect followed as the "malignant" people sprang up like "white ants" and descended like "locusts." "It is affirmed that these people considered themselves immortal;

seventy lives was the reward promised to every one of them who fell in action. A body of about 5000 had collected in the neighborhood of Narnaul, and were in open rebellion. Cities and districts were plundered." The insurrection was initially successful. It was defeated by a large imperial army sent from the Mughal court after a battle of epic proportions from which few Satnamis escaped with their lives.[60] The royal chronicler had no more space for the background and characteristics of these insurgents. We know little about the "ways of community" of these mendicant-householders who engaged in trade, agriculture, and a variety of other professions. If a contemporary writer found them merely "foul, filthy, and impure,"[61] Irfan Habib's account of the beliefs and practices of the Satnamis or Mundiyas of Narnaul is based on a text of the Sadh sect of Farrukabad that was compiled in the early nineteenth century.[62]

The Sadhs were possibly the descendants of Mundiyas—one of their myths situated the founder and the formation of the sect in Bijhasar in the Narnaul region—which scattered after the defeat of the rebellion over the upper part of the Doab from the area west of Delhi to Farrukabad. In 1832, H. H. Wilson published a description of the sect that originated with Birbhan. Birbhan received a miraculous communication from *satguru* (true guru), also known as Udaidas, who in turn was the servant of the one god. The tenets of the sect were known as *malik ka hukum* (the embodied word of god) and were communicated in *sabdas* and *sakhis* (detached stanzas). They were compiled into manuals and the substance was collected in a tract entitled *Adi Upadesh*, first precepts, which organized the entire code under twelve *hukums* or commandments.[63] The Sadhs believed in one god called *satnam* who created the universe with his will and was formless: "Acknowledge but one God who made and can destroy you, to whom there is none superior and to whom alone is therefore worship due, not to earth, nor stone, nor metal, nor wood, nor trees, nor any created thing. There is but one Lord, and the word of the Lord. Bow not your head in the presence of idols or of men."[64] The members of the sect did not have temples but met in a house or courtyard on every full moon when they ate together and spent the night singing and reciting stanzas attributed to Birbhan and the verses of Nanak and Kabir.[65] The boundedness of the group was manifest in the injunction to members to "avoid intercourse with all not of the same faith, eat not of a strangers bread," and in their denial of caste distinctions within the community.[66] It was accompanied by a rejection of rituals and local superstitions.[67] The sect construed the householder, the man-in-the-world, as an ascetic marked by disdain for wealth and authority. Members were enjoined not to assume the garb of a mendicant, solicit alms, accept gifts, harass the poor, or to keep the company of kings and wealthy men. The meetings of the pious were the only places of pilgrimage and god was the giver of all things.[68] The Sadhs worked toward a pure state of the body and senses: they had to wear white garments, shun intoxicating substances and evil influences—opium, tobacco, betel leaves, perfumes, gossip, calumny, music, and dances—and direct their energies toward praise of the creator. There were injunctions against lying and stealing, the use of violence and force, and an emphasis on monogamy where the woman had to be obedient to the man.[69] The twelve commandments were repeated in a variety of ways in both the *Adi Upadesh* and the *Satnam Sahai*. The variations do not add significantly to the basic pattern of Sadh beliefs and practices. The group also believed in the real but temporary existence of inferior deities and their incarnations. The community was concentrated in the main in a suburb called Sadhwara near Farrukabad where their number was estimated at two thousand.[70] The Sadhs were also known as Satnamis because of their worship of *satnam*. At the same time, Wilson emphasized, "this appellation more especially indicates a different, although kindred sect."[71]

Wilson was referring to the sect of Satnamis founded by Jagjiwandas in Barabanki district, near Lucknow, in the early eighteenth century. Jagjiwandas was born into a family of Thakur landlords in the Sardaha village in Barabanki district in the 1680s.[72] The change in Jagjiwandas's life came after his encounter, when still a boy, with Bulla Sahib, a disciple of the Sufi mystic Yari Shah who lived in Delhi between 1668 and 1725. A poor farm servant, Bulla Sahib did not believe in rituals and refused to initiate Jagjiwandas as his disciple. But Bulla Sahib's favor and potent touch were enough for Jagjiwandas. His soul awakened. A new sect was begun. These Satnamis were expected "to adore the true name alone, the one God, the cause and creator of all things, Nirgun or void of sensible qualities."[73] Members were prohibited the use of meat, *masur* (red lentils), liquor, and aubergines. Jagjiwandas's asceticism did not prevent him from continuing as a householder through his life. It spoke of a moral code that enjoined indifference to the world and an implicit devotion to one's spiritual guide while discharging everyday social and religious obligations. In spite of their belief in one supreme god, the Satnamis recognized the entire Hindu pantheon. They revered all incarnations, particularly Ram and Krishna, as manifestations of the nature of the true deity, and accorded a special place to the god Hanuman. The *Agh Binsh*, the sacred book of the Satnamis, contained stories from Puranas, lessons on morals, ethics, and divinity derived from Sanskrit religious texts, and rules of piety. Jagjiwandas also wrote several other texts featuring Hindu divinities. Caste distinctions were retained within the sect: "On the contrary, its professors seem careful not to interfere with caste prejudices and family customs. . . . The water in which the Guru's feet have been washed, is drunk only when the Guru is of equal or higher caste than the disciple."[74] The Satnamis gained a few adherents among different groups. Jagjiwandas had two Muslim disciples and a low-caste Kori disciple who "converted Chamars and other low caste Hindus to the faith." At the same time, most of Jagjiwandas's followers were Rajputs and Brahmans. While two of his disciples went north to Ambala and Amritsar, most settled in Barabanki near the village of Sardaha. A very high proportion of the near ten thousand members of the sect lived in the region around Barabanki, although they were notionally meant to have "spread across all parts of North India from Banaras to Amritsar."[75]

The Satnami sect founded by Ghasidas was almost exclusive to the Chamars of Chhattisgarh. Ghasidas was born in the village of Girod, next to the forest of Sonakhan, in the northeast of present-day Raipur district. Chisholm, a settlement officer, basing himself on oral testimony in the 1860s, dated Ghasidas's birth around 1770.[76] He was the fourth son of Mahngu and Amraotin, a family of farm servants. The boy Ghasi performed miracles such as producing sugarcane out of a fallow field while playing with his friends. As he grew older, Ghasidas seemed to spend more and more time in meditation. Mahngu and Amraotin, fearing that their son was turning into a *bahiya* (a man touched with divine madness), arranged to have him married to Safura. Ghasidas became a farm servant of Gopal Marar, a member of a vegetable-growing caste. Soon he fathered two sons, Amru and Balak. Ghasidas continued to perform the work of ploughing for his agricultural master as a means to support his family. The master felt that Ghasidas did not work properly until one day he saw that the plough being used by this farm servant was moving on its own accord. The master fell on Ghasidas's feet and accepted his authority.[77]

Ghasidas's fame grew. Chisholm was to later describe the unlettered man who would be guru.

> He was a man of unusually fair complexion and rather imposing appearance, sensitive and silent, given to seeing visions, and deeply resenting the harsh treatment of his brotherhood by the Hindoos. He . . . had the reputation of being exceptionally sagacious, and was universally respected. By some he was believed to possess supernatural powers, by others curative powers only, by all he was deemed a remarkable man.[78]

Ghasidas acquired a band of devoted followers. He decided to go into the forest of Sonakhan to meditate. In Satnami myths, Ghasidas was led to the forest because of his grief over the death of his children and his wife. The administrator's account, on the other hand, explained Ghasidas's move as a consequence of his desire to become a prophet, impelled by both his followers' "constant importunities" and his feeling of "personal vanity."[79] The followers spread the news of this withdrawal into the wilderness and intimated to the Chamars that Ghasidas intended to emerge, after six months, with a revelation.

> Chamars from all parts of Chhattisgarh began to collect in Girod to receive the message. The scene as described by an eye witness was strange and impressive. The roads leading to this hitherto unfrequented hamlet were traversed by crowds of anxious pilgrims. The young and old of both sexes swelled the throng—mothers carrying their infants, and the aged and infirm led by stronger arms. Some died by the way, but the enthusiasm was not stayed. Arrived at the spot, the plain skirting the rocky eminence presented to the eye a vast multitude of human beings, divided into different knots, discussing the strange crisis which had brought them together.[80]

After six months, in the quiet of the early morning, the crowd acclaimed Ghasidas's return as he walked down the mountain, which faced Girod. Ghasidas explained that he had been "miraculously sustained" in the forest and had "held communion" with a "higher power," *satnam*, who had instructed him to deliver his message to the Chamars.

Ghasidas became the guru of a new sect. The guru forbade his disciples idol worship, instructed them to believe only in *satnam* who was formless and the maker of the universe, and to follow a code of "social equality."[81] Satnampanth turned its members into Satnamis. Satnamis were forbidden meat, liquor, tobacco, and certain vegetables and pulses. They were asked not to use cows for cultivation or to plough after the midday meal. The Satnamis maintained their distance from Kanaujia Chamars—the major division of the Chamars in the region, who did not join Satnampanth and who in turn retained their separate identity.[82] Ghasidas lived to the age of eighty having survived several attempts on his life prompted by upper-caste hatred. When he died around 1850 Satnampanth had 250,000 members and the guru's teachings had become a "living element in society."[83]

The making of Satnampanth was both a response to and informed by processes of social change in the late eighteenth and early nineteenth centuries in Chhattisgarh: the discriminatory character of Bhonsle administration toward low castes and the growing rigidity of the ritual hierarchy of purity and pollution; the institution of *lakhabata* and revenue practices that allowed some Chamars to establish their own villages and pushed others to the margins of village society; and dislocations within the sociopolitical order and rapid displacements in the center of authority. Indeed, the simultaneous subordination of and assertion by Chamars provided the context for the creation of Satnampanth, an endeavor that fashioned its vision of the sacred and the divine by reworking the relationship of its members with the interlocking hierarchies of caste and centers of ritual power.

In the middle of the 1860s Chisholm stated that the "movement" was not more than fifty years old and had occurred between 1820 and 1830. Was this the making of a colonial myth that a low-caste monotheistic sect, which opposed the caste system, could come into existence only after the British superintendents had moved into Chhattisgarh in 1818? Chisholm's speculative history could indeed lend itself to such readings: but his rough chronology, based on oral testimonies, is corroborated by other sources. The Satnamis were not featured in a discussion of sects and ascetic customs in a detailed Marathi manuscript, compiled around 1818, which dealt with the history, inhabitants, and institutions of Chhattisgarh.[84] Agnew, a keen observer, also did not mention the sect in his account of religion in Chhattisgarh written in 1820. While the processes that informed the making of Satnampanth had been underway since the late eighteenth century, the actual construction of the subordinate initiative needs to be located over the second quarter of the nineteenth century. The period between the 1820s and the 1840s witnessed the creation and accumulation of myths about Ghasidas.[85] The truncated, abbreviated, and reworked versions of some of these myths were to then put in an appearance in the accounts of colonial administrators written in the 1860s.[86] The rituals and practices of Satnampanth became a part of the lived-in world of its members—which also included a small number of members of the Teli (oil presser) and Rawat (grazier) castes—by the middle of the nineteenth century.[87]

Were there links between the Satnamis of north India and the sect that developed among the Chamars of Chhattisgarh? The Sadhs and Satnamis of north India and Satnampanth of Chhattisgarh shared common features. The most obvious parallel here is the belief in one supreme god who went under the name of *satnam*. The notion of *satnam* could indeed have come from the north via mercenaries or pilgrims and formed a part of popular religious discourse, a fluid world of ideas, to be seized upon by Ghasidas and the Chamars of Chhattisgarh. Second, there were injunctions in all these sects against the use of intoxicants, and similarities between the Satnamis of Barabanki and Satnampanth of Chhattisgarh in the prohibitions on red pulses and certain vegetables such as aubergines. Third, none of these sects incorporated the overarching opposition between the man-in-the-world and the individual-outside-the-world—central to Dumont's discussion of caste and sect—and instead construed the householder as an ascetic. Finally, we find a parallel in the myths of these sectarian formations. The legends of the Satnamis of Barabanki recount that Jagjiwandas's guru Bulla Sahib was a farm servant of Gulal Sahib. Bulla used to lose himself in meditation while working in the fields. Once a displeased Gulal Sahib confronted Bulla who was ploughing the field with his attention fixed on another world. Bulla answered, "You are the master of my body and it is doing its work, but my soul is with her [the soul's] lord." Gulal was deeply ashamed and became a disciple of Bulla Sahib.[88] A myth of Satnampanth featuring Ghasidas's encounter with Gopal Marar, where the Chamar farm servant worked the fields without letting his hands touch the plough, eventually compelling the agricultural master to accept his authority, seems an elaboration and variation on the theme.[89] These beliefs and practices of the north Indian sects may well have been carried to Chhattisgarh by mercenaries, pilgrims, and other migrants who settled in the region.

It would be hasty, however, to make too much of these continuities. A number of the shared features and parallels between the Sadhs and the Satnamis of Barabanki and the Satnamis of Chhattisgarh will be shown to extend to other sects. There were also significant differences. The sects of the north had developed largely among twice-born castes, while Satnampanth of Chhattisgarh drew its motive force from reconstituting the untouchable status of its Chamar members. The beliefs of the Sadhs and Satnamis of Barabanki centered on the written word, the *Adi Upadesh* and *Agh Binsh*, respectively, and sectarian texts formed an important part of their religious practices. On the other hand, Satnampanth of Chhattisgarh was rooted within oral traditions and did not share the emphasis of the other two sects on the importance of the revealed word of god. The *satguru* of the Sadhs was the servant of god who carried the word of *satnam*, but in Satnampanth *satnampurush* was established as the embodied form of the true deity, *satnam*. It followed, therefore, that unlike the two north Indian sects Satnampanth, at least initially, had no place for the gods and goddesses of the Hindu pantheon. Finally, Satnampanth situated the characteristics it held in common with the Sadhs and the Satnamis of Barabanki alongside the beliefs and practices of other popular traditions.

Kabirpanth constituted a significant presence within Chhattisgarh. The Kabirpanthis of Chhattisgarh claim that Kabir (1448–1518 c.e.) began preaching in Rewa, north of Bilaspur, and that their first preceptor Dharamdass, a Bania, also belonged to Rewa. The center of the Kabirpanthis of Chhattisgarh was at Kawardha, the seat of the *mahant*. The *mahants* of Kawardha claim direct descent from Dharamdass.[90] Kabirpanth forbade the worship of idols and deities, the members were not allowed meat and intoxicants, and the sect had its distinctive rituals and practices. The members of Kabirpanth were, in the main, Pankas and Telis. Pankas are Gandas whose traditional caste occupation set them out as village watchmen. In Chhattisgarh, the Pankas have formed a separate division of Gandas. They are members of Kabirpanth, disown their connection with the Gandas, and hold that their name is derivative of *pani-ka* (from water), which establishes their affinity with Kabir who is said to have been found floating in water as a baby.[91] The Telis, whose traditional occupation was oil pressing, were divided into two groups, Kabirhas and Deotahas. The Kabirhas did not worship idols, images, or deities and refrained from meat and intoxicants, while the Deotahas worshiped deities, including images of Kabir, and did not observe restrictions on food.[92] However, the two groups did intermarry. Kabirpanth of Chhattisgarh had a well-defined ritual structure by the early nineteenth century.

Satnampanth drew upon the symbols and practices of Kabirpanth and situated them in a new context. The *chauka*, a square figure made with wheat flour, was altered and simplified, divested of its associations with the texts of Kabirpanth, and pressed into the service of *satnampurush* and Ghasidas in the Satnami modes of worship. The tying of the *kanthi*, a black string with wooden beads, signaled the incorporation of a neophyte into both Kabirpanth and Satnampanth, but the *mantra* (incantation) that accompanied this act of initiation was very different in the two sects.[93] All this was part of wider processes of intersectarian rivalry and the mechanisms of expansion of religious orders, where preexistent symbols were claimed and infused with new meanings to establish the distinction of a new sect and its modes of worship.[94] The accent was on differences between religious orders. Kabirpanthis—like the Satnamis of Barabanki who had attracted a few low-caste members—professed an indifference to the world but retained caste distinctions in everyday life. The reproduction of the sect was carried out through spiritual-genealogical links between gurus and disciples, and the issues of consanguinity and commensality in the life of the householder were left untouched.[95] In Satnampanth, on the other hand, the initiation by a guru, a critical event, was accompanied by a denial of distinctions between caste and sect. It was thus that while Kabirpanth permitted marriages between Kabirha and Deotaha Telis, Satnampanth—presided over by a householder guru—did not allow marriages and relations of commensality with Kanaujia Chamars who did not accept the authority of Ghasidas and continued with the practice of removing the carcasses and dealing in the skins of dead cattle. There were to be no distinctions within Satnampanth between Telis, Rawats, and Chamars once they joined the sect.[96]

Satnampanth combined the appropriation of elements from popular sects and traditions with a set of focal signs drawn from the ritual hierarchy of purity and pollution. The formation of Satnampanth, in fact, occurred within a symbolic universe filled with substances and practices inherently polyvalent and with multiple associations. Ghasidas forbade the Satnamis meat, liquor, tobacco, and certain pulses and vegetables. The injunctions were common to Kabirpanth, the Satnamis of Awadh, and other sects and also pressed dominant meanings within the ritual hierarchy of purity and pollution. These substances were sectarian markers, the bearers of impurity, and, often, the signifiers of a low ritual status. Satnampanth cast off impure substances and practices. The members of Satnampanth were prohibited the use of cows for cultivation and were asked not to plough after the midday meal. It is significant that the Marathas had undertaken steps toward the protection of cows in Chhattisgarh, and the Gonds of the region had given up the practice of using cows for cultivation.[97] The Satnamis, as Chamars, had removed the carcasses of dead cows, bullocks, and buffaloes within the village. They had a claim on the skins and the flesh (which they ate) of the dead animals. It was this association with the death substances of a higher being, the cow, which underlay their lowness, situating the group at the margins of village society, outside the central network of relationships defined by service castes. The prohibitions within Satnampanth effected a change in the Satnami relationship with the sacred cow, sought to end the stigma attached to their earlier caste practice, and established a claim to purity. This act of reworking their place within social and ritual hierarchies had led the Satnamis to reject the practice—the acceptance of substances of death pollution from the higher castes—which had defined their low position in the caste order.[98] Clearly, the Satnamis drew upon the ritual hierarchy of purity and pollution to question their subordination.

The accent within Satnampanth was on the purity of the body. This purity had to be maintained. The guru played a critical role here. After the initiation of Satnampanth, the guru's home became a major pilgrimage for its members.[99] Moreover, Ghasidas began the tradition of *ramat*, in which the guru and his sons traveled to areas with a concentration of Satnami population to provide *darshan* (vision).[100] In the pilgrimage to Bhandar and during *ramat* the Satnamis offered coconuts (and later money) to the guru and then drank the *amrit*, water in which they had washed the guru's feet.[101] Edward Harper and Lawrence Babb have both shown that *charanamrit* (nectar of the feet), a mark of "respect pollution," is a sign and practice embedded within the divine and ritual hierarchies of Hinduism.[102] In a fundamental act that repositioned a major sign of the divine and ritual hierarchies of the caste order, the *charanamrit* that was obtained from washing the feet of the deities of the Hindu pantheon (and of certain superordinates within the ritual hierarchy of caste society) had become a distinctive symbol of the substance of the guru's authority and purity. Ghasidas was fashioned as a guru who combined the characteristics of a saint, a shaman, and a healer. His *amrit* not only purified but also healed and regenerated the bodies of Satnamis. It cured snakebites, fulfilled desires for the birth of a child, and repaired bodies.[103]

Satnampanth not only drew upon, but it also rejected elements of the hegemonic hierarchies within caste society. The sect had no place for gods and goddesses who were active members of the cosmic order, the beings who defined and sustained a divine hierarchy. We know of the close connection between divine and social hierarchies within caste society. A person's ritual status is closely tied to his/her access to gods within the divine hierarchy.[104] This matrix is operated by gods and goddesses. But Satnampanth rejected the *devi-devtas* (gods and goddesses) who were themselves *murtipujak* (idol-worshiping) beings. In a dramatic move, which sought to abolish the marks of a low ritual status, Ghasidas countered the machinations of village gods and goddesses by throwing them onto a rubbish heap.[105] The guru established *maghi puno* (the night of the full moon in *magh*, January–February), *bhad athon* (the eighth day of *bhad*, August–September), and *dashera* (the tenth day of *ashwin*, October) as sacred dates in the Satnami ritual calendar.[106] In the constitution of sacred time for the Satnamis, these dates were associated with the gurus rather than the divinities of the Hindu pantheon. Moreover, Satnampanth had no temples. Its members were to worship *satnam* by repeating his name, morning and evening, facing the sun. This abolition of the divine hierarchy was accompanied by a rejection of the figure of the priest, whose place and function are closely tied to the ritual hierarchy within caste society. *Satnampurush* and the gurus were established as the mythic figures who displaced the gods and goddesses of the Hindu pantheon. Ghasidas established the position of *bhandari* who replaced the *purohit* within Satnampanth. The *bhandari*, as a nominated representative of the guru in a village, conducted the life-cycle rituals and played a major role in the festivals of the Satnamis. Finally, the rituals of Satnampanth came to underscore the closeness, the bounded nature, of the Satnamis. Here the entire Satnami population of the village participated. The rites were conducted in the name of *satnampurush* and Ghasidas by the *bhandari*.[107]

The formation of Satnampanth followed a process of symbolic construction that drew upon existent hegemonies and traditions and situated the symbolic forms in a new context.[108] The repositioned signs, placed together, reinforced each other as markers that defined the boundary of Satnampanth in relation to other groups. The appropriation and repositioning of the signs and practices of the ritual hierarchy of purity and pollution and the symbolic forms of other traditions led to the creation of Satnampanth as a pure body which in turn cleansed the bodies of its members of signs of impurity. The signs of purity embodied by the Satnamis worked alongside their rejection of the divine hierarchy and the figure of the priest, which are closely tied to social hierarchy, to question and contest the subordination of the Satnamis within the caste order. At the same time, there were limits to the challenge. The Satnami questioning of their subordination reproduced the significance of dominant meanings of purity and pollution and relations of authority centering on the gurus within Satnampanth. These themes are elaborated in the chapters that follow.

Malguzars, Gurus, and Missionaries, 1850–1900

In 1854, after Raghoji III died without an heir, the British acquired Chhattisgarh under the doctrine of lapse as part of the territories of the raja of Nagpur. The next decade saw revenue settlements and the establishment of a new set of property rights in land. The administrators' concern over the privileged position of *malguzars* (village proprietors) led to a shift in policy and legislation in the last three decades of the nineteenth century, but the few changes that were effected remained within the framework of the agrarian hierarchy and proprietary rights established during the 1860s. Even as the processes within the agrarian economy worked against the majority of the Satnamis, the new property rights fed into the authority of the gurus. The second half of the nineteenth century witnessed an elaboration of the organizational hierarchy and the practices of Satnampanth. The guru as the head of the organizational hierarchy and the owner-proprietor of Bhandar simultaneously acquired symbolically constituted attributes of royalty and embodied the power and the truth of *satnam*. Evangelical missionaries, bearing the cross and signs of civilization, made a bid to deprive the gurus of the allegiance of Satnamis. In 1868 Oscar Lohr, the first missionary of the German Evangelical Mission Society, began work among the Satnamis. A pioneer missionary had chanced upon a group of heathens whose faith enjoined them to believe in one god and to reject idolatry and caste. Was this not the hand of "Divine Providence"? Oscar Lohr, it seemed, had only to reveal the evangelical "truth" to the Satnamis before they would *en masse* "witness" and be delivered by Christ the Savior. The Satnamis did not see the coming of the millennium. The group did not go forward to meet its "destiny." The missionaries persevered. The halting enterprise of conversion to Christianity among the Satnamis grew through ties of kinship and the prospects of a better life under the paternalist economy of mission stations. These converts received missionary regulations through the grid of local cultures. The new masters reaped an unusual harvest.

Altered Contexts

After acquiring the territories of the raja of Nagpur the British reconstituted the administration. In 1861 the Central Provinces were created as an administrative region, and within Chhattisgarh Raipur and Bilaspur were established as separate districts. Land revenue policy and practices constituted the principal concern of British administration. Indeed, land revenue was the most important source of income for the state. It made for more than half of the total revenue of the province.[1] Moreover, the question of land revenue was closely linked to the efforts of the administrators to increase the prosperity of the region.[2] Finally, the wider system of law and order—constituted by civil and criminal judicial administration and the police—worked in tandem with revenue administration. The law courts and the police enforced the rules and punished the transgressions of the regulations of the revenue administration.

The years between 1854 and 1868 witnessed three summary settlements where the administrators sought to clearly define the rights of the government, *gaonthias*, and the cultivators through the introduction of British legal concepts of property and contract. These trends underlay a decision in 1860 by the administration of the Nagpur province to revise the land revenue and confer proprietary rights on village headmen. The detailed procedures for the land revenue settlements were embodied in the settlement code of 1863. The first question emerging concerned the proportion of landlord's assets to be collected as land revenue.[3] The new land revenue settlements were based upon prospective rather than existing profits. In Chhattisgarh, settlement officers expected a large increase of profits in the ensuing period and fixed on one-half to two-thirds of the *gaonthia's* assets as land revenue. This meant an imposition of "the largest increase that was practicable" in order to encourage a rise in rents and an entrepreneurial attitude on the part of the landlords.[4] The settlement officers, following an "aggregate to detail" method, estimated the produce and the revenue of a group of villages and then divided the sum among the villagers on the basis of their economic standing. Second, the Chhattisgarh districts witnessed settlements that were to last twenty years. Finally, surplus or uncultivated wastelands were divided into two categories: unoccupied village lands designed to provide villagers with ample adjacent land to extend cultivation and, beyond that, the waste/forest lands.[5]

The efforts of British administration were directed at encouraging an entrepreneurial spirit among the landlords of the Central Provinces.[6] The belief that the grant of proprietary rights was the best way to encourage agricultural enterprise was accompanied by a keenness to bestow them upon the "responsible" members of society. These rights were now to be conferred in Chhattisgarh on *gaonthias* who had earlier collected the government land revenue. In 1861 the chief commissioner of Central Provinces stated: "Rightly or wrongly, the opinion has prevailed with our officers that an estate cannot be managed without a responsible head residing in or belonging to it; that the occupant cultivators must be dependent for support and guidance on a landlord and that for the state to collect the land tax from individual cultivators is objectionable."[7] The policy of the upper levels of provincial administration had privileged the position of *malguzars* by constituting them as improving landlords. At the same time, the agrarian characteristics of Chhattisgarh marked by *lakhabata* (the periodic redistribution of land) and the migratory nature of the agricultural population made the district officials in Raipur and Bilaspur wary of the grand design of the provincial administration.[8] The cautionary, even dissenting, voices of district administrators anticipated some of the difficulties that emerged after the establishment of new proprietary rights in Chhattisgarh. Yet the provincial government went ahead with its policies.

At the end of an inquiry instituted in each village between 1864 and 1867 in Chhattisgarh, the *gaonthias* were given a formal patent that conferred proprietorship. The *gaonthias* were now styled as *malguzars*. The *malguzars'* lands were divided into *seer* (home farm), over which they had complete control, and *khudkasht* (land broken from village waste), in which the tenants were offered some protection. The rest of the village land was held by cultivators. The tenure of holdings of these cultivators was also investigated and the settlements of the 1860s created three grades of tenants: absolute-occupancy tenants, conditional-occupancy tenants, and tenants-at-will. The rents of absolute-occupancy tenants were fixed by the settlement officer, normally for the duration of a settlement. The rents of conditional-occupancy tenants could be increased by the landlord at periodic intervals through an application to revenue courts. The rents of tenants-at-will could be enhanced almost at the wish of the landlord.[9] The details concerning the distribution of land, revised rents, and particular customs in each village were now set down in a *wajib-ul-arz*, village administration paper.[10]

The effects of the graft of proprietary rights on an agrarian system characterized by a lack of fixed and inalienable rights in property, the institution of *lakhabata*, and the cultivators' tendency to migrate led to anomalies and anachronisms.[11] In the initial years the proprietary rights of the *malguzars* were not always understood and the *malguzari* status was not fully recognized.[12] The village headman, who had formerly only received a portion of the rental, had been transformed into a proprietor. The vast majority of peasants had been turned into tenants-at-will. The Commissioner of Chhattisgarh reported in 1868, "The consequences are now appearing, the people are reproachfully saying you have done everything for the Malguzars and made them Maliks [masters] and put us in a worse position than ever."[13] As we shall soon see, the *malguzars* came to understand and use the advantage of their privileges, position, and power.

Where were the Satnamis situated within the new agrarian structure established by the *malguzari* settlement? It is not easy to answer this question. The first difficulty stems from the problem of distinguishing the Satnamis from the rest of the Chamar population. The first census of Chhattisgarh was undertaken on 5 November 1866. The Chamars constituted a little less than a fifth—362,032 of 2,103,165—of the total population of Chhattisgarh. The census report added, "The Chamars of these provinces are almost confined to the country of Chhattisgarh. They in no way resemble the Chamars who are leather workers and dwellers of Northern India. Here the Chamars have thrown off Brahmanical influence, have set up a new creed, possess a high priest and priesthood of their own."[14] The statement, of course, indicates that the census did not distinguish between Satnamis and Chamars and assumed that all Chamars were members of the new sect. Two years later the settlement officer of Raipur commented,

> It is generally supposed that the names of the Satnamis and Chamars are synonymous but this is by no means the case, as the Satnami religion does not refuse to receive proselytes from any caste but as the Chamars form the majority of the sect and as no distinct laws of caste are admitted among its members, all incumbents of other castes become, in the eyes of the Hindoos, Chamars.[15]

At the same time, the colonial administrators—not unlike the local population—continued to use the terms *Chamar* and *Satnami* synonymously. It was only in 1891 that the census mentioned in passing that the Satnamis formed 88.5 percent of the total Chamar population of Raipur district, while in Bilaspur district this figure was 54.7 percent.[16] From 1901 the census enumerators started listing the Satnamis both under the heading of Chamars (including subcastes) *and* under the heading of Satnamis. Over the next four decades there was no significant variation in the proportion of Satnamis to the total Chamar population in Chhattisgarh (see Appendix 2). This does not, of course, allow us to establish the location of Satnamis as *malguzars*, occupancy tenants, tenants-at-will, and field laborers. Indeed, it is only on rare occasions that British administrators in their discussions of landlord-tenant relations mentioned the castes of *malguzars* and tenants. But a very rough estimate is possible. In Bilaspur in 1868, out of a total of 2241 villages, Brahmans owned 513, Banias and Marwaris 221, Rajputs 233, Marathas 46, Kurmis 207, Telis 85, and Chamars 156.[17] For Raipur, Crispin Bates has calculated the ownership of villages by different castes and tribes on the basis of the revised estimate of the second settlement (1885–89). Bates arrived at the estimates by aggregating the number of shareholders of different castes in relation to the total number of villages, since a single village could have several proprietors with rights divided according to a sixteen-anna share (one rupee was made up of sixteen annas). In Raipur in 1869, out of a total of 2097 villages, the caste breakdown of *malguzari* rights was as follows: Brahmans 380.8, Banias and Marwaris 172.5, Rajputs 145, Kurmis 182, Marathas 273.2, Telis 126.3, and Chamars 80.5.[18] It was, often, Brahmans, "Marathas" (meaning people originally belonging to the Maharashtra region, including Brahmans), Rajputs, Banias, and Marwaris who tended to be owners of entire villages. A large number of Satnami/ Chamar *malguzars* may have held only a small share within the villages.[19] Indeed, the Satnamis, described as peasants dependent on the produce of their land, which they cultivated themselves, were primarily tenants-at-will.[20] The Satnamis and Chamars constituted a little over 25 percent of the tenant population in the *khalsa* of Chhattisgarh. A large proportion of the Satnami/Chamar population lived in a corridor running from the area between Raipur and Durg towns, north and eastward on each side of the Seonath River, to the eastern border of Raipur and Bilaspur districts.[21]

Even as the settlements were being finalized, the regional economy was rocked by the famine of 1868–69. The famine came at the end of a succession of poor harvests and dismal monsoons since 1864. The year of 1868–69 began with "very fair" prospects and the first fall of rain in June 1868 was "copious and universal." This raised expectations. Large areas of land were brought under cultivation. Almost all stocks of seed grain were expended. The grain traders sold off their surplus stocks. And then the monsoon failed. The prices of existing supplies of grain soared. There was acute scarcity in Chhattisgarh. The scarcity itself produced few deaths but a severe epidemic of cholera and other fevers led to a high rate of mortality estimated, conservatively, at ten thousand in Raipur district. Moreover, strains of a virulent disease among cows, bulls, and buffaloes combined with lack of fodder led to a significant loss of cattle, "completely ruining many agriculturists."[22] McEldowney has shown that the Central Provinces administration evolved a policy of famine relief only at the end of the century.[23] In 1868–69 the attempts of the administration were inept. The people suffered but stayed on in Chhattisgarh. The famine did not lead to migration.[24] The picture of distress was complete.

In this wider context, with administrators enforcing strict revenue collection, influential upper- and middle-caste *malguzars* bought villages cheaply. A total of 248 villages changed hands. Similarly, "the lower classes . . . who had but lately been constituted [as] ryots [tenants] with certain status and rights of occupancy made over their patties to their Malguzars relinquishing all claims of any sort to right in the land and agreeing to remain in the village as mere tenants-at-will, in practice."[25] The upper-caste *malguzars* withheld customary aid to bring the cultivators to their knees and gain their *pattas*—papers that had constituted them as plot proprietors, occupancy tenants, and conditional-occupancy tenants.[26]

The *malguzars* were extending practices they had initiated well before the famine of 1868–69. In the years preceding the settlements the *malguzars* had deliberately encouraged *lakhabata* and the redistribution of land in order to prevent the accrual of occupancy rights.[27] The settlements had given enormous powers to *malguzars* over their tenants. The *malguzars* now invoked customary authority and selectively drew upon the British legal framework to acquire land and deny tenants their new occupancy rights.[28] In the year following the famine there were reports of tenants being forced en masse to resign their occupancy rights by *gaonthias* who refused them loans of grain and access to fallow lands. The Commissioner of Chhattisgarh commented that when the *malguzars* withheld assistance, "the inhabitants were at [their] mercy," and the *malguzars* became "masters of the situation."[29]

The administrators were indeed concerned about the situation. After the famine it was increasingly felt that tenant claims had been ignored. A shift in policy was inaugurated by George Campbell in 1868. It was ruled that the transfer of holdings no longer banned tenants from acquiring occupancy status, and now they were to acquire these rights retrospectively. Campbell believed that the cultivators had stronger claims on rights to land than the *malguzars*. He wanted to secure the principle that the occupancy status apply to persons rather than to land holdings. Campbell's concerns were taken over by later administrators, and a tenancy act passed in 1883 gave occupancy tenants the right to make improvements on their holdings along with a guarantee of compensation if they were ejected from a holding. Tenants-at-will were classified as "ordinary tenants" and given legal recognition. They could, however, still be ejected if their holding consisted entirely of *sir* (nonfarm) land or if they refused an enhancement of their rents. The rents of the occupancy tenants were fixed at each settlement. In 1898 the act was extended and the settlement officers were given the responsibility of fixing the rents of all tenants.[30]

Did this reworking of policy and the new legislation bring about changes in the pattern of agrarian relations? McEldowney has shown that the attempt of George Campbell to protect and support peasant proprietors in the 1870s did not, in practice, benefit the vast majority of tenants in Chhattisgarh. The modified *malguzari* system could do little for occupancy and other tenants who had gone off to cultivate land outside their villages and even less for those tenants who had lost their holdings. In the period between 1868 and 1890, many *malguzars* in fact managed to retain control over their tenants in spite of protenant laws, because almost every law or procedure protecting tenants had a loophole or a clause the *malguzars* could use to their advantage. For example, the *malguzars* could not legally eject tenants except for rental arrears. At the same time, they allowed the rental arrears to accumulate and then, taking recourse to the law courts, ejected a tenant for nonpayment of rent. Similarly, the *malguzars* used their customary powers: they withheld assistance—for instance, in the form of seed grains over which they had a monopoly—from the tenants who continued to be dependent on them. Finally, they increased rents, collected illegal dues in the form of *nazrana* (premium and consent money), and exploited tenants by turning to the institution of *begar* (forced labor). British administrators were usually aware of these practices and sought to counter them, but the laws eventually enacted remained within the basic framework set up in the 1860s. A law that closed one loophole often opened another. The effort to run the proprietary settlement of the 1860s on a broader basis did not succeed. The changes in law did little more than offset the growth of subtenancy. The proportion of tenants with protected status—compared to those without it—was barely altered. Finally, the privileged position of the *malguzars* remained unchanged. The tightening of the administrative structure made for difficulties for the tenants, and the creation of the occupancy rights did not, of necessity, offer them protection.[31] We find then that the setting up and elaboration of the *malguzari* settlement—the initial British gift of new proprietary rights that strengthened the hand of *malguzars*, the response of *malguzars* to the famine of 1868–69, and their strategies in the face of protenant legislation and policies of administrators—worked to the disadvantage of the vast majority of Satnamis who were tenants. These Satnamis lost out mainly to Brahman, Marwari, and Kurmi *malguzars*.

And what of Satnami *malguzars?* Although a section of Satnami *malguzars* benefited from the processes that worked to the advantage of village proprietors, the transfer of villages that began during the famine of

1868–69 led to the expropriation of several among their ranks over the next four decades. Crispin Bates, on the basis of settlement reports and district gazetteers, estimated the pattern of village ownership by members of different castes and tribes. In Bilaspur the number of villages owned by Chamars and Satnamis declined from 156 in 1868 to 148 in 1881–90 and to 81 in 1910. In Raipur there was an increase in the number of villages owned by Chamars and Satnamis from 80.5 in 1869 to 92.5 in 1885–89 and then a decline to 79 in 1912. In the district of Durg, which was formed in 1902 out of parts of Bilaspur and Raipur, there were (somewhat curiously) no Chamars and Satnamis entered as *malguzars*. The main beneficiaries of these processes were Banias (traders) and Brahmans. The Banias, largely Marwaris who also functioned as moneylenders, increased their ownership of villages in Raipur from 172.5 in 1869 to 298 in 1885–90 to 483 in 1909, an increase all the more remarkable since in 1909 members of the group also owned 160 villages in Durg. The Brahmans increased their ownership of villages in the *khalsa* of Chhattisgarh from 893.8 in 1868–69 to 931.5 in 1885–90 to 1190 in 1909–10.[32] A number of Satnami villages were, moreover, in areas with poor soil.[33] Finally, villages owned by Satnami *malguzars* tended to be populated primarily by members of their community. The continued practice of *lakhabata* in these villages, I show below, attested to the solidarity of the Satnamis. Did this solidarity also perhaps set limits to the gains made by Satnami *malguzars* at the cost of cultivators of their own community?

Satnami *malguzars*, tenants, and agricultural laborers were agents and players in an underdeveloped regional economy. Crispin Bates has made a persuasive case that the rice zone of Chhattisgarh developed in a subordinate relationship to the cotton zone of Berar within the economy of Central Provinces. As Berar came to specialize in the production of cotton, a cash crop, it was fed by exports of rice from Chhattisgarh. The opening of railways between Nagpur and Raipur in 1888 made for more effective links and a closer relationship between the two agro-economic zones. The increase in the production of rice in Chhattisgarh occurred through *malguzars* and tenants bringing previously uncultivated land under the plough. There were few changes in the methods of cultivation. Earlier broadcast methods continued and improvements such as transplantation were discouraged by the widespread fragmentation of holdings. These unaltered techniques and patterns of cultivation came under pressure through surplus appropriation from above on a fragmented system of land distribution. The growth of trade in turn did little to alter the lopsided development of Chhattisgarh. The Chhattisgarhi cultivators received a relatively low price for their grain. The benefits of trade went to a small section of intermediary traders and merchants with a "trickle-down effect" that barely went beyond the top third of the agrarian population.[34]

Some of the implications of this economic stasis for the Satnamis emerge in a brief account written in 1885 of the Satnami family of Manai who lived in the village of Padampur in Chhattisgarh. Manai's family consisted of his wife and his mother-in-law who was blind and could not work. Manai and his wife cultivated two and a half acres of land and supplemented their income through agricultural labor. They owned no cattle. Three days' labor entitled Manai to the loan of a plough and two bullocks for one day to work on his land. The family possessed no ornaments, owned only two brass pots, and lived in a small wattle and daub hut with two rooms. They survived on rice gruel for most of the year. Once or twice a month the family ate *bhat* (boiled rice). They spent less than fifteen rupees in a year on food and their annual expenditure, which included eight annas for the Satnami guru, did not exceed their income which, reckoned in money, was less than thirty rupees a year. Manai's family did not have any savings in cash but had kept some rice in store for difficult times.[35]

A rather fuller picture of Satnami "disabilities" emerges in an account written by the missionary Oscar Lohr around 1875. The low ritual status of the community meant that there were marked restrictions on clothes, ornaments, and accessories. Satnami men were not expected to wear a full-size *dhoti* and don a turban or appear in shoes before upper castes. Satnami women were denied a *saree* with a colored border and were not allowed silver and gold ornaments. An umbrella, fashioned as a distinctive cover of authority—arguably through a refiguring of the meanings of the *chhattra* (ornamental canopy) of rajas and gods that at once signified the divine attributes of royalty and the regal aspects of divinity—was reserved for use by upper castes. Forms of transport were also marks of status and rank within the caste order. It was in keeping with these cultural schemes that the Satnamis were forbidden from riding horses and elephants and using a palanquin during their weddings. Oscar Lohr was struck by the prohibitions imposed on the Satnamis in the domain of public space on account of their collective embodiment of the stigma of extreme pollution. The community was denied the services of the barber and the washerman. The group was also not permitted to participate in *melas* (fairs) and could not enter temples and the interior of public buildings. To the considerable chagrin of the indignant missionary, the Satnamis were not allowed to approach a provision store too closely and therefore could not examine merchandise before buying it. Finally, the institution of *begar* (unpaid labor rendered by tenants to their *malguzar*) led to the use of force by village proprietors, particularly during the busy season when the fields of the Satnamis needed attention. It virtually followed that landless Satnamis were kept as "serfs" and often worked for food and clothes, instead of being paid wages in cash.[36] The missionary's notes were governed by the need to expose the tyranny and oppression of the caste system, which in turn revealed the liberating power of Christ. Almost certainly it would have been impossible to uniformly impose these various discriminatory practices. At the same time, the restrictions and disabilities listed in Lohr's rough-and-ready inventory constituted the principles of subordination of the Satnamis, which derived from an interplay between meanings imbued with power within the ritual hierarchy of purity and pollution and the culturally fashioned authority of dominant castes.[37]

What was the Satnami response to the adverse processes in the agrarian economy and their own subordination in village life? Until the late 1860s the Satnamis, along with other cultivators, persisted with the strategy of flight from the *malguzar* of their village. Such resistance to the increase in rents, denial of rights in land, and the collection of arbitrary dues also fed the authority of *malguzars*, who welcomed cultivators from another village and then encouraged *lakhabata* in order to prevent their own tenants from gaining occupancy rights.[38] Soon after the famine of 1868–69, settled agriculture increasingly became the norm since tenants could acquire occupancy rights even if they had been involved in *lakhabata*, so long as they had lived in their village for twelve years.[39] By the time of the revision of the settlement in the 1880s a settlement officer stated that *lakhabata* rarely took place.[40] But the Satnamis continued with the practice. In 1869 the settlement officer of Raipur drew a clear connection between *lakhabata* and the Satnamis: "Simga tahsil is the hot bed of lakhabata. The Satnami Chamar is found in much greater numbers in that tahsil than elsewhere and this is the caste which apparently is most in favor of its redistribution."[41] At about the same time the settlement officer of Bilaspur wrote: "It [*lakhabata*] now prevails more among Chamar villages than among any other class, arising I am inclined to think from their entertaining among themselves rather strongly a vague kind of idea that all men have equal rights."[42] In 1880 an official called *lakhabata* a "perfect example of village communism." Twenty years later the settlement officer of Durg echoed these sentiments and attested to the continued practice of *lakhabata* among the Satnamis: perfect equality was at once an essential characteristic of the lakhabata system and a cardinal principle and the true essence of Satnami faith.[43] In these assertions, the discovery of the "truth" about the Satnamis had played tricks with official memory. The administrators seemed to have forgotten the contradictory dimension of the practice of *lakhabata* in the hands of *malguzars*. At the same time, among the Satnamis *lakhabata* does appear to have been carried on as a relatively egalitarian measure that also underscored group solidarity. The settlement officer of Durg found that in villages in which *lakhabata* took place there was a uniformity in the rents paid by the cultivators.[44]

In the late nineteenth century the relations between Satnami tenants and upper-caste *malguzars* were extremely tense. The combination of loss of land, discrimination in village life, and the effects of the famine years of 1896–1900 underlay the initiative of Satnami tenants against *malguzars* in the 1890s. They began a no-rent agitation and withheld rent from landlords.[45] The *malguzars* often disposed of Satnami tenants by fudging legal documents and through perjury. The Satnamis in turn looked upon civil court decrees as instruments of guile that were obtained by trickery. They cultivated the land and reaped the crops even after orders of ejection had been passed. When the *malguzars* did not give their tenants protection and assistance in time of need the Satnamis relied on moneylenders and learned to disregard the claims of *malguzars*.[46] The famine years of the 1890s, according to an administrator, saw the Satnamis at their worst: "To lie, steal, destroy cattle and commit arson are everyday affairs; whilst the bolder spirits indulged in burglaries, dacoities, and violent assaults."[47] In 1892 sixty Chamars, "a turbulent and lawless set," were arrested for rioting in Bilaspur district; in 1896 Chamars attacked a police officer investigating dacoities (armed robberies) once again in the same area; in 1898 a court official was attacked by the Chamars of Raipur when he went to seize cattle for the repayment of debts.[48] Almost twenty years earlier the census had reported, "When mortally wounded the Chamar would go to any length to injure an antagonist. His espirit de corps is worthy of praise, a Chamar will suffer considerable loss to do a good turn to a brother of the same fraternity."[49] It would not be mere conjecture to suggest that a majority of these so-called Chamars were actually Satnamis. In his discussion of the Satnamis Russell had stated:

> Over most of India the term Hindu is contrasted with Muhammadan but in Chhattisgarh to call a man Hindu conveys primarily that he is not a Chamar. . . . A bitter and permanent antagonism exists between the two classes, and this the Chamar cultivators carry into their relation with their Hindu landlords by refusing to pay rent. The records of the criminal courts contain many cases arising from collisions between Chamars and Hindu, several of which have resulted in riot and murder.[50]

Colonial administrators, worried about the solidarity of the Satnami initiative, had retaliated with tough measures that included the stationing of punitive police in turbulent villages.[51] This solidarity was rooted in the institutions and practices of Satnampanth.

The Organization of Satnampanth

Satnampanth had been established by Ghasidas. His second son, Balakdas, took over after his death around 1850 (see Appendix 1). In Satnami myths and other oral accounts Ghasidas is remembered as an ascetic householder. Balakdas in turn is cast as a conqueror who elaborated the organizational hierarchy and the regulations of Satnampanth. The successive generations of gurus functioned within the structure established under father and son. We do not have the evidence to provide a consistent chronological account of the development and changes in the institutions of the sect. What follows then is a picture of the central features of the organization—practices, norms, divinities, and beliefs—of Satnampanth in the second half of the nineteenth century.[52]

The first *gaddi* (seat) of the gurus was established in Bhandar. Ghasidas had built a house and lived in the village during the last years of his life. The village, populated for the most part by Satnamis, also had Rawat, Kewat, Muslim, and Ghasia cultivators.[53] Under Balakdas the wealth of the guru's family increased. In the 1860s a colonial official mentioned Bhandar, the home of the guru, as the ritual center for the Satnamis in which members of the group made "suitable offerings" to the guru.[54] After the initiation of settlement operations and the grant of proprietary rights in the 1860s the guru became the owner-proprietor, the "sixteen-anna" (or sole) *malguzar*, of Bhandar. The development of a market in land and proprietary rights after the revenue settlements and the famine of 1868 prompted Balakdas's only son, Sahebdas, to buy the village of Telashi. Almost a decade later a dispute over the repayment of a debt between Sahebdas and his uncle Agardas led to a division of the *gaddi* of Satnami gurus. Sahebdas stayed on in Bhandar, while Agardas moved to Telashi.[55] Other members of the patrilineage of Ghasidas also went on to acquire proprietary rights in different villages. Bhandar remained the symbolic locus of power, the effective seat of the Satnami guru.

Satnamis had begun flocking to Bhandar after Ghasidas settled there. The injunctions against the propitiation of Hindu gods and goddesses meant that the guru, the only anthropomorphic icon, became the living symbol of worship and belief for the Satnamis. Balakdas inherited Bhandar as a sacred space of Satnami pilgrimage, where the *darshan* and *amrit* of the guru carried the substance of his authority. The second guru also elaborated the pattern. The reconstitution of sacred time in the Satnami ritual calendar was pressed further into the service of the gurus when Balakdas institutionalized the practice of an annual *puja* of the guru on *dashera*.[56] The calendrical event attracted Satnamis in ever larger numbers to the seat of the guru. It also invoked the curiosity of the missionary Oscar Lohr who wrote of a visit to the guru in Bhandar on the occasion in 1868.

As I approached the village, I saw a great mass of people milling about and making their way toward me. Soon they had completely surrounded me. I tried to address them, but found this impossible. Then in the midst of this crowd of three or four thousand people, I saw the Chief Priest coming toward me.[57]

The establishment of Bhandar as a focal site of Satnami pilgrimage over the nineteenth century defined its preeminence in the structure of beliefs and practices within Satnampanth.

A serious violation of norms and taboos could occasion a visit to Bhandar. The Deputy Superintendent of Police, Raipur, in the context of the famine of 1868–69 noted:

> Even Satnamee Chamars who by the precepts of their faith are forbidden to indulge in animal food thought nothing of stealing, killing and eating buffaloes and cows or even of devouring such as they found dead. They also indulged in Mussor [a red lentil] and certain Bhajees or spinaches [sic] which in times of greater plenty they had prided themselves in abstaining from, about which unorthodox practices when taunted by their neighbors, who rejoiced in the reformers breaking through their rules and observances, they would excuse themselves by saying that necessity had no laws and all that they would have to do would be to obtain absolution from the Gooru.[58]

Thus the guru at Bhandar provided the Satnamis, who had broken rules and transgressed norms, the way to reenter Satnampanth. A Satnami in turn had explained that to accept *amrit* from the guru in Bhandar was not to speak or work against him, and thereby to rigorously observe the rules of Satnampanth.[59]

A pilgrimage to Bhandar was not the only way of having *darshan* of the guru and obtaining *amrit*. The institution of *ramat*—initiated by Ghasidas and put on a sound organizational basis by Balakdas—meant that the gurus traveled every year to villages in different parts of Chhattisgarh. The Satnamis would come and touch the guru's feet, drink *amrit*, and make an offering to him. The guru in turn settled matters involving the violation and transgression of norms of the sect. *Ramat* embodied the elements of a spectacle—Balakdas had outraged the feelings of the upper castes by going on tour wearing the sacred thread (the mark of the twice born in caste society) and riding an elephant—and had become part of the established order of Satnampanth in the second half of the nineteenth century.[60] The census of 1881 complained that "the present guru spent his time managing his own temporal concerns, and in making a sort of progress (tours) through the country, receiving presents, offerings, and homage from all, but enlightening none."[61] In 1890 P. N. Bose reported that the guru "went on tour in great state, with elephants, camels" and a large retinue.[62] Russell writing at the time of the famine ten years later had felt that the subscriptions to the guru had been significantly reduced.[63] The situation did not last very long and by the early twentieth century the gurus were again receiving large sums of money from the *bhandaris* in different villages.[64] The institution of *ramat* remained alive.

The offerings made by Satnamis on their pilgrimage to Bhandar and during *ramat* and the imposition and collection of fines from Satnamis who had erred provided the gurus with considerable wealth. Under Balakdas the appropriation of the sacred thread, which added to his bearing as the representative of *satnam*, and the simultaneous use of elephants and horses—the symbols of authority of the raja and dominant landholding groups—at once displayed the ascetic qualities of purity and truth and the regal attributes embodied by the guru. The acquisition of the proprietary rights of Bhandar and Telashi did not merely lead to a *malguzari* income. It also meant that aspects of the newly constituted authority of the *malguzar* as the controller of land and power came to be attached to the royal aspect of the Satnami guru. The missionary Oscar Lohr described the guru's house in Bhandar as "very extensive," built like a great temple without idols, and surrounded by an aura and abundance of wealth. The use of elephants, camels, and horses as modes of transport and the keeping of armament-bearing retainers reinforced this image.[65] The guru was both on par with and shared the attributes of a *raja-admi*, kingly person.[66]

A photograph from the late nineteenth century, taken by the missionary Julius Lohr, shows a Satnami guru with his retinue (see Figure 1).[67] The guru sits on a chair which resembles a throne in the center of the picture. He wears a *dhoti* of fine cloth, a short jacket of silk with a brocade collar, and sports a turban on his head and a large ring on the little finger of his right hand. The guru has taken off his shoes and his right foot rests on the right hand of a youth who is squatting on the ground with a *lota* (round vessel) in his left hand. The young Satnami is about to take *amrit* from the guru. The guru's retinue stands on his left and right, in front of and behind him. The retainers are dressed as soldiers and have a martial bearing. They are wearing turbans, jackets, a broad belt with what seems an official insignia on the buckle, loose white trousers and ornate shoes, and carry swords in their right hands. To the guru's right and left and immediately behind him are three men, the special body guards, who also bear a shield in their left hands. In front, on the left of the picture, stands a figure who looks like a *chaprasi* (peon). He wears a jacket, belt, and trousers but his turban seems smaller. He also holds a long stick rather than a sword in his right hand and, unlike the other retainers, he does not wear a scarf. The posed-for nature of the photograph underscores the twin aspects of the guru's authority: the provider of *amrit*; and the regal figure with his retinue of advisers, body guards, soldiers, and a peon.

Figure 1. *Satnami guru, circa 1898. Source: J. J. Lohr,* Bilder aus Chhattisgarh und den Central Provinzen Ostindiens *(1899)*

It was Balakdas who had invested the guru *gaddi* with attributes of royalty. His successors elaborated the theme. According to colonial administrators, by the late nineteenth century the wealth of the gurus had declined, they had become indebted, and golden pinnacles that had adorned the house in Bhandar had been stolen.[68] Satnami myths explain this decline as a manifestation of the principle of disorder, but they do not divest the figure of the guru of his regal attributes.[69] It is not surprising then that Satnamis continue to refer to the guru's house in Bhandar as a kind of palace, which once had golden pinnacles on top, and to the guru as the bearer of the truth of *satnam*, who commands elephants, horses, and, indeed, motor cars.

The structure of authority of the gurus was further secured through marriage. A marriage in the guru family cemented alliances. Satnami myths and oral testimonies recount that the members of the guru family were invariably married into the families of substantial cultivators and *malguzars* within the community. Partappurin, for instance, who married the three sons of Ghasidas in succession, was the daughter of the *gaonthia* of Partappur. The affines were—or, like Partappurin's father, went on to become—important figures within the organizational hierarchy of Satnampanth. This organizational structure extended from the gurus at the top to *mahants, diwans,* and, finally, down to the body guards and peons of the guru and *bhandaris* and *sathidars* in villages. Ghasidas had appointed *bhandaris.* Balakdas developed and formalized the structure. This was possibly refined even further by the later gurus.[70] Satnampanth had a firmly entrenched organizational hierarchy by the middle of the second half of the nineteenth century. A report from 1881 on "the religious leadership of the Satnamis" spoke of both the guru and his numerous lower representatives.[71] In 1890 P. N. Bose while reporting that the Satnami guru went on tour with "a large following" also added that the *bhandaris* collected what was due to the guru and represented him in "all social ceremonies."[72] Julius Lohr's photograph of a guru with his retinue of advisers, armed retainers, and a *chaprasi* confirms this picture.

We get a fuller description of the organizational hierarchy of Satnampanth that had developed over the nineteenth century in an account of Satnami religious practices written in the early twentieth century. A *mahant* regulated the community and upheld the norms of Satnampanth within defined territorial limits: the area under his control could range from five to a hundred villages. The *diwan* always accompanied the guru on *ramat* and was his adviser, while the *chaprasi* ran errands and did odd jobs for the guru. The *bhandari* was the representative of the guru in a village: he acted as a priest in life-cycle rituals and oversaw the feasts of the caste for the expiation of offenses. On these occasions he broke a coconut in the name of the guru and in return received eight annas or a rupee. The *sathidar* in a village issued invitations and gathered Satnamis for ceremonies and feasts and received four or five annas on these occasions. The *sathidar* and *bhandari* had taken on the respective roles of the barber—who issued invitations to ceremonies and rituals of all but the lowest castes—and the Brahman priest to constitute an alternative to the network of relations with service castes in the village, which excluded the Satnamis. The group had elaborated a pattern where members of the extended kin—agnates and affines—carried out the ritual functions that were performed by the service castes of priests, washermen, barbers, and graziers during the rites of passage of other castes.[73] Among the Satnamis, forms of disability were turned into designs of assertion.

This organizational structure meant that principles of caste and sect were intermeshed with each other within Satnampanth. A comparison with Kabirpanth of Chhattisgarh serves to clarify the issue. Members of all castes could, theoretically, be initiated into Kabirpanth. The guru did not admit distinctions of caste among his followers. All Kabirpanthis joined in the *bhandara*, the communal kitchen, and ate the food cooked by Kabirpanthi ascetics. At the same time, Kabirpanthi householders were governed by the norms of their respective castes in everyday village life. It was not only that rules of caste forbade interdining and intermarriage, for example, between Teli and Panka members of the sect, it was also that the guru of Kabirpanth had no say in matters involving marriage, commensality, and transgressions of caste norms among his followers. These questions were internal to each caste and were settled through the mechanism of the caste *panchayat*.[74] All this is expressed in the contrast that the Kabirpanthis draw between *samaj* (society) and *jati* (caste), on the one hand, and *dharm* (faith) and *panth* (sect), on the other.[75]

The Satnamis functioned with rather different principles. The Introduction has noted that contrary to Louis Dumont's ideal typical model of renouncers and their orders, sects adopt different approaches toward rules of caste. Satnampanth combined an acceptance of rules of caste in certain areas along with the rejection of these distinctions in other spheres. Satnampanth was a sect that admitted members of different castes through a rite of initiation. At the same time, the rules of admission were governed by norms that did not permit members of castes bearing impurity—for instance, Mehtars (sweepers), Ghasias (a caste that looked after horses), and Dhobis (washermen)—to be initiated into Satnampanth.[76] The rules became rigid under Balakdas.[77] Here the admission of a person who could be taken into Satnampanth involved his/her acceptance of a *kanthi* and giving a feast—a commensal act of group solidarity—to the Satnamis. The twin act signaled both, the initiation into a sect and the incorporation into a caste. Once a person joined Satnampanth there were no distinctions between high and low. Members of different castes—for instance, Telis, Rawats, and Chamars—became part of one body and were bound through ties of consanguinity, commensality, and the belief in a common guru.[78]

The guru as the head of the organizational hierarchy within Satnampanth regulated the prohibitions on food and the transactions with service castes. Apart from the restrictions on food that we have noted, the rules of Satnampanth prohibited Satnamis from getting their clothes washed by a washerman or their hair cut by a barber, or to eat sweets made by the village confectioner or drink buttermilk from the house of the village grazier. The Satnamis had always been denied the services of the barber and the washerman, but the transactions with the confectioner and the grazier were within the bounds of fair play in the caste order. The restrictions here articulated a set of new norms that negotiated the pattern of old exclusions. Together the prohibitions on interaction with the barber, the washerman, the confectioner, and the grazier seized upon the signs of subordination of the Satnamis and set them up as symbols of the self-reliance and the superiority of the sect. They formalized a clear alternative to the powerful network of relationships with service castes within village life. The regulations were overseen by gurus, *mahants*, and *bhandaris*. The *mahants* and *bhandaris*, as the representatives of the guru, had the right to impose a fine on the Satnamis who had broken the rules and, on their failure to pay, to ostracize and excommunicate them. They also informed the guru during his *ramat* about members of the group who had violated norms and regulations. The final authority in these matters rested with the guru. The rules concerning food and the transactions with service castes enforced the purity of the Satnami body.[79]

The control of the guru extended to matters of marriage. Indeed, the breaking of rules of Satnampanth and consequent ostracism and excommunication often centered on "matters concerning women." Satnamis were outcast when "(1) they ate in the house of a person of another caste (2) kept a woman of another caste (3) were caught doing wrong with a woman of another caste (4) did wrong with the brother's wife or the wife's elder sister or another relative."[80] During *ramat* the guru also imposed a *dand* (fine) on those men who contracted a relationship with another man's wife or with "a woman who had been abandoned by her first husband."[81] The reference here was to *churi* or *paithoo* (secondary marriages), where a person left his/her spouse and started living with another partner. The marriage was solemnized with the new husband giving the woman *churis* (bangles), paying a *behatri* (compensation for brideprice) to the earlier husband, hosting a ritual feast for Satnamis in the village, and paying a fine to the guru.[82] The settlement of *jati* (caste) affairs and disputes among the Satnamis was carried out by the *jat sayan* (caste elders), the *bhandari*, and the caste *panchayat*.

If the matter could not be settled in the village it was taken up by the Satnamis of a group of villages, which could include a *mahant*. The settlement at the level of a village or a group of villages involved the imposition and payment of a fine and a feast to the caste for the expiation of the offense. The guru usually received a portion of the fine when he went out on *ramat*. The number of people to be fed depended on the nature of the transgression and violation of rules and the status and standing of the offender. A failure to accept the decision of the caste elders led to excommunication. In such cases the readmission into Satnampanth required the mediation of the guru. The offender had to drink the guru's *amrit*, break a coconut, make an offering of money to the guru, and feed the Satnamis in the village.[83] The guru as the head of the organizational hierarchy of Satnampanth regulated the community, which combined the twin, closely linked features of a *jati* and a *panth*, a caste and a sect.

A set of symbolic markers served to define the boundary of Satnampanth. The *kanthi*, a string with wooden beads, was appropriated by Ghasidas from Kabirpanth. The *kanthi* signaled a neophyte's initiation into Satnampanth. Balakdas added to this process of symbolic construction. The guru distributed the sacred thread among the Satnamis. The appropriation of the sacred thread by a low caste is often interpreted through the lens of sanskritization. I will return to this issue later.[84] My point here is that the sacred thread, which was worn by a Satnami after he came of age and started following the rules of Satnampanth, was also a symbol of intersectarian rivalry and difference. Satnamis argue that the combination of *janeu* and *kanthi* distinguished them from Kabirpanthis, Vaishnavas, and Brahmans.[85] Finally, the Satnamis acquired another marker, during the nineteenth century, in the form of *jait khambh* (victory pillar), a high bamboo pole with a triangular piece of white cloth that served as a flag on top. The *jait khambh* in each Satnami settlement was a symbol of the guru's authority that also reminded the community of their boundedness as a group. The white flag, a sign of purity, was changed on *dashera*, the occasion of guru *puja*.[86] The markers within Satnampanth underscored the centrality of the guru who was the representative of *satnam*.

It would be much too sanguine, however, to assume that the Satnamis had effected a complete break with the beliefs and traditions of the past. In the late 1860s the settlement officer of Bilaspur observed that to a superficial observer most of the social practices of the Satnamis did not present anything peculiar and different from the arrangements of the Hindus. At the same time, he added that closer inquiry revealed the distinguishing features of the group.[87] The administrator's comment directs us toward a creative cultural process in which the Satnamis drew upon their membership of the new sect and upon preexistent traditions to fashion novel modes of belief and worship over the nineteenth century. This construction of deities and constitution of practices worked alongside the Satnami subversion of the divine hierarchy of the Hindu pantheon and the central role accorded to the gurus of Satnampanth.[88]

Apart from *satnam* and Ghasidas, Mahadev (Shiva) and Drupda *mata* emerged as the two major deities of the Satnamis.[89] The Satnamis, "make an earthen vessel and, believing a stone to be the phallus of Mahadev, put it on top [of the vessel] and a basil plant in the vessel. This is worshipped once a year. They light incense and break a coconut before it and say, O Mahadev Maharaj [see to it that] the grain, wealth, bullocks, and cows that we have now always remain with us."[90] Mahadev—the destroyer of the world in Hindu mythology and an awesome figure within the cosmic order—was a god known to be easily pleased and generous in granting boons. If this was the reason behind the worship of Mahadev, it is also interesting that the particular representation of the deity and the *puja* offered to him were peculiar to the Satnamis. Now, while the worship of a stone can fuse together attributes of the deities Vishnu and Shiva, an earthen vessel with a stone and a basil plant—the last a distinctive symbol of Vishnu—was a novel construction of Mahadev. Similarly, even as the burning of incense and the breaking of a coconut seemed to draw upon paradigmatic elements of Hindu *puja*, issues of fertility and the offering of milk, which are characteristic of the Hindu worship of Mahadev, were absent from the Satnami variation on the theme. Similarly, Drupda *mata* was a goddess fashioned by the Satnamis. Drupda or Drupta was a corruption of Draupadi, the heroine of the epic narrative *Mahabharata*. Chhattisgarh has an extremely popular folk version of the epic, the *Pandvani,* which is sung and recited as part of a vigorous oral tradition. In Hindu mythology it was Draupadi's marriage with five brothers and her subsequent inability to love all of them equally that prevented her from entering heaven. This also stood in the way of her deification. The Satnamis, on the other hand, seized upon the character of Draupadi from the dramatic performances of the *Pandvani,* gave it a new twist by celebrating the heroine's marriage with the five Pandavas, and provided her with the attributes of other goddesses to transform her into Drupda *mata.* She was worshiped by the lighting of a lamp and incense in front of the *jait khambh*—the symbol of the guru served simultaneously as the icon of the goddess—and the singing of songs in her praise. The Satnamis would "fall down and appeal, O Drupta Mata guard our children."[91] The fashioning of Mahadev and Drupta *mata* as distinctive deities of the community was a part of the Satnami innovation with and play upon preexistent traditions in the construction of their forms of worship.

The pattern replicated itself in the Satnami reworking of Hindu festivals. In *dashera,* established as a sacred date within the Satnami calendar, the celebration of the god-king Ram's victory over the demon Ravana was re-placed by *guru puja* and an annual pilgrimage to Bhandar. This perfor-mance of *guru puja* on *dashera*, in keeping with a larger cultural scheme of the practices of *rajas* during this festival, underscored the regal attributes of the Satnami guru.[92] But there was a little more to the picture. The mission-ary Oscar Lohr, on his visit to Bhandar on the occasion in 1868, had re-ported that the guru's body was dripping with sour milk, which had been poured over him by his followers. Now this was also part of a wider pattern where the icons and idols of major Hindu deities—Shiva and Vishnu—are bathed in curd and milk. Thus, the Satnami guru had taken the place of the god-king Ram, the seventh incarnation of Vishnu, and the sour milk rein-forced the deification of the guru as a god on earth.[93] The festival of *janmashtami* (the day of the birth of Lord Krishna) also evinced a transfor-mation at the hands of the Satnamis. Indeed, in the late nineteenth century the Satnamis seemed to have effected an inversion in the festival: they had thrown milk, buttermilk, and curd at each other and trampled upon them in a symbolic mocking of the Hindu celebration of *janmashtami*, a festival that interestingly was largely confined to the towns of Chhattisgarh at least until the 1930s.[94] Finally, the Satnamis responded to the forms of song and dance specific to particular castes in Chhattisgarh by developing *panthi geet* and *panthi naach* (songs and dance of Satnampanth). These folk forms re-told Satnami myths that celebrated the gurus of Satnampanth and were per-formed in marriages and other celebrations associated with life-cycle rituals and festivals.[95]

The Satnamis shared the wider pattern of beliefs that centered on threats to the village community. They worshiped Dulha Deo, the guardian deity of the village, whose *puja* was performed by a *baiga* (shaman) and who was accessible to members of all castes. In a related move, the Satnamis also joined the other castes to pay subscriptions to a shaman to protect the vil-lage from an illness, a mishap, or a misfortune.[96] A missionary employee observed—with a measure of satisfaction mixed with glee—that Satnamis believed in different harmful and evil spirits. A man who died after eating opium or in an accident or who committed suicide became a *bhoot*. A *mashan* kept dead men and women in his control through magic and incan-tation. A *shaitan* was a dangerous spirit. A man who died before getting married became a *rakshasa*. A woman who died in childbirth along with her baby turned into a *paretin*.[97] And then there were *tonhis* (witches). Ashen faced, malevolent, with a morbid sexuality, they cast spells and had a par-ticular penchant for sucking the blood of babies through a thread that trav-eled for miles before attaching itself to the navel of a new born. The Satnamis, in addition to seeking the help of the shaman, invoked their gu-rus for protection against these evil spirits and vile witches.[98]

The different festivals in the village that were tied to the agricultural cycle were critical for crops, rains, and seasons. Generally, they did not mark out the ritual subordination of the Satnamis and invited their participation. During *hareli/haryali* (July–August), one of the most popular agricultural festivals, the Satnamis put a red *tika* (mark) on, burnt incense before, and made an offering of *roti* and coconut to their agricultural implements, which had earlier been washed, and kept them in front of the cow shed. They also allowed their cattle to rest until midday, offering both the cows and the oxen specially prepared rice balls and a mixture of salt and wheat flour and garlanding them on the occasion. Often, Satnami women kept a fast for a day or two before *hareli* and (whenever possible) fed the cattle *ghee* (clarified butter), salt, and sweets. At noon on the day of the festival, when the *rawats* (graziers) came to collect the cattle to take them out to graze, the Satnamis joined other castes in making customary ritual gifts (generally rice) to these graziers. In some parts of Chhattisgarh, during *hareli* the Satnamis placed *londi*, a flour ball made with salt, in their fields for a good harvest and also arranged branches of the *belwa* tree (a mark of Shiva) there to ward off lurking evil. Although there is little direct evidence, the Satnamis may well have participated in the festivals of *jawara* and *aarti*, which fell before *hareli* in the agricultural year, to propitiate Mouli Mai, the earth goddess, and thus ensure a bountiful rice harvest. Later in the year, during *surhuti* (another festival in the agricultural cycle of the region), the Satnamis burnt *diyas* (earthen lamps) for Lakshmi (the goddess of wealth), washed their silver coins, putting a *tika* on them, and did a *puja* so that money would not leave their homes. Similarly, in *diwali* (festival of lights marking the victory of the god-king Ram over Ravana, and also a key festival in the agricultural cycle, celebrated in October–November), paddy from the fresh crop was cooked in a new utensil, an offering was made to the cows in the house, Mahadev was appealed to so that he would not let Lakshmi leave the household, and money was given to the village graziers who danced before the house. The Satnamis danced in their own group, separate from the other castes, in the village on *phagun* or *holi*, a festival celebrated with greater gusto in the towns rather than in the villages of Chhattisgarh. During *pora* (August–September), very much a festival of the poor, the Satnamis burnt incense and offered a *roti* to a clod of earth and to earthen figures of bullocks, and after that fed their kin.[99] A poor Satnami explained the matter to a missionary, "We have no Lakshmi [both, the goddess of wealth and money]. What shall we worship? A bit of earth in which Parvati [the consort of Shiva] resides."[100]

Satnami life-cycle rituals combined features shared with other castes in the village with their own emphases. Around the time of the birth of a baby, the Satnamis like most other castes prohibited a man from cohabiting with his pregnant wife for a specified period (generally a month before and a month after the delivery), the new born was placed on a measure of grain and money and then bathed three times, and the mother was not allowed to eat anything or bathe for four days. However, among the group it was a Satnami woman—and not the untouchable village midwife engaged by other castes—who cut the umbilical cord of the baby after whispering an incantation of the sect into its ear. During *chhatti* (ceremony on the sixth day after the birth of a child) the Satnamis followed the rituals of other castes, including bathing the mother and giving her herbs and food. Among the Satnamis, however, the *bhandari* officiated as the priest, and his act of breaking a coconut in the name of the guru was a central feature of the ceremony.[101]

And what about (primary) marriage? I recall here two complementary descriptions, one by a Satnami convert to Christianity and the other by a colonial administrator.

Whenever they [Satnamis] have money in their hands they fix a *shadi* or *bihav* [primary marriage] in the five months of *magh-fagun-chait-baisakh-ashadh*. When we go from our village to another to arrange a marriage we go to the house of a person who is not of our *gotra*. The people of that household ask what brings you here. We answer that we have heard that there is a girl in your house. If the householder then states that there is a girl in the house and we will give her to you, arrangements are made for food and a day is fixed for the engagement. When we go for the engagement money, clothes, and ornaments are given to the bride's parents in front of five people.[102]

The elders of the village . . . fix the date of the marriage by reference only to the convenience of the parties [without consulting an astrologer or a priest]. On the appointed day the bridegroom's party, seldom more than twenty in number, come to the house of the bride's father, stay there for two days and are entertained at the latter's expense. On the morning of the second day, a Marwa (temporary bower) is erected in front of the house, and the bride and the bridegroom walk around it seven times in the presence of the caste people, after which they receive the benedictions of the elders and are thenceforth looked upon as man and wife. No [Brahman] priest is called upon to officiate at the ceremony, and no set words like the Hindu "Mantras" are ever used. The next day after the marriage, the bridegroom's party leaves for home. The bride goes in a "Gara" (cart) if the bridegroom can afford one, otherwise she walks. . . . After two or three days residence at her husband's house, the girl returns to her parents, with whom she continues to live until puberty, notice of which is duly sent to the husband. A day for the "Pathoni" or home-taking is then fixed, when the husband comes with a lot of people to demand his wife.[103]

Although these descriptions are by no means exhaustive, we find two significant and distinct emphases here. On the one hand, the ritual prestations between the affines, the negotiation and payment of a brideprice, ceremonial feasts, and *pathoni* (the bride's formal move to her affinal home after reaching puberty) were not practices peculiar to the Satnamis, but were rather features common to marriages among several low and middle castes. On the other hand, among the Satnamis the auspicious date for the wedding was fixed by the elders of the community without consulting astrologers or priests, the *bhandari* represented the guru at the ceremony, which took place without any Hindu incantations and chants in front of the *chauka* of Satnampanth, the songs sung by the women of the group on the occasion celebrated Drupda *mata* and the Satnami gurus, and after *pathoni* the couple would sometimes visit the guru at Bhandar.[104]

The pattern was similar in the rituals around death among the group.

> At the time of a person's death he is made to drink a mixture of the leaves of basil, curd, pieces of coconut, grass, and the water in which the feet of five [Satnami] men have been washed. This is called *panchamrit* [nectar of five substances]. A calf is brought. This is brought because the person goes to *baikunth* [heaven] holding the tail of the calf. To hold the tail of the calf fulfils obligations to the nephew [sister's son] which gets rid of sin. After people come back from the burial—all of them, men with men and women with women, go to have a bath. Then all the people go for a bath after three days. On this day people from different villages come. All these people are fed. The feast is [given] on behalf of the father, the mother, and brother [family] of the person who has died so that s/he doesn't stay in this world and goes straight to heaven.[105]

We find that here too amid certain similarities with other castes—for instance, the significance of the calf, the ritual removal of death pollution, the feast—there were also significant differences. The *panchamrit* of the group was distinctive: the inclusion of water in which the feet of five Satnamis had been washed as a constituent of the solution was premised upon and signified the purity of Satnampanth and the boundedness of the community. Of course, this boundedness was inescapably gendered, since it was five men who contributed to the constitution of the (pure) boundaries of the community.[106] The *bhandari* once again served as the representative of the guru.

Missionaries, Satnampanth, and the Community of Converts

It was this central authority of the gurus that was sought to be replaced with the liberating power of Christ by the early missionaries. Mission work in

Chhattisgarh was begun by Oscar Lohr of the German Evangelical Mission Society, which remained the primary missionary organization in the region till the end of the nineteenth century. Lohr first heard of the Satnamis at a meeting of missionaries in Bombay in April 1868. The Rev. J. G. Cooper of the Free Church of Scotland in Nagpur had made an appeal for a missionary to work among "a peculiar sect of people" in Chhattisgarh. The appeal was backed by Colonel Balmain, the Commissioner of the Chhattisgarh Division. Lohr was told that the Satnamis spoke Hindi and that no missionary had ever worked among them. These were the two conditions laid down by the German Evangelical Mission Society for Lohr's missionary work in India. The Satnamis fit the bill. Lohr traveled to Nagpur and met Rev. Cooper who informed him that the Satnamis had given up idol worship under the "leadership of an apparently inspired man of their caste"; the Scottish Mission could not begin work among the group because of financial constraints. "Recognizing the will of the Lord," Lohr decided to begin work in Chhattisgarh. A fortnight later the missionary and his family were in Raipur.[107]

Lohr found a patron and an ally in Colonel Balmain in Raipur. In the postmutiny years, even as the colonial state sought to maintain its distance from the religion of its subjects, individual officers could take a keen interest in "civilizing" the heathen through the agency of missionaries and Christianity. The Chief Commissioner advised the missionary to acquire a site for a mission station and informed him that a large tract of government wasteland comprising 1544 acres was about to be put up for public auction. This dovetailed neatly with Lohr's plans to begin his "work out in the district right in the middle of these people."[108] He bought the land, which included a deserted village, with financial aid from Colonel Balmain and other British acquaintances. Within a few months Lohr's family had moved into a bungalow with outhouses. The missionary named the place Bisrampur (the abode of rest); the neighboring village, with an area of 265 acres, was called Ganeshpur. The missionary was registered as the *malguzar* of Bisrampur and Ganeshpur with proprietary rights that extended to the forest on his land.[109]

Lohr's first encounters with the Satnamis did not await his move to Bisrampur. The missionary set up a school for Satnamis soon after his arrival in Raipur. His effort was to instruct the Satnamis in elementary subjects and Christian truths while finding out more about their sect. This contact led him, on the occasion of the annual festival, to Bhandar.

> When we reached the Guru's residence he had me sit next to him, and after some semblance of order had been achieved with the help of considerable clubbing and beating, I was able to speak to this great mass. I explained to them that they really had no right to call themselves Satnamis, as they did not

know the "True Name" given to men that they might be saved, the name of Jesus Christ. For four long hours I continued speaking, then sat down, weary and exhausted. The Chief Priest himself now served me some refreshments of which I was in dire need. The next morning the crowd assembled once more and I was able to speak to them again. Later I met with smaller groups and answered their questions.[110]

The missionary was elated by the warm welcome he had received and stated that the Satnamis had stroked his beard to show him great honor and affection in their traditional way. "This enthusiastic welcome given to a missionary on his first visit to the people he had come to serve can probably not be duplicated in mission history."[111] But the stroking of Lohr's long flowing beard by the Satnamis was, perhaps, little more than an instance of Satnami curiosity. Was the serving of refreshments by the guru the extension of hospitality to a white *saheb*? Or had the missionary lost the initiative? Had his visit to Bhandar on the day of guru *puja*, along with thousands of Satnamis, unwittingly signified his acceptance of—and his incorporation as an affiliate in—the domain of the guru's authority?[112] The curiosity did not translate itself into conversions, the hospitality was to be replaced by hostility. Lohr's visit to Bhandar set the pattern of differential perceptions, which were a feature of the encounter between the Satnamis and the missionaries.

Oscar Lohr baptized his first three converts soon after moving to Bisrampur. The Christmas service of 1868 had been attended by a thousand Satnamis. The following Sunday a larger crowd gathered to witness the baptism of three Satnamis who had attended Lohr's school at Raipur and had moved to Bisrampur with the missionary. Lohr asked the Satnamis to remove their *janeu* (sacred thread), which they had received from the guru. The missionary's instructions created a furor. The converts who had gone through the motion of a public confession of their faith later recanted. The Satnamis launched an offensive. The thirty-five Satnamis who attended the school in Bisrampur immediately confronted Lohr and told him that they did not wish to convert and would leave the school if they were not permitted to wear the sacred thread. Lohr refused. Twenty-two of the twenty-five students returned that afternoon after Lohr assured them that they would not be forced to become Christians.[113] Until the critical moment of the first baptism, the basic principle of Lohr's teaching that a true Satnami had to believe in the "True Name" of Jesus Christ did not, perhaps, compromise the structure of beliefs of the Satnamis. It may indeed have seemed an elaboration, a variation on the theme of *satnam*. The missionary command to the Satnami converts to remove the *janeu* before baptism, on the other hand, challenged a principle of faith within Satnampanth. The initial millenarian hopes of Lohr were dashed.[114] The Satnamis became wary of the missionary enterprise.

A year later the missionary baptized four converts—two Satnamis, a Kurmi, and a Brahman—in January 1870.[115] The two Satnamis had been students of the training school established in Raipur and then transferred to Bisrampur, the Kurmi had been in mission service for two years, and the Brahman had come in a starving condition during the famine of 1868 and had made rapid progress in learning at the training school.[116] The Kurmi and the Brahman decided to become Christians after they survived a prolonged illness that brought them close to death. The miraculous healing powers of the Lord continued to figure prominently in missionary accounts as a driving force that compelled people to embrace Christianity. At the same time, the missionary fixed upon the natural ties of kinship as the basic building block for conversion among the Satnamis: "The two Satnamis . . . [as] members of large families . . . will become instruments of the conversion of many of their kinsmen."[117]

The missionary's hopes were well founded. Kinship did indeed prove critical to the growth of the Christian congregations. The early conversions of Satnamis in Bisrampur are a case in point. In the pioneer mission station Anjori Paulus was the first Satnami convert, baptized in January 1870. Almost two years later Lohr wrote, "Today I have again led twelve souls to Jesus through baptism: all of them Satnamis. . . . Among the people baptized were the father and mother of Paulus, one of his sisters and his eight days old suckling baby—also his grand parents, daughter and uncle."[118] By July 1872 forty-four people—twenty-seven adults and seventeen children—had been baptized and the same number were under religious instruction, "ready to embrace Christianity."[119] Nearly thirty of these converts and inquirers were members of the pioneer Satnami convert's extended family, which included affines and agnatic kin. The missionary enthused, "From these far spreading and numerous relationships among the Chamars, we may conclude, that hereafter the whole tribe will embrace Christianity."[120] The "whole tribe" proved elusive. At the same time, Anjori Paulus and his relatives were not alone. The early Satnami settlers of Bisrampur and other mission stations were generally followed by their relatives and, over time, a significant proportion of the family was baptized.[121] The missionaries described the process as the growth of Christianity from within. Ties of kinship and bonds of affinity were clearly natural. They were also seen to counter the materialist instincts of the converts.

The converts became a part of the paternalist economy that developed around the missionaries and mission stations. The mission employed the converts as coolies and servants and after a household had saved enough to buy a pair of oxen it was granted four acres of land. The converts who completed the course at the training school were employed as cat-echists, teachers in village schools, and Scripture readers. The missionaries trained the converts as masons, smiths, and carpenters. Most of them were employed at mission stations. The women converts were engaged as ser-vants and employed as bible women. The situation of the converts at mis-sion stations stood in marked contrast to what they had faced as cultivators in their village. They received loans at low rates of interest and the mission-ary, unlike other *malguzars*, did not exact *begar* but paid them for labor on public works such as the building and repair of roads and irrigation tanks.[122] The missionaries, the owner-proprietors of Bisrampur and Ganeshpur, Baitalpur and Parsabhader, held together the economic system of the mis-sion stations.

The authority of the missionary was closely intertwined with a set of key practices, the arts of civilization, initiated by the mission project. It was within the matrix of local cultures that the missionaries were fashioned as *sahebs.* An early map of the Bisrampur mission station shows the imposing, square missionary bungalow in the center; the other mission buildings were similarly placed at masterly discretion within the missionary's domain.[123] A church built in 1873 opposite the missionary's house completed the pic-ture.[124] In another context, Jean and John Comaroff have argued that mis-sion buildings and the spatial organization of activities among the church, the school, the dispensary, the printing press, and the fields, governed by Western notations and divisions of time and labor, formed a part of the attempt of the evangelists in South Africa to rationalize the indigenous com-munity through the geometric grid of civilization.[125] My point here is that the mission buildings and the spatial organization of work were imbricated in the everyday definition and reinforcement of missionary authority, the *saheb* who owned and regulated the fields, the forest, and the mission sta-tion. Moreover, the missionary healed bodies through Western medicine, and these new potions and practices were often seen to embody greater efficacy than local deities and specialists. He also controlled the production of the printed word. This needs to be set in the context of the importance Protestantism attached to the convert self-commitment to the "word" and the "book" as the sign of a true Christian and of the power of writing within an oral tradition. The ability to inscribe and to engender print served to underwrite missionary authority, and the cures that he conjured com-pounded his command.[126] Finally, the missionary was the model in the moral discourse about Christian decency, bodily shame, and physical mod-esty, which turned clothing into an emblem of indigenous Christianity. The men wore pajamas, shirts, and some even had shoes, the women wore full five-yard *sarees* and blouses, and the little girls wore dresses that were sent by rich benefactors from across the seas. These garments and accessories were, of course, not worn at all times. To church and Sunday school? Certainly. At other moments gestures of decency and modesty were enough. The days of loin cloths, *lugdas* (short *sarees*), uncovered breasts, and naked children lay in the past. The missionaries with their shirts, jackets, trousers, solar hats, and dresses—the insignia of the *saheb* and *memsaheb*'s power—presided over this public pantomime of propriety.[127] The gains for the converts were at once material and symbolic and they fashioned a distinctive understanding of missionary authority. A Satnami convert on being asked to perform a menial village duty, for instance, had replied, "No, I have become a Christian and am one of the Sahibs; I shall do no more *begar*."[128] At the same time, these key practices, the social instruments to make wilderness bear fruit and yield a harvest, had contradictory consequences: the "sons of wilderness" came to recognize the signs of civilization as attributes of the power of missionaries, but they could also deploy them in their interrogation of this authority.[129]

The missionary was the master of the mission station. He combined the powers of the *malguzar* and the pastor. The division between temporal and spiritual power became blurred and got lost as the provision of employment and aid to converts was accompanied by a drive to control and discipline the members of the congregation. The missionary in consultation with the local leaders—the catechists and school teachers—among the converts often defined regulations to order the life of congregations.[130] These regulations and institutions governing the community, viewed through the grid of local cultures, show continuities with the rules of Satnampanth. Under the new rules the indigenous congregations retained the concern with norms of purity and pollution and were expected to shun all substances and practices—for instance, carrion, liquor, opium, and marijuana—that were viewed with disfavor by the local population, particularly the Satnamis. Moreover, the principles of endogamy—albeit in the form of marriages with fellow converts—were reinforced through an insistence on ritual feasts to the extended kin and affinal group and members of the community to signify the sanctity of marriage. A marriage with a non-Christian was valid if s/he had joined the church and the wedding feast signified the incorporation of a new member into a bounded group. This seemed to mirror the rules of the sect.[131] Finally, the organization of the congregations was premised upon the institutions of village life. The constitution of the church council with its *prachin* (elders) was fashioned along the lines of the *jat panchayat* with its *sayan* (old/wise men). The church council settled disputes, regulated the life of the congregation, and relied on the mechanism of excommunication, which characteristically "outcasted" the members who transgressed the norms of the community.[132] All this suggests that the rules and institutions set up to govern indigenous congregations involved a reworking and rearrangement of the regulations of Satnampanth within the relocated communities. The missionaries, often unwittingly, participated in the creation of an indigenous Christianity.

And what of breaks with the past? In Protestant ideology marriage, for example, was a sacred contract between individuals and the monogamous household was the basic unit for the conduct of a Christian life. For civilization to flourish the Christian family had to triumph over the moral murk, sloth, and chaos of the heathen world. The missionaries' concern with monogamy and their fear of adultery, a snare and trap of Satan, meant that the converts were forbidden the practice of *churi* or secondary marriages. However, this was a critical arena in which the converts exercised considerable initiative and consistently flouted missionary authority to form what their masters designated as "adulterous" relationships of secondary marriages. Even at the level of transgressions, the institution of marriage showed significant continuities between Satnampanth and the community of converts. The Satnami converts did not replicate a modernized social order in the image of missionary masters and had their own uses for the "truth" offered by the missionaries.

The myths of Satnampanth were reordered among the converts. The key issue was the place of missionaries and Christ in the teachings of Ghasidas. Colonial administrators writing in the late 1860s had found that the basic tenets of Satnampanth—a monotheistic sect opposed to caste and idolatry—resembled Christianity.[133] Oscar Lohr's enthusiasm at the prospect of working among such a people had soon given way to disappointment and caution. The missionary's early reports from the field did not have anything to say on the links between Christianity and Satnampanth. A little later in 1894, von Tanner, who stayed at Bisrampur, mentioned that Ghasidas had been influenced by Christian missionaries whom he had met during his travels: the Satnami guru had prophesied that he would be followed by a White Guru who would deliver the Satnamis. Von Tanner claimed that the Satnamis had identified Oscar Lohr as that White Guru but refused to accept his teachings because of their belief in a crude religious system, a "satanical travesty" of Christian teachings, that had developed since the death of Ghasidas.[134] Was this pure missionary invention? Or had the Satnami converts contributed to the making of this myth? In Satnami myths, as we shall see, Ghasidas's initiation of Satnampanth had come about only after his encounter with *satnampurush*. This *satnampurush* was *shwet* (white), which connoted qualities of purity and truth. Had the converts seized this white attribute of *satnampurush* and assimilated it to the white missionary *saheb*? Or had the links been established by the missionaries? What was in evidence, perhaps, was a coming together of two processes. The converts worked upon the myths of Satnampanth to forge connections between missionaries, Ghasidas, and Oscar Lohr within their oral traditions. The missionaries seized and reordered the myths to fashion them into an alternative history of the Satnamis. The two processes fed each other. In the 1930s the pooled resources of the convert and the missionary were to result in an "authoritative" account of Satnampanth situated on the axis of the inexorable logic of the truth of Christ.

At the turn of the century the population had declined, the land reduced to fallow.[135] According to the reports of colonial administrators, their tough measures—including the stationing of punitive police—combined with the blows of the famine years had broken the spirit of the rebellious Satnamis and laid them "at the feet of their Malguzars." There was of course much more to the picture. Members of the group devised new strategies such as carting of grain and goods to claim some of the benefits of the trade with Nagpur, and out of the experience gained during famine years developed the practice of seasonal migration to supplement their income from land.[136] Most Satnamis who had converted during these years as a strategy of survival in a time of want and misery returned to "the fold of their religion."[137] The small number of Satnami converts at mission stations continued to function within the contours of the distinctively designed institutions and rules governing their communities and defied missionary logic in fashioning their understanding of Christianity, marriage, and sexual transgression. The community as a whole persistently confounded missionary hopes of mass conversions. The unity revealed by the Satnamis in their continuance of *lakhabata* and opposition to *malguzars* was retained in the structure of the myths and the practices of Satnampanth. Perceptions of the unjust measures of an often treacherous *sarkar* and the actual loss of their land had become a part of the group's history.

Satnamis in Village Life, 1900–1950

Adversity and loss, authority and discrimination, virtue and power and their negotiation by the Satnamis in everyday arenas in the first half of the twentieth century are the key themes discussed in this chapter. The main features of the agrarian economy of Chhattisgarh in the late nineteenth century were elaborated between 1900 and 1950. There were also shifts, modifications, and changes as the region came to be more closely integrated—particularly, through the growing trade in grain with the cotton zone of Berar—within the Central Provinces. The Satnamis adapted, through a variety of means, to the changing economic circumstances, but they also lost out in significant ways and key arenas. The economic difficulties of the group were compounded by the principles of its subordination within the caste order. The play of idioms of authority and forms of discrimination was accompanied by diverse Satnami responses to these processes in the domains of the familiar and the everyday in village life. All this raises new questions for explanations of the nature of power in caste society in South Asia. Issues of gender in the community—centering mainly on ritual, sexual exploitation, and kinship—imbued these cultural schemes with further intricacies of the dynamic between meaning and power.

Adversity and Loss

At the end of the nineteenth century, the Satnamis and Chamars were primarily tenants who constituted roughly a fourth of the total tenant population of the districts of Raipur, Bilaspur, and Durg. The other members of the group were located at opposite ends within the agrarian hierarchy as agricultural laborers and *malguzars*. The picture was not significantly altered in the first half of the twentieth century.[1] Several reports for different parts of Chhattisgarh from the period mention the Satnamis (along with Chamars) as a principal caste who constituted between 22 and 30 percent of the total tenant population. At the time of the land revenue settlement of the region between 1927 and 1932, about two thirds of these Satnami tenants were in "average circumstances." A little over 20 percent of the Satnami tenants did not have cattle, were heavily in debt, and, in general, in very poor circumstances, and only about 12 percent were rich or well off with an adequate measure of control over productive resources.[2] As for Satnami *malguzars*, the processes of decline that had seen a reduction in their numbers from 111 to 79 in Raipur and from 156 to 81 in Bilaspur between 1868–69 and 1910–12 continued and form a significant theme within Satnami oral accounts. We do not have detailed statistics, but a number of reports from the period mention the Satnamis along with the Gonds as groups who lost their *malguzari* rights in particular to Banias and Marwaris. This loss consisted of the transfer of all or, more often, a part of their share in the *malguzari* of the village.[3] The land hunger of the Marwaris, Banias, Brahmans, and *malguzars* of other castes was prompted by the increase in the value of land.

The appreciation in the value of land began during the period of recovery that followed the famine years at the turn of the century. In 1927 an official spoke of an increase in the demand for and the price of land and a rise in the subleting values and the price of food grains since the beginning of the twentieth century.[4] This increase was manifest in the value of tenancy rights, where the average rate per acre for sale of tenancy land rose from ten rupees at the close of the nineteenth century to forty-six rupees for occupancy land in 1933.[5] The appreciation in the value of landed property both accompanied and was a consequence of a rise in the price of grain and an increase in the occupation of agricultural land. By the late 1920s the price of rice and wheat in different parts of the region had variously risen by between 75 percent and 108 percent since the turn of the century.[6] Similarly, there was an increase in the area occupied by agriculture. In Raipur, Bilaspur, and Durg Districts, occupation had spread virtually to the margins of cultivation by the end of the 1920s.[7] Finally, the period witnessed a rise in the population of Chhattisgarh: a rapid increase between 1901 and 1911, a period of slow rise or even decline over the next decade, and after 1921, once again, a time of quick growth. The increase in the pressure on and value of land and the rise in prices combined with the inability of the *malguzars* to raise rents—on account of the protection of tenants against increases—led the village proprietors to formalize the practice of levying *nazranas* from the early years of the twentieth century. The term *nazrana* was used loosely to denote both the "consent money" extracted by a *malguzar* on the transfer of land between two tenants and the premium s/he obtained for letting out land to a tenant on rent. The Commissioner, Chhattisgarh Division, explained the former practice.

> The tenancy law of the province makes it illegal for an occupancy tenant to transfer his rights. . . . Such transfers are, however, in fact a matter of everyday occurrence but the illegality makes it possible for the proprietor to take a considerable share of the value of property sold as consent money for non-interference in the illegal transfer. The consent money varies from 25 to 50 percent of the transfer price; 33 percent is the common figure.[8]

The *malguzars* also collected very large sums in allotting land to new tenants in their villages. The amount varied according to different qualities of soil and ranged from 30 to 100 rupees an acre. In most cases the *nazrana* was much greater than twenty-five or thirty years of revenue assessment per acre.[9] The tenants generally had to borrow the money—often from the village proprietors, who often functioned as moneylenders—to pay the *nazrana*.

The advantage for the *malguzars* was clear. The practice of levying a *nazrana* meant that the village proprietors pocketed the entire unearned increment; whereas, if they had relied on an increase in rents a part of the enhanced sum would have had to be remitted to the government at the next settlement. The system was of course made easier by the rapid and enormous rise in prices and in the value of land, which left the margin between economic rent and the government assessment so wide that very large sums could be exacted without much effort.[10] It is not surprising then that *malguzars* all over Chhattisgarh opposed the revenue resettlement of the *khalsa* since it cut into their share of *nazrana* even as it provided them with higher rents.[11] The institution of consent money as *nazrana* also worked to the substantial benefit of village proprietors.

The overwhelming majority of the Satnami and other Chhattisgarhi tenants found themselves in a no-win situation. In order to improve their lot they had to get hold of land from the *malguzar* or secure a transfer of right from another tenant. The second option tended to be increasingly more viable given the rise in occupied area and the reduction of waste land. At any rate, in both cases the tenant had to pay a heavy *nazrana* to the *malguzar* as premium or as consent money to effect an illegal transfer. Moreover, the premium and consent money that was paid was borrowed at a minimum of 12 percent interest.[12] There were two consequences. The practice of *nazrana* siphoned off the profits from agriculture that the cultivators could derive from an expansion of cultivation in the context of a rise in the price of grain and an increase in the value of land. Second, *nazranas* prevented the near two-thirds of tenants in "average circumstances" from substantially increasing their holdings and could even lead them into debt, while the tenants who sold and transferred their occupancy rights lost out because of the institution of consent money. *Nazranas* simultaneously capitalized on and set limits to the attempts of Satnami and other tenants to increase their holdings, which was the main way of deriving increased returns from cultivation given the wider constraints to the development of agricultural production.

These constraints, involving an increasing partition and fragmentation of holdings and a lack of innovation in methods of cultivation, emerge in a survey of a typical village, Sargaon in Raipur *tahsil.*[13] The survey found that between 1868 and 1923 there had been a steady decline in the size of the average holdings of cultivators—excluding the *malguzari* and the holdings of plot proprietors—from twenty-seven acres to a little under ten acres.[14] A major factor behind the reduction in the size of holdings was the law of inheritance. Each male member of the family was entitled to a roughly equal share in the family property from the time of his birth, which he could claim at any time. An example from Sargaon illustrated this process of the partition of and reduction in the size of land holdings. In 1868 Raisingh owned 23.05 acres; by 1886 land had been divided between Ramnath who owned 11.23 acres and Sunhar who held 11.19 acres; by 1907 the holdings had been further subdivided so that Nandoo and Bhunoo owned 5.03 acres and 6.20 acres of Ramnath's land and Nandlal and Santroo 5.20 acres and 5.69 acres of Sunhar's land.[15]

The problems of partition of land were compounded by the fragmentation of holdings. It was not only the individual holding that tended to become smaller, but the size of the fields comprising the holding was also constantly reduced. The laws of inheritance combined with the consequences of the institution of *lakhabata* to produce widespread fragmentation. The practice of *lakhabata* had led to a system of distribution of land that was made block by block in keeping with the diversity of soils in Chhattisgarh. All cultivators were given a share in each block of the village. It followed that when a paternal holding was divided among sons, all of them not only got their share of the total holding but also a share in each of the different qualities of land that made up the holding. J. C. McDougall explained the process:

> Suppose . . . an original 10 acre holding consisted of five fields of equal size and that these fields differed in quality the one from the other. To ensure an equal partition each son would be given two-fifths of an acre in each field. In this way the holding comes to consist of a large number of minute fields scattered all over the village area. In other words it becomes "fragmented."[16]

In Sargaon a selection of twenty holdings showed that the biggest block of land owned in one place by a cultivator was 2.61 acres and the average size of a block was less than half an acre. The close correspondence between the number of blocks and plots in each holding revealed that a cultivator very rarely possessed two adjoining fields. Official opinion stressed that the fragmentation of holdings led to a lowering of the agricultural produce of the village due to the useless multiplication of field boundaries, the loss of crop land, and the loss of time in going about from one field to another, while the small and scattered plots prevented cultivators from effecting permanent improvements on their land.[17]

The partition and fragmentation of holdings also came in the way of the introduction of changes and innovations in the methods of cultivation in Chhattisgarh. The method of transplantation of rice is a case in point. At the end of the 1910s there was a veritable official crusade for substituting the *biasi* system—in which rice was sown by being broadcast by hand—with transplantation, but the method did not come to be widely adopted despite strenuous efforts of the agriculture department.[18] The small and fragmented character of the holdings prevented the cultivators from adopting the system since their transplanted fields were damaged by the "passing to and fro" of men and cattle working in neighboring fields and by the general custom of allowing the cattle to graze on the young rice crops until the end of the *biasi* operation.[19]

It actually made perfect economic sense for Satnami and other Chhattisgarhi cultivators to persist with the broadcast method of rice cultivation. The rice crop occupied the fields for about five months. It was in the interest of cultivators to grow their crops under a system that ensured the best distribution of their labor over the rice-growing period, and also gave them time to sow and weed the other crops. In the agricultural pattern of Chhattisgarh, the method of transplantation of rice meant that the greater part of labor operations was crowded between mid-July and mid-August when other crops required attention. On the other hand, under the *biasi* system, once the rice crop had been sown it required no further attention until the sowing of other crops was complete. Further, the first step in the *biasi* method did not require extra labor, and the main agricultural operation of weeding that required outside labor was carried out between mid-August and mid-October when there was little else to be done. The *biasi* system had a dual advantage for cultivators: it gave them a much longer period to weed so that it could be carried out with fewer laborers; and the tending of rice did not interfere with the care of other crops.[20] In any case, the inability of the poor quality of cattle in Chhattisgarh to carry out the heavy work of puddling meant that switching over to the method of transplantation of rice was not really a feasible alternative.[21] The combination of the *biasi* system of rice cultivation and the fragmentation of holdings, "minute fields scattered all over the village," also led to the lack of popularity of new and improved agricultural implements in Chhattisgarh.[22] Clearly, modern harvesting implements were out of place in a small rice field, and they could not be used for different crops sown along with each other but harvested at different times. The conservatism of the Chhattisgarhi cultivators—the bane of the modernizing agriculture department and settlement officials of the Central Provinces government—reveals a logic and rationality rooted in the conditions and circumstances of agricultural production. At the same time, the simultaneous partition, reduction in size, and fragmentation of holdings in conjunction with the continuation of earlier methods of cultivation and agricultural implements, which were not geared toward a rapid increase in agricultural production, meant that such growth had to depend on the extension of cultivation.

The relationship of dependence that bound the rice zone to the cotton zone with its increased demand for grain did provide a stimulus for greater agricultural production in Chhattisgarh. However, much of the increase in rice cultivation in the region came about as *malguzars* and tenants brought large portions of their previously uncultivated holdings and waste lands appointed for each village under the plough. By 1930 occupation had reached the "margins of cultivation." The period between the late nineteenth century and the third decade of the twentieth century also witnessed an increase in the irrigated area, which came about because of a gradual rise in the number of water tanks in villages, rather than government schemes of canal irrigation. The major benefit of irrigation was to allow greater opportunities for double cropping of marketable crops with rice.[23] Double cropping, known as *utera*, involved the scattering of seeds—of linseed and urad (a lentil)—broadcast by hand into a standing rice crop in the middle or end of September.[24] The seeds germinated between the rice plants and then grew into full-fledged plants amid the stubbles after the paddy crop had been reaped. By the early 1930s oil seeds were the second most important crop of Chhattisgarh and the *utera* crop of a rice field often yielded one-third to one-fourth of the value of the rice crop.[25] However, the

difficulty for the cultivators here was that the double-cropped area fluctu-
ated from year to year since its extent depended entirely on the character of
the late monsoon.[26] The extension of cultivation and the growth of trade did not primarily
benefit the ordinary Satnami and other cultivators. A great deal of the advantage was reaped by the intermediaries involved in the trade in grain.
Cultivators marketed only 27 percent of the surplus paddy they produced,
while wholesale merchants and people engaged in petty trade marketed almost 68 percent of the surplus of husked rice and paddy. Although the price
of rice rose rapidly after the extension of the railway into Chhattisgarh in
the late nineteenth century, the cultivators continued to receive a relatively
low price for their grain. Crispin Bates has argued that surplus appropriation in Chhattisgarh in the first half of the twentieth century was "determined by the demands of trade with Nagpur, a condition of economic dependence in which traders and merchants were the chief beneficiaries."[27]
These were made up primarily of Marwari dealers but also included petty
traders and itinerant merchants. The benefits of the developing trade with
Nagpur were much more limited for agricultural producers.

The Satnamis worked within the interstices of this structure of trade to
cope—albeit partially—with adverse processes in the agrarian economy.
Members of the group along with Telis took a lead role in the carting of
agricultural produce in the twentieth century. In the Durg *tahsil* both these
castes engaged in petty trade in carting grain to Bhatapara, a prominent
grain market. The report for Durg, in fact, described the subsidiary occupation of Satnamis as the carting of grain from virtually all parts of the district
to its major grain markets and towns.[28] By carting grain the Satnamis
claimed some of the profits of the major trade of Chhattisgarh. Indeed, the
group's participation in the carting of goods extended to timber and forest
produce from neighboring *zamindaris* and metal for the building of roads in
different parts of Chhattisgarh. The Satnamis also traded in cattle and bullocks and some became cattle dealers who bought cattle at large markets
such as Baloda Bazar and sold them in small village markets.[29] Was all this an
instance of the Satnami idea and practice of self-dependence? At times petty
trade helped Satnamis stay clear of debts. At least one report drew an explicit connection between the carting of goods by the Satnamis and their
freedom from indebtedness in some group of villages in the Durg district.[30]
The other subsidiary occupations of the Satnamis within Chhattisgarh included working on roads, railways, canals, and other public works. But there
were also certain rewards that lay outside the region.

Migration from Chhattisgarh had begun during the famine years at
the end of the nineteenth century. Over the first three decades of the twentieth century, the temporary migration of Satnami individuals and families

to coal mines and steel works of Bihar and Bengal and cities such as Calcutta and Nagpur became a regular feature of village life in Chhattisgarh. A settlement officer clarified:

> Small tenants [of all castes], whose number is fairly large, take to various other occupations [in Chhattisgarh] in the non-working season . . . while the more adventurous Satnami emigrates temporarily after each harvest to Calcutta, Kalimati and other centers of trade, to obtain the best market for his labor and returns with the beginning of the year to resume agricultural operations. It is not an uncommon sight to see villages denuded of a large part of their population during January, February, March, April and May each year, on account of the temporary exodus.[31]

The Satnamis would leave after the final agricultural operations of the rice harvest and return in time for the new agricultural season.[32] The officials reporting on the coal mining industry confirm this picture. Most of the laborers were primarily agriculturists who treated mining as a secondary occupation and periodically disappeared to their villages to cultivate their fields. The laborers had no fixed hours of work and preferred the system of piece work. By 1920 there was an increased tendency for cultivators to travel to mines with their families.[33] During these temporary forays the Satnamis carried some of the rhythms of work and practices rooted in village life into the new arenas of labor in mines, industries, and cities.[34] Seasonal migration offered what the Satnamis perceived as reasonable returns for their labor, while they continued to cultivate their land within the bounds of the agricultural cycle in Chhattisgarh.[35]

What are we to make of the situation of the Satnamis within the regional economy of Chhattisgarh? The limits to the development of agricultural production in Chhattisgarh meant that Satnami cultivators had to extend their holdings in order to seek profits from agriculture. The increased occupation of land and the system of high *nazranas* made this a difficult venture: almost two-thirds of the Satnamis were tenants in average circumstances, and 15 percent were no better than agricultural laborers. It is significant that in a situation where 60 to 92 percent of tenants in different areas of Chhattisgarh were considered free from debt, the Satnamis—subsumed under the generic Chamar—were described as a group with a "fatal facility" to fall into debt and without a desire to repay it.[36] There was a relatively high level of indebtedness among the Satnamis who borrowed from moneylenders (often *malguzars*) at a rate of 25 to 37.5 percent interest, and from cooperative banks, which they regarded as *naram saokari* (soft moneylending).[37] The repayment of debts often led to the transfer of the tenancy rights of Satnami cultivators. The close participation of Satnamis within wider economic processes—carting and other subsidiary occupations—could also leave them susceptible to fluctuations in the market for agricultural products and labor such as the period of the Great Depression. Even seasonal migration could create difficulties regarding the holdings of Satnami cultivators within the village.

The fate of Santram, a poor Satnami cultivator of the village of Kapisda in Bilaspur District, was intertwined with these processes. Santram, who had borrowed fifty rupees from a moneylender in 1929, lost his land to his codebtor both because he was tricked into signing a sale deed—instead of a mortgage deed—and because of the machinations of his adversaries during his frequent absences to coal fields to earn his livelihood between 1929 and 1938. Santram's loss of land and his act of striking and killing the codebtor's brother with a stick to avenge his loss of face was also rooted in the domination exercised by the members of a higher caste over a Satnami cultivator.[38]

Authority and Discrimination

The principles of the ritual subordination of the Satnamis were structured in everyday village life. The community's effort to reconstitute its status invited upper-caste derision, scorn, and abuse. Here I bring together written evidence from the interwar years and oral accounts collected during field work in 1989–90 to trace the interplay of authority and discrimination in village life during the late colonial period. The account implicitly engages with and extends influential theories of the nature of power in caste society in South Asia, theories which were discussed in the Introduction.

In the second half of the 1920s Baba Ramchandra, a Maharashtrian Brahman whose acquaintance we have already made earlier in this account, lived among the Satnamis and under the pseudonym Santdas drew up a list of the "particular losses and insults" suffered by the members of the community.[39]

> 1. In the learning and teaching of knowledge. 2. In access to gods. 3. In drawing and being helped to draw water from the common wells. 4. In the matter of getting their hair cut. 5. In not being able to get their clothes washed. 6. In buying things from the market. 7. In bringing and taking loads on common roads. 8. In the giving and taking of loans. 9. In day to day interaction. 10. In relationships involving the exchange of food and daughters. 11. In the access to ponds and banks to wash clothes. 12. Over clothes, shoes, umbrellas, and sitting on cots. 13. In the exchange of greetings. 14. In not being allowed to recite the sacred texts and perform sacred sacrifice. 15. In matters relating to

courts. 16. In getting medicines. 17. In the giving and taking of loans. 18. In the farming and grazing of cattle. 19. In using modes of transport to enter and leave the village. 20. Instead of Satnamis addressing them as Chamra. 21. In villages and small towns, the area with Satnami houses being called Chamra *para* [neighborhood]. 22. At the time of the tour of the gurus saying that the guru of the Chamar folk has come. 23. In calling the drivers/coachmen of carts carrying goods of Satnamis on roads Chamars and in claiming to abuse and beat them. 24. In the terrible behavior of police, the *panchas* of *panchayat*, the peons of courts, and sepoys and village watchmen of Hindu caste and following their example other castes. 25. In the behavior of *patwaris* and peons in villages and rural areas. 26. Discrimination in selling goods on the market. 27. In going and coming from Calcutta, Kharagpur, Jagannath to do labor [what they have to face] waiting at stations and rest houses, at the time of buying tickets and while on trains the behavior of ticket collectors and the police. 28. In the arguments of barristers and lawyers. 29. In spite of paying huge fees not getting work in factories. 30. At the time of fairs.[40]

Baba Ramchandra's effort, as we shall see, was to reform the Satnamis. The list was drawn up to appeal to the Deputy Commissioner of Bilaspur to institute a government inquiry that would redress Satnami grievances and solve their problems. It was constructed as an authentic statement—"I have seen a number of activities with my eyes and have particular proofs with me"—of the forms of discrimination and exploitation faced by the Satnamis.[41] The statement began by emphasizing the difficulties of Satnamis on account of denial of education. Then in a comprehensive move it brought together the forms of discrimination implicated in the definition of high and low faced by the Satnamis in transactions of everyday life (2–13, 19–21), rituals and ceremonies (14, 22, 27, 30), and in Satnami efforts to earn a livelihood and carry on production and their engagement with authority at different levels (15–18, 23–30). A number of these issues resonate in Satnami oral accounts of village life, collected for the most part in 1989–90.

The metaphor of *gaonthia zamana* (the era of landlords) orders the Satnami memory of the experience of discrimination in everyday life in the past. A few Satnamis specified that they were speaking of a time forty, fifty, or sixty years ago. For all the older Satnamis, between sixty and eighty years, the category was self-evident and self-referential. *Gaonthia zamana* was the era of the *angrez sarkar* (British government), a time they had witnessed and experienced. At the same time, Satnami recollections of *gaonthia zamana* amounted to more than a collection of disconnected individual voices. The individual accounts were bound together by a broad area of agreement and a shared sense of community experience. There is, of course, a danger that the older Satnamis I talked to about their recollections of caste discrimination in the late colonial period were not actually recalling their own experience. Instead they were retelling what had become a standardized list of untouchable disabilities of the kind drawn up by Baba Ramchandra—although, it needs to be pointed out, he had taken away the unpublished manuscript when he left Chhattisgarh in 1929—that came to be popularized by politicians of the "depressed classes" during the interwar period and which became an absolutely routine part of the rhetoric of major untouchable leaders such as Dr. Ambedkar. This was, however, not the case. In discussing the difficulties of the past, Satnamis made a clear distinction between what they had seen and lived through, on the one hand, and what they had merely heard about, on the other. When a seventy-year-old Satnami stated that their ancestors were made to carry a *jhadu* (small broom) tied to their hips and were expected to walk with their bodies hunched and bent, heads low, eyes on the ground when moving through the village, the others present asked the *sayan* (elder) not to get carried away. The storyteller backtracked and argued that he was merely trying to explain that Brahmans, "descendants of a prostitute," had always oppressed Satnamis and that he was, in any case, speaking of their ancestors. The old man was firmly told to stick to what he had seen with his own eyes.

It would, of course, be naive to argue that Satnami oral narratives are authentic and relate true stories only due to the fact that they privilege experience and discount hearsay in the telling of the past. The interplay between the experience of the past and an inherited and transmitted oral tradition underlies the enactment of Satnami narratives. At the same time, the Satnamis' claim that their oral accounts address an immediate and lived past has validity. Satnami brevity about the terrible conditions at the time of the hoary past of their ancestors contrasts with the passion and anger, detail and resentment that characterizes their accounts of an era they have experienced. Moreover, the immediacy of this past carries with it a force of crisis. During my field work in 1989–90, 1994–95, and 1996, Satnamis often expressed the worry that informing an outsider—particularly, an educated Brahman like me—of what had happened to their *panth* ran the risk of a return to the fearsome rule of the past. The *gaonthia zamana* in Satnami oral narratives was the time of *angrez sarkar*, and the accounts elaborate the economic processes mentioned by colonial administrators and the issues in the charter drawn up in the late 1920s. They encapsulate the Satnami ordering of their past in the late colonial period. The narration of the accounts in turn serves to organize the memory of the Satnamis as a bounded community. The solidarity of the collective orchestrates individual voices.

Most accounts of *gaonthia zamana* opened with the theme that service to the *malguzars* always took precedence over a Satnami cultivator's work and concerns.

> During harvest operations we had to cut the *malguzar*'s crops first. Then the cultivators would cut their own crops. In monsoon, at the time of sowing of seeds, the *malguzar* would say, "So-and-so, tomorrow you bring your plough to work in my fields." The cultivator would reply, "*Gaonthia*, tomorrow my family is going to sow." The *malguzar* would then say, "*Bhosdi ke* [bastard], you can't cut wood from trees of my village, your caste won't be allowed to cut wood, the village grazier will not graze your cattle." What could a poor man do? The orders had to be followed.[42]

> The *malguzars* would tell the *kotwar* [village watchman], "Go to that [Satnami] neighborhood and bring the people from there." The watchman would come and even if we were going for a bath or to defecate, whether we had eaten or not, would take us to the *malguzar*. We had to run errands, bring liquor. If we did not, we were beaten up with shoes at the *gudi* [the meeting place of the village *panchayat*]. The rule of the past was fearsome. We were made to carry goods, luggage.[43]

> It was the rule of *malguzars*. The constable would come and the *malguzar* would say take this [Satnami]. And we had to carry large beddings from one village to another.[44]

The *malguzar*'s demands led to a disruption of rhythms of labor and a break with the routine of daily activities that were further compounded by the indignities—beating, excommunication, and abuse—heaped on the cultivators.

These arbitrary demands were an instance of the officially sanctioned and institutionalized practice of *begar*, nominal unpaid services rendered under custom—codified by British administration—by cultivators to *malguzars* and, by extension, to local officials. Although the share of *begar* to be performed by a tenant was recorded at each settlement, a settlement officer noted that there were instances where *malguzars* kept no cattle or farm servants and got their "home farm ploughed and sown gratis" by their tenants.[45] In other words, there was a widespread infringement of the rules and conditions governing *begar*. In Satnami oral accounts these infringements are constructed as the norm defining *begar* during *gaonthia zamana*. Some Satnamis recollected that *malguzars* in exacting *begar* were equally harsh on all cultivators; others contended that Satnamis, Chamars, and tribal groups were the worst hit. All agreed that they faced an enormous burden.

In our days *begar* was harsh. *Zamindari* and government officials would make us carry their loads from one village to another and prepare their camp sites. Being untouchables we did not have to fetch water or cook food or massage their body. The *gaonthia* would make us run errands and render free labor. Refusal would invite their anger, abuse, and physical beating.[46]

Malguzars oppressed us in different ways: put pressure on us, shouted at us, abused us, and oppressed us. They used to make us work for them. *Begar*. [The *malguzar* would say], "You shall go to work in my field. Ten people shall go. Your plough and bullocks shall all go." That is it. If we did not do it we would be beaten up. That was *gaonthia zamana*.[47]

The government and *zamindari* officials combined with the *malguzars* to demand *begar*, where ploughing, weeding, and reaping for the *malguzar* were accompanied by the shouldering of the burden of service to *malguzar* and *sarkar*. During the revenue settlements of 1927–32 the administration decided that the revised papers defining the rights of tenants and *malguzars* should not contain a reference to *begar*. The settlement officer of Bilaspur invoked the unfree-free opposition and the obvious charms of modernity: "Very little of the patriarchal idea now survives in the relations between landlords and tenants, and there is no reason why this relic of a medieval custom should be entered into the record of rights, particularly when there is so much cry against forced labor all over the world."[48] Satnami oral accounts suggest why the formal withdrawal of a "relic of a medieval custom" from settlement papers had little practical effect.

In Satnami perception the exaction of *begar* by the *malguzar* stemmed from his pervasive desire, shared by all upper castes, to keep the Satnamis backward. A hint of improvement in their status was met with envy and hatred.

For the *malguzar* there were always jobs to be done. If I had ten animals in the house, the *gaonthia* would say, "Bring one load of grass to my house." If I pleaded that it wouldn't be possible for me to take the load of grass, the *malguzar* would say, "Bastard, you can keep so many animals in your house but can't bring me grass. *Bahen chod* [sister fucker] if you don't bring it tomorrow then I will beat you with my shoe."[49]

This was my field and next to that was the field of a Brahman *malguzar*. There was a plough working in my field. If the *gaonthia* of the village saw that the work of my field was being done before his, he knew that there would be more rice in my field. He would get angry. He would say, "Bring your plough and labor to my field tomorrow." His work would get done, mine would be left incomplete.[50]

The settlement officer of Bilaspur actually drew a connection between *bhet begar* and the tendency of *malguzars* to increase their home farm since they could, without entailing additional expenditure, get their lands cultivated by tenants within the village.[51] Now we know that the Satnamis had continued to lose land in the first half of the twentieth century. The oral accounts of the group elaborate these themes by emphasizing that the adverse effects of *begar* within the work process and in village life were accompanied by their loss of land to *malguzars*. The figure of the land-grabbing, upper-caste (often Brahman and Bania) *malguzar* constructed out of a compound of contempt, anger, resentment, and irony is a familiar villain within Satnami accounts of their past.

> If a piece of land was in the *malguzars* holding, they would harass and loot and put pressure—if a Harijan's land was in their holding, they would beat us up, impose a fine, implicate us in a criminal charge. The high [caste] *malguzars* used to grab a Satnami's land.[52]

> In *gaonthia zamana* whatever land was there was kept by them [*malguzars*] in their holding and right. They used to take the land in all the strips. That time land was cheap and we were paid very little for our labor. They grabbed all the land.[53]

> Satnamis held land under British government and some were *malguzars*. But they were illiterate and simple, and by trapping them the upper-caste *malguzars* looted them. Whatever good land the Satnamis had was taken away. Only the light [unproductive] land has remained with the Satnamis. In Sendri [village] the Brahman *malguzar*—he isn't there now—had three hundred acres of the good land in the village. This is what *malguzars* of other villages also used to do. The real thing, the land that produced vegetables and paddy, was taken away by the *malguzars*.[54]

The loss of land was common to all Satnamis, both ordinary cultivators and *malguzars*. It was, in fact, illiteracy among the Satnamis, along with their simplicity, that created the space for the upper castes to practice their duplicity and deceit. The twin factors of Satnami gullibility—born of their lack of education and understanding—and what was remembered as the upper-caste—particularly Brahman—dishonesty and command of writing deprived the Satnamis of their land.

> In *malguzari* times—till forty or fifty years ago—they [*malguzars*] used to take our land from us through the writing of accounts and loans. The people were poor. They would ask for two measures of paddy from the *malguzar*. If the

person's circumstances turned bad and he could not pay back quickly at the end of the year the two measures would become six measures. The rate of interest was not higher for the Satnamis. But the *malguzar* had the real weapon in his hands. If the *malguzar* wrote fifteen instead of five [measures of grain that were borrowed], it had to be paid back, if he wrote thirteen measures, that had to be given back. If the payment could not be made, the *gaonthia* would take the land. *Malguzars* built their holdings that way. We have paid this way to Brahmans and are still paying them.[55]

If we took a loan, the *malguzars* would grab our land. They would write a larger sum and when we could not pay they would take our land. That is how they now own most of the land. The big people and local officials used to come to the *gaonthia*'s house. We were poor. They took our land. We are still poor and our land is still being taken from us.[56]

The statements reveal and concur with the Satnami perception of the era of landlords as *gaonthia raj*, a time when the norms and the law were defined and set up by upper-caste village proprietors. *Gaonthia raj* was marked by *kada shasan* (strict rule) and the *malguzar* had control over village society: "British government had given [the right to] rule to the *malguzars*." The same commentator soon added, "There was no [true] *sarkar* [government] at that time."[57] The rule by *malguzars* then constituted the reverse of order and legality for the Satnamis. The frequent references to the abuse heaped upon the group and the indignities and beating suffered by members of the community that followed their refusal to do *begar* are illustrative of this pattern of arbitrary authoritarian control. If there was trouble in the village, "the *gaonthia* acted as a Judge and collected a fine."

And what of the village *panchayat*?

There was no real [village] *panchayat.* The *panchayat* was hastily assembled. Four people were called and the *gaonthia* would point to a man and say, "Was it his fault or not?" The assembled group would say, "Yes it is his fault." Then the man was given punishment on the orders of the *gaonthia.*[58]

The punishment could consist of a beating with a shoe at the *gudi* (meeting place of the *panchayat*), the focal point in the village where people congregated, along with the imposition of a fine and/or excommunication from the village, which involved stopping the services of the village grazier, restrictions on the cutting of trees, and prohibitions on the use of ponds and tanks in the village.[59] Another account emphasized that the *malguzars*' grip over village matters and the poverty of the Satnamis, itself promoted by village proprietors,

meant that the group was often compelled to accept its position under landlord rule.

> What could a poor man do? The orders had to be followed. A rich man may
> have done otherwise. He was in a position to withstand pressure. But a poor
> man? And our caste people have been poor. Ninety-five out of one hundred
> are poor. Our ancestors were poor. Our caste was oppressed. One Brahman
> *malguzar* could take care of a large Satnami population. Why? Because they
> had the weapon [of writing]. Let us take an example. Even today without Rajiv
> [Gandhi, the former Prime Minister of India who was later assassinated in
> 1991] saying so, we cannot move a leaf in the village, only if he says so can we
> do something. This is what used to happen earlier. He [Rajiv Gandhi] is the
> king of the world. The *gaonthia* was the raja of the village. What he wanted was
> the way things were arranged.[60]

The reference to the *malguzar*'s wielding a *hathiyar* (weapon) along
with his construction as a raja is significant. In Satnami perception writing
was the key weapon in the hands of the *malguzars*. A critical sign and instrument of *malguzar* domination, writing facilitated their drive to grab the
lands of Satnamis and also allowed the village proprietors to carry out the
will of the colonial government, the power that had turned them into rulers
of villages. And then there was the complicity between the *malguzars* and the
functionaries of British administration: "The big people, *thanedar log* [bear-
ers of authority] used to come to the *gaonthia*'s house," and together exacted *begar* from the Satnamis. The Satnamis fixed upon their construction
of the *malguzar*'s monopoly over formidable aspects of domination—the
command of writing, the right to control and rule the village conferred by
the government, and links with the subordinate officials of colonial administration—to fashion him into a raja of the village.[61]

There were other rites that went into the making of the figure of the
raja.[62] The upper-caste *malguzar*, as the principal member of the village community with considerable powers under colonial administration, was a powerful patron of the *panch pauni* (five fingers [of a hand]: service castes), *nai*
(barber), *dhobi* (washerman), *rawat* (grazier and water carrier), *kumhar*
(potter), and *purohit* (priest). The nature and significance of the services of
these castes extended far beyond the washing of clothes, the cutting of hair
and beards, and the grazing and milking of cattle. The service castes have
played a critical role in rites of passage and in village life. Instead of providing here a detailed catalogue, I will take a few examples centering on marriage among Brahmans—remembered by Satnamis as rapacious *malguzars*
during *gaonthia zamana*—which also have a wider significance. It is customary among Brahmans in Chhattisgarh to go for marriage negotiations with

the barber and the grazier who serve the family. Their presence constitutes a guarantee and proof that the family belongs to a particular *jat* (endogamous group) of Brahmans. At the time of the wedding, too, both families have their own barber and the grazier, where their services establish that the families have not been ostracized by the elders and members of the caste within the village. During the wedding the grazier and his wife grind pulses for ritual *badas* (fried savories). The grazier distributes the *pattal* (leaf plates) on which food is served. The barber works with the grazier in distributing leaf plates and leaf cups and also shaves and massages the groom. The *nain* (barber woman) assists the bride. Before the completion of the marriage ceremony the bride takes *suhag* (vermilion), a signifier of the auspicious married state, from the *dhobin* (washer woman) and the *kumharin* (potter woman). In a bid to remain a *suhagan* (married woman) until her death, the Brahman bride (who cannot remarry) rubs the parting of her hair against the parting of the hair, which contains the *suhag*, of the *dhobin* and the *kumharin* since they are considered *sada suhagan* (eternal brides) because they can remarry. The marriage ceremony is marked by a pattern of different ritual prestations to the *purohit* and all the participants from the service castes. The *nain* and the *rawatin*, for instance, get a *lugda* (short *saree*) during the wedding. While there are variations in particular customs among different dominant landholding castes such as Banias, Rajputs, and Kurmis, the roles of the men and women of service castes are equally important in the marriage ceremonies among all these groups. Similarly, the variations do not alter the critical place of ritual exchanges and the significance of service castes.[63] The performance of a life-cycle ritual without the barber to issue invitations or a grazier to fill water is, indeed, unthinkable. The smooth running of relationships and social life within village society has been premised on the participation of service castes. Stopping the services of the barber, washerman, and grazier, in fact, forms the most effective and complete form of social ostracism and boycott, used as a final sanction against an offender within the village. Moreover, village settlement records of the late colonial period distinguished between village servants and servants of the *malguzar*, but the formal distinction, as Satnami accounts emphasize, was often lost in practice. The *malguzar* stood in a special relationship with the service castes and village servants and called the shots in the matter of social boycott.

The Satnamis stood outside the intricate and powerful web of relationships that featured the service castes. As in the nineteenth century, the low ritual status of the Satnamis and the norms and concerns of *chhua* (touch pollution) meant that the Satnamis did not have the critical services of the Brahman priest, the barber, and the washerman. The *rawat* grazed the cattle of Satnamis and also milked their cows in return for paddy and milk but did not participate in their ceremonies. Indeed, one of the few ceremonies that admitted the Satnamis along with the members of the other castes was the setting up of a pole in the middle of a freshly dug pond in the village to avoid inauspiciousness and prevent the water from drying up. The Satnamis together with the other castes were asked to touch the pole, which signified that the village was united, before it was taken into and erected in the pond; however, the group was not allowed to participate in the *puja* performed by the Brahman priest. It is, of course, true that the Satnamis had developed their own functionaries and invoke them without fail to establish their self-sufficiency and dignity and indeed their superiority over upper castes, a theme to which I will return soon. At the same time, the denial of the *panch pauni* continued to define the exclusion of the Satnamis—along with other untouchable groups—in key areas of village life and served as a reminder of their low ritual status. It simultaneously underscored the fact that the *malguzar*'s special relationship with the service castes was integrally constitutive of his dominance. In Satnami perception the forms of power derived from colonial administration fused with a culturally and ritually resonant notion of a land-holding dominant caste to produce the figure of the *malguzar* as the raja of the village.

The Satnamis were not allowed into the temples and worship of higher castes since it was believed that their touch desecrated Hindu gods and goddesses and their presence polluted the priests and participants at the place of *puja*. Similarly, *chhua* was the key determinant in the pattern of spatial segregation of the Satnamis. The houses of the Satnamis were in a separate neighborhood, invariably situated at one end of the village and condescendingly referred to as Chamra *para* by the upper castes. In the *panchayat* too, "We were made to sit at the side separately. The *malguzar* would shout, '*Beti chod* [daughter fucker] Chamar, sit in that corner.'"[64] Water and food were substances charged with the significance of potential pollution. "We had a separate *ghat* [bank] in the *ghatonda* [village pond] to bathe and wash our clothes," and the Satnamis drew their water from separate wells. The elders of the higher castes did not attend the Satnami *chauka* or *puja*. The children of the higher castes, curious onlookers and bystanders, would only be given and accept bits of coconut, and nothing that had been cooked. After a life-cycle ritual—for instance, *chhatti* (ceremony on the sixth day after the birth of a child), marriage, *dasgatri* (ceremony on the tenth day after death)—the Satnamis would send a coconut and uncooked rice and pulses to their friends of a higher caste.[65]

The Satnamis were prevented from using clothes and accessories and modes of transport that were the signifiers of rank and status within village society. Satnamis emphasized that although upper castes wanted these restrictions to be followed as invariant rules they could not be uniformly enforced in all villages. But in villages where Satnamis were few and upper castes were strong, shoes, umbrellas, and turbans became focal signs of contest.

> If we wore shoes and crossed a Rajput he would say, "Bastard Chamar, take off your shoes." We had to take them off. We had to take off our shoes and carry them in our hands when passing in front of Brahmans and Thakurs and while crossing the streets in their neighborhood.[66]

> We could not carry an umbrella nor wear a turban. They were taken away from us.[67]

The imposition of restrictions on clothes was rare and often confined to villages and areas with a significant Rajput population.

> In village Birkona if a Satnami wore a new *dhoti, kurta,* put on shoes and good oil in his hair the *malguzar*'s men and others would laugh and say, "The Chamar has become one of the gentry." The clothes were taken off.[68]

Satnamis were forbidden to ride a horse or travel in a palanquin. To wear shoes, carry an umbrella, or ride a horse constituted a public assertion and challenge that questioned the principles of the subordination of the group. The upper castes in turn jealously guarded their privileges. They prevented the Satnami claim over public space by opposing, for example, a Satnami marriage procession moving to the accompaniment of music within the village.[69] The restrictions were geared toward maintaining the rites of rank within village society. The low position of the Satnamis arose from the articulation of the difference that separated them from dominant castes with their location within the ritual hierarchy of purity and pollution.[70]

Indeed, against the grain of dominant anthropological theories of the nature of power in the caste order, Satnami oral accounts about *gaonthia zamana* underscore that relationships of power and the privileged position of the *malguzar* in Chhattisgarh involved an intermeshing of the ritual hierarchy of purity and pollution, the culturally and ritually constituted dominance of landholding castes, and the forms of power derived from colonial administration.[71]

The Satnami resistance to these principles that shaped everyday interactions took various forms. In the early twentieth century Satnami women had worn nose rings to show their contempt for the upper castes and Satnamis traveling on trains had, seemingly accidentally, touched and defiled the upper castes.[72] This challenge could also assume a more direct aspect. Asaram told the story of his brave uncle, quiet aunt, and an arrogant oilpresser.

My maternal aunt had gone to the village pond. A Teli, who was proud and wealthy, had slapped her three times for using the pond and polluting the water. She had not said anything as a woman. [But] when her husband heard this he went to the Teli's house with his friend, a barber, and entered the courtyard. He challenged the Teli: "You have slapped my wife, come out and I will slap your wife, six times." The Teli bolted his door and refused to come out.[73]

Another man recounted an anecdote about his maternal uncle and two Rajputs. The Rajputs had taunted his uncle, a well-built man, about wearing the sacred thread and had called other kinsmen to prevent him from walking through the street in front of their house. A few days later when the Rajputs brought their horses to drink at a pond near his house he told them, "If I can't pass your street, you can't stop at this pond."[74] The uncle sent the Rajputs away. There are, arguably, as many such vignettes highlighting contest in daily life as Satnamis who remember *gaonthia zamana*.

Among the Satnamis the *bhandari* had replaced the Brahman priest within the village, and this allowed the group to challenge claims about the ritual purity of the Brahman *purohit* (priest).

Our *bhandari* was the real *pandit* [priest/learned man]. In a Hindu *puja* the Brahman *pandit* got up five times in the middle to go and urinate. His mind was not on any of their twenty gods as he blankly repeated his lines but on his erection and the young Brahman girl who was the cause of it. But our *bhandari* would sit through ceremonies for hours, his mind completely on Ghasidas and *satnam*.[75]

The old Satnami explained that Brahmans were not only envious but worried that if they did not keep the Satnamis on the margins of the Hindu social order they would lose their position of dominance. In Satnami perception, the *bhandari* and the *sathidar* (who had taken the place of the barber to issue invitations within the village) also defined the group's self-reliance compared to other castes.

We would do everything ourselves. Our clothes were not washed by washermen, we would not take water from graziers, our women did the work of midwives. We did not call the village *maharin* [midwife]. What about upper castes? The midwife goes into their house, the grazier gives them water. Now do you understand why upper castes have resented us?[76]

In this statement and other Satnami oral accounts the community's self-reliance and purity, inviting the resentment of upper castes, went hand in hand.

The gurus and the modes of worship of the Satnamis provided the group with dignity, a means to counter the upper-caste assertion of their low ritual status.

> Why should we turn to Hindu gods? Our Ghasidas and s*atnam* are true. Can you find a *satpurush* [true man] like Ghasidas anywhere? No, never. Then and now we have been and are the only true believers. Those people [upper castes] invented lies when they called us Chamars.[77]

> We also had ceremonies for birth, marriage, death. But among us they were always pure and done in the name of Ghasidas. There was no meat, tobacco, or liquor. But you see other castes. Whenever there is *chhatti* [ceremony on the sixth day after the birth of a child] they—yes, Brahmans too—get drunk and openly or quietly eat meat. We refrained from all of this.[78]

In these ceremonies the women sang *panthi geet* (songs of the panth), which were based on the myths of the guru of Satnampanth. "We have always remembered our gurus and Ghasidas. *Kathas* [legends] of gurus are a part of our bodies. In the time you are asking about every little child knew the *itihas* [history] and *kathas* of our gurus."[79] Satnami myths, discussed in the next chapter, questioned and challenged the relations of power that defined the subordination of the group.

This discussion of the relatively quieter and regular acts of contest in a religious idiom is not designed to obscure the more dramatic but less frequent violent confrontations between Satnamis and other castes, which have continued throughout the twentieth century. Two points stand out here. These moments of dramatic confrontation were also replete with ritual resonances, involving challenges to schemes of rank and honor and corresponding moves where a higher-caste person on being beaten by a Satnami had to expiate the offense through the rite of a feast to the caste group within the village. Second, the Satnamis also joined other castes in opposing rival tenants and village proprietors. Both these themes featured in a dispute in the early 1930s when Satnami cultivators combined with tenants of different castes to oppose a family of *malguzars* in village Murlidih in Bilaspur District. The tension was rooted in differential perceptions of the changes introduced by the land revenue resettlement of the village between 1927 and 1932. The conflict centered on rival claims over the village waste and the land adjoining the village pond used for growing sugar cane, over the payment of rent and interest, and the issues of repayment of debts and of forced labor. There was also the intrusion of the notion of *swaraj* (freedom), reworked and reinterpreted by the tenants. The tenant initiative opened with the customary social boycott within village life, *nai dhobi bandh*, in which the critical services of the barber and the washerman are stopped. Only this time the *malguzars* were at the receiving end. The boycott was comprehensive. The *malguzars* were shunned. There was a ban, enforced by oaths in the name of relatives, on verbal interaction with them. The social boycott was, of course, a form of censure, also expressed in other ways. The tenants would smear the doors of the *malguzars'* houses with shit and throw the polluting substance into their compounds. The homes of the village proprietors were pelted with stones, their chili plants uprooted, their compound walls broken. The tenants of Murlidih had initiated and sustained a major offensive. To effect a complete social boycott of the *malguzars*—who called the shots in matters of censure and in relation to service castes in everyday village life—was to establish an alternative, oppositional center of authority. The tenants went on to tear the bonds that inscribed debts to *malguzars* and stake a claim on their property. The "tenant party"—a joint venture of Satnamis and cultivators of other castes—brought the *malguzars* to their knees in Murlidih.[80] This is one tale. There are other stories. At the same time, my focus on the rather more commonplace Satnami negotiation of upper-caste dominance has attempted to highlight the group's engagement with the principles of its subordination to resist the interplay of authority and discrimination in everyday village life.

In Satnami perception their self-reliance and modes of worship underlay the unity of the group.

> The Satnamis unite whenever there is tension and enmity with other castes. There are, of course, always divisions and rivalries among people of kin. But when it comes to facing another caste the Satnamis forget their divisions and unite against the members of the other caste. That is why Satnamis alone can face and defeat all other castes. The Satnamis on one side and all Hindus on the other. It is only when there is real disunity among us (there are bad people everywhere) that the Hindus win.[81]

Two disputes between Satnami families from the 1920s and 1930s, which centered on transgressions of the norms of kinship and neighborhood, played out these questions of unity and division within the group. An altercation and fight between Satnami families of Itwari and Chandu on the morning of 15 July 1927 in Karkhena village in Bilaspur district resulted in the death of Itwari. Chandu and Itwari were Satnami cultivators, distant relatives and also neighbors who held adjoining fields. Kachrin, a young woman, occupied a key role in the drama. A few months before the fight Kachrin left her husband Hagru, who was Itwari's son, and started living with Ramdayal, the son of Chandu who had given her *churis*. Hagru, instead of taking the matter to the Satnami *panchayat* filed a complaint in a lower criminal court against Chandu and Ramdayal for having enticed Kachrin to leave with her ornaments. We do not know the details of the court proceedings but Chandu and Ramdayal were fined. As Chandu later stated: *"Han nalish ki thi aur jurmana hua tha—more gawahi badal diye* [Yes, there was a case and a fine was imposed. My testimony had been changed]." After a few days Chandu and his two sons had beaten up Itwari, the man who had tricked their family. Hagru filed another suit. The hearing fixed for 14 July 1927 was postponed. The next day Chandu's family once again thrashed Itwari's family. During the fight Chandu said, "You have got us fined so we shall bathe in your blood." Matters concerning marriage, along with other internal affairs of caste in the village, were normally settled by the Satnami *panchayat*. The fine was constructed by Itwari's family as the result of a transgression. The transgression was caused by an enmity. The enmity was rooted in ties of blood. Itwari's family stepped beyond the bounds of fair play and disregarded the important principle of settling a dispute within the *panchayat* to maintain Satnami unity. Arguably, Chandu had reaffirmed notions of legality and the principle of unity among the Satnamis when he told the ploughmen who had interceded to prevent the fight that the sticks of Itwari's family, which had been seized by his family, would be returned only before the Satnami *panchayat*.[82]

Another dispute in the small village of Darri in Bilaspur district in the late 1930s also had its beginnings in an elopement. A young Satnami ran away with his aunt. They returned after a few days. The youth's family did not take the matter to the Satnami *panchayat*. Instead, they asked the village *panchayat*, controlled by the landholding dominant caste, to settle the issue. The village *panchayat* denied the facts of the elopement and decided that too much fuss had been made about a nonevent. Barring a few families, the main body of Satnamis in the village were incensed. They questioned the decision of the dominant members of the village community. The group was beaten up for sticking to its claim that matters concerning marriages, elopements, and affairs of caste should be settled by the Satnami *panchayat*.[83] During field work I discussed this dispute with a Satnami companion as we traveled back together from a rather remote village. At the end of our journey my escort sighed, "Among us, disunity always brings beating and loss." And then followed a laconic lament, "If we leave property aside, women are the cause of so much trouble."[84]

Virtue and Power: Questions of Gender

Recent years have seen new analytical emphases in the study of kinship and gender in patrilineal India.[85] These newer accounts variously articulate a live engagement with women's voices and realities, all marked by a close attention to the many ambiguities and ambivalences inherent within the ideologies and practices of a hegemonic kinship system, and each intimately concerned with the politics of gender in everyday arenas. As a result, these studies have questioned an exclusive emphasis on the corporate, lineal nature of North Indian kinship, highlighting the pitfalls of arguments that stress the unambiguous and total incorporation of a bride into her husband's family.[86] At the same time, these analyses have been wary of seductive but schematic formulations concerning, for example, the divergent devolutions of property in patrilineal North India, to sons through inheritance and to daughters through dowry, formulations that subsume and imprison marriage prestations in a discourse of purely economic rights and valuations.[87] Taken together, this scholarship has revealed the severe limitations of singular, univocal cultural constructs and propositions in explaining the presence of various gendered perspectives and several representational possibilities regarding marriage, affinity, and kinship.

The issues foregrounded by the new emphases in the study of kinship and gender in patrilineal Hindu India bring to mind the distinction that Pierre Bourdieu has drawn between "official kinship" and "practical kinship," between kin relationships perceived in the shape of "objects" versus kin relationships understood in "the form of the practices which produce, reproduce, and use them by reference to necessarily practical functions."[88] Thus,

> official kinship is opposed to practical kinship in terms of the official as opposed to the non-official (which includes the unofficial and the scandalous); the collective as opposed to the individual; the public, explicitly codified in a magical or quasi-juridical formalism, as opposed to the private, kept in an implicit, even hidden state; collective ritual, subjectless practice, amenable to performance by agents interchangeable because collectively mandated, as opposed to strategy, directed towards the satisfaction of the practical interests of an individual or a group of individuals.[89]

Some of the categories and distinctions rehearsed by Bourdieu are not without their own problems,[90] but the larger, epistemological force of this passage derives from its suggestion that dominant—therefore, official—representations of the logical patterns of kin relationships override the nitty gritty of practices of kinship in everyday arenas, rather in the manner that, plotted onto the geometric space of a map, neat lines showing metalled roads and railway tracks bracket the complex networks of beaten paths, "paths made ever more practicable by constant use."[91]

Quite in keeping with an emphasis on the concerns of practical kinship, indeed reinforcing its epistemological and political significance through considerations of gender, the revisitations of patriliny in north and middle India have studied women's song and speech genres, rituals, and pilgrimage to focus on "female self-images that are simultaneously sexy and motherly,"[92] the ambiguity of women's ties to natal kin—including their own multiple and shifting reconstructions of these bonds, at once as wives and sisters—and the uses of this ambiguity in the construction of gendered subjects, in the tenor of everyday lives, and in practices of pilgrimage,[93] and women's poetic discourse on power and the possibility of their resistance to "patrilineal authority and patrilineal pronouncements on female identities."[94] These discussions involving questions of hegemony and agency, ideologies and subjectivities, reveal that kinship is a contentious analytical domain, a contested lived arena, made up of a complex interplay between nuances of meaning, possibilities of subversion, and articulations of power. They highlight the need to recognize the multiply textured and many-layered nature of the relationship between patriliny and gender, a task that I take up in somewhat different ways from ethnography through the means of historical fieldwork, an interchange between the archive and the informant.[95] My effort here also goes beyond a sole consideration of kin relationships, to discuss issues of gender among the Satnamis that were embedded within ever wider networks of power, involving the sexual exploitation and discursive domination of Satnami women by upper-caste men as part of larger agendas of sexualities, communities, and the nation.[96]

In the early years of the twentieth century, *tahsildar* Durga Prasad Pandey described what he thought was the Satnami rite of initiation.

A person was initiated as a full member of the Satnampanth through a ceremony called Satlok [world of truth]. Satlok took place within three years of the marriage of a Satnami or after the birth of the first son. It was considered to be the initiatory rite of a Satnami, so that prior to its performance he and his wife were not proper members of the sect. When the occasion was considered ripe a committee of men in the village would propose the holding of the ceremony to the bridegroom, the elderly members of his family would also exert their influence upon him, because it was believed that if they died prior to the performance their disembodied spirits would continue a comfortless existence about the scene of their mortal inhabitation, but if after that they would go straight to heaven. When the rite was to be held a feast was given, the villagers sitting round a lighted lamp placed on a water pot in the center of the sacred chauka or square made with the lines of wheat flour; and from evening until midnight they would sing and dance. In the meantime the newly married wife would be lying alone in a room in the house. At midnight her husband went to her and asked her whom she should revere as his Guru or preceptor. She named a man and the husband went off and bowed to him and he [the person named by the wife] then went in to the woman and lay with her. The process would be repeated, the woman naming different men until she was exhausted. Sometimes, if the head priest of the sect was present, he would nominate the favored men, who were known as Gurus. Next morning the married couple were seated together in a courtyard, and the head priest or his representative tied a kanthi or necklace of wooden beads round their necks, repeating an initiatory text.

> Bhaji churrai bhanta churrai
> Gondli karai chhaunka
> Lal Bhaji ke churrawate
> Gaon la Marai chauka
> Sahib ke Satnam; Thauka.

[We have given up eating leafy vegetables, we eat no brinjals. We eat onions with relish. After leaving *lal bhaji* the *chauka* has been placed in the village. The true name is of *satnam*, okay.][97]

It seems likely that Durga Prasad Pandey's account brought together and conflated two distinct rituals among the Satnamis: the Satnami rite of initiation, and *jhanjeri chauka* or *satlok* (world of truth/*sat*[*nam*]). The Satnami rite of initiation emphasized the closeness, the bounded nature, of the community. It was performed at the time of marriage or at a somewhat later date, which was, indeed, decided on by the elders and members of the Satnami *panchayat* in the village. The entire Satnami population participated. The rite was conducted and the final act of incorporation was performed by the *kanphunkia* (one who addresses the ear) guru who tied *kanthis* around the neck of the married couple and whispered a *mantra* (incantation) in their ears.

Jhanjeri chauka—also it would seem known as *satlok*—was quite different from the Satnami rite of initiation.

> *Jhanjeri chauka* was held when a woman had not borne children after several years of marriage. It has not been held for at least sixty years. The Satnamis were not the first to perform it. It was first performed at the time of *Ramayan* by raja Dashrath when he did not have a son. Ram, Lakshman and Bharat were the result of *jhanjeri chauka,* born from the sage Vashisht. It was then held before *Mahabharat.* What else explains the existence of a hundred Kaurava brothers? Kunti [the mother of the five Pandava brothers also] had *jhanjeri chauka* done on her. This matter [then] goes back a long time. Among

Satnamis it was performed by a *jhanjeri potne wala guru* [guru who performs the *jhanjeri chauka*]. This guru was different from the *kan phunkne wala guru*. He had nothing to do with the guru at Bhandar. This guru was invited when a person didn't have a child. The men would assemble together. The affines and men of the village. There was a *puja* done by the guru. The woman would sit naked, her hair open, in the aspect of a *devi*. The *chauka* was fearsome. After the *puja* the guru was the first to go to the woman. He had intercourse with her. The guru decided on the other men. Only men who had sufficient courage would then approach the woman and, one after the other, have sexual intercourse with her. [On my asking if it was only members of the family who approached the woman] It could be anyone chosen by the guru. The woman had remained barren so why should it only be members of the family. Seven or eight men went up to the woman, at times only two or three succeeded. It required great courage to face a woman, naked with open hair, like a fearful *devi*. If a man failed to perform the *devi* cast a spell on him. A lot of men would go with their eyes closed, "fail" inside, and turn away rather than climb on the woman. It was only men who were special who could perform the task.[98]

All this raises important questions about the ordering of gender within Satnampanth.[99] My inquiries—of necessity, guarded and cautious—revealed that Satnamis, in fact, had another ritual *sukh dekhna* (envisioning of happiness) in which the close agnates of a man had intercourse with his wife. We do not know if *sukh dekhna* was an intermediate step carried out before the holding of *jhanjeri chauka*, although the statement that the "woman had remained barren so why should it only be members of the family" does lend credence to the conjecture. It is significant that the "sowing of the seed" in a "barren" woman required the energies and the participation of Satnami males beyond the immediate agnatic kin. The ritual reversed the dominant patrilineal emphasis that sees a barren woman as the source of childlessness and implicitly underscored men's responsibility for women's barrenness.[100] In *jhanjeri chauka* the sharing of a woman by Satnami men at once offered a cure for barrenness and possibly turned the woman's body into a site for the reinforcement of the solidarity and brotherhood of men within Satnampanth. It is worth asking, however, if the woman was only the passive instrument of male desire. Durga Prasad Pandey's account states that the woman chose the men during the ceremony. Similarly, when I raised the question of the woman's role in choosing the men who had intercourse with her I received a defensive reply, "A *devi* could ask for anything." This perhaps implied a recognition of women's agency in maintaining the boundaries of the group. A series of questions remain. Was the ritual a momentary (but no less significant) celebration of female sexuality? Was the construction of women's agency in terms of their sexuality double edged? Was the enactment of the ritual, with its attendant liminality, a male project to negotiate women's sexuality and agency? Did motherhood—and not merely wifehood—divest a woman of her threatening sexuality?

We can possibly do little more than raise these questions. It is important to remember that upper castes in Chhattisgarh—including, perhaps, the Brahman *tahsildar* Durga Prasad Pandey—have seized upon *jhanjeri chauka, satlok,* and *sukh dekhna* as instances of the sexual profligacy of an "unclean" and "inauspicious" people to discredit and marginalize the Satnamis. These moves have served simultaneously to feed the voyeuristic fantasies and desires of upper-caste men. Indeed, the theme was played out all too often in the statements of upper-caste men during my visits to the field. In the words of a Brahman doctor, "The Satnami women have a 'natural' smell, very dirty but exciting, which forces you to look at their taut bodies."

This means that Satnamis defend *jhanjeri chauka* and counter upper-caste assertions through an innovative play with the *Ramayana* and the *Mahabharata.* In the *Ramayana* raja Dashrath had difficulties begetting children. The sage Vashishta advised Dashrath to perform a sacrifice for the birth of sons. Out of the sacrificial fire emerged a dark figure carrying a bowl of *payasam* (a sweet made by boiling rice in milk). The raja divided the *payasam* among his three wives, giving two halves to Kaushalya and Kaikeyi who in turn shared their portions with Sumitra. (In some popular accounts of the story, the *payasam* is replaced by a fruit divided in the same order and proportion among the three wives of Dashrath.) This boon of substance worked wonders: Kaushalya gave birth to Ram, Kaikeyi to Bharat, and Sumitra to Lakshaman and Shatrughan. The Satnami account seized upon the efficacy of external agency in the birth of Dashrath's sons: the *payasam* or the fruit had become "seed" or semen (incidentally, in its texture, consistency, and appearance *payasam* resembles semen and fruit is, of course, born of seed), and Vashishta was turned into the main protagonist who sired the four sons of the raja. And what of the *Mahabharata?* In the epic, the five Pandava brothers were born of different divine figures to Kunti and Madri, the two wives of the accursed king Pandu who could not copulate for fear of death: the paternity of Yudhishthir, Bheem, and Arjun, the sons of Kunti, is attributed to Yama (the god of death), Vayu (the wind god), and Indra (the king of gods) respectively; Nakul and Sahdev, the youngest brothers, were born to Madri from Ashwini Kumar. The hundred Kaurava brothers were the progeny of the blind king Dhritarashtra. Here the Satnami oral testimony reworked Kunti's encounters with cosmic beings and implicitly questioned the credulity of one blind man to produce a hundred sons by turning both the birth of the Pandavas and the Kauravas into instances of *jhanjeri chauka.*[101]

At the same time, these rhetorical moves placing the ritual at the heart of the sacred texts and traditions of Hinduism are only a part of the larger picture. The upper-caste offensive also implies that there are well-defined limits within which the group is willing to discuss *jhanjeri chauka*. It is one thing to set the record straight and clear legitimate doubts but a totally different matter to indulge an outsider's seemingly inevitable prurient curiosity. Memories are fresh—the claim that the ritual has not been performed for sixty years was accompanied by the disclosure that a *jhanjeri potne wala guru* still lives somewhere near Mungeli—and upper-caste abuse abounds. I am not sure of an answer to the Satnami who asked me, "Why are you so interested [in *jhanjeri chauka*]? Do you [a Brahman] also want to run us down?"

In almost every arena, it was difficult for Satnami women to cope with upper-caste men. The low rank and the alleged promiscuity of Satnami women were turned into instruments of their sexual exploitation. The limits to *chhua* (touch pollution) for upper-caste men were set by their liaisons with Satnami women. Sexual exploitation began with the advent of adolescence. The rich upper-caste superordinates did not spare an opportunity. An anger burns in the Satnami expose of hypocrisy and double standards of upper-caste "vultures." I rehearse the eloquent and ironic voice of an old Satnami woman who grew up during *gaonthia zamana*.

Growing girls received special attention. Boys exhibited often. Some would show "it," others wanted us to touch and hold it. This happened in lonely houses, fields, and scrub forests. Nubile girls of fifteen and sixteen were much sought after. We had often to go out to collect cow dung and fuel. We went out in groups of three and four. But we had to separate, and to look for dung and fuel wood in different directions. Boys of our own community were also interested, but those of rich upper-caste families were aggressive and shameless. Shouting for help was no use. Often there was no help. Our elders too were helpless. Sometimes there were quarrels. Everyone advised keeping quiet. After all it was no use shouting about the loss of our *laj* [modesty]. Happenings like these were not uncommon. If you live in water, you cannot have enmity with the crocodile.

When indebted our parents/elders had to work as laborers. Or else they were engaged as *saonjia* on an annual contract. They worked in the fields or threshing grounds. The rest of the family had to help out both at home and in the fields. Girls had to carry food for fathers and relatives. As untouchables we could not enter the homes of clean castes, but women and girls were never left unmolested. The game was played in several ways—sweet words and force. But we had no escape. We had to accept our fate.

Women were specially vulnerable when their men folk went out on *begar*. When detected, this caused some flutter. But that was all. All this was happening all the time. Some officials demanded women, especially young girls. If parents/elders were away, even force could be used. To avoid trouble (and beating) some people sent their sisters, daughters, and daughters-in-law without much protest. Some women were lured with gifts and money, although there was little open prostitution. Not all men were vultures, some of them were loving and showed consideration. But many fulfilled their lust and later did not even show recognition.

Things are changing now. But not much. Wolves will remain wolves, vultures will be vultures. We can be angry, we can resist, but after the deed is done it cannot be taken away. We have to live with them. We cannot protest too much. Our bodies are made of bones and flesh, not of silver and gold.[102]

It was not only upper-caste men who claimed the bodies of Satnami women. The members of the organizational hierarchy of Satnampanth also came under trenchant criticism for sexually exploiting the women of the group when a project to reform the community was domesticated and directed at sanitizing the Satnami household.[103] Nor was this merely a product of the imagination of upper-caste benefactors of the Satnamis. Mogra, during a second meeting with the anthropologist S. C. Dube stated: "Religious functionaries, *mahants* and their men always needed women. For fear of their curses their demands had to be met. They had a license to do whatever they taught their followers not to do."[104]

In the opinion of upper castes in Chhattisgarh, on the other hand, the rituals of *sukh dekhna* and *jhanjeri chauka*, along with the institution of *churi* and the frequent remarriages among the Satnamis, confirm the promiscuity of the women of the group.[105] *Churi* has been a widely prevalent form of remarriage among all but the highest castes—Brahmans, Rajputs, and Baniyas—in Chhattisgarh, where a married woman could marry another man if he gave her *churis* (bangles). While the broad pattern was similar, specific customs regarding *churi* varied across castes. Among the Satnamis, if *churi* took place with another member of Satnampanth, the matter was deliberated by the caste elders and *panchayat*. They fixed a certain *behatri* (compensation for brideprice), which the new husband had to pay to the earlier husband and his family. The new husband also had to give a feast to the Satnamis—the number was decided by the Satnami elders in the village—which symbolized the incorporation of the woman into his home and the acceptance of the marriage by the community. The earlier husband in turn had to feed the Satnamis within the village in the form of a *marti jeeti bhat*, a symbolic statement that the woman was dead to him. Finally, the new husband could be asked to pay a *dand* (fine), a portion of which was kept for the guru and the rest used by the Satnamis in the village. There is nothing intrinsically illicit about the structure of remarriages among the Satnamis as compared to other low and middle castes here. But the group did have an extremely high incidence of *churi* and Satnami men were known to accept their wives rather easily if they returned after having run away with another man.[106] A construction of these practices as irrefutable evidence of the lax morals of the Satnamis, reinforced by the distinctive rituals centering on reproduction and sexuality among the community, has fueled the blatant statements and insidious innuendo of upper castes. Satnami women are widely cast as deviant harlots who, withered by age, become despicable harridans.

What were the implications of the structure defined by *churi* for Satnami women? The control of women's sexuality within the caste system is closely tied to the phenomenon of the maintenance of the boundary of a caste. A sexual breach is simultaneously the violation of the boundary and a transgression of the norms of caste.[107] The concerns of caste and boundary maintenance did not apply in quite the same way to Satnami women. Satnampanth admitted members of other castes—except, recall, castes that embodied ritual impurity—through a rite of initiation. If a Satnami woman was given *churis* by a man of an acceptable caste he could become a member of Satnampanth. The man had to accept the authority of the guru—by making an offering to him and drinking his *amrit*—feed a specified number of Satnamis, and have a *kanthi* tied round his neck and a *mantra* whispered in his ear in order to be initiated into and incorporated within Satnampanth. We should not, however, make too much of this picture. An easier alternative for higher-caste men was to have sexual liaisons with Satnami women and then abandon them if their caste intervened in the matter. Moreover, Satnami kinship was part of a wider patrilineal and patrivirilocal system with distinct regional emphases, a matrix of constraints and possibilities.

The ideology and practice of Satnami kinship—and the wider milieu in which they were embedded—valued the labor of women: the institution of brideprice—and its compensation at the time of secondary marriages— was a recognition of women's prospective contribution to the household economy; and in the case of *churi*, a woman had to state that she had "come of her own will to live and earn" in the new house in order to be incorporated into the domestic unit (and into Satnampanth if she belonged to another caste). Maya Unnithan-Kumar has argued that the ideology of brideprice does not value the labor of wives because it constructs them as dependents of men. Among the Girasia of Rajasthan, for example, brideprice is seen as a compensation for the money that a father has spent on his daughter rather than as payment for the loss of her labor.[108] This is all the evidence that Unnithan-Kumar adduces for her argument, which is quite inadequate since she does not have anything concrete to say here about how Girasia men and women—wife givers and wife takers—actually construct women's contribution of labor to their affinal homes. Indeed, it is curious that Unnithan-Kumar casts the issue in terms of continuous—and, implicitly, lifelong—contributions of labor within the natal home while dealing with patrilineal kinship in which the normative accent is on the desirability of daughters to marry at a young age and move to the husband's home in accordance with wider principles of patrilocal residence. Second, the formal principles of patrilineal kinship do broadly constitute wives as dependents of men: but this does not inherently deny the possibility of value and significance being accorded to their labor in different ways. The Satnamis, for example, were clear that the ideology and practice of brideprice was related to importance of a woman's work within her husband's home.

It is also important to keep in mind that in particular situations secondary marriages have set greater binds and restrictions on women, a point made forcefully for the Girasia of Rajasthan by Unnithan-Kumar.[109] However, the weakness in this argument once again stems from its somewhat exclusive focus on aspects of control exercised over women, which is arguably only one side of the larger story. Moreover, there seem to be certain important differences between the Girasia and the Satnamis in the domain of secondary marriages: among the Girasia the brideprice is returned by the woman's natal kin who along with the collective male *jaths*—exogamous patrilineages—exercise control in the matter of her choosing a new husband, and the new partner has to make an excess payment over and above the initial brideprice. It should be clear from my discussion that all these features are absent from the practice of *churi* among the Satnamis. Thus, while I agree with Unnithan-Kumar's larger argument that women do not escape structural inequalities of patriliny under brideprice arrangements and secondary marriages, it also seems to me that to stop at this point is to shy away from the necessary task of exploring the many variations in the relationship between patriliny and gender.

At the same time, in keeping with these emphases, it is equally important to recognize that the wider structures of patrilineal and patrilocal kinship also meant that Satnami daughters, sisters, and wives were denied the security of patrimony, clear entitlements within the natal home, and firm rights in the affinal group.[110] It was within these limits then that *churi* could provide Satnami—along with other low- and middle-caste—women with a degree of autonomy and space for maneuver to negotiate principles of kinship that were weighted against them.[111]

In order to elaborate these issues of how the institution of *churi* provided Satnami women with a space to negotiate marriage(s), motherhood, possessions, and property within the wider structures of patrilineal kinship let me tell a little tale. It is a fragment of a story about the middle and last years of Puna, a Satnami woman whom we encounter for the first time in these pages. However, given the larger paucity of the historical record—regarding intimate matters in everyday arenas, particularly those involving subordinate groups—we will have to make do with this tale that is not always easy to follow (for which my apologies, patient reader). The fragment serves as a register of how Satnami women constructed their place within a wide-ranging dynamic of gender, kinship, and power. Indeed, it is hardly ironic that Puna's short story is contained in what Simon Schama condescendingly deems as a "record of incrimination."[112] The Satnami woman's last husband, Samelal was convicted for her murder by the Bilaspur Sessions Court in June 1947.[113]

Puna lived in Kormi, a small village about four kilometers from the Bilaspur railway station. In Kormi Puna is remembered as a very beautiful woman who had several suitors.[114] We do not know the name of Puna's first husband who initially brought her to Kormi, but she soon left him for Uderam Satnami who gave her *churis*.[115] After seven years of living with Uderam, Puna had deserted him for Sewar Satnami for a year but had then returned.[116] Puna and Uderam once again started living together and now had a daughter, Lainmati.[117] Ten years later Puna once again left Uderam, this time for Samelal Satnami.

Samelal had given Puna *churis* and had fed the caste, but had not paid any *behatri* to Uderam. Instead, Puna and Samelal had soon gone off to Calcutta. The beginnings of Puna's liaison with Samelal and the couple's move to Calcutta were indeed closely linked moves. We have seen that while most Satnamis migrated temporarily, others lived away for longer periods in order to earn money from their labor before returning to their village. Here Samelal's meager landholding in Kormi made work in Calcutta an attractive proposition.[118] As for Puna, Samelal and Calcutta, a home and protection, money and affection, interest and emotion were possibly part of a package deal. Now we do not know anything about the relations between the couple in Calcutta. All that the case tells us is that they earned money and after two years had come back to Kormi. On their return to the village, Samelal and Puna lived in one of the two houses of Santokhi (Samelal's father).[119] Chintadass Kotwar added, "Samelal lived separate from his father because of his having contracted this relationship with Puna."[120] But Puna was soon to chart a course independent of both Samelal and Santokhi.

The depositions of witnesses in the trial and the remembered history of the dispute in the village agree in presenting the relationship between Puna and Samelal as one marked by frequent quarrels. After one such fight, soon after their return from Calcutta, Puna built a house in the compound of Sawat Satnami, an older man of their caste. The quarrels continued and Puna and Samelal would come together and again fall and live apart after short intervals. "When they separated, Puna used to live in her house [in the compound of Sawat] while Samelal would go and live with his father."[121] A little after Puna built herself the house, she also bought a piece of land and registered it in her own name.[122] Here the gutsy Satnami woman used the money she had earned together with Samelal in Calcutta so that she was no longer dependent on him.[123]

Serious fights with Samelal also led to other responses on the part of Puna. After one such quarrel, "she lived and dined"—a turn of speech implying sexual relations—with Khekhi Satnami.[124] On two other occasions Puna went and lived with Uderam, her second husband. "Whenever she came to me she had quarreled with Samelal. During these periods she did have marital relations with me but I never took her as my *churi* wife."[125] When Puna returned to Samelal's house after living with Uderam, Samelal had to expiate the offense and feed the caste. This was not the only financial setback faced by Samelal. Puna's "desertions" were marked by her carrying away of ornaments and goods from the house she shared with Samelal. She gave some of these ornaments and goods to Lainmati, her daughter from Uderam.[126] According to Samelal, Puna had carried off ornaments and property on three occasions. The third time was a few days before Puna was killed. Puna came to Uderam's house to tend to her daughter who was ill. According to Uderam she brought "paddy and she was wearing Bahuta and Hamel. These ornaments were of silver. . . . She gave these two ornaments to her daughter Lainmati."[127] Puna had evidently stripped the hut bare and removed the materials to Uderam's house.[128] Samelal was terribly disconcerted and asked Uderam to keep her since she had a daughter by him. But nothing came out of this desperate entreaty.

Samelal sought a way out of his predicament. He met the *malguzar* of the neighboring village, Banakdih, with a view to sell the tenancy land he held there in order to raise money to sue Puna for the property that she had carried away and for a field that "stood in her name though he [Samelal] had purchased it out of his earnings in Calcutta."[129] Samelal's son (from an earlier wife), a young man called Bhukhan also reached there. The *malguzar* declined to buy the land. Samelal was despondent. Bhukhan commented that "this dispute between Samelal and Puna would not end until one of them lost his [sic] life."[130] A few days later Puna was dead. An old Satnami who was a lad at the time claims that Samelal had asked Bhuru, a relative who had earlier killed his wife in Kormi, about the conditions and life in a jail. Both Bhuru and Samelal had given themselves up to the police.[131] In the Sessions Court, Samelal denied having killed Puna and said that he had been framed by the police. At the same time, he admitted the history of his relations with Puna. The admission confirmed how Puna had managed family and property before she was put to death in a forest near her home.

We find that the Satnami woman had functioned within the interstices of the flexible structures of *churi* to negotiate and get past the principles that denied her firm rights within affinal group(s), rights over children, and entitlements to property. She had acquired land, built herself a house, and carried away ornaments and goods from her affinal unit to give them to her daughter from an earlier marriage. Puna had also expressed her emotions and obligations of motherhood by moving into her former husband's home to tend to her ill daughter. The course charted by Puna reminds us of the need to attend to the variations, nuances, and differences in the many-sided relationship between the analytical domains of patriliny and gender. Puna's many moves and maneuvers, remarkable for their deft adroitness, were part of a larger pattern. The practice of *churi* could help Satnami women to carve out strategies and negotiate marriages and migration, murk and misery, and motherhood and men.

It is difficult to draw neat conclusions at the end of this discussion about the ordering of gender in Satnampanth. Kinship among the Satnamis valued the labor of women but excluded them from the formal arrangements of the devolution of patrilineal property and firm entitlements in the affinal group. The flexible marriage practices centering on *churi* afforded Satnami women a degree of space to negotiate—and on occasions subvert—the principles of patrilineal and patrilocal kinship. Upper-caste men, with land and power, turned the alleged promiscuity of Satnami women into an instrument of their sexual exploitation. Both historical evidence and contemporary oral testimonies indicate that members of the Satnami organizational hierarchy too used their privileges to gain access to the women of the group. *Jhanjeri chauka*, which drew upon itself the enormous condescension of upper-caste self-righteousness, suggests that women were much more than inert victims of processes to reinforce male boundaries but also poses seemingly intractable problems of interpretation. These complexities are further compounded by Satnami myths, where sexuality invested women with agency, and the mediation of feminine guile and desire led to divisions, disputes, and disorder. For the most part the myths of Satnampanth articulated a "heroic history," but gendered disruptions put this to an end. It is to these myths that I now turn.

CHAPTER FIVE

A Contested Past:
The Myths of Satnampanth

The repertoire of Satnami myths, a part of a vigorous oral tradition, pro vided the group with a powerful statement of its past. The myths were written down by Baba Ramchandra, the leader of the Kisan Sabha movement in Awadh in north India between 1918 and 1920, in the late 1920s in a manuscript called *Ghasidasji ki Vanshavali*. This chapter discusses the text and its relationship with the Satnami oral tradition to examine the myths of Satnampanth. It explores the creation of a new mythic tradition and focuses on the symbolic elaboration of Satnami conceptions of the past encoded within their myths. My account of the myths begins with the initiation of Ghasidas and ends with the conflict between members of the fourth genera-tion of the guru family when the weakness of the later gurus, manifest in the uncontrolled sexuality of their wives, led to a division of the seat of the guru and endemic conflicts within the guru family.

The *Vanshavali*

Ghasidasji ki Vanshavali was the outcome of an interesting historical encoun-ter. In the early 1920s, a few leading lights of Satnampanth got together with local Hindu reformers and Congress leaders in Chhattisgarh to set up an organization called the Satnami Mahasabha. The Satnami Mahasabha was an effort to reform the Satnamis and to participate in the network of elite organizational and constitutional politics within the region and in the Central Provinces. In the winter of 1925, Naindas and Anjordas, the prominent leaders of the Satnami Mahasabha, traveled with a small group of Satnamis to the Kanpur session of the Indian National Congress. In the course of the Kanpur Congress the Satnami contingent and its leaders met Baba Ramchandra.

Shridhar Balwant Jodhpurkar, aka Baba Ramchandra, a Maharashtrian Brahman had left home at an early age, wandered through central and western India, worked variously as a coolie, a vendor, a laborer, and in 1905 had gone to Fiji as an indentured laborer, married a beautiful Chamarin (a woman of the Chamar caste), and lived there for several years.[1] Baba Ramchandra had left his wife in Fiji, and on his return to India involved himself in organizing and leading a militant and radical Kisan Sabha movement between 1918 and 1920 in the Awadh countryside.[2] In 1925 this leader of the Awadh peasants seems to have been disenchanted with a "capitalist Congress."[3] The Satnamis fired his imagination. The private papers of Baba Ramchandra reveal that he traveled back to Chhattisgarh with the Satnamis, stayed there till the late 1920s, and was closely involved in shaping the organization of the Satnami Mahasabha. The writing of the *Vanshavali* was one of the several consequences of the encounter between Baba Ramchandra and the Satnamis.[4]

Is the *Vanshavali* a reliable guide to Satnami myths? The manuscript is in the handwriting of Baba Ramchandra. The script is Devanagri in a running hand. Its language is Hindi, Chhattisgarhi, and, very occasionally, Marathi. The text, unlike Ramchandra's other writings among the Satnamis, bears the impress of a rapid noting of the myths as they were narrated by his informants. The *Vanshavali* does not mention the month or the year when it was written by Baba Ramchandra. Moreover, we cannot be certain of the use for which it was intended. It is possible that Baba Ramchandra's writing of the *Vanshavali* was a preparatory exercise, the myths a set of hurriedly jotted preliminary notes, toward giving the Satnamis an authentic and canonical history as a means to reform the group. Equally, Baba Ramchandra may have been persuaded by the leaders of the Satnami Mahasabha, who were illiterate, to write down the myths. At any rate, Baba Ramchandra published his official history of the Satnamis in 1929. *Satnam Sagar* reveals Baba Ramchandra's familiarity with the pattern of Satnami myths.[5] I think it likely that the *Vanshavali* was written sometime between 1926 and 1928, after Baba Ramchandra got to know the Satnamis well enough to be initiated into their knowledge, but before he composed *Satnam Sagar.*

We need to pose the question of the relations of power within which the *Vanshavali* was constructed. In this text, an alive, continuously performed oral tradition was fixed in writing. Moreover, the *Vanshavali* was compiled in the context of the activities of the Satnami Mahasabha, where Baba Ramchandra's efforts were often directed toward appropriating Satnami beliefs to the concerns of a largely Brahmanical Hinduism. We need to be wary of the imprint of a Brahmanical "tradition" Ramchandra could have left on the text. In other words, we cannot presume that the *Vanshavali* necessarily provides us with a direct Satnami statement of their myths.

Studies of the interface between orality and writing in various contexts underscore that texts made possible by literacy can be rooted within an oral matrix.[6] Jonathan Schaeffer, for example, has argued that the thought and writing of Giambattista Vico was grounded in—and drew its motive force from—the oral matrix of rhetoric.[7] Juan Ossio has shown that in a seventeenth-century Peruvian narrative the devices of a literate tradition remained subordinate to mythical categories that gave the work its real meaning.[8] These writings from distant lands, other cultures, suggest the need to take a closer look at the *Vanshavali* and its relationship with the Satnami oral tradition.

The construction of the *Vanshavali* underscores that the myths were hurriedly written as they were narrated: the attempt to form complete sentences is given up very soon, and the text conveys a sense of Ramchandra groping for words and drawing upon his knowledge of Hindi, Marathi, and Chhattisgarhi.[9] In an effort to capture the basic pattern of the myths, sentences break off and there are jumps to key episodes within a story, an attempt to hold on to the thread that held the tales together. Baba Ramchandra's endeavor was to retain the continuity of the narrative. In the *Vanshavali*, the imprint of Brahmanical and upper-caste traditions exists, in an important sense, in the use of particular words and forms of expression. Baba Ramchandra did not have the time to work upon and transform the myths. The text, as we shall read, carries the immediacy of face-to-face interaction characteristic of oral traditions. Baba Ramchandra's other writings among the Satnamis, in fact, had greater polish and were often more didactic than the *Vanshavali*. Indeed, *Satnam Sagar*, Baba Ramchandra's rather more official history of the Satnamis was organized along separate lines and followed a different trajectory from the *Vanshavali*. Thus, *Satnam Sagar* opens with an elaborate cosmological account of the origins of the universe, various Hindu gods and goddesses occupy a significant position in the narrative, and the Satnami gurus put in a cameo appearance in what is actually a highly sanitized account of Satnampanth, reconstructed in the image of a reformed Brahmanical tradition.[10] Baba Ramchandra, it would seem, was uncomfortable with several aspects of the Satnami myths and jettisoned them when he tried to give the Satnamis a more appropriate history.

I also found during my field work in 1989–90 and 1994–95 that the myths recorded by Baba Ramchandra have been an important part of the Satnami oral traditions. The *kathas* about Ghasidas and Balakdas that I heard, discussed, and recorded in the field did not vary significantly from the myths in the *Vanshavali*.[11] Is it possible that the myths in the *Vanshavali* fed into and became a part of the Satnami oral tradition? The myths were not mere manufactures of the moment, a creation of the 1920s. The events and episodes, the plots and the subplots, of these discursive dramas put in an appearance in the accounts of colonial administrators writing in the late nineteenth and early twentieth centuries. The manuscript also does not seem to have stayed in Chhattisgarh for long enough to have been disseminated among (the very few) literate Satnamis. In the early 1930s Baba Ramchandra had carried it away to Awadh, where it was found among his papers in the 1970s. By the middle of the 1930s the Satnamis were, once again, looking for a literate sympathizer to write down the history of their gurus. The Satnami *mahant* Naindas had requested Sunderlal Tripathi, a Brahman Congressman of Chhattisgarh, to write down "the *kathas* [legends] and *itihas* [history] of the gurus." Sunderlal Tripathi had refused. When I asked the eighty-four-year-old man the reason behind this request, his answer showed a clear if derisive understanding of the symbolic power of writing within oral traditions: "Who knows? The illiterate like written things."[12] Similarly, a Satnami *mahant* who knew Naindas and Anjordas told me that they had wanted to publish the *kathas* of the gurus so that the "other Hindu people" could read them. But the two Satnamis had not been successful.[13] In the *Vanshavali*, it seems to me, the basic structure and relations, the internal organization of the Satnami mythic order, was not inherently compromised by the written form.

The myths in the *Vanshavali* had developed over a hundred years, a creative cultural process that involved accretions and, within limits, deletions and improvisation. At the same time, the writings of the administrators on the Satnamis in the second half of the nineteenth and early twentieth centuries dealt with these myths principally as an instance of the gross superstition of an ignorant folk, which had destroyed the initially strong edifice of a monotheistic sect opposed to the caste system and idolatry. Similarly, the interest of evangelical missionaries in Satnami myths did not go much beyond attempts to appropriate, rework, and fashion a few of the tales into true stories, Christian fables, an aid to proselytize and spread the "word." What these sources describe are abbreviated versions of certain Satnami myths. Moreover, the thinness of official records and the tendency within Satnami myths to conflate discrete events into a dramatic episode do not permit a consistent dialogue between the two sets of sources. All this makes it very difficult to construct a chronological account of the development of Satnami myths over the course of the nineteenth century and through to the period they were written down by Baba Ramchandra.

These limits suggest other possibilities. First, the corpus of Satnami myths tells a full story that elaborates the group's cultural construction of its past and embodies its representations of history. Indeed, the Satnami rehearsal of myths in multiple contexts—a story in summer and a winter's tale, fables for children and ramblings of the old, accounts woven into inextricably bound rhythms of labor and leisure, and the performance of oral narratives as *katha* and *panthi geet* (songs of Satnampanth) in weddings, rituals, *chauka*, and *puja*—ordered the past of Satnampanth. Second, the internal order and structure of the myths reveal the symbolic constitution of Satnampanth. The specific symbols within the myths were implicated in the definition of the boundary of Satnampanth. Third, Ghasidas and Balakdas, the major mythic figures of Satnampanth, effected resolutions and negotiated figures of authority who populated the cosmic and social order to define the boundary and orchestrate the construction of Satnampanth. The three movements served to reaffirm Satnami identity, reinforce their solidarity, and interrogate the relationships of power constituted by the ritual hierarchy of purity and pollution, the culturally and ritually constituted centrality of kingship and dominant caste(s), and colonial authority within Chhattisgarh. But the death of Balakdas also signaled the end of the bold narrative of Satnami myths, which were now replaced by more fragmentary and tendentious tales. Among the later gurus weakness replaced resolve and they did not command the truth of Satnam. The mediation of feminine guile and desire led to disputes. The guru *gaddi* was divided. Untamed female sexuality manifested principles of disorder. The work of gender brought to a close the heroic history of the myths of Satnampanth.

The Initiation of Ghasidas

The *Vanshavali* opens with Ghasidas's encounter with his landed master, a critical step in the constitution of the mythic status of the guru.[14]

> Ghasidas made his *tapsthan* [place of worship] in Girodpuri. After performing *tap* [worship], he took up the work of ploughing in the field of a Marar [a caste which, traditionally, grows vegetables]. Ghasidas picked up the plough on his shoulder. His master started walking behind him. The master saw that the plough was suspended in the air, above Ghasidas's shoulder. When they reached the field the master joined the plough to the bullocks. Once again,

he saw that Ghasidas's hand was above the handle of the plough which was moving on its own.[15]

As we have seen, until the revenue settlement operations carried out by the colonial regime in the 1860s, the plough was the basis of assessment of land revenue in Chhattisgarh. A *nagar* (or a "plough" of land) was an elastic measure intended to represent the area one plough and four oxen could cultivate. The plough was the basis both for the apportioning of land and the revenue demand of the state within the village. In a land-surplus situation, within a social order in which the plough was charged with cultural significance, the *nagar* was a critical metaphor of power within the work process and in everyday village life. The plough was, in a manner at once substantive and symbolic, constitutive of the relationship between a ploughman and his master. Ghasidas worked for his Marar master, but he did not carry the burden of his master's plough on his shoulder, and his hand remained above the handle of the plough. Ghasidas had effected a move to transform his relationship, mediated by the plough, with his agricultural master.

The myth emphasizes that the master became worried since he could not ascertain if Ghasidas was a holy man or a trickster. But the Marar master's uncertainty about Ghasidas was to end soon. It had only to await Ghasidas's meeting with *satnampurush*.

> Ghasidas ploughed the field and left the bullocks to graze. The field was next to a mountain and the bullocks went there. When Ghasidas went there to bring back the bullocks *satnam* emerged. It was there that Ghasidas met the pure white form of *satnam*. *Satnampurush* said to Ghasidas, "I had sent you to reform the lineage, but you forgot and have started working for others. This entire Chamar lineage has got spoilt. Have you forgotten this? Intoxicated by meat and liquor, these holy men have got ruined. You spread the name of *satnam*. I am *satnampurush*, know me." So Ghasidas said, "Who will believe my word since in order to look after my wife and two children I work for other people?" *Satnampurush* answered, "I shall bring all the Chamars to you. You give them betel leaf and make them repeat the name of *satnam*." Ghasidas, once again, refused. But *Satnampurush* tied two pieces of coconut to Ghasidas's clothes.[16]

Ghasidas is the person who had been sent by *satnampurush* to reform the Chamars. The Chamars, in turn, are a *vansh*, a lineage. The use of a metaphor of kinship emphasizes the bondedness of Chamars as a community: a collectivity whose destiny could be orchestrated by it's mythic figures. Ghasidas had forgotten to reform his own people, his lineage, and was working for others. The Chamars, as a result, had taken to *mas madira* (meat and liquor) and had been ruined. Second, it was of essence that the Chamars, who were holy men, be restored to a state of purity. They had to be reformed through their coming to know *satnam*. The name of *satnam* had to be spread. *Satnampurush* was to bring the Chamars to a reluctant Ghasidas. Finally, Ghasidas's refusal to follow the orders of *satnampurush* was a consequence of his working for other people. He had to accept the apparent subordination that followed this labor in order to support his wife and children.

> Ghasidas took the plough and the bullocks to the master. The master said, "Ghasidas I shall not have you work because your body appears peculiar to me. It seems as though you have a crown, four arms, and a conch shell. I have never seen your body like this." The master, overwhelmed by the form, cried "Jai Guru Ghasidas." He fell on Ghasidas's feet.[17]

The reversal that had begun with the change in the relation of Ghasidas's body to the plough had been completed by the submission of the Marar master. The master's act was brought about by the change in Ghasidas's form, directed by *satnam*. It occurred after Ghasidas's encounter with *satnampurush*. Indeed, the crown, the four arms, the conch shell, signs of the deity Vishnu, had fleetingly transfigured the lowly Ghasidas into a supremely divine being, on par with the greatest of gods, where the signs of a particular deity were metonymically extended to refer to wider distinctions of divinity, the embodiment of *satnam*. This proved the final step in effecting a resolution of the contradiction between the authority of Ghasidas—a low-caste laborer and ploughman—and his higher-caste agricultural master.

Yet, much more was to happen before Ghasidas was initiated into his new status as a guru. For what lay ahead were trials, ordeals, and obstacles, and all these had to be overcome by Ghasidas.

> When Ghasidas returned from the Marar's house his children ran up to him and ate the pieces of coconut [that had been tied to his clothes by *satnampurush*]. Ghasidas's wife gave him water and food. After eating, when he sat down, the children died. His wife and neighbors were bewildered and anguished. The children were buried with the advice of the *jati* [caste]. After three days Ghasidas took the ritual bath, finished other *jati* rituals, and slept with his wife who died. She too was buried.[18]

What is striking is the very ordinariness of the acts of Ghasidas, of eating and of sleeping with his wife, which led to the deaths. The acts spoke of routine domesticity and of ties within the family. With the death of his children and his wife the ties were broken, the domesticity was no more.

Ghasidas was left alone, a mood of renunciation set in. He went to a mountain in Sonakhan. There *satnampurush* assumed the form of a tiger and ran towards him. So Ghasidas said, "Yes, you have eaten three; eat me as well." The tiger bowed his head. Then *satnampurush* assumed the form of a python. Ghasidas went up to him and asked to be eaten. The python bowed his head. When night fell, Ghasidas climbed a Tendu tree and put a noose around his neck. The noose left him and he sat down. Ghasidas thought that he had not tied the noose properly. A second time he tied his neck tightly to the Tendu tree. The branch of the tree bent down and reached the ground. *Satnampurush* assumed the four armed form and stood aside. He then said to Ghasidas that he had again forgotten to worship *satnam*. He was asked to spread the name of *satnam* and make the place into a site of pilgrimage and get it worshipped: "You worship here for six months and the Chamars nearby will come to this holy place. You feed them betel leaf, get them to worship the name of *satnam*; the idols of gods and goddesses in their houses should be thrown out." Ghasidas replied that his wife and children had died and he was being asked to get a name worshipped. He could not do it. So *satnampurush* said to Ghasidas, "I will make everyone alive, but the name of *satnam* should be spread. I am telling you to worship here. After six months I will make your son and daughter alive." After saying this *satnampurush* disappeared and Ghasidas started worshipping there. In the meanwhile, people of the caste and family tried to find Ghasidas. When they could not find him, they gave the funeral feast. For six months Ghasidas purified his body. For six months he left all food and drink. After six months *satnam* emerged in the same form. Ghasidas recognized that form and touched the feet of *satnam*. A pond emerged at the place where *satnam* had kept his feet. From that pond *amrit* [nectar] was obtained. In that water *satnam* made Ghasidas have a bath and then gave him the *amrit*. *Satnampurush* then asked Ghasidas, "Now have you experienced *satnam?*" Ghasidas answered, "Maharaj, I have experienced your form." . . . Telling him the rule of making disciples *satnampurush* brought Ghasidas to the real/original place of worship and asked him to give coconuts and betel leaves and spread the name of *satnam*. *Satnampurush* said, "I shall give all the Chamars the dream of this name and send them to this place," and then went back to his world.[19]

This can be read as the story of the initiation of Ghasidas that was directed by *satnampurush*. *Satnampurush*, in various guises, put Ghasidas through the ordeal of death. The revelation by *satnampurush* of his true form, after Ghasidas failed to see that it was he who held the noose, was a statement of the power of *satnampurush*. Ghasidas's mistake was that he still did not know *satnampurush*. He had not worshiped and spread the name of *satnam*. *Satnampurush* instructed him on what had to be done for the creation of Satnampanth. But Ghasidas refused. The assurance that he would make Ghasidas's wife and children alive resolved the problem. In their first meeting *satnampurush* had emphasized, *"Mein khud satnampurush hoon mujhe pahchan* [I am *satnampurush,* recognize/know me]." The later events resulted from Ghasidas's inadequate recognition of *satnam.* It was after he carried out the instructions of *satnampurush* and cleansed his body by renouncing food and drink and performing worship that full recognition followed. To know/recognize *satnampurush* was to accept *satnam.* *Satnampurush* created the *kund* (pond), gave Ghasidas *amrit* (nectar), and purified him. In brief, he conducted Ghasidas's rite of initiation. *Satnampurush* also provided that little extra—the rule for creating disciples, a vision to the Chamars—that gurus need. The conditions of possibility of Ghasidas becoming the guru of a reformed *vansh* of Chamars, of the creation of Satnampanth, had been fulfilled.

Obeyesekere has discussed the classic pattern in which a figure new to a mythic tradition passes through ordeals and trials set up by the supreme deity till the final moment when the mythic figure recognizes the deity's powers and is simultaneously incorporated into the existent pantheon and the mythic tradition.[20] What we find in Satnami myths is a play on the familiar theme. The relationship between *satnampurush* and Ghasidas is ridden with tension. The tension, I suggest, is linked to the specific character of the myths of Satnampanth. The Satnami mythic order was a new construct. Both Ghasidas and *satnampurush,* unknown in their specific form, had to be established within this mythic tradition. This involved a double movement: Ghasidas had to pass through trials and ordeals set up by *satnampurush* before he was initiated as a guru, and Ghasidas, in turn, put *satnampurush* through tests. From the moment of their first encounter, at each step, *satnampurush* had to counter the resistance offered by Ghasidas. In the trials Ghasidas underwent with the tiger and the python, the tables were turned. Ghasidas recognized that it was *satnampurush* who had come in the form of the tiger and the python. When he addressed *satnampurush* he offered a challenge: "Yes, you have eaten three, eat me as well." The tiger, the python, and the branch of the tree bowed down before Ghasidas. The note of resistance was struck, once again, when Ghasidas refused to follow the orders of *satnampurush* because his wife and children had been taken away from him. All this is related to the fact that Ghasidas, in spite of a mood of renunciation, is not quite a "world renouncer." More about the specific nature of his asceticism a little later. My point here is that Ghasidas's resistance bore the mark of, and carried forward the ambiguity in, the relationship between these two mythic figures. It was by tying the pieces of coconut to Ghasidas's clothes, effecting a separation between Ghasidas and his wife and children, setting up ordeals, providing the assurance that his wife and children would be made alive that *satnampurush* was recognized in his true form by Ghasidas. Two new mythic figures were established within a new mythic tradition.

The constitution of Ghasidas as a guru was premised on diverse attributes of asceticism, which at once combined features of the "individual-outside-the-world" and the "man-in-the-world" with elements drawn from popular traditions. Ghasidas had to "renounce" his wife and children, to be dead to the world, and to cleanse his body. He was a novice who was purified by *satnampurush* through *amrit* before he was initiated into his new status. At the same time, Ghasidas went through the exercise only after *satnampurush* gave him his word that the wife and children would be brought back to life. To a significant degree, Ghasidas's renunciation was framed by his desire to go back to being a householder. Moreover, after his initiation, Ghasidas did not come back as a renouncer. He was brought to the world, reclaimed by his *jati* people, who had presumed him to be dead and had already gone through the motions of a symbolic burial. In the mythic tradition of Satnampanth, Ghasidas's wife had both been sleeping and been dead for six months. It was only after Ghasidas woke her up, brought her back to life, and fixed her broken arm that Chamars started becoming Satnamis in large numbers.[21] Finally, Ghasidas possessed the characteristics of a saint, a shaman, a healer in popular traditions. He fulfilled his followers' desire for the birth of a child, gave a blind *banjara* (gypsy) the gift of sight, cured snake bites, and repaired bodies. Ghasidas healed the bodies of members of Satnampanth.

Guru Ghasidas, a Gond Raja, Angrez Sarkar, and Danteshwari Devi

The establishment of the authority of Ghasidas required him to displace other figures of authority within the social and cosmic order. The classic manner of displacement within a mythic tradition takes the form of a mythic figure totally eclipsing the other mythic figures.[22] This was the fate of village gods and goddesses who were thrown onto a rubbish heap by Ghasidas and the Satnamis. At the same time, in Satnami myths the gurus also effected displacements by demarcating their separate sphere of authority. The exercise, once again, served to constitute the boundary of Satnampanth. To illustrate this process I shall take three examples: Ghasidas's encounters with a tribal Gond raja, with *angrez sarkar* (British government), and his relationship with Danteshwari *devi*, the tribal goddess whose propitiation required human sacrifice.

The first of these encounters took place very soon after the establishment of Satnampanth.

The Gond raja of Sonakhan [an estate north of Raipur] got the news that a Chamar by the name of Ghasidas was accumulating money and coconuts in his kingdom. The raja told Ghasidas that he wanted half the money and coconuts as his share. Ghasidas replied that he had only betel leaves and coconuts and no money, and agreed to give a share of the betel leaves and the coconuts if the king desired. The king took half the coconuts and then said, "I am in debt; help me pay the debt of fifty thousand rupees or I will kill the money lender."[23] When the king killed the money lender Ghasidas knew that *pap* [sin] had entered the place and it would be better for him to move out. On the day of *maghipuno* [the day and night of the full moon in the month of *magh,* January–February] the king sent soldiers to Ghasidas's house. There were a few of Ghasidas's men among the soldiers. It struck them that they had surrounded the guru's house, but if they were to catch him it would be a grave insult to Satnampanth. They began to sing *bhajans* [devotional songs]. All the soldiers then became devotees of Ghasidas, broke open the door to the house, and prepared the way for Ghasidas to escape. Ghasidas reached a village; the villagers started celebrating *maghipuno*; the king of Sonakhan attacked; Ghasidas had to leave. This happened again and again as Ghasidas went from one village to another.[24]

Each celebration of the festival of *maghipuno* led to attacks by the raja and his soldiers. *Maghipuno*, established as a sacred date in the Satnami calendar by Ghasidas, marked the boundary of Satnampanth as the community came under attack for its distinctive celebration of the power of Ghasidas.

There is also, however, an important subplot in this story: the relationship between Ghasidas and the king of Sonakhan. Ghasidas's response to the king's demand for money and coconuts served to demarcate their respective spheres of authority. Ghasidas said that he had only betel leaves and coconuts and no money. The betel leaves and coconut—offered to the guru by his disciples and an important medium in the rituals and practices of Satnampanth—were comprehensive icons of Ghasidas's authority. Similarly, Ghasidas did not dismiss the authority of the king and readily agreed to part with a share of the betel leaves and the coconuts.[25] The difficulty was that the king was unjust and had been visited by *pap* (sin). The soldiers, the instruments of the king's unjust authority, were won over by the just and moral authority of Ghasidas. Ghasidas had, in any case, made up his mind to leave. The soldiers now provided him with a way out of a place contaminated by sin. Ghasidas's move from one village to another, all of them celebrating *maghipuno*, was a statement of his authority and of the spread of Satnampanth.

Ghasidas's second key encounter, now with *angrez sarkar*, was equally charged with the interplay of meaning and power.

Ghasidas had built a house in Bhandar which he had to abandon because of the attacks by the raja of Sonakhan. After rule had been established by the British, he returned to Bhandar. Ghasidas had lived there for ten years when the *angrez raja* [English king] received the news about the guru. Soldiers carrying the orders of Agnew *saheb* and Mulki *saheb* came from Raipur. Ghasidas had been summoned to the capital. Ghasidas went to Raipur sitting in a *doli* [palanquin].[26]

In a characteristic move, the *doli*, reserved for their use by the upper castes, a signifier of status and rank within the caste hierarchy, had been appropriated by Ghasidas.[27] The act of appropriation was an expropriation of the dominant. The upper-caste expropriators had been divested of their monopoly over a symbol that was constitutive of their domination. Ghasidas had adequately answered the summons of the *saheb.*

And so it was that very soon,

Ghasidas arrived in Raipur.[28] His authority in the capital was awesome. Tens of thousands of Satnamis reached there. As a result, Ghasidas had to sit on a *chaupai* [a small cot], high up on a tree, where he could be visible to all.[29] The *chaprasi* [peon] gave the news of Ghasidas's arrival. The *saheb* demanded Ghasidas's immediate presence, but Ghasidas's response was to delay.

To see and to be seen by Ghasidas was *darshan*, a spectacle, which affected thousands of Satnami devotees. The substance of Ghasidas's authority, in the seat of the *angrez raja,* was transmitted through sight.[30] Moreover, to wait upon a superior is an aspect of subordination. Ghasidas obeyed the *saheb*, but deliberately took his time, arriving with dignity in the evening. It is barely surprising then that the *saheb* subjected Ghasidas to tests and trials.

The *saheb* got the peon to give Ghasidas a *lota* [a small vessel] of *sharbat* [a sweet drink] which contained poison. Ghasidas drank it. He returned to his *aasan* [seat] on the tree. When the night was over the colonial authorities sent the peon to see whether Ghasidas was alive or dead. They were informed that he was alive. Ghasidas had passed the trial. The *saheb* called Ghasidas again, and both the *saheb* and the *memsaheb* did *salaam* [saluted him]. Ghasidas said *satnam* and put both his hands on their heads.

Ghasidas's authority as a guru had been recognized by the *angrez saheb.* But the *saheb* still considered him a *kachha* (weak) guru who had to be tested further. He wrote down the name of Danteshwari, the man-eating goddess, on a piece of paper. The *saheb*'s command was not merely expressed in, but was also shaped by writing. Indeed, the written form bore the mark and was constitutive of the *saheb*'s command, which was a concrete form of colonial authority.[31]

Ghasidas was sent with a *chaprasi* (peon) to Danteshwari *devi* in the chiefdom of Bastar.

> It was an eight-day journey to the *devi*'s shrine. After being taken there, Ghasidas was put inside the *devi*'s temple and the doors were locked. The *devi* emerged from water. The doors of the temple opened.

The encounter between Danteshwari and Ghasidas demarcated the separate but complementary spheres of authority and the different spaces inhabited by the two mythic figures. Danteshwari lived in water, and Ghasidas on land. The goddess addressed Ghasidas as *bade*. In Chhattisgarhi this is a mode of address reserved for the *kurra sasur*, the husband's elder brother, a relationship characterized by mutual avoidance.[32] In the kinship network of the Satnami cosmic order the relationship between Ghasidas and Danteshwari bound them through mutual avoidance.

> Danteshwari asked him, "Why have you come here?" Ghasidas answered that he was there because he was obeying the king, and insisted that Danteshwari should eat him. The goddess replied that she ate all *jatis* [castes/communities] except Satnamis, and asked Ghasidas to spread the name of *satnam*. Ghasidas pledged that he would not betray Danteshwari and tempt her by allowing *mas* [meat] and *madira* [liquor], the substances she devoured, in Satnampanth. The goddess instructed Ghasidas further that if he spread the use of coconut, *pakka bhojan* [food cooked in clarified oil], and *chauka*—substances which carried purity—among his devotees she will never trouble the beings in his *teerth* [place of pilgrimage].

It was the purity of Satnampanth, the avoidance of meat and liquor, which made Danteshwari encourage Ghasidas's endeavor. The space inhabited by Satnampanth was a *teerth*, a holy place. The reinforcement of the boundary of this space, through a continuous purification of the body, maintained the distance between Danteshwari and Ghasidas. In Satnami myths, this maintenance of distance was the mutual acceptance by Danteshwari and Ghasidas of each other's authority and of the relationship of avoidance that bound the *devi* and the guru. Once more, Ghasidas negotiated and displaced the purchase commanded by a key player within the social and cosmic order by demarcating his own sphere of authority. In all three cases, this served to establish Satnampanth.

Balakdas, *Janeu,* and Conquest

After Ghasidas's death—which I discuss later—his son Balakdas took over as guru. In Satnami myths Ghasidas had initiated the challenge both to caste hierarchy and to colonial authority. Balakdas also took this up, although in rather different ways. This emerges in the myth about Balakdas and the *janeu.*

It was on the day of Ghasidas's funeral feast that Balakdas told the Satnamis who had assembled that Ghasidas had appeared in a dream and told him, "I had given the *kanthi;* you spread the *janeu.*" Now, there is a complicity here between the writing of British administrators and the upper-caste people to whom I talked about the incident. Both depict it as an act born of the inordinate vanity of Balakdas. This fits well with their shared stereotype of the Satnamis as an arrogant people. The Satnami version, on the other hand, emphasizes the continuity with the past. The wearing of the sacred thread by the Satnamis was the last wish of Ghasidas. It was conveyed on the day of the funeral feast, the last life-cycle ritual, of Ghasidas. Balakdas was to honor Ghasidas's word and build upon the beginning that had been made with the *kanthi* through the spread of the sacred thread. The *janeu* was to become a principle of Satnami faith. According to the myth, the enterprise had the critical support of members of the guru family and key members within Satnampanth. When they went to Balakdas wearing the *janeu* the guru was pleased, "Our *kul* is fortunate."[33]

We have noted earlier that the appropriation of the sacred thread by a low caste is, often, subsumed within the master discourse of sanskritization.[34] Here I find several problems with such an approach. First, if Satnampanth appropriated the signs afforded by the ritual hierarchy of purity and pollution, it also drew upon popular traditions, which had negotiated and challenged the caste order in different ways. Second, it rejected and overturned key elements of the divine and social hierarchies within caste society. Finally, the *janeu* was an addition to Satnampanth, a part of a process of symbolic construction that situated the sign in a new context and questioned the caste system.[35] The concept, it seems to me, can prove to be much too facile. It circumvents an analysis of the processes and the logic of the symbolic construction of a low-caste endeavor. It follows that placing the Satnami appropriation of the sacred thread within the framework of sanskritization would miss out on the simultaneity of the critique of caste society and a questioning of British rule under Balakdas.[36] The wearing of the sacred thread by the Satnamis, an oppositional step, led to a conflict with the upper castes and brought colonial law into play. Thus:

> The news about the *janeu* spread from one village to another. The ignorant
> Hindus created an organization which resolved to kill Balakdas. But the Hin-

dus were worried. Balakdas had to be found alone for their plan to succeed. Once Balakdas was traveling with a few companions. The Hindus initiated a quarrel but could not harm Balakdas. The Satnamis appealed to colonial authorities. There was an enquiry. The Raipur *kutcherry* [court] asked Balakdas if he had distributed the *janeu* among Satnamis. The guru, of course, did not lie. He won the case. The officials were given a bribe of a thousand rupees by the Hindus. They arrested five Satnamis who were kept in a *hawalat* [jail]. The *sarkar* in order to test the Satnamis and to get more money from the Hindus went "against its law" and gave each of them five large measures of grain to grind. The Satnamis said that they would perform the evening purificatory practice and then grind. They prepared themselves by defecating and taking a bath in the evening. The Satnamis then put the grain in the *chakki*, the mill, in front of soldiers. As soon as they said *satnam* and moved the handle, the mill burst. The peon informed the officials, who thought that the Satnamis had deliberately, as an act of mischief, broken the mill. The officers called the five Satnamis and in front of the Hindus asked, "What is your caste?" The answer, "Satnami. The decision about food and drink was taken by Ghasidas. When he heard about the *janeu*, Balakdas has made us wear it. *Satnam* is *sancha* [true/pure], any other name is *asancha* [false/impure]. This is all we know." In front of the Hindus the officers wrote on small pieces of paper. The papers contained orders. Wear the *janeu*; put on a *tilak* [mark on the forehead]; keep a *choti* [or *shikha*, tuft of hair allowed to grow long at the back of the head]. After this the *janeu* started being worn in many villages.[37]

There are two closely linked themes in this story: the truth of *satnam* and the legitimacy of the Satnami endeavor; and the relationship of the Satnamis with colonial authority. It was critical for the Hindus to find Balakdas alone. We have seen that in Satnami self-perception they are defeated only when there is a division within their ranks or when they are disunited. Balakdas had only a few companions, which was an invitation for the Hindus to attack. But the few Satnamis were united. Balakdas could not be killed. The Satnamis were also loyal subjects. After the quarrel it was they who appealed to the *sarkar*. In the court it was the straightforward answer of Balakdas, the power of his word, which carried the truth of *satnam*, that won him the law suit. The government was, however, corruptible. The five Satnamis were jailed because the officials had been bribed. Moreover, the *sarkar* went against its own law when the Satnamis were given five measures of grain to grind. The Satnami mythic tradition drew upon the language of colonial law and used it to criticize the *sarkar*, the power that defined its lexical rules. At the same time, the Satnamis once again obeyed the king's orders. They first created the conditions in which *satnam* could operate. It was after they had purified themselves that they faced the ordeal of grinding five measures of grain in the mill within the confines of the jail. In Hindi the phrase *chakki peesna* commonly refers to the practice of prisoners grinding grain in a mill. It evokes subjection within the disciplinary institution of the prison. The power of *satnam* burst the *chakki.* The *sarkar* did not recognize what lay behind the breaking of the mill, which was understood as a deliberate act of Satnami mischief. It was, in fact, after the Satnamis stated the truth of *satnam* in a brief and simple fashion that recognition came to the *sarkar.* At each step, the loyalty and obedience of the Satnamis to the *sarkar* was accompanied by the questioning of colonial law. The truth, legitimacy, and power of *satnam*—a glimmer, perhaps, of an alternative legality—had triumphed over the *sarkar,* which at different points had shown itself to be corrupt and ignorant, unjust and unlawful. At the same time, once the *sarkar* had been compelled to act as a properly constituted moral authority, the Satnami claim over the *janeu, tilak,* and *choti*—the symbols of upper-caste domination—was established through the orders of government officers, which were, characteristically, inscribed in writing on small pieces of paper.

In Satnami myths Balakdas is cast in the mold of a conqueror. The myths engaged with the patterns and properties of ritually constituted kingship to fashion the guru as a figure who possessed regal attributes and, significantly, was on par with the king. Ghasidas's encounter with the Gond raja had demarcated the separate sphere of authority of the Satnami guru. Balakdas built upon and consolidated this move but also added a royal dimension to the seat of the guru. As we have seen, Balakdas had formalized an organizational hierarchy that extended from the guru at the top to *mahants, diwans,* and, finally, *bhandaris* and *sathidars.*[38] The organizational structure of Satnampanth constituted an alternative ritual and symbolic center of power to kings and dominant caste groups. Now,

> Balakdas called his men and asked them to get ready to go to villages. The Satnami population had to be acquainted with the holy men and the members of the organizational hierarchy. Balakdas was [on the one hand] accompanied by Sarha and Judai—two warriors of Satnampanth who were adept at using swords and guns—and four thousand other brave men, and [on the other] by hundreds of pious Satnamis. The guru [embodying the attributes of purity and royalty] put on a *janeu* and *tilak* and carried a spear, a sword, and a gun and rode on a decorated elephant. The impressive cavalcade moved from one village to another. Satnamis came in droves and thronged the guru. Their joy was unbounded and the sound of *panthi geet* [songs of Satnampanth] rent the air. After the guru's *darshan* they showered Balakdas with gold, silver, and clothes.[39]

Clearly, Balakdas had begun his dramatic conquest.

In the course of his tour Balakdas encountered figures of royal author-ity. The king of Nandgaon took a horse from a Satnami and broke the *kanthi* of a few others. Balakdas got the news. He made it clear that as a guru he did not fight with anyone. Instead he cursed the raja, the throne of Nandgaon could never have a legitimate heir. According to the myth, the curse has continued to this date. The raja of Khairagarh decided to test Balakdas. He had meat put in a *katori* (a small round vessel), which was then covered with a piece of cloth. The king asked Balakdas what the vessel contained. Balakdas said that it had pieces of coconut. When the vessel was uncovered the ritually polluting meat had, indeed, turned into pure bits of coconut. The raja gave Balakdas a prize and declared that he was a true guru. The raja then got a letter from the Hindu king of Bilaspur to kill Balakdas. The letter was returned with the reply that the one who kills shall be put to death. An order was passed against the killing of Balakdas in the kingdom of Khairagarh. Balakdas was called by the raja of Kawardha who asked the guru to sit next to him. The raja had heard that Balakdas's body had the imprint of the ten incarnations of the god Vishnu and wanted to see it. Balakdas took off his clothes and showed the signs on his body. The raja was happy. He worshiped the guru and gave him money from his treasury. The spheres inhabited by the king and Balakdas were complementary: the raja, as the ruler, rewarded Balakdas with money; and the king was the supplicant who worshiped Balakdas, the guru. The final measure of Balakdas's triumph in Kawardha was his entry into the inner space, the female and feminine do-main, of the house of the raja. The raja's sister called him inside and ac-cepted him as her guru. Balakdas's spectacular success was also the triumph of his community.[40]

Marriage Matters

In the *Vanshavali* the Satnamis are cast as a *vansh*, a lineage. We encoun-tered this metaphor early in the narrative when Ghasidas met *satnampurush*. The metaphor operates, and is operated by, the nature of relationships be-tween the gurus, members of the organizational hierarchy, and ordinary Satnamis. The members of Satnampanth, particularly the *mahants* and *bhandaris*, who had a crucial place in Satnami life-cycle rituals, also played an important role at the critical points of the life cycle of the guru family. To understand the workings of this metaphor of kinship I shall focus here on marriage.

In matters of matrimony the members of the organizational hierarchy of Satnampanth played the role of matchmakers for the guru family. When Ghasidas decided that Balakdas should get married and Balakdas in turn wanted a bride for his brother Agardas and a groom for his sister Agroti, the gurus conveyed their desire to the *mahants* and *bhandaris* of Satnampanth. The members of the organizational hierarchy duly conferred, searched, found, and presented suitable boys and girls. A marriage in the guru family cemented alliances. In the myths, as in practice, the marriages were invariably in the family of Satnami *malguzars* who were also important figures in Satnampanth. Moreover, the scale and grandeur of the wedding was a spectacle, which displayed the authority of the Satnami gurus. At the same time, the spectacle was understood as a *jati rivaz* (a caste custom) in which, according to the myths, all Satnamis participated. It was the common property of Satnampanth.[41]

The affairs of marriage of the gurus were indeed closely tied to the norms and desires of the community. Balakdas, on the advice of *mahants* and other Satnamis, decided to build a *mahal* (a castle). The work of decoration and painting was done by Chetari, a member of the *chitrakar* (artist) caste. The Chetari had a daughter by the name of Radha. Radha was adept at the art of singing. One day Balakdas went to see the work being done on the house. Radha was also there. She was enamored of Balakdas. When Balakdas was returning, Radha caught hold of his hand. Balakdas had heard her sing earlier. He did not turn down this invitation. They made love. The girl became pregnant. After five months Radha's parents noticed that she appeared to be an unwed mother. They asked her to tell the truth about the father of the child. She replied that the child was of Balakdas. The people of the caste assembled on *puranmasi* at Bhandar. A *panchayat* decided that the guru in impregnating a girl of another caste had committed a grave sin. The guru, the *panchayat* discussed, was no longer capable of giving *amrit*. Balakdas got the news. He called the people present and asked them to stop whispering things secretively among themselves and, instead, to state that which was bothering them clearly. The *mahant* of Nawalpur took the lead and said, "People say that the *chitrakar*'s daughter is carrying your child. The guru should bring a *nam* (name/male child) through an act with a girl of one's own *jati*. You have tainted *satnam* by doing this deed with another caste. How can we take *amrit* from you?" Balakdas laughed and answered that he would solve the problem:

> When I assumed the incarnation of Ram my father sent me off to the jungle with my brother and wife. There a demoness by the name of Surpanakha attracted me. I told her that the two of us can't be together in this era. I was Krishna in the next era and Surpanakha was born as Kubri. She asked me for a boon. She wanted a son. I answered that in the next era you will be born as Radha; and then the two of us will come together. It is because of the previous life that we have come together. This explains the incarnation in her stomach.

The gathering of Satnamis at Bhandar told Balakdas that it did not believe this statement about his previous life. Only if Balakdas married the girl in front of all present would they know the truth and believe him. *Chitrakar* was summoned and asked to join the Satnami *vansh*, the *jati*. He did not, however, wish to spoil his caste. But when Radha was questioned about her wish in the matter she replied, "I have become of your caste, marry me quickly." The girl's father was satisfied with bridewealth. Balakdas married Radha. The guru was taken to the house in Bhandar. After the guru's *aarti* the Satnamis took *amrit* from Balakdas.[42]

Satnampanth, the *vansh*, was a powerful instrument of sanction and censure in the matter of marriage of gurus. The ingenious explanation of Balakdas, an innovative play with the elements of preexistent mythic traditions—of the *Ramayana*, the *Mahabharata*, and the Krishna legend—was not enough. The decision of the caste *panchayat*, which had met on a sacred date (*puranmasi*, the night of the full moon), was final. Balakdas had to accede to the wishes of his *vansh*, marry Radha, and give her *churis*. Radha was incorporated into Satnampanth, and Balakdas retained his mythic status.

Deeds of Death

The death of a guru was the disruption of the cosmic order of Satnampanth. The critical event occurred in situations of disorder, and it was characterized by patterns of betrayal. We find then that toward the end of Ghasidas's life, Satnampanth was in a bad way. The Satnamis had forgotten to worship *satnam*. *Satnampurush* had assured Ghasidas that he would take a human incarnation and sort out the problems of Satnampanth. When Ghasidas's daughter-in-law became pregnant, he asked his associates within Satnampanth if the child would be a boy or a girl. The guru was told that it would be a girl. But Ghasidas was expecting a boy, the incarnation of *satnampurush*. The prophecy of the birth of a girl meant that he had now to take on the responsibilities of Satnampanth all over again. The guru verbally chastised *satnampurush* and once more appealed to his mentor to take a human incarnation, yet to no avail. Ghasidas had withdrawn from the world, but had now to go into it again.

Ghasidas started building a house. When the workmen ran short of wood for the beams of the roof, he gave an order to look for a tree. The only tree to be found was a *bel* under which someone had buried a *trishul* (trident) long ago. *Bel* and *trishul* are the marks of Mahadeo, the god Shiva. Ghasidas remembered *satnam* and struck the tree five times with his *tangiya* (axe). Truly it was an awesome conspiracy of circumstances within the divine order. The tree fell and Ghasidas sat down. The branches of the tree spread all over the guru's body. The entire body became extremely hot. Ghasidas asked the servants to bring the tree and went home. The guru, racked by pain, had food and went off to sleep. After this unfortunate encounter with Mahadeo, Balakdas's first wife, Neerabai, gave birth to a girl. Balakdas and other Satnamis were called at night. Ghasidas told them that *satnampurush* had betrayed them. He had promised a boy but a girl was born. Ghasidas announced, "I shall go to *satnampurush* . . . and ask him that since you were going to take *avatar*, why has the opposite happened?" Ghasidas left his body with the Satnamis for two and a half days during his sojourn to meet *satnampurush*. It was another betrayal at this stage that established the finality of Ghasidas's death. On discovering that Ghasidas's body was being guarded, his son Balakdas stated that the dead do not return. When Ghasidas came back after two and a half days he found that his last rites had been performed. The guru had to go back to the other world.[43]

It was the combination of disorder and betrayal which, once again, lay behind the death of Balakdas. In the course of his tour Balakdas reached Bilaspur. The raja of Bilaspur, recall patient reader, wanted Balakdas dead. Balakdas made matters worse by camping in the village of Amara Bandha, which was the heart of enemy territory. The Rajput Kshatriyas held a meeting and passed a written resolution: "The *shikar* (prey) has come into our house. We should not delay. He must be killed tonight." The night was ominous. It was cold and dark. The full moon of *pus* (December–January) had been eclipsed by a cloud cover and torrential rain. The right eyes of Sarha and Judai, the two legendary Satnami warriors, were fluttering. The constellation of stars spoke of a battle that night. Balakdas and his group were to eat the evening meal at the house of Kariya Chamar. Kariya had taken money from the Kshatriyas and was on their side. A Satnami had betrayed Satnampanth.

Balakdas tempted fate. He decided not to go to eat and sent off his group. There was only one Satnami with Balakdas in his tent. The Hindus attacked. They could identify Balakdas because he was sitting on a chair wearing gold ornaments. The first blow of the sword hit the chair. The second claimed the life of Kodu Bahiya. In a dim light, from a fire burning outside, the Hindus thought that they had killed Balakdas. Yet the terror of the night was not over. Sarha and Judai were returning after the meal. They took the enemy to be their companions. The warriors were killed. The Hindus, convinced that they had completed their task, were going back when they heard the guru's companions shouting, "Balakdasji come this way." The Hindus started looking for Balakdas. The dark night was suddenly illuminated by a flash of lightning. The Hindus saw Balakdas in his gold ornaments; they asked him who he was; the guru did not lie. A major fight broke out. Balakdas was killed amidst chaos. Horses and elephants left their places and ran, people ran helter skelter and fought and killed, not recognizing each other. In death too Balakdas had lived a belief of Satnampanth: Satnamis can be defeated only when they are disunited.[44]

Sexuality, Desire, and the Division of the Guru *Gaddi*

Balakdas was succeeded by Agardas, Ghasidas's youngest son (see Appendix 1). The first act of the new guru was to give a feast in order to perform the last rites of his older brother and to accumulate merit.

> Satnamis from all directions came. A great sacrifice was performed. A ritual feast of seven maunds of rice and lentils along with a hundred maund of sweets was prepared. Many kinds of food were made with great fanfare to the accompaniment of a conch shell and musical instruments. The food was distributed. The *matas* worshipped the guru.[45]

This complex of rituals once again underscores the importance of the attributes of kingship in the constitution of the authority of the Satnami guru. The guru gave gifts to accumulate merit and performed a sacrifice, which are critical functions of a Hindu raja. The specific form taken by the *dan punya* (the ritual giving of gifts to accumulate merit) and the *yagya* (sacrifice) was a feast for the Satnamis: members of the group replaced the Brahman as the receivers of the benefaction and prestations made by the rajalike guru, Agardas. The feast was spectacular. Various dishes were cooked in legendary proportions to the accompaniment of a conch shell and musical instruments for the thousands of Satnamis who came to Bhandar. The scale and spectacle of the death rites of Balakdas confirmed that his successor Agardas embodied the attributes of a king.

A regal aspect and rituals of royalty were a concomitant and prerogative, a defining feature, of the figure and the seat of the Satnami guru. The theme, established by Balakdas, was played out by later generations of gurus. A photograph taken in the late nineteenth century represents a Satnami guru as combining the closely interwoven characteristics of the raja and the guru. The myths about the later gurus, similarly, present them as holding court in palatial homes, traveling on elephants, camels, and horses followed by an elaborate retinue, and dispensing *amrit* to the members of Satnampanth. At the same time, this is arguably the principal element of continuity between Balakdas and the later gurus. Ghasidas and Balakdas, the protagonists of a "heroic history," had orchestrated the construction of Satnampanth. The later gurus did not possess the essential attributes of the two major mythic figures.

The death of Balakdas signaled a change in the relationship between the guru and the women within the family.[46] In Satnami myths, woman's sexuality forms the overriding concern, the key trope, in the construction of the figure of the guru *mata*, the wife of the guru. Wives, ever the outsiders in male perspectives within patrlineal kinship, rather than mothers and sisters, were the principal players. Sexuality invested the women with agency. For a guru to be in control was to master his wife's sexuality and divest her of agency. Where the early gurus had succeeded, the later ones failed.

What are we to make of this picture? To preempt the narrative, the images at play are unhesitantly vivid and deeply disturbing. What strikes us immediately, even as we glance through these myths, is the singular manner in which overlapping sketches of motherhood and wifehood and cohabitation and marriage are first blurred and then ceaselessly gathered onto another canvas.[47] Upon this canvas, the now fuzzy lines and already indistinct tones of these images are made to blend with, indeed they are at once overwhelmed and orchestrated by, the perspective of a fully finished portrait, a highly colored picture of the subversive (when untamed) sexuality of the wives of the gurus. This canvas, these myths, this perspective have no place for other pictures, other stories, other envisionings: for example, what was the relationship between sex and marriage as overlapping means, among others, for the empowerment of the guru *matas*? If such a distinction is possible, did the guru *matas* sexually seek the gurus or desire the authority they commanded? How did wifehood, sexuality, and motherhood simultaneously mediate and mutually transform each other? And what about the mystery of the missing sister (in *her* agnatic and affinal contexts)?[48] The answers to these questions are premised upon nuances, details, and textures, upon fine lines, distinct etchings, and broad strokes that have all been erased from the canvas of Satnami myths, where a singular and grotesque portrait now stands. Yet, we must ask these questions. For to do so is to underline the possibilities of other imaginings of desires and sexualities, *matas* and motherhood, and masculinities and femininities, including within the guru family. Besides, questions sustain and generate images, and an interrogation of men's controlling strategies in their wider depiction of women's subversive sexuality may even lead us to something of a montage.

Clearly, these Satnami stories present us with an extraordinarily gendered set of images and ideas that at once map the salience of the heroic attributes of Ghasidas and Balakdas and define the limits of the contestatory nature of the myths of the community. At the same time, these ideas and images also have an aura of naturalness about them, constructed in a language that imbues them with a certain it-could-not-be-otherwise character, which in turn blunts the edge of moral censure. It is within the interstices of these simultaneous movements that we need to locate constructions of the subversive sexuality of *matas*, and their uses as a strategic resource. *Sui gen(d)eris* the early gurus had kept their wives under their thumbs, but with Agardas the situation was reversed and the gurus were overwhelmed by the sexuality of the *matas* of Satnampanth.

Let us turn to the chequered career of Partappurin *mata* (who, over time, married the three sons of Ghasidas), which illustrates this pattern.

> After his encounter with Danteshwari *devi*, Ghasidas returned to Bhandar and arranged the marriage of his eldest son Amardas with the daughter of the *malguzar* of Partappur in Bilaspur district. The wedding took place in Partappur. The bride and the groom came back to Bhandar. On the first night, when Partappurin *mata* came to sleep with Amardas she found him meditating sitting in the yogic lotus posture. Partappurin returned saying that she would come back soon. Partappurin's lust remained unfulfilled. One afternoon when Amardas was lying in bed Partappurin caught him off guard and in a lascivious move started rubbing his feet. Amardas was equal to the occasion and drew upon his inner reserves to frighten off his wife with yogic illumination. Partappurin ran off screaming loudly. Amardas set off, a spear in his hand, in hot pursuit. The guru followed the *mata* from one village to another. Before he could catch up with her Amardas reached the village of Chattua. It was *janmashtami*. The villagers worshipped Amardas and invited him to dance the *panthi naach*. Amardas, immersed in the *panthi*, died in Chattua.

It is significant that Partappurin *mata* was the daughter of the *malguzar* of Partappur. We have noted that marriages in the guru family cemented alliances of kinship with families of important Satnami land owners, *malguzars*, and key members of the organizational hierarchy of Satnampanth, where such alliances generated "cultural capital" in wider networks of the "economy of practices" of Satnami kinship.[49] Yet, in Chhattisgarh as in several other contexts, bonds of kinship, particularly with affines, are double edged. The ties which bind are, on the one hand, the basis of mutual support and (particularly in the case of the family of the Satnami gurus) a source of varieties of capital, and, on the other hand, these bonds are always fraught with risk, ever pregnant with threats of envy, disruption, and betrayal, a constant danger for families, groups, and communities.[50] Further, mapping these ties onto the tension-ridden relationships of a woman's agnates with her natal kin—a tension that translates itself into a lingering ambiguity from the woman's perspective—where control over the bride's body and possessions is at stake, we find the stage set for a colored, characteristically masculinist representation of the attributes of the guru *matas*. With these wives' ever threatening subversive sexuality inextricably bound to their status as dangerous outsiders, the two images work in tandem, each reinforcing the other, mutually defining a singular portrait, all held in place by schemes of village exogamy, tensions with wife givers, and (male) perceptions of (female) sexuality within patrilineal kinship. Thus, the very name of Partappurin *mata* invoked her alien, natal home, her father as the *malguzar* of Partappur was something of a rival figure to the gurus within configurations of local kingship, and left untamed her sexuality was unbounded, all too capable of overwhelming her husbands, the Satnami gurus.

Amardas had curbed his sexual instincts and countered Partappurin's desire through celibacy and meditation. At the same time, it was the unfulfilled lust and desire of Partappurin that broke Amardas's meditation and led him to Chattua, unto his death. If Amardas's death on *janmashtami*, as he danced the *panthi naach*—recall, these are both marks of distinction within Satnampanth—conjoined the critical event of a guru's end with signs defining the boundary of the community, it was Partappurin's sexuality that ordered this past.

Balakdas, ever the masculine hero, could not be similarly undone by concerns of celibacy. He was in complete charge in his dealings with Partappurin whom he married after the death of Neerabai, his first wife. Partappurin's obedience to Balakdas was total. She was the first member of the guru family to make sacred threads when Balakdas embarked on the enterprise of distributing *janeu* among the Satnamis. The *mata* was happy at Balakdas's decision to marry Radha, the girl who had seduced Balakdas but who afterwards had remained under his control.[51] And then Balakdas died young.

Partappurin stood transformed after the death of Balakdas. Now implicit obedience was replaced by the assertion of a dominant sexuality, and the *mata* acquired the aspect of a *devi* through the mediation of desire.

> At the feast for Balakdas's last rites the *matas* performed worship. The time unto midnight was spent in this work. Agardas went to sleep in this place. The *mata* [Partappurin] dressed up and went to Agardas to make love. The woman said to Agardas, "See what form I have taken and come. Look at me carefully." At that moment that woman's being had eight arms and seemed full of [the attributes of] many different kinds of characters. Seeing this otherworldly form, Agardas became worried. He thought to himself, where can I run. Agardas started pleading with this woman with folded hands. Then she said to Agardas, "Do *keli* [make love] or I will turn you to ashes." To this Agardas replied, "Whatever you say I am willing to do, just don't kill me." *Mata* Partappurin told him, "Listen to me and make me your *patrani* [most prominent wife, literally queen who sits on the thigh]."[52]

The time and the place set the stage for the encounter between Partappurin *mata* and Agardas. Balakdas's last rites had been performed, the *matas* had paid their respects and worshiped the dead guru. It was just after midnight. Agardas had gone to sleep at the site of the feast. Partappurin *mata* struck swiftly, at the first opportune moment, after Agardas became the new incumbent to the *gaddi*. Agardas was caught unaware and off guard. At any rate, he did not stand a chance. Partappurin, dressed for the occasion and driven by her desire for Agardas, had been transformed into a figure of another *lok* (world). The guru recognized that there was no escape. Partappurin's form had eight hands and was full of aspects of "many different kinds of characters." The tale emphasizes Agardas's total submission to Partappurin *mata*: he pleaded before her with folded hands, agreed to satisfy her desire so that she spared him his life, and no sooner had she expressed the command, married her so that she became his *patrani* (queen).

Clearly, the legendary acts of Ghasidas and Balakdas, cast on a grand and epic scale, did not find a sequel among the later gurus of Satnampanth. The transformation in the figure of the guru was worked through the motive force of sexuality of the women who had been incorporated into Ghasidas's lineage through marriage. Sexuality invested Partappurin with agency and, indeed, imbued her with the aspect of a *devi*. Agardas was putty in the hands of this *mata*. It followed that Partappurin quickly moved into a dominant position within Satnampanth. Thus, the morning after Agardas's encounter with the *mata* a gold *kalash* (pinnacle) was placed on top of the palace at Bhandar. If the golden pinnacle measuring seven arms in length symbolized the royal aspect of the guru of Satnampanth, it was Partappurin who occupied the key role in the ceremony to install the *kalash*. She was the first among the *matas* to offer *puja*, and under her direction the *matas* established a new rite of precedence in the performance of the ceremony by relegating the *mahants* of Satnampanth to a secondary position.

Soon after the installation of the pinnacle, Radha Chetari, the third wife of Balakdas, was filled with desire for Agardas. The matter lay in the hands of Partappurin *mata*. Radha said to Partappurin, "One day I too want to make love with Agardas." With Partappurin's permission this act was done. If Partappurin took charge of Agardas's affairs, she also assumed responsibility of fixing the wedding of the heir to the seat of the guru. When Sahebdas, Balakdas's son from Radha Chetari, was to be married both *mata* Partappurin and guru Agardas called the pious Satnamis and asked them to look for a girl. They were informed about a girl called Bahi. Sahebdas was married to her. Unlike the past, when only the guru, in consultation with the *mahants* and *sants* fixed the weddings within the family, now both Partappurin and Agardas conducted the search for and decided on Sahebdas's bride.[53] Partappurin had wrested the initiative from Agardas.

139

The relations between the guru and *mata* within Satnampanth stood reordered and transformed. The change underlay a shift in the construction of the figure of the guru. With the death of Balakdas, the "heroic history" of Satnampanth was replaced by a more fragmentary narrative featuring tensions and divisions among the gurus.

Sahebdas desired the guru *gaddi* and contested Agardas's position as the guru as soon as he came of age.

> Sahebdas moved to Bhisodi as there was illness in Bhandar. There he did a *puja*. He slept and had a dream. An old woman emerged from a basket holding something in her hand. She said to Sahebdas, "I was coming to meet you but now you have come to meet me." He replied, "One work of mine hasn't got done." The apparition stated that in six years time his work would be done.[54]

Sahebdas's dream was a part of a recurring pattern within the myths of Satnampanth. We need to recall that *satnampurush* had appeared in a vision to all Chamars, deep in slumber, and ordered them to accept Ghasidas as their guru. Similarly, Balakdas's act of wearing and distributing the *janeu* had been directed by Ghasidas through an elaborate dream sequence. Now the nature of the dream had undergone a transformation. It was no longer a matter of *satnampurush*, Ghasidas, or Balakdas guiding the destiny of Satnampanth through the medium of a dream. An old woman had replaced the mythic figures of Satnampanth in Sahebdas's dream. Sahebdas was not working for the good of Satnampanth. His sole quest was the acquisition of the seat of the guru. Consequently, members of Satnampanth expressed surprise and doubted the veracity of Sahebdas's account of the dream.

In these circumstances, Sahebdas's pursuit of the *gaddi* was aided by Partappurin *mata*. After the episode of the dream,

> Sahebdas came to Bhandar and asked Partappurin if Agardas had got the *gaddi*. Partappurin replied, "You are the *malik* [master] of the *gaddi*." On receiving this answer, Sahebdas acted with stealth and cunning. He took a minister and slipped off quietly to Raipur. There he gave an application and got the *gaddi* registered in his name. It was only on Sahebdas's return to Bhandar that people found out that he had become the guru. The royal canopy was put in Bhandar and Sahebdas was installed on the throne. Agardas was understandably upset and Sahebdas could not be invested with a *tilak* to complete his succession as the guru. The conflict between Agardas and Sahebdas came to a head over the repayment of a debt to Gokuldas of Jabalpur. The debt went back a long way in time and had been calculated at thirty-four thousand ru-

pees. Sahebdas had earlier told Agardas that they should get together and repay it. Agardas in turn had replied that he did not have enough money. The issue had not been resolved. The estrangement between Agardas and Sahebdas, on account of the *gaddi*, now translated itself into a fight over the repayment of the debt. The *gaddi* was divided into two parts. Bhandar and Telashi were the main places. The organizational hierarchy too was divided into two groups. After the proceedings Sahebdas stayed on in Bhandar. Agardas, *mata* Partappurin, Dulhapuri, and Mutki *mata* of Ratanpur went to Telashi.[55]

The account of the conflict between the gurus centered upon and invoked a notion of disorder. It was women—both the old hag in Sahebdas's dream and Partappurin *mata*—who played a key role in directing the course of events, while Sahebdas, driven by his relentless pursuit of the *gaddi*, practiced stealth and deployed cunning to trick his uncle and members of Satnampanth. The events that followed were a symptom and consequence of the disorder. Sahebdas's investiture ceremony was aborted. The gurus could not repay their debt. The guru *gaddi* was divided.

The division of the guru *gaddi* was formalized and settled through the intervention of the institutionalized power of writing commanded by the colonial government. The gurus of Satnampanth lost an opportunity.

After the death of Partappurin Agardas and Sahebdas were summoned to meet the English *saheb*. The court met early in the morning. The *jila saheb* [district magistrate] asked Agardas, "Do you want to govern?" Agardas said, "I am a guru, I do not know law. Since I do not know politics I cannot do this work." The district magistrate read the Victoria paper which had come. [He said to Agardas] If you rule the following things are yours: *janeu, tilak, palki/dola* [palanquin], law. All this has come for you. Agardas replied, "Maharaj, I do not want to rule." Sahebdas was called and asked the same question. Sahebdas stated that what his uncle had said was true. They were told, "You are missing an opportunity at this time. You will suffer later. Every year the Victoria paper comes for you but the Hindu people here give money and suppress it. Give one thousand rupees and take back the paper." In the paper Sahebdas was entered as the *zamindar* of Bhandar and Agardas as the *zamindar* of Telashi.[56]

The domain of the guru and the space of rules, regulations, and the law of the colonial government were separate. Agardas and Sahebdas did not take up the offer to rule and govern the Satnamis, which was inscribed in the paper that had come from Queen Victoria, because they did not understand politics and law.

We have seen that this demarcation between the sphere of the guru and the domain of colonial government had been staged earlier in Satnami myths. The gurus Ghasidas and Balakdas, a law unto themselves, had kept within the bounds of colonial law. We also need to recall, however, that Ghasidas's authority had been recognized by the *saheb* and Balakdas had triumphed over the *sarkar*. The two gurus had forced recognition upon colonial power through the truth of *satnam*. But now the situation had changed. The colonial government of its own accord had offered the gurus the right to rule. Agardas and Sahebdas in spurning the offer (and by not paying the thousand rupees) had played into the hands of the Hindus, who bribed the government every year to suppress the charter that gave the Satnamis a right over the symbols of upper-caste domination. The colonial government though corruptible was no longer ignorant and had sought to help the Satnami gurus. The recognition of the division of the guru *gaddi* came about as Agardas and Sahebdas could not sort out their differences. It was also accompanied by their failure to establish a claim over the sacred thread, *tilak*, palanquin, and the law for the members of Satnampanth. The destiny of Satnampanth was closely tied to the fortunes of the guru *gaddi*. These were hard times for members of Satnampanth.

The difficulties were compounded further when Agardas and Sahebdas died soon after their encounter with the British official.

> Agarmandas and Ajabdas of Telashi had come for the death rites of Sahebdas. There was a *panchayat*. Karri *mata* [the widow of Sahbedas, his second wife] told Ajabdas, "What shall I do? I am in my youth. You keep me and stay with me in Bhandar." Ajabdas answered, "My wife is pregnant. I cannot do this." After saying this Ajabdas moved off. Karri once again called Ajabdas from Telashi. Ajabdas said to her, "You have called me. Now who will pay off Gokuldas's debt ?" Karri assured him that she would pay the debt. Ajabdas believed her. He came to Karri in Bhandar. Karri *mata* kept Ajabdas as her *mukhtiyar*, the man-in-charge of the *malguzari*.[57]

Karri, like Partappurin, was a dangerous outsider within gurus' patrlineage, and also like Partappurin she was drawn toward her husband's younger brother because of her youth and sexuality. Ajabdas's qualms of conscience on account of his wife's pregnancy could not prevent him from getting ensnared in Karri's trap. Karri tempted him with the offer to repay Gokuldas's debt. The *mata* had initially suggested that Ajabdas should "keep her." But it was Ajabdas who had to leave his seat at Telashi and come to Bhandar where he was "kept" by Karri. A guru had come to serve a woman. The debt was not repaid. Feminine guile had triumphed over a weak guru to elaborate a principle of disorder.

The *Vanshavali* closes by rehearsing an account of the conflicts over the succession to the *gaddi* between members of the guru family. What stands out in the midst of the confusion that marks the narrative is the central role of Karri in the unfolding of the drama. To begin with, when Agarmandas, the son of Agardas, on the advice of *mahants* appealed that he should be made the guru because he was the son of his father's first wife, it was Karri's evidence in court that gave him the *gaddi* at Telashi. Once again, a few years later, it was Karri's cunning and guile that made Muktavandas, her son from Ajabdas, the guru at Bhandar. Karri bribed the local officials and testified in court that Muktavandas was in fact Sahebdas's son. Atibaldas, the son of Ajabdas from his first wife Gautri *mata*, appealed against the decision. He argued that Muktavandas was not Sahebdas's son, but was born to his father Ajabdas and Karri after they were married in the *churi* form. In other words, Atibaldas and Muktavandas were half brothers, and Atibaldas was the older son of their father Ajabdas. But when asked by the magistrate to prove these claims, Atibaldas could only produce a document that mentioned his father as the *mukhtiyar*, the man in charge of the *malguzari*. The *saheb* told Atibaldas, "Your father is a *mukhtiyar* so you cannot be given the right over the *gaddi*. The *gaddi* remains in the hands of Muktavandas."[58] Karri had dictated this course of events. She had seen to it that the documents mentioned Ajabdas as a *mukhtiyar* and declared Muktavandas as Sahebdas's son. At this point the *Vanshavali* breaks off. From the 1920s the tensions and conflicts between the gurus got linked to and were played out in the arena of formal institutionalized politics. Agamdas, the third son of Agarmandas, emerged as the guru of Satnampanth and the head of the newly founded Satnami Mahasabha, and it is time we moved on to the next installment of this (hi)story.

CHAPTER SIX

Reform and Authority: The Satnami Mahasabha, 1925–1950

In the early 1920s a few influential members of Satnampanth got together with local and provincial politicians to set up the Satnami Mahasabha. Its aim was to press the government of the Central Provinces and the local authorities for demands made on behalf of the community and to reform the Satnamis. The Satnami leadership enlisted the help of G. A. Gavai, a politician of the "depressed classes," and worked closely with Baba Ramchandra. The interventions of these outsiders helped to shape this initiative. The leaders and the members of the community in turn inflected the interventionist voices and measures of their benefactors in diverse ways. The Mahasabha also successfully negotiated the threat from rival Satnami endeavors.

The Introduction has set out the different approaches to the study of caste associations and movements. This discussion of the Satnami Mahasabha has different emphases from the existing literature. The Satnami initiative can be seen within limits as a product of "political opportunity," but the importance of British administration for the Mahasabha extended far beyond the mere definition of an avenue of institutional politics in which the Mahasabha leaders jockeyed for position and privilege. The Satnami Mahasabha drew upon the symbols and resources of the language of colonial administration and situated them alongside a set of key signs within Satnampanth. This served to fashion a new legality, the true law of Ghasidas. Moreover, the illiterate Satnami leaders of the Mahasabha did not actually conjure a new ideology of caste unity or construct elaborate ideological formulations rooted in traditional symbols. Instead they worked within the interstices of relationships of intervention and appropriation—idioms of authority and law and agendas of gender to reform the household and the community—to forge a reworked Satnami identity, which was at once tied to the languages of caste associations and a reconstituted Hindu tradition, and to the symbolic forms within Satnampanth. Indeed, the Satnami participation in a wider political game, through the mediation of more established players, inaugurated tensions and contradictions at the heart of the programmatic endeavor. The members of the community had their own uses for the activities and emphases of the Mahasabha.[1] Finally, these issues suggest the need to focus on themes that have been incorporated in the literature on caste associations only in fledgling ways: idioms of law, order, and command, which in turn were tied to relationships of authority within the community, projects of the domestication of reform to reorder conjugality, gender, sexuality, and nurture within the household, and the ways in which dominant interventions were refracted through grids of the categories of the community—all parts of processes involving the fashioning of traditions and the making of a colonial modernity.

The Satnami participation in the wider elaboration of caste associations in the first half of the twentieth century also brings up another significant issue, the group's negotiation of the culturally and politically constituted categories of Hindu and (by implication) Hinduism, particularly as they were played out alongside government measures with regard to religious and caste communities in the domain of institutionalized politics of the colonial state. Now, we know that since the earlier decades of the nineteenth century, broad, supralocal religious categories—for example, an all-India Hindu community, an all-India Muslim community, a distinct Sikh identity—acquired a particular salience and were constructed in novel ways in the larger context of the series of Western appraisals of Indian religions and of the socioeconomic changes and cultural shifts brought about by colonial rule.[2] These categories were profoundly shaped by many of the crucial underlying premises and key classificatory schemes of colonial knowledge(s).[3] Similar processes also underlay anticolonial nationalism's early demarcation of the spiritual domain as its "sovereign territory" and its later "political battle with the imperial power," and the picture was not very different for the wide-ranging making of ideologies by non-Brahman and untouchable-caste initiatives that forged new unities and established dis-

tinct divisions within indigenous Hindu society.[4] Yet, as some of the important recent scholarship on South Asia has been at pains to emphasize, the
overarching unities of both religious communities and nationalism were
reworked and reinterpreted by large sections of the South Asian population
through the grid of local cultures, translations and renderings filtered primarily through imaginings of *jati, panth,* and *biradri,* caste, sect, and kinship.[5] It is precisely within the interstices of these simultaneous movements,
of the fashioning of large-scale and homogeneous constructs of communities and the nation and of their reworkings in local arenas that we can trace
the Satnami negotiations of the politics of caste associations and nationalist
endeavors to reform the community, and the group's elaborations of that
key category of the Hindu community.

We have seen that through the nineteenth and early twentieth centuries the Satnamis constructed their vision and practice by carving out a
separate identity through reworkings and contestations of the intertwined
hierarchies and centers of ritual power within the caste order. This fashioning of a distinct Satnami identity—a fusion of the features of a caste and a
sect—occurred within an evocational field of Hindu symbols and practices,
but it also served to both deepen and broaden an awareness of us-and-them
distinctions between the Satnamis and other Hindu castes, distinctions that
were elaborated in different ways depending on concrete and changing
contexts. Here the untouchable and marginal status of the Satnamis meant
that its marks of difference were imbued with a certain salience in the hierarchies of "otherness" within the Hindu caste order. Now, from the 1920s,
under the aegis of the Satnami Mahasabha, as we shall soon see, the
Satnamis negotiated different, institutionalized political constructions of
the Hindu community in various ways. Thus, the Satnami Mahasabha emphasized the low ritual status of the community within the Hindu social order when it drew upon the linguistic resources of the depressed-classes
movement to petition the provincial government, and while working with
upper-caste nationalists the Mahasabha leaders sought to highlight the
Hindu nature of the signs and practices among the Satnamis: but both these
moves, in rather different ways, went against the grain of the emphases of
Satnampanth that provided its members with a distinct identity, and thereby
introduced tensions at the very heart of the endeavors of the Satnami
Mahasabha. It is barely surprising that when a rival to the Mahasabha, a
body that called itself Shri Path Pradarshak Sabha (Society of the Light of
the True Path), ranging itself against Gandhi's newly coined category of
"Harijan" for the Scheduled Castes, sought to secure an unambiguously
Hindu status for the Satnamis, its efforts also met with little support from
the community (or from the provincial government). Indeed, the Satnami
Mahasabha's efforts to recast the relationship of the community with a

reconstituted Hindu tradition in its bid to reform the community were re-worked by Satnamis in local arenas through a selective appropriation of certain paradigmatic signs and practices of Hindu hierarchies, appropriations that served to extend the Satnami challenge to Brahmans and the caste order.

A third general point follows from the first two. The Satnami Mahasabha and its allies among upper-caste nationalists and provincial politicians articulated a vision of nationalism that drew a connection between country and community, where several "'communities' (religious or otherwise) together constituted the nation; and service to the Community went together with, and indeed to a large extent implied, service to the Country."[6] In fact, this understanding of the country/nation as being made up of several communities came to be consistently challenged from the 1920s by a vision of the modern state which, as Partha Chatterjee has argued, held "the single, determinate, demographically enumerable form of the nation" as the only viable form of community within its jurisdiction.[7] However, the Satnami Mahasabha and its allies persisted with a conception where the improvement and reform of the community was equated with service to the nation. Gyanendra Pandey has argued that the "character of this latter equation speaks of the limits of Indian liberalism in the nineteenth and early twentieth centuries, a liberalism that was manifestly inadequate for its own project of building a liberal nation of free and equal citizens."[8] This argument, it seems to me, tends toward endorsing Eurocentric self-representations of "liberalism" and "nationalism" as transcendental and immaculate conceptions. Thus, the community comes to be configured here as "a premodern remnant that an absentminded Enlightenment has somehow forgotten to erase,"[9] and the elaborations of nationalism in communitarian ways are understood primarily as the failure of the idea of the nation to realize itself in history. At the same time, a rather different but equally immaculate conception, now of "the idea of community," underlies Partha Chatterjee's argument that "by its very nature, the idea of the community marks a limit to the realm of disciplinary power."[10] As we shall see, both these arguments are held in place by a binary divide between state and community.[11] My point here is that the Satnami Mahasabha, caught in the nitty gritty of historical practice, paid little heed to the niceties of an abstract liberalism in its elaborations of the ideas of the country and community. Equally, the Mahasabha's articulation of community featured what Chatterjee identifies as a rhetoric of "kinship, austerity, sacrifice," a rhetoric that could fairly regularly strike an "antimodernist, antiindividualist, even anticapitalist" note:[12] but this went hand in hand with reworkings of the disciplinary imaginings of the state within the community as part of the fashioning of a colonial modernity.

The Formation of the Mahasabha

David Baker has shown that the politics of the Central Provinces underwent major shifts and changes in the 1920s. Until 1918 Maharashtrian politicians had been in control of the Congress and provincial politics and there had been limited political activity in the Hindi-speaking regions. The Montagu-Chelmsford reforms created an elected legislature with constituencies representing every district. In the 1920s politicians from Chhattisgarh and Jabalpur took control of the Congress and opposed the government in the legislature. To counter the activities of the Congress politicians, the government encouraged various interest groups to work the Montagu-Chelmsford reforms.[13]

One of the consequences of this policy was its stimulus to the politics of the depressed classes in Nagpur and Berar under the leadership of G. A. Gavai. The Depressed Classes Association was set up in 1920 in Nagpur as a separate platform for untouchable groups with the aim of seeking greater representation at local and provincial levels, ameliorating their condition, and charting a political course independent of Brahman and non-Brahman groups.[14] Unlike the non-Brahman movement's stark opposition to Brahman politicians, the Depressed Classes Association was willing to cooperate with individuals and institutions who were not "antagonistic to its creed."[15] Gavai, a nominated member of the legislative council, had close contacts with the Brahman Tilakites of the region but also maintained links with the Congress leaders from Chhattisgarh like Raghavendra Rao and R. S. Shukla. After 1928 Gavai was to lose his leadership to the emerging all-India leadership of Dr. B. R. Ambedkar. In the early 1920s Gavai played the reservation game and sought to extend the activities of the Depressed Classes Association at the provincial level.[16]

The Satnami Mahasabha was formed in 1925. Satnamis credit Naindas and Anjordas with taking the first steps toward creating the organization. They recount that in the early 1920s Naindas, a Satnami *mahant* and, perhaps, a member of the district council of Raipur, enlisted the help of Anjordas, another *mahant*, to stop the killing of cows in slaughter houses in the districts of Raipur and Bilaspur.[17] The step formed a part of a Satnami initiative to check the government, officials, and other castes from continuing to refer to Satnamis as Chamars. The efforts of the two Satnamis brought them in touch with G. A. Gavai and Sunderlal Sharma, a Hindu nationalist from Rajim.[18] Sunderlal Sharma, influenced by the Hindu proselytizing vision and practice of Dayanand Saraswati and the Arya Samaj, had distributed the sacred thread among untouchables in 1919 and organized a temple entry venture for low castes—which did not include Satnamis—in the Rajiv Lochan temple in Rajim in 1924.[19] The first reference to the

Satnami Mahasabha occurs in a letter of 24 October 1925 from G. A. Gavai to Pandit Sunderlal Sharma. Gavai had asked, "Did you prepare the constitution of the Satnami Mahasabha?" and had instructed Sunderlal Sharma to send a copy to "any vernacular newspaper."[20] It would seem that the Satnami Mahasabha was set up as a result of the joint efforts of Sunderlal Sharma, G. A. Gavai, Naindas, and a few well-to-do Satnamis with substantial land holdings.[21] Ratiram, the president of the Mahasabha, was the *malguzar* of Keotadabri; and Anjordas, the vice president, was the *malguzar* of Deori.[22] They were soon joined by Agamdas, a guru of Satnampanth.

The members of the Satnami Mahasabha registered their presence in the arena of nationalist politics by attending the 1925 Kanpur session of the Indian National Congress. The Satnami contingent of five members had gone to Kanpur with their leaders Naindas and Anjordas. We have noted that in the course of the Kanpur Congress Baba Ramchandra, former leader of the Awadh Kisan Sabha movement and now progressively disenchanted with a "capitalist Congress," had met the Satnamis.[23] Baba Ramchandra observed, "It was at this meeting that the Satnami brothers from Raipur, Bilaspur, and Durg were purified."[24] The leaders of the Indian National Congress had performed a collective rite of initiation by purifying the Satnamis, gifting them the right to wear the sacred thread, and reclaiming them within the fold of Hinduism to provide the group with a new ritual and political status. By the winter of 1925 the defining features of the organization of Satnami Mahasabha stood sketched. Anjordas and Naindas, who were to play a critical role within the Mahasabha, had emerged as the Satnami leaders of the initiative. Moreover, there were close and effective links established with upper-caste nationalists and provincial politicians. Finally, after his meeting with Naindas and Anjordas, Baba Ramchandra traveled with the Satnamis to Chhattisgarh and was closely involved in specifying the direction of the Mahasabha over the next few years.

Recasting Identities: A Petition

The Satnami Mahasabha launched its first major initiative, a petition to Sir Montagu Butler, the Governor of Central Provinces, in January 1926.[25] The petition, drafted by G. A. Gavai and occasioned by the Governor's visit to Chhattisgarh, defined the position of Satnamis within Chhattisgarh, listed their grievances, difficulties, and the root cause of their backwardness, and suggested remedies and solutions to the government. It began by situating the Satnamis within the hierarchy of Hinduism, "In Hindu society there are castes and subcastes, high and low, and about one-fifth of the Hindu world is depressed and untouchable. The Satnamis of Chhattisgarh Division come in the category of 'depressed classes'." There were, however, important qualifications. The Satnamis did not carry out the work of Chamars. Their occupations were agriculture and menial work, but the lack of education among the Satnamis had deprived many village proprietors and thousands of ordinary families of their lands and divorced them from agriculture, the principal occupation of the community. The last statement, in fact, takes us toward the Satnami Mahasabha's diagnosis of the affliction that plagued the Satnamis.

The problem lay with illiteracy and ignorance. "We are the most backward community. Illiteracy is the root cause of our backwardness." Satnami students were refused admission in most schools and where admitted were subjected to discriminatory treatment. Similarly, illiteracy had deprived Satnami village proprietors and tenants of their land and forced them to become "drawers of water and hewers of wood." Satnami ignorance also meant that they were forced to work for others either for very low wages or without payment and that members of the group could not intervene through the agency of the law courts, which were ineffective in redressing their grievances. Finally, the attitude of high-caste Hindus, who reacted to religious, social, and political awakening among the depressed classes of the province by sanctioning social boycott and imposing further hardships, compounded the problems and sealed the fate of the Satnamis. The vicious circle of illiteracy and backwardness stood fully drawn.

What were the solutions offered by the petition? The issue of nomenclature was primary and critical: "We pray your excellency may be pleased to order a circular to be issued to the effect that the Satnamis should be called the Satnamis and not the Chamars." Second, in relation to the vexed problem of illiteracy/education the petition proposed that if primary education was turned into a provincial subject—instead of remaining in the hands of local bodies—it would become more accessible to the members of the community. Third, the Mahasabha requested that an impartial officer or committee enquire into and redress Satnami grievances of loss of land and the exaction of forced labor. The problem of social boycott and discrimination by upper castes was to be addressed by the government, giving the Satnamis legal protection. Finally, the petition took up the issue of reservations of jobs and seats in provincial and local governments for Satnamis by demanding an increase in the number of nominees to the legislative council from among the depressed classes, a liberal observance of the principle of nominating depressed-class members to local bodies, and the removal of the customary discrimination of government officers in appointing members to posts of constables in the police department and as menial servants in other departments.[26]

What was the government response to the petition? After being presented with the document by the Satnami Mahasabha on 27 January 1926 the Governor, Sir Montagu Butler noted, "The petitioners saw me today at Bilaspur. The Commissioner and D.C. were present. I heard them but did not make any promise. Please now find out from the Commissioner at Raipur how the land lies with respect to the following headings (1) Right to be called officially Satnamis (3) Complaint about forced labour (6) Request to be nominated to the bodies."[27] The Commissioner of Chhattisgarh and the Chief Secretary of the Central Provinces had agreed that Satnami was a nomenclature of long standing and that there was nothing wrong in entering the sect as a distinct caste in government papers. The complaint about forced labor, the Commissioner reported, affected all castes but the lower castes were particularly badly hit. Finally, the group was represented in local government: after 1921 two Satnamis had been nominated to the local bodies in Raipur and Durg, and in Bilaspur, in the absence of a "suitable Satnami," a Syce (Kori, a caste whose ascribed occupation is to look after horses) had been nominated to the municipal committee. The Chief Secretary added that the government had approved a proposal to enhance the representation of the "depressed classes" at the provincial and local levels.[28]

The Central Provinces government also asked various officials in Chhattisgarh to report on the legitimacy of the claims made by the Satnami Mahasabha. The Deputy Commissioners of Bilaspur and Raipur wrote that Satnami Chamars were rarely employed as menial servants and had not offered their services as peons but seemed content with employment near their homes as field servants, laborers, and at times as *kotwars*.[29] And what of Satnami recruitment to the police force? The Deputy Inspector General, Eastern Range, stated that enlistment to the force was already difficult in Chhattisgarh and the nomination of Chamars would only make it worse. The "movement by the Chamars to wear the sacred thread" made the proposal all the more inopportune. The officer was convinced that the enlistment of Chamars would keep away potential recruits from the north and lead to "wholesale" resignations, apart from the problem of other men refusing to fall in line with the Chamars and the grave nuisance of "water difficulty"—because of the observance of norms of purity and pollution—in the ranks.[30] The Inspector General of Police concurred and pointed out that no other department of the government entered so intimately into the everyday life of the people: the enlistment of Chamars would merely lower the prestige of the force and reduce its efficiency; and there were bound to be serious difficulties, particularly in the matter of house searches. It was, therefore, most undesirable to force the pace in such matters in the police department.[31] On the issue of exclusion of the Satnamis from the list of the depressed classes, it was pointed out that Satnamis were mixed with other Chamars and they did not find a place in the list because they had "always been included in the genus of Chamars who did find a place in the list."[32]

There was a consensus among the officials regarding the Satnami Mahasabha's complaint about discriminatory treatment in local schools. The responsibility lay with Chamars/Satnamis and their lack of interest in educating their children. The most liberal statement of this consensus was voiced by the Commissioner, Chhattisgarh Division, "I have not the slightest doubt that in the majority of schools Satnamis are not given a very warm welcome but at the same time it is notorious that their desire to enter schools is not strong. The complaint of the Mahasabha must be read in the light of the well known reluctance of all lower classes in Chhattisgarh to share in the benefits of education."[33] Other officials, however, found the complaint a "clear lie."[34]

The largely negative and hostile response of officials in Chhattisgarh was tempered by the provincial government, which was actively pursuing the policy of encouraging the depressed classes within the framework of the Montagu-Chelmsford reforms. A printed circular informed the president of the Satnami Mahasabha, Ratiram Malguzar, that the requests made in the petition had been duly considered by the government. Satnamis were to be shown under a separate category in the next census returns and general instructions had been issued to the effect that the group was not to be referred to as Chamars in official papers. As for the grant of educational facilities, the Satnamis were to be included explicitly among the classes who received special concessions. The issue of labor for inadequate wages was to be looked into by settlement officers at the next revenue resettlement of the districts of the Chhattisgarh Division. The number of nominated members from the depressed classes to the C.P. legislative council was to be increased from two to four and general instructions had been issued for the nomination of depressed classes to local bodies. This was to include Satnamis, as distinct from Chamars, where they were found in large numbers. The Satnamis were reminded that they enjoyed the same protection under the law as other communities, but their request to be employed more fully in government departments had to await a change in public opinion.[35]

The Satnami Mahasabha had won a number of its demands. Satnampanth's reconstitution of Chamars as Satnamis had finally been accepted by the government, and this led other groups to initiate moves, of reform and the writing of petitions, to rid themselves of the stigma of being called Chamars.[36] In 1926 Ratiram, the President of the Satnami Mahasabha, was nominated as a depressed-classes representative to the C.P. legislative council.[37] Indeed, the oral accounts of present-day Satnami leaders celebrate the petition as a charter of victory. The victory had its costs. The petition needed the intervention of an outside agency. What strikes us immediately, even as we glance through the petition, is the highly formalized language in which it is constructed. The language drew upon and was

structured by the rules and conventions of an elaborate constitutional political game played by caste associations in the early decades of this century.
It is not only that Satnami leaders of the Mahasabha wanted to play this
game, it is also that illiteracy among the Satnamis enabled an elite who commanded the power of writing to align themselves with the Satnamis. This
created tensions and contradictions.

Satnampanth had drawn upon the hierarchies and centers of ritual
power of the Hindu caste order to question and contest the signs, rituals,
and practices that defined the low ritual and social status of its members.
The petition from the Satnami Mahasabha, on the other hand, accepted the
system of *varna* ranking and situated the Satnamis at the lowest rung of the
Hindu social order, the "one-fifth of the Hindu world that was depressed
and untouchable." Similarly, in distinguishing Satnamis from Chamars the
petition did not refer to the elaborate structure of myths and rituals of
Satnampanth that constituted it as a pure body, separate and distinct from
the Chamars. Instead, it invoked the principle of occupation. The Satnamis
did not work with leather but on land and did menial jobs. The apparent
acceptance of a low ritual status, the momentary aphasia of the myths, and
the invocation of the secular principle of occupation went hand in hand
with the privileging of illiteracy as a comprehensive explanation for Satnami
backwardness. They constituted—each separately and taken together—an
effort to negotiate and articulate the emergent politics of caste associations
in the early twentieth century. The petition from the Satnami Mahasabha
was located in the political context of depressed-classes initiatives. To adopt
the figures of speech and the grammatical rules of the language of these
movements was to accept—however momentarily—a redefined Satnami
identity. At the same time, the petition also hinted that Satnamis had been
malguzars and owners of land in the past. We have seen that the group had
lost land over the nineteenth and early twentieth centuries and that in
Satnami notions of the past they appear as owners of land who were deprived of their status and position within the region through the trickery
and deceit of upper castes. What was at work in the petition then was a
coming together of two processes: a redefinition of Satnami identity and a
selective drawing upon and reiteration of the beliefs and traditions within
Satnampanth. The simultaneous and at times contradictory movement lay
at the heart of the Satnami Mahasabha.

Constructing Reform: Tensions and Contradictions

We have noted that the Satnami Mahasabha drew an equation between the
reform (and improvement) of the community and service to the country.

To this end, the leaders of the Mahasabha embarked on the project of rein-vesting the community with the signs that had been a part of Satnampanth. Old Satnamis remember "the time of Naindas and Anjordas" as a watershed when the *janeu* and *jait khambh* once again became the distinctive signs of the community. "They were there before. But it is in my living memory when people started wearing the *janeu* with the *kanthi* again. Naindas and Anjordas used to come and see to it that people were wearing them."[38] In the remote village, Devarmal, Kamaundram recounted, "I know of only three real gurus. Ghasidas, Naindas, and Anjordas. Naindas and Anjordas would go from one village to another. The *jait khambh* you can see was placed at that time. This happened in many villages."[39] The traditional signs reinforced the boundedness of the Satnamis. At the same time, the Satnami Mahasabha's endeavor to rework the relationship of the community with a reconstituted Hindu tradition in the image of upper-caste nationalists also meant that the signs were pressed into the service of a redefined Satnami identity.

> Balakdas had given the *janeu*. But as a *kasam* [vow], *janeu* and *kanthi* were distributed by Naindas and Anjordas. Balakdas couldn't get a record made. He didn't make a record of the importance of the *janeu*. It was because of the recognition of *gaubhakti* [veneration of cows] that record of *janeu* was made. Everyone started wearing *janeu* and *kanthi*.[40]

Under the aegis of the Satnami Mahasabha, *janeu* and *kanthi* became inter-twined with the veneration of cows and a refurbished Hindu identity of the Satnamis, and *jait khambh*, which was simultaneously a sign of Ghasidas and an icon of Drupda *mata*, became the symbol of a reformed Satnampanth.

The contradiction within the Satnami Mahasabha—which also fea-tured tensions between its leaders and rival Satnami gurus—was played out in an effort on 23 February 1929 to sort out matters within Satnampanth. We get a glimpse of this initiative from a published leaflet and two frag-ments written by Baba Ramchandra.[41] The leaflet was a call to Satnami brothers, particularly *mahants* and *bhandaris*, to assemble on *maghipuno* at Girodpuri, the birth place of the revered and ancient Guru Ghasidasji Baba. The assembly was aimed at correcting wrong customs within Satnampanth, an attempt to lead the group on a straight and narrow path. The pamphlet began with a proverb, "thieves do not like moonlit nights." Next, it went on to announce that presence at the meeting was a test of the good character and morals of a true Satnami, and also held out sanctions—the imposition of fines and the forfeiture of the *janeu* and the *kanthi*—to Satnamis who would not attend the meeting. Later, at the Mahant Conference in Girodpuri, the *mahants* Naindas, Anjordas, and Bisaldas scored a victory.

"Untruth was vanquished" when the three *mahants* persisted in the face of difficulties to make Atibaldas, Muktavandas, and Jagtarandas—Satnami gurus and brothers all—wear the *janeu* for the cause of the reform of Satnamis.[42] We need to untangle the threads of this drama.

The problems were tied to tensions within the Satnami Mahasabha and to internal conflicts within the Satnami leadership. The authority and power of the leaders of the Satnami Mahasabha were linked to their position in the world of the organizational, institutionalized politics of locality and province: Naindas was a member of the district council of Raipur; in 1926 Anjordas had contested the elections to the legislative council with the support of the Swarajists; the leaflet was published by the district council, Raipur; and the Satnami Mahasabha had connections with important local political figures. This leadership now took upon itself to persuade Atibaldas, Muktavandas, and Jagtarandas, who occupied the *gaddi* at Bhandar, controled a section of the members of the organizational hierarchy of Satnampanth, and were opposed to the Mahasabha's links with the upper castes to fall in line with the Satnami Mahasabha and its patron guru Agamdas.

In spite of Satnami Mahasabha's attempt to recast the Satnami identity in terms of a reconstituted Hindu order, the task of reforming the members of the community drew upon the authority of the gurus and the symbolic order of Satnampanth. The meeting was to be held on the day of *maghipuno*, a sacred date in the Satnami calendar and a critical marker within the mythic tradition, and its venue was Girodpuri, the birth place of Ghasidas. A Satnami not attending the meeting was disobeying the orders of the guru. It followed that the sanctions held out against the members of the community who did not attend the meeting involved a similar play with key Satnami symbolic forms. The *kanthi*—a focal sign of Satnampanth—was to be taken away from the defaulter who also had to pay a fine to the guru and *kachi pakki*, another fine, to other Satnamis at the time of *ramat*, the tour of the guru. The Satnami Mahasabha operated through the organizational hierarchy of Satnampanth. It sought to influence and win over the *mahants*, *bhandaris*, and *sathidars* as an enduring step to reform Satnampanth.[43]

These efforts to redefine the Satnami identity and to reform the Satnamis did not always sit well with contending figures of authority within Satnampanth. The Satnami *mahants* of the Mahasabha ranged themselves against Atibaldas, Muktavandas, and Jagtarandas. We have seen that the three brothers, who lived in Bhandar, had a claim on half of the guru *gaddi* and were the rivals of Agamdas. Agamdas was a patron of the Satnami Mahasabha which in turn supported him as the main guru of Satnampanth. Atibaldas, Muktavandas, and Jagtarandas were opposed to Satnami Mahasabha's close association with upper castes and its efforts to provide a refurbished Hindu identity to the Satnamis.[44] Thus, if the orders of the Satnami Mahasabha invoked the sanctity of the guru, the relationship of the endeavor with the gurus of Satnampanth who contested its authority was ridden with tension. This tension is underscored by the note on which the leaflet ends: "Any guru who asks a *mahant, bhandari, sathidar,* or *sant* not to come . . . will have to think about himself and do it."[45] The leaders of the Satnami Mahasabha held out a barely concealed threat to the guru brothers that if they tried to subvert the plan of holding the assembly they would have to consider the consequences. Similarly, at the assembly, Naindas, Anjordas, and Bisaldas, with great difficulty, made Atibaldas, Muktavandas, and Jagtarandas wear the *janeu.*[46] According to Baba Ramchandra, the *mahants* had effected an inversion. In past times it was the gurus who used to reform the disciples, but now it was the disciples who were engaged in reforming the gurus.[47] Let me reiterate the contradiction: despite its wider political links and efforts to forge close connections with the Hindu universe of its upper-caste benefactors, in order to command authority, the Satnami Mahasabha had to draw upon the power of the gurus and the symbolic forms within Satnampanth; at the same time, in the attempt to reform the Satnamis, the Satnami Mahasabha came up against the authority of the gurus and practices legitimated by the myths and rituals of Satnampanth and had to direct itself against them. The problems that the Satnami Mahasabha sought to address through the Mahant Conference at Girodpuri were rooted in this contradiction. The problems and the contradiction continued to be played out in other ways.

Imperatives of Education and Authority

The Satnami Mahasabha placed a premium on education in its effort to redefine Satnami identity and reform Satnampanth. We have seen that the petition from the Satnami Mahasabha had pointed to illiteracy as the root cause of Satnami backwardness and to education as the antidote to these ills. Illiteracy and education were, in fact, immensely powerful organizing principles that served to define the perspective, the self-image, and the political articulation of low-caste movements in the early twentieth century.[48] After 1920 the C.P. government had encouraged the depressed classes to gain education and had aided and supported the efforts of the untouchable caste of Mahars to enter schools. The Mahar initiative had been guided by G. A. Gavai who had close links with the Satnami Mahasabha. The Mahasabha started a boarding house in Ganjpara, Raipur in order to educate the Satnamis.[49] The Satnami Ashram was set up with the help of local upper-caste leaders, particularly Nathuji Jagtap and Sunderlal Sharma.[50]

Naindas and Anjordas played a critical role here. The two Satnamis, along with Sunderlal Sharma, initiated the practice of *katori*: in grain markets Satnamis—and the occasional upper-caste person—would contribute a small measure of grain for the upkeep of Satnami boys and the expenses of running the boarding house.[51] The boarding house was in existence when Baba Ramchandra reached Chhattisgarh in early 1926.[52] Under the guidance of Baba Ramchandra the boarding house was fashioned into a school.[53]

A resolution drafted the constitution of the school and defined its aims. The name of the school was unanimously changed from Satnami Ashram, Chhattisgarh to Satnami Jagat Gurukul, All India and Other Nations.[54] As a next step the resolution provided a statement of the aims of the school.

> (1) Boys of all castes can gain education. (2) Boys from seven to ten years can take admission and can continue till they are fifteen years. (3) Fathers and mothers are told that the boys will be kept [in the school] till fifteen. (4) All the languages of the nation will be taught. (5) After passing out of the Gurukul the boys will have to serve the Gurukul for three years. After receiving the certificate from the Gurukul they will be eligible for an appropriate place. (6) When students pass, those in the third and fourth standard will be given scholarships. (7) After passing out of the Gurukul the boy will be married. Other boys will be married from within the Gurukul. The boys will be educated about *brahmacharya, grihasthashram, vanaprastha.* It [education] can be imparted to both a boy and his wife.[55]

The act of changing the name of the school was significant. The Satnami Ashram in its refashioned form as a *gurukul* sought to gain greater credibility by approximating to both Brahmanical and Arya Samaji constructions of the ideal place of learning within the Hindu social order. The play with links and connections within a wide geographical space—Satnami Jagat (world) Gurukul, All India and Other Nations—was rather more than a mere example of exaggerated ambition. A *gurukul* provided the classical blueprint for a universal place of learning. The aims of the school offered a confirmation of the *gurukul* ideal. Only boys were to enter the school at a young age, stay there till they were fifteen years, be educated in accordance with the principles of the high Hindu notion of four stages in a man's life— *brahmacharya, grihastha, vanaprastha, sanyasa*—and serve the *gurukul* for three years after they finished their education. Under normal circumstances the boys were to marry after they passed out of the *gurukul;* but if they were married within the *gurukul* both the boys and their wives were to be educated together within this institution. All this was, of course, evidence of Baba Ramchandra's imposition of strands within Brahmanical Hinduism and cues taken from the educational ventures of the Arya Samaj on the Satnami Mahasabha.

The third step of the resolution was to define the organizational basis of the Satnami Jagat Gurukul. The most important place was that of the general Mahasabha (committee). The decisions of the Mahasabha were law. It decided the dates of meetings. If any official went against these rules he was given orders by the Mahasabha, which had to be obeyed. The officials of the Satnami Mahasabha were to sort out matters among themselves so that there were no obstacles in the work of the Gurukul. All the *gurus, mahants, bhandaris, sathidars,* and officials and members of the Satnami Mahasabha were to help out annually, as their financial circumstances permitted, with the expenses of running the Gurukul. It was also decided to form a smaller committee that would officially tour different parts of India and the world to raise money for the school. Finally, much was made of financial contributions by members of the Mahasabha, which were to decide their official position.

> 1.Those who deposit Rs. 10,000 will be given 50 rupees per month, transport, a peon whose income won't be less than 10 rupees per month, uniform, armaments, and 2 rupees for daily expenses. 2.Those who deposit Rs. 20,000 will be given twice this [money/privileges].

At the same time, if an official or a member of the Satnami Mahasabha did not turn up for a meeting at the appointed time—decided by the general committee and announced in a letter—the result was a punitive deduction of a day's salary.[56]

In constructing the organizational rules of the Satnami Jagat Gurukul, the Satnami Mahasabha drew upon and replicated different structures of authority. The emphasis on the supreme power of the collective will of the committee and the importance of the regimentation of time was a play upon the idiom and forms of liberal constitutional politics. This was pre-eminently the language of caste movements, the Indian National Congress, and indeed colonial administration. But in addition, the Satnami officials were also offered some of the substantive symbols of a *saheb*'s authority: a fixed high salary, a mode of transport, and a peon who in turn had a defi-nite and regular income, wore a uniform, carried armaments, and was en-titled to an allowance for daily expenses. The Satnami Mahasabha, like the myths of Satnampanth, sought to appropriate the forms and symbols that underwrote the power of the colonial *saheb* and upper-caste superordinates.

How successful was Satnami Jagat Gurukul? We do not have figures for the number of boys who enrolled in the school and went on to finish their education, although the decision to impose fines on the parents of boys who left midway (to recover the money spent on them) suggests that the organizers had to cope with the problem of students dropping out. Nor do we know what became of the aim to give scholarships and certificates. The plans to "impart education about *brahmacharya, grihasthashram* and *vanaprastha*" and to teach all the languages of the nation were abandoned as the drive to raise funds for the Satnami Gurukul led to confusion over the money that was collected. Baba Ramchandra in his capacity as the organizing president of the Satnami Mahasabha wrote an angry letter to Agamdas, Naindas, and Anjordas: Had they not been entrusted with the task of collecting donations for the Raipur Satnami Ashram? How much money and grain had they accumulated? Where were the accounts? Who had given them the right to spend the money? What was the amount spent? Where was it spent? Did they seek the permission of members of the main committee before spending the money?[57] The Satnami Gurukul had found itself in a financial mess despite the efforts by the Satnami Mahasabha to build a tight organizational structure.[58] In 1933 Naindas met the missionary M. P. Davis and "boasted" that some years ago the Satnamis had begun to show signs of new life by starting a private school with the aim of opening up avenues for Satnami youths to enter government service. On being pressed further, however, Naindas had admitted that the school had to close down because of financial difficulties. The Brahman who took care of the school had left with all the money.[59] At the same time, the boarding house continued to function. The Satnami literate elite remember the Ashram as the origin for a new generation of leaders of the community who followed Anjordas and Naindas. Naindas was a little more circumspect when he told the missionary M. P. Davis that students of the Satnami Ashram had joined government service and been appointed police constables. In the perception of Satnami leadership the educational venture had not been a failure. It had led Satnami boys to become a part of the law and order machinery.[60]

Idioms of Order and New Legalities

The resolution concerning the Satnami Gurukul had gone on to construct a charter of rules for the Satnami Mahasabha.[61] The Mahasabha informed the *panchas* that in districts, *tahsils*, and villages when *panchayats* were held a number of weaknesses remained in their deliberations. In order to remove these weaknesses the Satnami Mahasabha had created the post of the *sabhapati* (chairman). The chairman, Agamdas, and the ministers, Naindas and Anjordas, had the full right to deliberate matters in the highest *panchayat*, which had been created in Raipur. The appellants were to make an appeal on a one rupee stamp paper. The criminal was to be punished according to the law based on *Manusmriti*. At the same time, if the charter of rules was tampered with and a guru-*mahant-sathidar-sant* of Satnami *samaj* or a guru of any other community went against the rules he was liable for prosecution under the Indian Penal Code.[62] There was a simultaneity about this establishment of a highest *panchayat* designed to correct the weaknesses of the local Satnami *panchayats* by administering a law based on *Manusmriti*, on the one hand, and the insistence on a one rupee stamp paper for the appellants and the invocation of the Indian Penal Code, on the other. This provided a blueprint for the manner in which the Satnami Mahasabha engaged with idioms and languages of the law.

In a note addressed to the government, written in the late 1920s, the Satnami Mahasabha complained about Baliya and Thagwa, Satnami *malguzars* of Amera village, who were disobeying the commands of Ravidasji and Ghasidasji.[63] Such people, the Mahasabha indicated, endangered the lives of Satnami who wore a *janeu* and were reformed. The benevolent *sarkar*—"under whose rule our caste has benefited a great deal and is likely to improve further"—was appealed to keep a check on Baliya and Thagwa since they were going against Satnami *kanun* (law) and destroying the orders of Ghasidasji.[64] Moreover, the appeal was made in a *jalsa*, a public meeting, legitimated by the presence of the *thanedar* (chief constable), the local representative of governor *saheb* and colonial power, who was to convey the opinion of the Satnami Mahasabha, formed at the assembly, that unless the recalcitrant Satnamis improved their ways, their *kanthis* would be taken away. Finally, the check on the lawless activities of the Satnamis was to be effected through surveillance and policing by the colonial administration.[65]

The Satnami Mahasabha deployed the language of law to ward off possible threats from outside. When the main *panchayat* of the Satnami Mahasabha issued certificates—a borrowing from colonial administrative practices—for the reform of the Satnamis and distributed the sacred thread for the service of cows and *shastras*, it also issued a warning.[66] If there were any questions about this matter they were to be addressed to the Satnami Gurukul Ashram, Raipur. People of all castes—"Malguzar, Hindu, Satnami, Muslim or Christian"—who did not clear their doubts with the apex body at Raipur and went on to harm a *janeu* wearing Satnami or his relative or tampered with any of his possessions were guilty under the Faujdari (Penal) Code, which had been established by the colonial government and now underlay the work of the Satnami Mahasabha.

The legal idiom also offered the Mahasabha a characteristic mode to sort out matters among the Satnamis. The daughter of a "pure" Satnami could be married into a Satnami family who ate meat. The Mahasabha advised the parents of the girl to issue a "notice" to their affines who ate meat. The unlawful people were given a clear message.

> Our Satnami women have been married into your homes. Among us, our caste and our guru have on the basis of the true law of Guru Ghasidas passed a resolution to reform eating and behavior. All of you are informed that you should reform your eating and behavior within six months. After the time has passed our girls will be called under the law of the government from your homes. If you don't think after reading or listening to this notice then once the date is passed the *sarkar* will proceed to take action against you.[67]

The reform of Satnampanth was at once predicated upon invocations of the rules and strictures of the true law of Ghasidas and the legal machinery of the colonial government.

To take a final example, the complex place of law as language and resource for the Satnami Mahasabha was further underscored in another of its appeals, written by Baba Ramchandra, to the *sarkar*. A request was made on behalf of the Satnami Mahasabha that until such time as members of their caste learned English—described as the *rajbhasha* (national language)—the government was to look after the affairs of the Satnamis. The officials of the *sarkar* were to manage matters in the manner of caste *panchas*. The community was to be disciplined, regulated, and punished in accordance with the *panchayat's* law. The money from the fines imposed on offenders was to be kept by the government and the *panchas* were to get a commission.[68] Even in this apparent capitulation to colonial authority, directed by Baba Ramchandra, the *sarkar* was only to administer the rules of the Satnami *panchayat*, and a fusion of colonial and *panchayat* law underlay the new legalities constructed by the Satnami Mahasabha. Indeed, in the oral accounts about the Satnami Mahasabha, Baba Ramchandra is remembered as a great man who had been a retired Sessions Judge before he came to Chhattisgarh: "Montagu Butler had accepted the *niyam* [rules] of Ghasidas. With the help of retired Sessions Judge Ramchandra, Naindas, Anjordas, and other *mahants* gave the Satnamis *kanun* [law]."[69] The government's acceptance of some of Mahasabha's demands and the intervention of Baba Ramchandra allowed the leadership of the Satnami Mahasabha to invoke colonial law and the *kanun* of Ghasidas, fashion new legalities, and cast its working in idioms of order and command.

The Satnami Mahasabha intervened to punish the transgressions of rules and norms of the community. The reports of missionaries from the period mention that the endeavor of reform among Satnamis centered on the collection of fines from villagers for breaking taboos of food—particularly carrion eating—and marriage. In 1934 M. P. Davis in his notes on the Satnamis hastily jotted,

> [Satnamis] continue to be despised as Chamars by all. . . . Yet closely organized . . . 23 *mahants*. . . . Each village where several or more Satnami families—a *bhandari*. . . . Had [Agamdas] guru's camp near Parsabhader one year. . . . He had Brahman *mukhtiyar* as convert. . . . Police-clerks-servants-*chaprasis* (plus four women) with him. . . . Collected fines of men: whose wife ran away; who took other's wife; ate meat; rebelled against guru, or *mahant*, or *bhandari*.[70]

An eighty-year-old *bhandari* commented, "Naindas and Anjordas used to tour the villages and see to it that people were following the Satnami law and faith."[71] The Mahasabha deployed the symbolic resources offered by colonial administration to restructure the organizational hierarchy of Satnampanth. The earlier pattern of *mahant-diwan-bhandari-sathidar* was enlarged with the introduction of different ranks of *mahants*. The new ranks were based primarily on colonial administrative categories: the *rajmahants* at the top were followed by *jila* (district), *tahsil*, and *sarkil* (circle) *mahants*.[72] Similarly, the leaders of the Satnami Mahasabha tightened the organizational basis of the Satnami *panchayat* to secure an effective mode of intervention in the affairs of the community. Instead of the more fluid arrangements of the past where *panchas* were chosen, depending on the situation, from among the *sayan* (elders) of the village, the *rajmahants* now intervened to choose the men who would be *panchas*. These *panchas* sat with the *bhandari* and *sathidar* to deliberate matters concerning Satnamis within the village.[73] The group of villages that had deliberated matters that could not be settled by a *panchayat* in a village were, in turn, given a firm institutional basis and constituted as the *athgawana* (committee of eight villages).[74] The altered organizational structure defined by the Satnami Mahasabha had been established by the mid 1930s.[75] In 1961 an ethnographer-administator described it as the "traditional social organization" of the Satnamis, a testimony to the rapid fashioning of traditions in the realm of colonial (and postcolonial) modernities.[76]

(En)Gendered Agendas and the Domestication of Reform

The idioms of order and command at the heart of the Satnami Mahasabha were allied to efforts to regulate the intimately linked arenas of marriage, sexuality, and nurture in the Satnami household. Baba Ramchandra sought to reorder conjugal and gender relations within Satnampanth, mainly through the writing of the unpublished "Satnami Panchkanya Dehati ki Jeevni" or the lives of the five pure Satnami girls.[77] It was intended to be read by *bade log*, the important people, within the Satnami hierarchy who were to then take the initiative of reforming Satnampanth through the reform of the household.

> I came out to tour the villages. My work is to organize. That is why without first reforming the household it is impossible to improve the rest of society. For this reason sages have praised this institution by stating, Great is the Household Mother. As a result, in India women of other castes are looked upon with respect. But this Satnami caste which is reformed in every sense why should their women be looked upon with such lack of respect? Thinking about this, whatever answers struck my limited understanding, I have offered them in the name of five pure girls.[78]

The passage introduces us to the key emphases of "Panchkanya Dehati": motherhood; the best means to the morality and economy of the Satnami household; a contrast between Satnami women and women of other castes; and the opposition between home and outside. These emphases tied together the six basic parts that constitute the main text of the "Satnami Panchkanya Dehati": a long poem called the song of dawn; a narrative, including a charter of demands, written—like the rest of the text—by Baba Ramchandra but attributed to a fictitious Satnami woman called Vidyavati; excerpts from Tulsidas's *Ramcharitamanas*; a short piece directed against the Satnami practice of selling grain in the market; another that lashes out at meat-eating Satnamis and eulogizes Naindas; and, finally, an elaborate "Mold to Produce Children." Each separately and taken together, these different parts of the "Satnami Panchkanya Dehati" elaborated a new code of morality of the household fashioned by Baba Ramchandra. Now if this code addressed certain problems of Satnami women such as those of sexual exploitation, it only did so within a matrix of restraints that arrogated power in domestic and intimate arenas in the hands of Satnami men and through measures designed to contain a more fluid pattern of gender relationships in Satnami kinship networks. This meant that Baba Ramchandra's code of morality and economy of the household imposed mechanisms of hierarchical and ritual control on Satnami women, further distancing it from their concerns and desires.

The "Panchkanya Dehati" appropriately opens with a *pad prabhati* or the song of dawn, an exhortation to wake up to truth. The poem is interspersed with a call to Satnami women to rise from slumber, which signifies indifference and ignorance. The *prabhat*, the dawn, is the light that illuminates the darkness shrouding Satnami women. Moreover, it is the worship of *satnam* that heralds the dawn. This is underscored through repetition. At the same time, the defining features of the new light of dawn are knowledge and virtue that are directed toward being good mothers who truly nurture their sons. There is a special value accorded to the male child. Finally, the exhortation to wake up is worked out in terms of a contrast. Women of all other castes have awakened, but Satnami women shamelessly sleep on, and the world laughs at these ignorant beings. In order to realize their humanity Satnami women must reform and improve.[79]

The *pad prabhati* is followed by Baba Ramchandra's construction of a short narrative containing a charter of demands made on behalf of Satnami women by their imaginary sister, Vidyavati Satnami. Brief but evocative descriptions of Baba Ramchandra and Vidyavati Satnami set the stage here. Ramchandra, carelessly attired and full of disdain for what he is given to eat, is cast in the mold of a saint and an ascetic in popular traditions. The fictitious figure of Vidyavati in turn is presented as combining all the essential qualities of a good woman. Educated but totally unspoilt, Vidyavati's learning not only leads her to better serve the *sasural* (affinal home) but also makes her shy, reticent, and obedient, which now become the ideals of Satnami womanhood. Thus it was in keeping with her character, the text argued, that Vidyavati was writing what she had learned under the tutelage of Baba Ramchandra. With the legitimacy of the Ramchandra and Vidyavati team established, the "Panchkanya Dehati" appealed to the organizers of the Mahasabha and important people within Satnampanth to redress the problems of Satnami women.

(1) Don't marry us off at an early age. (2) Teach us enough knowledge so that we can rid our lineage of its black mark and provide happiness to our sons. (3) *Panch* or *sarpanch*, guru or *mahant, bhandari* don't turn us into prostitutes . . . keep us pure. (4) Make us capable of serving our husbands. (5) Make us capable of serving the guru which improves the domestic and social situation so that we gain honor in the world. (6) Don't make us wear [ornaments of] brass, copper, artificial silver, and artificial gold. (7) Give up the practice of selling grain produced by the labor of the household at cheap rates. (8) You make us wear clothes of *pachees-tees* [the nationalist weave], in the same way give us another one and a half arm length of cloth to cover our receptacles of milk. (9) Don't send us to work outside the home. When we go to work in someone's house the master, his sons, and his servants have intercourse with us like our husbands. Get rid of this or tell us how we can maintain our creed of fidelity to the husband. (10) When guru, *mahant*, and *diwans* come on *ramat* don't send us girls before them. *Sipahis* and guru *mahants* call us on pretext of massaging them with oil, serving rice, to give water or some other work. We go respecting them as our true gods but when we reach there they lower our

prestige and destroy our faith. If we say anything their companions surround us from all sides and tell us that the guru ought to be given everything. Leave aside the gurus. After the guru has finished, the *mahants* and *sipahis* climb on us. For this reason we pray to our mothers and fathers and to our mothers-in-law and fathers-in-law to protect us from this cruelty. (11) If you take a debt from someone that must be repaid quickly so that you don't get to hear abuses, don't have to go to court, don't have to sell at cheap rates goods bought with the money earned by the household, and don't have to sell silver, gold, ornaments, and animals. This should be the direction you should take and make others take. (12) When a calamity strikes make a way that we married girls are not left behind alone at home. Our husbands go to earn [a living] at Calcutta and Kalamati [coal mines]. Their parents turn us into a means to make money. Even when they take us to other lands, there the guards, clerks, sweepers, and white and black *sahebs* of the factories engage our husbands in odd jobs here and there and turn us into prostitutes. (13) Make a way so that we don't have to marry in a household which eats meat or consumes tobacco or liquor. (14) We thank Naindasji *mahant* of our lineage who lives in Saloni. He will arrange for these thirteen things and obtain honor for us so that we and our children can be faithful to god and to country and remove our marks of shame.[80]

These demands suggested a particular understanding of the place and duties of women within an authoritatively mapped domain of Hindu tradition, a world of idealized domesticity constructed by Baba Ramchandra. Women of all castes enjoyed a high status in the Hindu order of family and marriage, but Satnami women had been doomed and relegated to a low position. Baba Ramchandra was possibly referring to the upper-caste perception of the alleged sexual deviance of Satnami women here. The way out consisted of emphasizing motherhood, *pativrata dharma* (the creed of complete fidelity and unflinching devotion to the husband), and modesty as both tenets for Satnami women and a proper moral code for the household. This involved, on the one hand, the protection of Satnami women from different forms of sexual exploitation to help retain their *pativrata dharma* and, on the other, a move to retain marks of status and the economic self-sufficiency of the domestic unit. The themes were linked and structured by an all-encompassing opposition between home and outside.

The charter demanded an end to the early marriage of Satnamis girls and made a plea for their education. Moreover, this learning and knowledge were to be geared toward the virtues of domesticity and the practice of motherhood, the service of the husbands and the guru—"which improves the domestic and social situation so that we gain honor in the world"—and ridding the Satnami lineage of its black marks of shame. Finally, this pervasive shame also had to be addressed in other ways. An appeal was now made to Satnami leaders to provide an extra bit of cloth to cover the breasts of Satnami women. The reference to breasts as receptacles of milk (*doodh ke bartan*) divested them of erotic and playful meaning—repeatedly rehearsed, for example, in the genre of short poems called *dadaria* that form an important part of the romantic and sexual banter between women and men within everyday rhythms of labor and leisure in Chhattisgarh—and construed breasts solely in terms of the function of nurture. Modesty and motherhood worked in tandem to counter shame.

The notion of the *panchkanya* that appears in the title, in fact, refers to five goddesses within the Hindu pantheon who are mothers, embody different virtues, and are marked by the purity that attaches to prepubescent girls. The married status of a woman—of being a *suhagan* (one who puts vermilion in the parting of her hair), the embodiment of an auspicious state—is privileged and celebrated within the complex of Hindu rituals and practices. The message of the value of the married state is, often, transmitted in negative terms. The figure of the married woman stands in opposition to the widow and the prostitute.[81] We find then that the demands against sexual exploitation in the "Satnami Panchkanya Dehati" evoked the figure of the prostitute. Satnami women were to be kept *pat* (pure) and not turned into prostitutes. They had to be defended against the transgression of sexual norms by various figures of authority: *panch* and *sarpanch* (Demand 3); the master, his sons, and even his servants (Demand 9); at the time of *ramat* (the tour of the guru) the guru, *mahants, diwans,* and *sipahis* (guards of the guru), and in day-to-day life *bhandaris* and *mahants* (Demands 3 and 10); finally, in places away from home, the white and black *sahebs* of factories, guards, clerks, and sweepers (Demand 12). Satnami women were to be confined within the home and not sent outside to labor since this led to a disruption of the pattern of conjugal rights of the husband over the wife's body (Demand 9). The norms that were invoked attached to the married woman and the mother—the embodiment of fidelity—and were, like the woman, situated within a construct of the morality of the household. At work indeed was the opposition between home and outside.

The demands set out in the "Satnami Panchkanya Dehati" do not appeal to any single center of authority and there is no superordinate who is completely absolved of guilt. The excesses of the gurus and superiors within Satnampanth are sought to be countered through the parents-in-law and parents; and when the parents and parents-in-law are complicit in using Satnami women by selling their bodies the appeal is made to the gurus. All figures of authority are guilty at one point or another and each is appealed to at different moments in the narrative. The responsibility for implementing the new code lay in the hands of male superordinates within the home and the guru of Satnampanth. Women's modesty and chastity were symbols of male honor in the new code of morality of the household.[82]

The home/outside opposition was also implicated in the creation of a moral economy of the household. The household, the domestic unit, was engaged in the production of grain. What was protested was the selling of grain at cheap rates outside in the market (Demand 7). Incurring a debt created similar problems. Failure to repay it led to abuses, insults, and the selling of goods, ornaments, and animals. The goods, like grain, were produced by the labor of the household. Ornaments of gold and silver and cattle were marks of status. In order that goods, ornaments, and animals be retained within the household, debts were to be repaid quickly. Similarly, when a calamity forced Satnami men to leave home to work in factories or coal mines, with the women left behind, the consequence was a disruption of the code of morality and economy of the household (Demand 12). Finally, with the household privileged and situated as the focal point of the new code, it stood to reason that girls should not be married into a home where the family ate meat or consumed tobacco or liquor (Demand 13).

Chastity and modesty as the defining characteristics of Satnami women also put in an appearance at the end of the narrative written by Ramchandra but attributed to the imaginary Vidyavati. The importance of the *pativrata* ideal was emphasized through the section that quoted excerpts from Tulsidas's *Ramcharitamanas*: Satnami women were to follow Anusuia's instructions to Sita on what went into the making of a perfect woman, wife, and mother.[83] They were, once again, exhorted to wake up and raise brave and devoted sons who embodied the characteristics of legendary Kshatriya warriors.[84] Moreover, the Satnami practice of selling grain in the market was criticized in a long passage addressed to all Satnamis. The passage emphasized the tremendous difficulties and hardships faced by Satnamis in carrying grain to markets in towns and the insults suffered in selling it there: vagaries of nature, insubstantial food, and abuses suffered during a long and arduous journey, carried out characteristically after the carts were loaded at home, served to define the home/outside opposition; and the absolute lack of care with which the grain was treated and the low price at which it was bought contrasted with the love, nurture, and labor of the household that went into its production.[85] All this underscored the need for a morality and economy of the household. Finally, the issue of immoral practices within the household was also addressed in a long passage that lashed out at the eating of meat by Satnamis.

> O sisters, we are the ones who are spoiling our sons. Children are after all subordinate to us. One day I was going from my village to my natal home. On the way I passed in front of a village. What did I see? A bullock was lying dead.

Some women and men were standing there. Here and there crows and vultures were croaking. In places dogs had attached themselves. In places boys were walking to and fro carrying meat. On the road a *janeu*-wearing Satnami passed in front of me.[86]

This conjures up a hellish vision of men and women like crows and vultures, boys like dogs. They are all predatory creatures. The contrast is emphasized through the figure of the *janeu*-wearing Satnami. The message was clear. Satnamis had to give up eating carrion to reform the household and rid Satnampanth of its sullying black marks of shame.

The drive to reform the household found its culmination in an elaborate set of rules, consisting of forty-six points, in the "Mold to Produce Children," which appears at the end of the "Satnami Panchkanya Dehati." This was a remarkable compilation that brought together characteristics of different kinds of food—for instance, chickpeas and milk as substances that replenished the virility of men—ideas about intercourse, pregnancy, and childbirth with varied bits of folk wisdom. The sexual act was to be marked by purity and geared toward procreation: the birth of a healthy and strong, brave and devoted male child.

> 1. Bathe and wear clean clothes 2. Spread clean clothes on the floor 3. On the fourth day of the month, after midnight 4. Hang pictures of brave devotees in the house 5. The woman should say to the husband that in order to beget a son donate semen 6. Half the stomach should be filled with sweet food 7. The thoughts and mind of man and woman should be one 8. Don't go to the woman after being angry 9. While having intercourse both should talk about knowledge 10. After intercourse the husband should clean his genitals and have milk or grams [chickpeas] or drink water 11. After intercourse the woman should turn to her left and after an hour get up and have a bath and cleanse herself, that's all 12. During pregnancy no intercourse should take place.

The virtues of strength, devotion, and bravery were to be nurtured and inculcated in boys by giving them the right food at the right time. The girl child was not ignored. But boys were privileged.

> 14. Boys instead of being breast fed ought to be given small amounts of fresh juice of grapes, pomegranates, and other such fruits . . . 16. If boys cry don't give them milk 17. Don't feed children milk after coming in from work or getting up after sitting next to the stove 18. After children turn a year old don't feed them stale grain . . . 23. Make children drink ground basil leaves [dissolved in water]—they won't fall ill.

The children—particularly the sons—had to be educated, kept away from immoral influences, and brought up in the correct way.

> 15. Don't keep boys and girls naked . . . 19. Don't teach children abuses from a small age 20. When mothers and fathers, brothers and sisters, mothers-in-law and fathers-in-law meet children they should say good things to them . . . 24. Don't wear or make your children wear dirty clothes 25. Teach them yourself or send them to a school after they turn three 26. Climbing on horses, exercise, using a stick, swimming, climbing trees, running, climbing walls and jumping off them, walking bullocks, bringing grass for cows, learning devotional songs—these are tasks which parents should learn and teach sons or get others to teach them.

The children also had to be protected from threats of envy, risk, and the ubiquitous evil eye.

> 13. To escape the trick of an evil woman and man a black thread ought to be tied to the waist [of the son]—this does good . . . 21. Don't send children alone anywhere 22. Don't put ornaments of gold and silver on children.

Finally, the text defined the mode of managing the Satnami household economy by providing instructions on how to negotiate journeys outside the home and setting out a code of correct practices rooted within the domestic unit.

> 27. If you go to another land or any place both women and men should go together 28. Don't keep money with you. If you have to sleep on the way, you sleep until others are up, then get up and let others sleep 29. At the time of going to another land keep useful implements and take a trusted man from the village 30. Don't stop at anyone's house away from home 31. Eat food which you cook with your own hands 32. Don't tell anyone the sorrows and secrets of your home 33. Do good to yourselves and then do good to others 34. Wherever you are going learn about it's surroundings 35. Take decisions leaving out considerations of your own caste and religion in situations of crisis 36. While you are alive don't leave your fields, country, woman, dress, and pattern of behavior, thought, caste, gardens, rivers and ponds 37. Knowledge and virtues should be learned from all who possess them 38. In this world and the other it is held that caste is of deeds. For this reason do good deeds to change your caste and *varna* 39. Don't keep the debt of anyone—eat little, wear torn clothes, but repay the debt 40. Don't leave your faith because of a threat or greed 41. Don't go anywhere without being called 42. Remain subordinate to the true word and consider another woman as your mother 43. Be-

come productive and get rid of poverty 44. Both wife and husband should learn to read 45. Don't sell your fields, it is better to sell grains 46. Even at the cost of losing your life don't sell your cow, daughter, or land. Donate them to a good person.[87]

There are echoes here of concerns expressed throughout the other parts of "Satnami Panchkanya Dehati." The "Mold to Produce Children," a detailed guide to proper conduct, was also held in place by the encompassing home/outside opposition. Clearly, the improvement of Satnampanth was to be carried through a reform of the Satnami household.

What were the implications of the new code elaborated by the "Panchkanya Dehati" for Satnami women? It is evident that the normative and prescriptive text addressed the problem of the sexual exploitation of Satnami women. We have seen that in the detailed oral testimony of Mogra, a Satnami woman who grew up in the late colonial period, sexual exploitation had figured as a critical element in the structuring of experience in everyday life. Other Satnami oral narratives about the past also rehearsed the theme in somewhat more fragmentary ways. The most eloquent voice here was that of Pitambar, an older Satnami man.

> The upper castes would not touch us. They would never eat with us. But they were always ready to fornicate. For "doing it" our women were not untouchable. Great is caste. Even after licking the privates of Satnami women, they would not lose their purity. Zamindari and government officials could be obnoxious. All of them wanted good quality rice, milk and *ghee*. Some wanted *daaru* [liquor]. Many—especially police, excise and forest officials—wanted women. It was difficult to refuse them. The rich supplied the food and the drink. We had to run errands and supply women.[88]

At the same time, Baba Ramchandra intended his new code to be an effective mode of intervention and control. The rules for proper conduct and the morality and economy of the Satnami household were to be implemented by male superordinates within the family and Satnampanth.[89] The privileging of motherhood, modesty, and absolute obedience and fidelity to the husband as dominant ideals for Satnami women and the celebration of the brave and devoted male child within the reformed Satnami household, sought to contain a more fluid pattern of gender relationships that were, no doubt, asymmetrical and informed by a patrilineal and patrivirilocal ideology. The creed of *pativrata dharma,* implicitly at the very least, attempted to control the practices of *churi* and the sexuality of Satnami women. The "Satnami Panchkanya Dehati" addressed the issue of the sexual exploitation of Satnami women within a matrix of impositions, controls, and constraints. All this was informed by a wider logic. Baba Ramchandra's new code situated gender within a "hierarchical and coordinated cluster of relationships" within the Satnami household and Satnampanth.[90] The project of the domestication of reform was premised upon an implicit recognition that the effective exercise of power required "mechanisms of politico-ritual control to impose their domination on the more diffuse domains of production, exchange, sexuality and nurture" within the Satnami household.[91]

The leaders of the Satnami Mahasabha took up only some of the concerns of Baba Ramchandra's highly interventionist project of reform. The Satnami household was sought to be sanitized through a decision to give the boys respectable names that connoted valor and purity. In the early 1920s Naindas told the missionary M. P. Davis that the Satnamis in a mass meeting had decided to cease giving their children such despicable names as Khubra (crooked), Mehtar (sweeper), Pachkaur (valueless), and Thanwar (stable boy). These "despicable" names, actually given to boys to avoid the risk of an envious evil eye, were to be replaced by "respectable" names such as Singh and Das.[92] Similarly, at a meeting attended by about two thousand Satnamis under the presidentship of guru Agamdas in February 1927 it was decided that Satnami women should wear blouses. If they did not follow this rule their families were fined.[93] Finally, the more enduring steps for the reform of the household were taken through the enlarged and reconstituted hierarchy of Satnampanth. The critical place was that of the *athgawana* (committee of eight villages).

> The *athgawana* was first made about 1928, two-three years after the visit to Kanpur. All marriages had to take place either within the *athgawana* or, if outside, with the permission of the *bhandaris* and the *panchas*. Why? So that rogues, bad people wouldn't come and spoil our girls and households. It kept the Satnamis united, our religion alive.[94]

The leaders of the Satnami Mahasabha strictly enforced the rules of marriage and commensality. "Under the Mahasabha a man who took another wife had to feed the caste. There was no escape."[95] In 1933 the missionary M. P. Davis wrote, "The Mahant [Naindas] had come to the village in order to discipline several followers whose wives or daughters had been wronged by the herdsman. In place of punishing the latter, who belongs to another caste, he merely outcasted a father who should have taken better care of his roaming daughter."[96] Several Satnamis stated that Naindas and Anjordas used to come and see to it that people were obeying the *kanun* (law) of the Satnami *samaj*. Otherwise they would beat the disobedient and recalcitrant ones with sticks. Legality, the idiom of command, and the reform of the household were closely tied to each other in the activities of the Satnami Mahasabha.

Hindu Emphases and the Satnami Response

We have seen that the Satnami Mahasabha had sought to rework the relationship of the community with a reconstituted Hindu order in the image of upper-caste nationalists. Aspects of Satnami religious practice allow us to trace both the community's uses for the emphases of the Mahasabha and the group's inflection of the interventionist voices of its upper-caste benefactors. I focus on the spate of temple-building activities—often sponsored by Satnami *malguzars* but which drew much wider participation—that was inspired by the reform and religious revival under the Satnami Mahasabha. We do not know if these ventures had anything to do with Gandhi's Harijan "upliftment" tour of 1933 in which he had stopped at Baloda Bazar in Raipur district.[97] Satnami oral testimonies and accounts written at the time certainly do not make the connection. "Earlier we had two, three temples. In Bhandar, Girod and somewhere else. From that time [of Naindas and Anjordas] Satnamis have liked to build temples."[98]

The catechist Prabhudas Karim Munshi, a Satnami convert to Christianity, wrote a brief report on the Satnami temple at the village of Kukda, built in the early 1930s.

> The old Satnami *malguzar* Gangaram did not have a son. He prostrated himself with folded arms and prayed to Ghasidas, "Maharaj if you give me a son I will construct a temple in your memory." The man had a son who died after nine months. The people of the village told the *malguzar* that his son had died because he had not built the temple. He then got a temple constructed but died before he could put a pinnacle on it. His brother Amarsingh has the key to the temple. He opens the temple during festivals when Satnamis break coconuts and pray to Ghasidas.[99]

In the temple, a bamboo pole with a piece of white cloth stood in place of an idol. The Satnamis lit earthen lamps before this *chinha* (sign) of Ghasidas. The Satnami Mahasabha had generated the impetus for the building of the temple. At the same time, although the act of erecting a temple—instead of a pilgrimage to Girod or Bhandar—to fulfill a vow was influenced by the concerns of Hinduism, the pattern of worship within the structure centered on Ghasidas and was rooted in the modes of belief and practice within Satnampanth.

A second temple completed in 1938 also had its beginnings in a vow made by a Satnami *malguzar*.[100] The village proprietor wanted his two wives to bear him sons: to obtain the boon, he built the temple on the site of the grave of a former guru. The missionary Baur reported that the outer walls of the temple were adorned with "all sorts of idols."[101] We do not know much about these idols but they do not seem to have included the major gods and goddesses of the Hindu pantheon. The disconcerted missionary's attention, for example, was captured by the depiction of a man, "holding a woman by the naked breast and she in the act of lifting her scant loin cloth."[102] Similarly, the temple was guarded by an enormous twenty-five-foot-tall idol of Bhimsen, the village deity of rain, holding a club over his shoulder.[103] Inside the temple there were no idols. The grave was covered with green glazed tiles. The pilgrims circumambulated the temple, bowed before the idols on the outer walls, and worshiped Bhimsen. The *samadhi* (memorial) of the guru made the temple a site for Satnami pilgrimage. The main act of pilgrimage was obeisance to the *samadhi*, which embodied the guru's authority. A guru *mata* was ensconced next to the *samadhi*. The Satnami pilgrims touched her feet and made an offering of money and a coconut. The guru sat at a short distance from the temple in a tent. His feet were washed and the *charanamrit* was sprinkled on a surging crowd, which was not allowed to reach the tent. The placing of a golden pinnacle on top of the temple, which signified its completion, was held on *puranmasi*, the night of the full moon.

> We [found] the cooks busily preparing food in the river bed. A line of twenty *chulhas* [stoves] had to be dug into the sand each capable of holding twenty large pots of rice. At one time four-hundred pots could be lifted from off the stoves and carried up the hill near the temple and the cooked rice deposited in huge piles there. The *dal* [lentil] was cooked and placed into two large cement tanks about six by eight feet square.[104]

The cooking and distribution of food among thousands of Satnamis, a spectacle of commensality, underscored the solidarity of the group. The evidence of wealth highlighted the well being of Satnampanth. The placing of the golden tip on the steeple brought forth cries invoking *satnam*, Ghasidas, and the living gurus. At the same time, walking amid the crowd, the missionary found "numbers of small groups sitting in devout attention and listening to Hindu Scriptures."[105] The veneration of gurus and the playing out of the boundedness of the Satnamis was accompanied by the retelling of stories of gods and goddesses of the Hindu pantheon. A Satnami pilgrim told the missionary, "This [occasion] shows that our Satnam religion is still alive and the momentum of this gathering will carry us on for another one hundred years"; and a *mahant* explained to a Brahman that the Satnamis were really Hindus. The two statements, which replicated the dual emphases of the Satnami Mahasabha, went together.

Money for the building of temples could be raised in other ways. The tightening of the organizational structure of Satnampanth initiated by the Satnami Mahasabha, for example, generated the funds for the construction of a temple in the village of Charakpur.[106] In 1932 the Satnamis in the village found they had collected close to 250 rupees. The person who filed the report on the temple explained:

> There are various ways of collecting this money (i) When a man makes a second wife some money is needed (ii) In fights the [Satnami] *samaj* imposes a fine (iii) If a man goes wrong with a woman he is fined (iv) A person is fined when he eats meat or fish. There are several such means through which money is collected in the *samaj*.[107]

In 1935–36 Ghasiya *bhandari*, Baniya, Kulbal, and Deonath of Charakpur realized that the funds were growing and decided to build a temple. Work on the temple was begun in 1937. It was a collective endeavor. The Satnamis in the village made additional contributions and brought the stones for the construction of the temple in their carts. The temple did not contain an idol and, significantly, was constructed at the site of the *jait khambh* of Ghasidas in the village. It was to be used for religious discourse and the narration of epics such as the *Ramayana*. This task, however, was to be performed by a Satnami priest. The villagers were clear that they would not employ a Brahman for the purpose. Clearly, the Satnamis fashioned their own uses for the key practices within Hinduism that were new additions to Satnampanth.

Oral accounts about the Satnami Mahasabha once again underscore the critical place of reworkings of the ideas and practices of upper-caste nationalism along with the legality of the venture.

> In 1918 it was Lord Government. The British government had opened a *buchadkhana* [slaughter house] near Baloda Bazar. Thousands of cows used to be cut there every week. Naindas could not tolerate this within his heart. Why? [He thought] In our Hindu country the British are killing thousands of cows. This is against my principles. I cannot tolerate it. He took two or three companions and reached the slaughter house. There he beat up the butchers with *lathis*. For eight days Naindas wielded the stick. The spirit of the butchers was broken. There was an explosion. The British government went to catch Naindas, the others were left alone. He was locked up in *hawalat* [jail]. The Government asked him, why did you stop our income of lakhs of rupees? Naindas answered, "*Sarkar*, according to Hindu religion, *gau mata* [the cow] is

175

our highest mother. She protects us and is our guardian. She was being cut and I could not tolerate it. The cow is my mother. Till I am alive I will not let the butchers here function."[108]

We have seen that the Chamar handling of the carcasses of dead cattle was implicated in their constitution as untouchables and that the signs and practices of Satnampanth had worked to reconstitute this status by turning the Chamars into Satnamis. In Satnami perceptions, Naindas elaborated on this theme. The British were an alien presence. To prevent the slaughter of the cow, the highest mother, by the British government was to defend the honor of the Hindu country against the intrusion of outsiders. The predators of the past were transformed into true sons of the sacred cow. The movement underwrote the legitimacy of the Satnami endeavor. The Satnami *lathis*, which broke the spirit of the butchers, articulated the idiom of command that had defined the Satnami Mahasabha.

In the court of the first class magistrate Naindas told the Brahman judge, "I tried to save the cow. I didn't know that to save the Hindu faith was anything wrong." The judge, Shukla Brahman said, "Naindas, since you have risked your life to save the cow this court gives you two swords, two shields, a gun and four policemen. As long as you are alive, this court shall honor you and give you a chair. Second, since you have prevented the murder of cows you are exonerated of seven murders. No charges will be brought against you even if you kill seven people." The court gave proof in writing with the seal of the judge. Within two years of Naindas's release, there was no sign left in Raipur, Bilaspur, and Durg that once cows used to be slaughtered there.[109]

It is instructive that Naindas made a Brahman concede that a Satnami was the true defender of the Hindu faith. The Satnami protection of cows, a reversal of the stigma attached to the community, lay behind the decision of the judge to invest Naindas with retainers bearing arms—symbols of official power—and accord him a position of equality and honor in the court. Moreover, the account seized the widely held notion that to kill a cow is equal to seven murders, reversing its emphasis: the successful bid to stop the slaughter of cows had exonerated Naindas of seven murders. In Satnami oral accounts the legality of the Satnami Mahasabha was inextricably bound to its defence of Hindu norms.

There was also a twist to this tale of the valiant Satnami defense of the cow.

After Naindas put an end to the slaughter of cows, the governor Lord Montagu Butler called him to Kanpur. He asked Naindas, "How do I welcome you? The work which you have done, Brahmans and Thakurs haven't been able to do. You are greater than them. Satnami religion is superior to all other faiths. For this I give you the *janeu.*" Naindas replied, "Saheb, it is very good you are giving me the *janeu* but people will think that I am a Brahman." Then the governor welcomed him with both the *janeu* and the *kanthi.* From that day the Satnamis wear both the *janeu* and the *kanthi* because we are protectors of cows.[110]

The account conflated discrete events—the meeting of the leaders of the Satnami Mahasabha with Lord Montagu Butler in Bilaspur and their presence at the Kanpur session of the Indian National Congress—and replaced Hindu nationalist superiors with the Governor of the Central Provinces. This was a part of a rhetorical move indicating that the Satnami Mahasabha's efforts to protect cows and defend Hindu norms simultaneously distinguished the Satnamis from Brahmans. The combination of *janeu* and *kanthi* was a mark of distinction that established Satnami superiority over upper-caste Hindus.

The Rivals of Satnami Mahasabha

The authority of the Mahasabha was challenged by rival initiatives in the community. In 1936 a group of Satnamis in the village of Tumgaon in Raipur got together with M. D. Singh, a catechist of the American Evangelical Mission, to set up the Shri Path Pradarshak Samaj (Society of the Light of the True Path).[111] The presence of M. D. Singh, who was accorded the title of *acharya* (teacher), meant that the Shri Path Pradarshak Sabha flirted with the ideas and tenets of Christianity. The vows taken by members, for instance, included the acceptance of "only that Scripture which teaches the true name Satnam" and a pledge against committing adultery, and the constitution of the Sabha opened with a biblical verse, "The bush continues to burn but does not become consumed" (Exodus 8:2).[112] At the same time, the overwhelming emphasis of the initiative was a drive to get the Satnamis recognized not as Harijans—the term coined by Gandhi for the Scheduled Castes, which still marked them out as untouchables—but rather as a distinct Hindu caste. The repetition of this theme underlay Shri Path Pradarshak Sabha's plan to reform the Satnamis.

> The Satnamis have to be reformed which includes the following written dictates. (a) Satnamis are to be turned into Hindus by being given the status of Hindus. (b) The Satnamis who do the work of Chamars are to be removed from the community or, according to rules, are to be included within the

community. (c) In government papers our caste has to be entered as Hindu Satnami. (d) Wherever it is difficult to do so to seek the help of the government. (e) To make the Satnamis Hindus and get them out of the slot of Harijans and into the slot of Hindus, that is turn them from Harijans into Hindus.[113]

This program of action was rooted in Shri Path Pradarshak Sabha's construction of a new past for the Chamars.[114] The Chamars had Brahman ancestors and, as Satnamis, had later started wearing the sacred thread and given up eating beef. In keeping with this reworked account of the group's origins, Shri Path Pradarshak Sabha appealed to the C.P. Legislative Assembly that the Satnamis be classified as caste Hindus—although without giving up the political benefits they received as a Scheduled Caste—instead of being considered Harijans, which still retained the stigma of their being outcastes.

The Government of the Central Provinces was not impressed. After a meeting with the Secretary and members of the Sabha the Deputy Commissioner, Raipur reported:

> Though the Secretary of the Samaj is a Christian, it appears that the persons who have sponsored the applications are Satnami Hindus. Their real grievance appears to be that they are included among Harijans. . . . All they appear to wish is that, in the Scheduled Castes, they should be included not under the term Harijans, but separately as a distinct Scheduled Caste. To this distinction, they attach importance as a mark of superiority over other Scheduled Castes.[115]

The Chief Commissioner, Chhattisgarh division felt that since the petitioners wished to remain "within the fold of Scheduled Castes and thus not sacrifice their political privileges," it was not necessary to make the fine distinction between Harijan and Hindu Satnami.[116] The Chief Secretary was clear that all Harijans were Hindus and Satnamis did not lose their identity by being included under the category of Harijans. Two weeks later the Minister for Education of the Central Provinces met the members of the Shri Path Pradarshak Sabha at Raipur and told them that the government would reach a decision after consulting the Satnami Mahasabha. The Mahasabha did not support the demand of the Path Pradarshak Sabha.[117] The petition was rejected by the government in July 1938.

The leaders of the Sabha did not give up their efforts. They now decided to forego the political privileges accruing to the community due to its being listed as a Scheduled Caste. The Sabha appealed to the Minister for Education of the Central Provinces to be allowed to reform the community by "removing our name from the Harijan list and classifying us with high-caste Hindus so that we may regain our original position and rank."[118] The Shri Path Pradarshak Sabha also went on to define its differences with the Satnami Mahasabha, which had no qualms about the Harijan status of the Satnamis. It argued that a claim based on the Hindu sacred texts could not be judged according to the whims of the Mahasabha. Moreover, the Satnamis were divided into two sections. "We belong to that section whose object is to ameliorate the condition of the Satnamis . . . while the other section holds quite opposite views."[119] The managing committee of the Path Pradarshak Sabha was willing to consider the decision of the Mahasabha only if its rules were accepted in turn.[120] Finally, the Satnami Mahasabha did not have a legal standing: "The Mahasabha is not a registered body nor has it got any rules of its own by which it can do anything." A body without rules was powerless to effect reforms. Was it surprising that the condition of the Satnamis was deteriorating?[121] The Shri Path Pradarshak Sabha seized upon the fact that the Satnami Mahasabha was not a registered body and turned it into an instrument of its indictment. It carried the critique further when a notice, obviously directed at the Mahasabha, expressly forbade any other organization from prosecuting the aims and objectives of the Path Pradarshak Sabha.[122] In 1940 the Sabha made its final effort to organize a large gathering of Satnamis to press the government to categorize the Satnamis as Hindus rather than as Harijans.[123] This endeavor once again failed. The Path Pradarshak Sabha did not have any success with the provincial government but within a few years, in the early 1940s, the All India Satnami Mahasabha, still under the leadership of Naindas, Anjordas, and Agamdas, had changed its name to the All India Hindu Satnami Mahasabha.[124]

The other challenge to the Satnami Mahasabha stemmed from divisions between the gurus in the claim over the *gaddi*, which came to be articulated in the realm of institutional politics in the 1940s. The Satnami Mahasabha had projected Agamdas as the guru of the Satnamis. Agamdas had acquired a bungalow in Raipur, developed effective links with the Congress leader Ravishankar Shukla, and had been nominated a member of the C.P. legislative council.[125] During the civil disobedience movement a few Satnamis had courted arrest during forest *satyagrahas* in Baloda Bazar and other parts of Raipur, and during the 1937 elections to the legislative council the Satnami Mahasabha had supported the Congress. Agamdas and his allies Naindas and Anjordas had become members of the legislative council.[126] At the same time, Bhandar, the original seat of the guru, had remained in the hands of the brothers Muktavandas, Jagtarandas, and Atibaldas. In 1937 Muktavandas had been imprisoned for seven years for "inciting" his servants to beat up a tenant.[127] Soon after the guru's release he was contacted by members of the All India Scheduled Caste Federation (AISCF). Muktavandas and the AISCF sought to replace Agamdas and the Congress and laid claim to the allegiance of the Satnamis.[128]

The All India Scheduled Caste Federation had been formally set up in July 1942 under the patronage of Dr. Ambedkar as a national political platform of the depressed classes.[129] Over the next two years the AISCF made vigorous efforts to develop branches all over India.[130] The connections between the AISCF and Muktavandas were forged by H. C. Kosare, an Assistant Public Relations Officer in the Employment Exchange, Raipur, Ramdas Mahar, a protege of Dr. Ambedkar and clerk in the Raipur District Commissioner's office, and Khemji Bhiwande, a Sanitary Inspector in the Municipal Council at Raipur.[131] The three non-Brahman Maharashtrians had set up the Chhattisgarh chapter of the AISCF in 1945. In February 1946 Muktavandas had traveled to Nagpur to meet the leaders of the Schedule Caste Federation and had been offered the presidentship of the Chhattisgarh Scheduled Caste Federation.[132] Muktavandas had accepted the offer. By the end of 1946 fifty-three prominent Satnamis had become members of the Scheduled Caste Federation and Muktavandas had directed the Satnamis to have faith in Dr. Ambedkar and not to support the Congress, which did nothing for their community.[133] The Chhattisgarh Scheduled Caste Federation launched a drive to win the support of the Satnamis in October 1947. It decided to hold a meeting on 24 October, the day of *dashera* and the *puja* of the Satnami guru at Bhandar. A pamphlet issued in the name of guru Muktavandas extended an invitation to the leaders of the Scheduled Caste Federation and directed Satnamis to be present for guru *puja*. Ten thousand Satnamis were expected to attend the meeting, which was to be addressed by P. N. Rajbhog, General Secretary of the AISCF, and Bal Gaekwad, President of the Bombay provincial SCF. The meeting at Bhandar was a part of a larger endeavor by the leaders of the Scheduled Caste Federation to organize the Scheduled Castes on a separate electoral basis for elections to the Parliament.[134] In their speeches in the Central Provinces, the Scheduled Caste Federation spokespersons had criticized the Congress and its leadership, particularly Gandhi—opposing caste Hindus and capitalists, they spoke in favor of labor-kisan and Scheduled Castes unity. Before the meeting at Bhandar the government was worried that the "object of Rajbhog and other Scheduled Caste leaders was clearly to utilize this religious gathering to do propaganda of the political type, as they had been doing in Bihar and elsewhere, in which they had been preaching things likely to cause enmity between castes and communities, subversive of public safety and tranquillity." In a preemptive move the government arrested Rajbhog, other Scheduled Caste leaders, Muktavandas, and three Satnami *mahants*. The guru *puja* was held without the guru. The promised speeches were not delivered. Only a thousand Satnamis were present.[135]

The Satnami Mahasabha responded to the alliance between Muktavandas and the Scheduled Caste Federation leadership by organizing a fair and a guru *puja* on *dashera* at Khadua, the village of Agamdas. Evidently it also drew up an effective strategy of propaganda to counter its rivals. A day after *dashera*, Rajbhog in a brief letter in Marathi to Dada Saheb Gaekwad wrote, "our rival party consisting of Satnamis and Harijans have conceived another meeting and have issued leaflets. This party is being supported by the Government Khandikar party and these people have prejudiced the people that (1) Satnamis and Ambedkar's party will be converted to Islam. (2) Ambedkar's party has been donated a sum of rupees two crores [twenty million] for the purpose."[136] A group of Muktavandas's supporters issued a leaflet that criticized the provincial government's action of arresting the guru and SCF leaders, and countered the allegations of the Satnami Mahasabha by emphasizing the Hindu credentials of the Satnami guru.[137]

We do not know what came out of Muktavandas hitching his fortunes to the cause of the All India Scheduled Caste Federation. From the end of the 1940s the divisions between the gurus were articulated and played out along factional divides within the provincial Congress. For the moment the Satnami Mahasabha had triumphed. In 1950 Agamdas was chosen as a Congress parliamentary candidate from Chhattisgarh and won the election. In the words of a Satnami, Agamdas had established the guru *gaddi* in the *rajdhani*, the capital, Delhi. This moment of success was possibly all the sweeter because different histories, seeking to transform the Satnamis, now lay in the past. It is to these histories that I now turn.

CHAPTER SEVEN

Contending Histories: Old Stories and New Pasts

During the late 1920s and 1930s different efforts to transform the Satnamis and redefine their identity turned the past of the group into a disputed terrain. History was seized upon as a negotiable and reworkable resource by contending accounts of the past, which sought to articulate the present. At work here were processes of the constitution of truths, the fashioning of traditions, the making of myths, and the institutionalization of pasts featuring a wide-ranging interplay of meaning and power in the construction of three distinct histories of the Satnamis, the subject of this chapter.

In the wider context of the activities of the Satnami Mahasabha, Baba Ramchandra gave the Satnamis the gift of what he considered a canonical history. This was a part of his larger bid to regulate and reform the community. The Maharashtrian Brahman's preliminary notes in the form of the *Vanshavali* had not compromised the internal order and meaning of Satnami myths. In *Satnam Sagar*, his effort toward an "authoritative" history, many of these myths were jettisoned, the others fundamentally transformed. The Satnami gurus were divested of their attributes of authority and imbued with the aspect of anonymous ascetics, bit players in an essentially Brahmanical drama. The salvation of the Satnamis now lay in following the path of the Vedas.[1]

The past also loomed large in the constitution and the endeavors of the Shri Path Pradarshak Sabha in both its incarnations, when the Sabha initially engaged with the tenets of Christianity and upon its later turn to the task of ridding the Satnamis of the stigma of being Harijans. In the beginning, the former catechist of the American Evangelical Mission, M. D. Singh, variously cited recent historical events, drew upon Satnami myths and conceptions of the past, and engaged with critical elements of contemporary popular political discourse and the ruses of orality to authenticate his address and present himself as the bearer of the word of *satnam.* Afterward, the Sabha's efforts to get the government to classify the Satnamis as Hindus, rather than as Harijans, led it to construct a genealogy of the group. The casting of Ghasidas as the successor of the Buddha and Ravidas, a discussion of beef eating in ancient India, and an invocation of the rhetoric of non-Brahman movements all played a role here. But the central place went to the radical twist that the Sabha gave to the ancient laws of Manu in its construction of the origins and the past of the Satnamis. This history confounded the classificatory schemes of caste, held in place by the principles of hypergamy and hypogamy, and reworked the symbolism of the seed and the field, which maintains the boundaries of caste in patrilineal Hindu South Asia.

The final foray into the terrain of the Satnami past discussed in this chapter was closely linked to the missionaries' millenarian master plan of mass movements. Early missionary work initiated by the German Evangelical Mission Society in Chhattisgarh had centered on the Satnamis. As the missionary enterprise grew—there was an increase in the number of missionary organizations and an expansion of evangelical efforts—there was a corresponding move to work with other social groups. The Satnamis had persistently confounded and frustrated missionary hopes, but they continued to remain a tantalizing prospect for the project of mass conversions. In 1935 a missionary followed Baba Ramchandra in constructing a history for the Satnamis. The writing of *Satyanami Panth aur Shri Gosain Ghasidas Girodvasi* was closely tied to the evangelical effort of M. M. Paul, an Indian missionary, to initiate a mass movement among the Satnamis.[2] The tract forged a complex relationship with the oral traditions of Satnampanth and the Satnami converts. The myths about the gurus were reworked to unfold and play out the truth of Christ.

These three endeavors involved the determined appropriation of the past of the Satnamis to other histories. It is perhaps only in order that my final steps in constructing a history of the Satnamis should discuss these efforts, which both consciously and inadvertently underscored the significance of their past for members of the community. There could also be another lesson here. In separate ways, these rival narratives claimed to relate true stories and map authentic genealogies, and often led to unintended consequences. Yet none of them succeeded in their common objective—toward different purposes—of fixing the meaning of the Satnami past within a final authoritative homogenized history. In other words, this chapter focuses on the fashioning of histories which failed to realize their end in the past.

Sacred Genealogies

In the midst of the workings of idioms of authority and the drawing up of engendered agendas, Baba Ramchandra's attempt to reform the Satnamis also led him to give them a formal history. Under the pseudonym of Santdas Sant he wrote the *Satnam Sagar* which claimed to be an *itihas* (history) of the group.[3] The text was dedicated to the "Mentor of True Religion," Saheb Agamdasji Maharaj, the universal preceptor of Satnamis. It reproduced a photograph of the Satnami guru (see Figure 2). Agamdas was pictured with his chest bare but for a *janeu* and a *kanthi*, and wearing a simple white *dhoti* (a garment tied around the waist). Here the guru sits before two books, which look like Hindu sacred texts, placed next to a *patra* (vessel) containing *gangajal* (holy water from the river Ganga) and other implements of Hindu *puja*. In the representation of the guru's authority, elaborate retinues and prerogatives of royalty had been replaced by the insignia of the Brahman *purohit*. As the next step, the text was fashioned as the Satnami *Gita*. In two verses from the *Bhagvad Gita*, Krishna explained to Arjun that he took an incarnation whenever sin increased to protect the pure, destroy the wicked, and restore order and faith in the world.[4] The *Satnam Sagar*, like the *Gita*, was constructed in the form of a dialogue between a master and his disciple.

The master was cast as a Vaishnava ascetic who had conquered desire. The disciple, a seeker of truth, was dissatisfied with the selfish and hollow people who inhabited the world and with the general futility of life. He met the master in a serene forest next to the village of Girod, which stood in the middle of the "home of true happiness, a beautiful land by the name of South Kosala."[5] If the reference to Girod as the abode of the master was a concession to the Satnami veneration of the village as the birthplace of Ghasidas, the dialogue between the *gosain* (ascetic master) and the *satkhoji* (seeker of truth) turned the tables on the Satnami pattern of beliefs. Baba Ramchandra rehearsed the ideas and categories of classical Hindu philosophy. The account began with a description of the nature of god and life. The fashioning of god as *satnam*—who was formless, undivided, and homogeneous—was rooted in Advaita or Vedantic beliefs. All life was grounded in

Figure 2. *Satnami guru, circa 1928. Source: Santdas,* Sanskshipt Satnam Sagar, Bhag 1, Itihas *(Raipur, 1929)*

nature, which was composed of three ingredients: *sata* (goodness), *raja* (passion), and *tama* (darkness). It had eight divisions: the principle of primordial essence, ego, sound, touch, effulgence, taste, smell, mind, and blossoming. This rather esoteric description of nature derived from Vedic and Puranic notions and Sankhya philosophy.[6] The Satnamis were also introduced to Puranic notions of time. In a dense and long passage they were told about celestial years and human years, partial deluges and great deluges, destruction and creation, and the time according to Brahma.[7]

And what were the Satnamis to do as they lived through the ebb and flow of life, interspersed with partial deluges and great deluges? The answer lay in following the Vedas.[8] Through the mediation of the figure of the ascetic master, Baba Ramchandra voiced familiar themes, many of which had been played out in "Satnami Panchkanya Dehati." The path of the Vedas, the Satnamis were instructed, enjoined them not to eat meat or to drink liquor. Men and women had to undertake and fulfill the vow of nonviolence. The body and the senses were to be kept pure. The sexual union between a man and a woman, husband and wife, was to be geared toward procreation, and the control over *vyabhichar* (wrong sexual behavior) required a man to treat another man's wife as his mother. The Satnamis were asked to inculcate modesty, calm, patience, kindness, and simplicity. These virtues allowed men to face criticism, cope with adversity, and remain detached from worldly concerns. True knowledge, words, and deeds led the traveler of the path of truth to the abode of liberated souls. This was the way of *karma yoga*, the path of performing the duties of one's station without an expectation of results.[9] Of course, there was nothing new about this construction of the ascetic-householder, which derived from both Brahmanical Hinduism and the emphases of popular sectarian formations. Some of the themes in fact echoed the concerns of Satnampanth. At the same time, the text emphasized that the normative order was encoded in the Vedas, which were "the essence of all religions/sects, the pure voice of true religion."[10] For Satnamis to believe in *satya dharma* (true faith) and *satnam*—now constructed in terms of the principles of Vedanta—was to follow the Vedas, which embodied the word of god.

How then did *Satnam Sagar* handle the problem of the low ritual status of the Satnamis? The text offered a solution by working with the notion that caste was premised not on birth but on a right way of life. In *satya yuga* (the epoch of truth) everyone walked along the path of truth and honesty, consequently there were no divisions between human beings.[11] In *treta* and *dwapar*, the epochs that followed, swarms of selfish men had imposed differences between human beings. Ram and Krishna had come down to earth and had restored order and faith in the world.[12] With the advent of *kali yuga*, the final epoch of evil, men had become violent, lustful, and angry. As a

result, differences and divisions had been reimposed between human beings. The struggle against these evil practices and the drive to establish the
path of truth underlay the efforts of the Buddha, Shankaracharya, and
Ravidas.[13] The text emphasized that divisions of caste were artificial and the
essence of true faith lay in following the right mode of life.

And what of the Satnami gurus? The *Satnam Sagar* selectively invoked
the myths of Satnampanth to situate the gurus within the tradition of Hindu
saints. Ghasidas was cast as the successor to the Buddha, Shankaracharya,
and Ravidas.[14] While the account briefly recounted aspects of the family life
of the guru, the miracles and encounters of Ghasidas, which played a
prominent role in Satnami myths, were removed from the picture. Ghasidas
had to await old age for the confirmation of his status as a holy man. It was
only when *gosain* Ghasidas had fulfilled his obligations as a householder
that *jagdish* (Lord of the World) appeared before him. Ghasidas, overwhelmed by the experience, became a renouncer and started meditating
under a tree outside the village of Girod.[15] After a year, he was visited by a
lion who asked for food. Ghasidas offered his body. The lion revealed himself as an incarnation of god and asked Ghasidas to prevent killing and violence in the world.[16] The Satnami myth had undergone a fundamental
transformation. The lion had acquired attributes of Narahari or Narsingh,
the fourth incarnation of the god Vishnu, and the resistance offered by
Ghasidas to *satnampurush* had been replaced by willing submission and
complete obedience to the Lord of the World. Ghasidas followed the
master's instructions and revealed the true path of abstinence and nonviolence to the Satnamis.[17] Satnami myths were also recast in the construction
of the figure of Balakdas, where the guru's regal attributes were substituted
by the aspect of a mendicant.[18] The vows of Balakdas in turn had been fulfilled by Agardas, Agarmandas, and Agamdas.[19] The *Satnam Sagar* incorporated Ghasidas and Balakdas into a mythic tradition composed of an as-
sorted amalgam of Brahmanical and upper-caste beliefs. The Satnami gurus
were presented as saviors of the Hindu faith.

We have little direct evidence for the ways in which Baba
Ramchandra's text was read and understood by the Satnamis. The complexity of language and the unfamiliar ideas distanced it from the religious
universe of the Satnamis. At any rate, the group inflected the interventionist voice of its upper-caste benefactor by selectively appropriating certain Hindu practices. Satnamis recount that it was from the late 1920s
that Hindu religious texts came to form a part of the modes of worship
within the community. "Under the Satnami Mahasabha, All India and
Chhattisgarh our people started reading the *Ramayan*, *Gita* and
Satyanarayan ki Katha."[20] We do not know if there was a corresponding move
to win the services of the Brahman *purohit.* Satnami oral accounts interpret

the absence of the *purohit* as the group's continued rejection of these religious functionaries. "We were self-sufficient. No, there was no place for the lying coward of a Brahman *pandit.*"[21] Satnamis with a measure of literacy came to narrate *Satyanarayan ki Katha,* read the *Gita,* and recite verses of *Ramcharitmanas.* A reading of these texts was increasingly situated alongside a recitation of the *kathas* of the gurus during the life-cycle rituals among the Satnamis.[22] The Satnami appropriation of the sacred texts of Hinduism could extend their challenge to Brahmans. A fifty year old delighted in the irony: "Our *samaj* learned the *Puran* and *shastras.* When Brahmans from Benares came Satnami *pandits* beat them in *shastraarth* (debate over the meaning and interpretation of shastras)."[23] The Satnami Mahasabha's reworking of its relationship with more mainstream Hindu traditions, actively promoted by *Satnam Sagar,* was thus accompanied by a challenge by the members of the community to the authority of Brahmans.

Nonetheless, Baba Ramchandra's charter for the Satnamis found its way into the genealogy of the group mapped by the Shri Path Pradarshak Sabha. We have noted in chapter 6 that this organizational initiative, a rival of the Satnami Mahasabha, had initially flirted with principles of Christianity before launching a drive to irrevocably invest the Satnamis with Hindu status. History was central to its efforts. The very moment of the constitution of the Shri Path Pradarshak Sabha was premised upon a play with the past.

> When Edward VIII gave up his throne and George V [sic] took his place, when provincial freedom [autonomy] was arranged. Then the word of Satnam reached me, M. D. Singh, and it said, O son of man rise and go amidst my Satnamis, and announce to the heavens to listen and to the earth to pay heed, for Satnam says that I have nurtured these children [the Satnamis] but they have fought with me. Oh, how this caste is full of sinners. This group is laden with irreligion. The people of this lineage have committed such immoral deeds. These children have got ruined. Those who were village proprietors are now peasants, and the peasants of the past have been turned into forest dwellers. Their country is in the hands of aliens. Oh, their condition is terrible, there is no one to look after them, leopards and jackals born among their midst are ruining them. So listen O son of man, you rise and go among my beloved Satnamis and warn them that if they continue to sin they will suffer further. [Tell them] Turn to me and give up sin, then I will turn to you and my blessings on the lineage will increase its honor in the world, this is the word of Satnam.[24]

In this announcement, the former catechist of the American Evangelical Mission, M. D. Singh was the bearer of the voice and the word of *satnam.*

The first step in securing the authenticity of the address was the citing of definite and very recent events of political history involving English kings and the British government, which also served to reinforce its authority. *Satnam*'s command to M. D. Singh to go among the Satnamis and redeem the community from its fallen condition was reminiscent of the words spoken by *satnampurush* to Ghasidas in their early encounters that were retold in the myths of the group. It also played upon the Satnami conception of their being the original inhabitants of Chhattisgarh, later displaced by outsiders who continued to usurp the lands of the group. The reference to the occupation of Satnami land by aliens/foreigners was possibly also a simultaneous and veiled critical hint at the rule of the country by the British, which was an important part of contemporary political and cultural discourse.[25] Finally, the voice of the leaflet seemed to conflate the voices of Satnam and M. D. Singh. Was this, perhaps, another example of the written form being rooted within orality, where it did not really matter who made a particular statement so long as it carried divine import? Or was the move more deliberate? M. D. Singh went on to become the *acharya* (revered teacher) of the Shri Path Pradarshak Sabha. But the Sabha itself soon altered its agenda and a different order of history came to the fore.

Shri Path Pradarshak Sabha's drive that the Satnamis, instead of being categorized as Harijans, be classified along with higher Hindu castes rested upon its claim to the origins of the group. The initiative addressed the community.

> Today we want to tell you what place you occupy in the sacred texts, and the category to which you belong. As it is written, *Karavera Nishadatu Charmakarah prasyute* (see Manusmriti X-36) or the Chamar Karavar was born of a Vedhi woman from Nishad. Now, Nishad is the son of a Brahman (Manu, X-8) and Vedhi is the product of a Vaishya father and a Brahman mother (Manu X-11–17). So think [about] who you are. In a way both the seed and the field are good, why then is the name of the resultant fruit different from that of the seed. Is this rule of difference proper. It emerges from [true] law that the fruit should be no different from the seed, but this is not what actually obtains.[26]

This claim to the upper-caste origins of the group, also reiterated by the Sabha in its appeal to the government of the Central Provinces, seized on the laws of Manu to turn them upon their head.[27]

The account's actual citation of evidence from the *Manu Samhita* did not deviate from the master text.[28] Karavara, the leather worker, was indeed born of the union of a Nishada male and a Vaideha woman: Nishada was the product of the *anuloma* (hypergamous) union of a Brahman father and a Shudra mother, and Vaidehaka the progeny of a *pratiloma* (hypogamous) marriage of a Vaishya man and a Brahman woman. But there was also more to the code compiled by Manu. Tambiah has argued that "the permutations and derivations of new castes through mixed unions [of Varnas] and the assignation of status positions to them on the basis of *anuloma* and *pratiloma* principles . . . exemplify a mode of formal derivation of a complex system of classification."[29] In this matrix, the *anuloma* marriage of a Brahman with a woman who was three Varna degrees lower led to the birth of Nishada, where the son stood "distinctly downgraded" and censured. Here the union of the parents, although in the right direction, was explicitly in violation of the law because it crossed the barrier between the twice-born Brahman and the once-born Shudra: the offspring was, therefore, said to have the duties of Shudras, namely the catching of fish. Vaidehaka, in turn, was the progeny of a *pratiloma* union, which by going "against the hair" was in the inverse order of castes and for this reason was heavily censured and morally condemned. Manu categorized Vaidehaka, guardians in the harem, as third from the top in the hierarchical order that characterized his list of six *pratilomas*, where the issues of all such unions were declared to be excluded from the community of Aryans: the "distinctive character of these *pratiloma* progeny is that they are assigned to an infinite number of base occupations practiced in general today by a varied number of polluted castes, the majority of them falling into the category called Harijans." Now, according to the laws of Manu, Karavara's status as the offspring of the union between issues of a condemned *anuloma* (Nishada) and a despised *pratiloma* (Vaidehaka) reproduced and increased the initial degradation built into these marriages.[30] And the entire scheme was held together by the conception of the seed and the earth—provided by the man and the woman, respectively—in the symbolic elaboration of social and biological reproduction. The limits to the acceptability of "good seed" falling upon "bad earth" were set by the degree of difference in their quality, and "bad seed" entering "good earth" constituted a moral outrage.[31]

The sharp interpretative turn of the little leaflet and the short statements drawn up by the Shri Path Pradarshak Sabha introduced a radical innovative twist to this larger tale. The Sabha claimed that the Satnamis embodied a high ritual status because they had descended from Brahman stock. The original Charmakara, Karavara was born of a union where his father and mother—the seed and the earth—were both pure. This invocation of the essential purity of the seed and the field at the moment of the origin of the group questioned its ascribed status as low untouchables. The new history paid no attention to the rules governing the generation of hierarchies of caste through mixed unions of Varnas and also reworked the principles underlying the symbolism of the seed and the earth that were implicated in the maintenance of boundaries of caste and the creation of new *jatis.* Instead, the laws of Manu were confronted with a novel legality in which the fruit could never be different from the seed. In this scheme, the purity of the original partners of a union that begat a caste inhered and decided its status in the present. It relegated the regulations of hypergamy and hypogamy to the margins and rendered them useless. Clearly, the past fashioned by the Shri Path Pradarshak Sabha confounded the classificatory scheme of castes, informed by *anuloma* and *pratiloma* principles, that lay meticulously codified in the *Manu Samhita.* It also invested the symbolism of the "seed and the earth," which is closely linked to the reproduction of the patrilineal Hindu caste order in South Asia, with new meanings. The classification of Satnamis as Harijans was patently mistaken and unjust.

The Shri Path Pradarshak Sabha reinforced its account of the superiority of Satnamis over Harijans by staking further claims on the past. It argued before the government that according to Hindu sacred texts the Aryans used to eat beef, and it was regarded as prized meat meant to be served in honor of guests. Only after the intervention of the Buddha did the Aryans, including Brahmans, stop eating beef. Similarly, among the Chamars of Chhattisgarh, guru Ghasidas had put an end to the practice of eating beef. The Chamars became Satnamis, a civilized caste, and stopped eating impure substances and shunned all intoxicants.[32] At any rate, the Sabha argued, the Satnamis belonged to the lineage of Ravidas who was a Brahman in his previous birth. Earlier the group was pure and used to wear the sacred thread, but it had then left the path of good and taken to the ways of evil. The account cited the *Bahakta Birdavali* of Satnam Press, Banaras and Baba Ramchandra's *Satnam Sagar* here.[33] The patient and pure, brave and calm Ghasidas had been born into Ravidas's lineage. He had once again made the Chamars walk the straight and narrow path of virtue and turned them into Satnamis.[34] Finally, the Shri Path Pradarshak Sabha seemed to seize upon and rework the rhetoric of non-Brahman movements and wider Satnami conceptions of their origins when it claimed that they were the original inhabitants of India, and therefore distinct from Harijans. All this served to establish the ritual status of the Satnamis as fallen Brahmans who were on par with the service castes of the barber, the washerman, and the ironsmith, and also with the Panka, who were largely Kabirpanthis.[35] In tune with this testimony of the reordered origins and pasts of the Satnamis, the Sabha had appealed to the government that the group should not be classified as Harijans but as Hindus. We have seen that the initiative had failed. More than fifty years later, during my field work, a Satnami who vaguely recalled his maternal grandfather's association with the Shri Path Pradarshak Sabha had repeatedly reiterated that Brahmans had descended from a prostitute. Was this perhaps a radical oral reworking of the earlier written charter's invocation of Nishada and Vaidehaka, where Nishada was removed from the picture, the Vaideha woman (as member of a caste who were the guardians of the harem) was turned into a prostitute, and the Satnamis were replaced by Brahmans as her descendants? Are we, by a somewhat long shot, in the face of one of the many possible unintended consequences of the history constructed by the Sabha, in this case played out in 1990? In the 1930s there was another past awaiting the Satnamis.

Satnami Myths, Convert Tales, and Missionary Stories

The 1920s and 1930s witnessed the reformulation of the policy of the different missionary groups. Chhattisgarh was witnessing what a missionary ruefully referred to as a "lull in conversions."[36] The missionaries were disillusioned with the practice of settling converts on mission stations, which served to perpetuate their dependence without making further gains to the faith. These converts at mission stations in turn had continued to defy the missionaries in fashioning their understanding of marriage and sexual transgression and could also question and challenge missionary authority. In the 1930s, for instance, the converts of the mission station at Bisrampur drew upon the missionary injunctions against adultery and the principles of maintenance of boundaries of groups, embedded within rules of caste and sect, to invoke the threat to the chastity of "virgin Christian sisters" and turn the honor of women into an evocative metaphor for order within the community and a symbol that constituted its boundary. Indeed, the converts' criticism of the missionaries here highlighted their uses of Christianity. Their initiative centered on a pervasive us/them, community/outsider divide. The community was formed primarily around the converts of Bisrampur, and all employees who did not belong to the mission station were outsiders. What was protested was the increasing intrusion of these outsiders into the affairs of the community. Moreover, efforts by missionaries to dismantle the ties of dependence of the converts and to make the congregation self-dependent got entangled with their defense of these outsiders. There was a disruption of the normative economy—the pattern of expectations and obligations—of the Christian community of Bisrampur. The figure of the missionary was transformed from the benevolent master of the past into a tyrannical *malguzar*. Finally, the assertion of independence by the Christian congregation of Bisrampur involved a defense of the paternalist ties that had bound them to the missionaries through complex ties of dependence and control: deference to the missionaries was one part self-preservation and one part the calculated extraction of land, employment, and charity. The converts worked on missionary rhetoric in their practice and their challenge to missionary authority was constructed in an idiom of evangelical Christianity.[37] The alternative measure of letting converts continue to live in their original homes in the hope that they would draw in other members of kin, caste, and village had created its own attendant problems. The converts, rather than winning fellow adherents to Christianity, often sought to be readmitted into their caste after the payment of a fine, and the missionaries and their workers found it difficult to counter the pressure to take this step, exerted on the converts by kin and caste elders, *malguzars* and dominant members of the village community.

The answer lay in turning the attention from individuals and families to entire groups. This tied in with the increasing missionary concern with the "indigenisation of the church." The missionaries saw themselves as engaged in training the Christians of India. Their aim was the eventual transfer of the church into the hands of Indian leadership.[38] The Indian nationalist movement and the idea of a free India as a possibility put the issue forcefully on the missionary agenda. The missionaries, in fact, took a cue from the efforts at large-scale mobilization under the umbrella organization of the Indian National Congress and the programmatic endeavors of the Arya Samaj and Gandhi to bring the untouchables into the fold of Hinduism. They formulated their alternative vision and policy of mass movements. If India had to be transformed into a Christian nation, a matter of certain urgency, it could only be carried out through large-scale mass conversions of entire groups and sections of the population.[39] Here, the Gandas and the Satnamis constituted two groups who held the possibility of the beginnings of a mass movement in the area covered by the American Evangelical Mission. At the same time, the real possibilities of the Gandas lay in the Khariar (western Orissa) chapter of the mission. The Satnamis of Pithora offered the way forward for Christianity in Chhattisgarh.

Pithora was a *zamindari* due southeast of Raipur. It had first formed an outstation of the mission establishment in the town of Mahasamund. In 1930 an Indian pastor, the Reverend M. M. Paul took charge of the substation. Large parts of Pithora, along with the surrounding *zamindaris*, were covered by forests. The open areas of the *zamindaris* were inhabited by settled agriculturists who were, for the most part, Gonds and Satnamis, and the forests by tribes who followed methods of slash-and-burn cultivation.[40] Moreover, Pithora lay close to Rajim, the heartland of Chhattisgarhi Brahmanical conservatism. Rajim was, in fact, the home base for activists like Sunderlal Sharma, the Hindu Congress leader who had adopted Arya Samaji tactics of *shuddhikaran* (purification) and the distribution of sacred threads to reclaim low castes into the fold of Hinduism. The twin factors of social geography—the pattern of distribution of population and the proximity of the area to Rajim—helped to set the agenda for the missionaries. The influence and pull of Hindu conservatism, Arya Samaji activities, and the tightly knit social organization of the Gonds in the area made them hostile to the missionaries.[41] The missionaries in turn did not have the resources to work among the various tribal groups who migrated because of their pattern of slash-and-burn cultivation. This left the Satnamis as the obvious target group who fit the bill for the evangelical plan of mass movements.

The Satnamis of the Pithora and Phingeshwar *zamindaris* and the surrounding areas had been left relatively untouched by the reform initiatives sponsored by the Satnami Mahasabha. Moreover, the Satnami relationship with the Arya Samaj leaders had been uneasy here. The Satnami converts to Christianity who had been reclaimed into the Hindu fold through *shuddhikaran* (purification) had continued to face the problem of not getting the services of the barber and the washerman.[42] M. M. Paul and his band of catechists countered the initiatives of these activists. The missionary invested his hopes of a mass movement among the Satnamis in a short tract, *Satyanami Panth aur Shri Gosain Ghasidas Girodvasi.*

The entire text, including the title, involved a play with *satya* (truth). The tract seized upon and selectively appropriated aspects of the myths and legend history of Satnampanth to reorder and fashion them for an alternative account. The plot, according to which events unfolded in this narrative, centered on the "truth" of Christ. It led the Satnamis inevitably and inexorably to their destiny in Christ. The appropriation of *sat* for Christianity was sought to be achieved through *bhajans* (devotional songs), which were addressed to *satnam*. The refrain, "I sing your virtues *satnam*, I sing your virtues," rings through the songs. *Satnam* is not only a form of worship but a mode of being: "I live for you I die for you I shall give up my life for you. In life and death you are my *thakur* [personal god]."[43] The persuasive power of the songs, in fact, derived from their construction in a specifically vernacular idiom. The device of repetition underscored the note of *bhakti* for *satnam*, and the rhythmic pattern, cadence, and texture of the *bhajans* followed the structure of Satnami devotional songs. Moreover, the motive images and metaphors of the new *bhajans* were drawn from the belief system of the Satnamis. "I shall not worship the gods of the past, I shall throw them out of the house, I shall worship the god whose form is like the wind and *satnam* shall be mine." The discarding of the idols for a boundless god was evocative of Ghasidas throwing the idols of the gods and goddesses of the Hindu pantheon onto a rubbish heap. Similarly, *baikunth* (heaven) and *amrit*, critical elements in the patterns of belief among the Satnamis, figured in the vision of heaven within the songs. At the same time, these *bhajans* effected a major change within the familiar structure of rhythmic patterns and images. It emerged at the end of the songs that the *satnam* worshiped, venerated, and lived was Guru Yishu, Jesus Christ.[44]

The narrative opened with a rhetorical strategy that established a claim to authenticity. Nineteen years earlier, the author had met the ninety-year-old man, Anjori Paulus, who in his youth had stayed with Ghasidas and had then accepted Jesus Christ. During this meeting Anjori Paulus had narrated the life and teachings of Ghasidas and the despicable deeds of the later gurus. The authentic voice—Anjori Paulus had observed Ghasidas, seen the later gurus, and witnessed Christ—validated the missionary narrative. Second, the author, an inveterate and relentless seeker of truth, had discussed what Anjori Paulus had told him with other Satnamis who had raised little objection. Finally, the account had been accepted by key members within the organizational hierarchy of Satnampanth. The need for the tract had arisen due to the ignorance and confusion among Satnamis.

> When I go into a village I find a number of people addressing each other with [the greeting] Satnam. Then I ask them who is Satnam and I get the answer, "One who is within us." So I get another opportunity to ask how many such Satnam are there who are within everyone. Most people say, "What we know is that our Guru Ghasidas is in every house."

The passage played upon the lack of a fixed anthropomorphic form of *satnam* and the conflation of the identities of *satnampurush* and Ghasidas among the Satnamis. The tract sought to end this confusion and ignorance.[45]

The missionary drew up a history for the Satnamis. The account began with the sect of Satnamis founded by Jagjiwandas in north India, which we have discussed in chapter 2.

> This [Satnam]Panth was started in 1760 by Shri Jagjiwandas. The Panth was first found in villages near the Lucknow district. Shri Jagjiwandas was born in 1738 in the village of Sarda in Ayodhya. . . . After Jagjiwandas's death in 1761 his followers buried him in the village of Kotwa in Lucknow where a memorial now stands.[46]

The passage used standard accounts such as gazetteers and the earlier writings of missionaries and cited dates, names of villages, and identifiable landmarks such as a *samadhi* (memorial). At the same time, the account also abandoned chronology when it stated that Jagjiwandas had close contacts with Ramanuj, Kabir, and Ghasidas.[47] The conflation of four hundred years of chronological-historical time, at first sight, seems to contradict the apparent emphasis on accuracy of dates and factual detail. At the same time, the use of specific markers along with the abandoning of chronology served to display learning. The narrative, in what appears as a reiteration of orality, had spatialized time and established genealogical connections between gurus of kindred sects. The two simultaneous movements combined to augment the authority of the narrative.

The early life of Ghasidas described in the account drew upon Satnami myths about the guru, particularly his devotional bent of mind in spite of a low station in life. A little later, however, the missionary narrative introduced a variation on the theme. Ghasidas, bereaved after the death of his favorite child and disillusioned with gods and goddesses who could not save him, did not retire to a forest near Girod. Instead he set off for Lucknow. In Satnami myths the trials and ordeals that Ghasidas had to undergo were set up by *satnampurush* in the forest mountain of Sonakhan, while the missionary account cast these as problems encountered during a long and difficult journey to Lucknow. In villages near Lucknow, Ghasidas encountered people who greeted each other with a sublime and sacred word, *satyanam*. On making further enquiries the Chamar from Chhattisgarh found out that these people were devotees of Jagjiwandas who preached a belief in a true god. Ghasidas met Jagjiwandas, agreed to become his disciple, and stayed with him to learn about *satyanam*. When Ghasidas decided to leave, Jagjiwandas gave him a guru *mantra* (incantation) and bade him farewell. An illiterate Ghasidas forgot the incantation but remembered the other things he had heard and learned. After the return of the intrepid traveler the Chamars were happy to see him alive. Ghasidas's acts of piety and devotion increased. There was a rise in his stature. People began to respect him.[48] The variation introduced in the missionary account was critical for the unfolding of the narrative. It removed *satnampurush* from the picture. It was through the agency of Jagjiwandas that Ghasidas had learned about *satyanam*. He had been primed and prepared for his role as the bearer of others' voices, words, and visions.

Ghasidas was ready to meet the missionaries. His many admirers asked Ghasidas to go on a pilgrimage to Jagannath Puri.

> He started on the journey with his older brother. They reached Cuttack and decided to spend the night there. When Ghasidas went to the bazaar to buy provisions he saw that a crowd had gathered there. On reaching near he was amazed to hear the word *satya*. He peered over the crowd and found himself looking at preachers of truth who included a *gora* [white] *saheb*.[49]

The most striking feature of the discourse of the preachers was its sustained and engaging play with *satya*. *Satya* initially drew Ghasidas's attention to the missionaries. The refrain of "Satya Guru Satyanam Satya Ishwar [god]" rang through their speech. The rehearsal of the eternal verities of the Savior—embodied in the "word"—served to fix the meaning of *satya* in Christ. This deity was blameless and offered the only way forward for the redemption of humanity in heaven. The missionary rejection of the idols of the Hindu pantheon and supreme disdain for distinctions based on caste found a resonance in Ghasidas's experience. The new message inscribed itself within Ghasidas's heart. Jagjiwandas had prepared Ghasidas. The missionaries completed the transformation.

Ghasidas returned to Girod. When the Chamars came forward to receive the *prasad* (food of the gods) from Jagannath Puri and bowed before Ghasidas he turned the tables on their expectations and beliefs.

> O brothers you have come to me to get *prasad*. But these are useless things. Listen, I met *pendra* [white] *saheb* and he patiently told me the story of *satyanam*—and said that it sets you on the right path—so listen to me brothers—I am not your guru—I am a Ganda like the Gandas in our villages who announce the orders of *sarkar*. In the same way I have turned into a Ganda to repeat the orders of *saheb sarkar pendra* guru—*pendra saheb* has come with only one *satyanam*—he has come from the north—he has brought the *Jumma Dabdar* [Bible] with him—that will destroy the religious books of the Brahmans—the Book cries out the name of *satnam* and tells his story. And whoever believes in it and lets it enter his heart that person becomes a *satya yugi*. *Pendra saheb* will make his bungalow at every twelve *kos* [a measure of distance, about two miles] and these twelve *kos* will be illuminated by light—now give up killing goats and pigs, give up taking the name of Ram, and throw out gods and goddesses and *mata* and worship only *satnam* which *pendra saheb* has brought to us.[50]

The textual force of this passage derived from its construction in a rustic rural Chhattisgarhi idiom. The mode of writing followed the immediacy of face-to-face interaction rooted within oral traditions. This was no mere imposition of the author. The passage drew upon the repertoire of the myths of Satnami converts to Christianity about Ghasidas and the missionaries that had developed over seventy years. The Satnami conversion to Christianity had led to a reordering of the myths of the sect among the group. The figure of Ghasidas was not erased from memory. It was transformed. In Satnami myths, Ghasidas had been initiated by *shwet* (white) *satnampurush*. The *shwet*, which connoted qualities of purity, was seized upon and assimilated to the figures of *pendra saheb*, the white missionaries. *Shwet* and *satnam* were signs capable of pressing new associations when situated within the reworked matrix of the myths of Satnami converts. The missionaries and Christ had displaced *satnampurush*. Ghasidas in turn was the watchman of the missionaries who fulfilled his duty of spreading the truth among the people as the bearer of the command of the white missionary *saheb*.

It would be safe to conjecture that both missionaries and Satnami converts contributed to this novel mapping of a Satnami-Christian tradition: a complex interplay and combination of Satnami myths, the oral traditions of the converts, and truths learned from missionary masters. The textual reconstruction of the bold declaration of Ghasidas after his return from Cuttack to Girod chose elements from within this matrix. At the same time, this was not only a matter of a faithful indexing and reproduction of the myths of Satnami converts. The inscription of these beliefs and legends within the text lent them authority and authenticity. Their meanings came to be more securely fixed and systematized by being situated on the axis of the inexorable spread of Christianity.

The text stole from the converts' myths to replace them with the missionary story. It also embellished the tale further. Now,

Ghasidas preached the sermon of *satyanam* between 1820 and 1830 only after he had met the missionaries and discovered the truth of Christ. After his return from Cuttack, in fact, Ghasidas was a man possessed who could only chant the name of *satyanam*. He renounced the world and started meditating in the jungle of Sonakhan. This marked the beginning of Satnampanth. The Chamars came to hear of Ghasidas's devotion and flocked to him in large numbers. Ghasidas performed miracles, granted boons to his followers, and cured the afflicted including barren women with *amrit*. Ghasidas asked his followers to believe only in one *satyanam*, to condemn idol worship, to love others the way one loved the self, and to give up superstitious beliefs in ghosts and demons. There were prohibitions imposed on liquors and intoxicating substances and on meat, red vegetables, *masur*, egg plants, and gourds. He also asked the disciples to control anger, keep their house clean, protect the body from bad habits and intoxicants, keep away from evil, live with each other in harmony, believe in one guru, and remain pure.[51]

The themes and emphases are familiar. But the variation too is significant. The tract reordered the Satnami past through the introduction of broad Christian tenets into the teachings of Ghasidas and by remolding it along the principles of Christianity. The basic teachings of Ghasidas were, however, not enough for an ignorant people. It was possible to glean the existence of one god in Ghasidas's teaching, but he could not put an end to evils such as religious ceremonies and festivals that corrupted minds.[52] The gap could, of course, have been breached by following the way of Christ. Instead, after the death of Ghasidas in 1850 his descendants widened the gap into a chasm, a bottomless pit of degeneration.

The missionary account of the condition of Satnampanth under the later gurus once again drew upon the myths and the legends of the group.

However, this past was reordered by emphasizing the havoc wrought by Ghasidas's descendants. There were two persistent and interrelated themes here: the inordinate vanity, pride, and greed of the gurus and the evils of sexual deviation and profligacy among the Satnamis. The disastrous results of the playing out of these themes were further compounded when Satnami gurus emulated Hindu beliefs and practices. Indeed, according to the missionary, it was this combination of greed and vanity along with Balakdas's efforts to repeat the sexual exploits of the god Krishna that had resulted in the practice of *satlok* in which the guru claimed the first right on all Satnami women, leading to the loss of their chastity. The pattern was also replicated, M. M. Paul continued, when Balakdas ordered the Satnamis to start wearing the *janeu*: the guru's command stemmed from his conceit, the need to emulate Brahmans, and his desire to collect money from the Satnamis among whom the sacred thread was distributed. The distribution of the *janeu* was further accompanied by injunctions to the community, following the rules that governed caste society, not to accept food or water touched by members of other castes including Brahmans. In this way, the missionary argued, caste had not been discarded but had become far more rigid among the Satnamis. Other practices initiated by Balakdas led to a further decline in the morals of the group. The missionary mentioned the practice of *jhanjeri*. It was so loathsome that he could not write about it in the presence of Christ. If "Balakdas had tarred the prestige of the *gaddi* with his despicable practices and had spoilt Satnami minds through his illicit words and deeds," his successors completed the picture of ruin.[53] The missionary's comment was unequivocal: "The guru, his wives, and his son would go in different directions. In this way several groups of beggars were formed and the condition has been falling ever since."[54] At the time of the writing of the account, a guru, Muktavandas, had been imprisoned for fourteen years on a charge of murder, an inheritance of the "sins and worthless pride" of the past gurus. The missionary used broad strokes and fine lines to paint the fall of Satnampanth. At display was a vivid picture of a devastated community.

The way forward for Satnampanth, of course, lay in the adoption of Christianity. This "truth" was secured through a contrast between Hindu rule and British governance. In an unabashed reiteration of the colonial mythology of progress under British rule the missionaries and *sarkar bahadur* (British government), working in tandem, were cast as the twin bearers of "the light of the western lamp."[55] Under Hindu *rajya* (rule), Satnamis had been treated worse than dogs and had faced discrimination in the details of everyday life. The Western missionary and British government combination, on the other hand, ceaselessly directed its efforts to combat this situation through education and the law. A number of Satnamis now stood on an equal footing with Hindus and Muslims. There were, however, limits set by the Satnamis themselves. Some Satnami leaders did not accept the true *satya* guru because they feared the loss of their income, which accrued from the community's belief in another *satnam*. Similarly, the efforts to promote education among the Satnamis by British administrators had been rejected by their gurus. Was it at all surprising then that the large mass of the Satnamis were not progressing despite the incentives and facilities provided by the government?[56]

The tract characteristically ended with an appeal to the Satnamis.[57] There was a move back to the teachings of Ghasidas, which were turned into prophecies later fulfilled by the missionaries. Ghasidas had stated, "*pendra saheb* was going to come bringing in *satyanam* with him": it was plain for all to see that the missionaries had arrived in the midst of Satnamis and went from house to house preaching about *satyanam* Jesus Christ, carrying the Bible.[58] What is significant about the brief description of the Bible that followed was its economy of presentation. Instead of spending time on the story of Genesis, the missionary account moved on quickly and succinctly to how the Lord Jesus Christ was a human incarnation of god, born from the womb of the Virgin to save and redeem humanity. It emphasized that Christ was the real *satyanam*, whose arrival had been prophesied by Ghasidas. A disciple was one who walked according to the instructions of his guru. The path of *gosain* (ascetic master) Ghasidas led to *satyanam* Jesus Christ.

How was the text read, understood, and apprehended by the Satnamis? The circulation of the tract began with its being sold along with other evangelical literature by the missionary and the preachers of the Pithora station. We do not have a breakdown of the exact number of copies of the tract that were sold. In 1935–36 M. M. Paul along with the preachers and catechists of his station sold 211 tracts, 105 gospel portions, and 5 New Testaments. By 1938–39 the numbers had increased to 3 Bibles, 11 New Testaments, 450 Bible portions, 970 tracts, and 2000 leaflets.[59] In the three intervening years *Satyanami Panth aur Shri Gosain Ghasidas*, it would seem, was the most significant addition to the body of literature sold by the missionary and the catechists. On an impressionistic reckoning then the tract was popular. It contributed to more than a three-fold increase in the number of tracts that were sold.[60] M. M. Paul had commented, "My small tract on Satnamis . . . is now printed and sells to people. Also illiterate people are found buying my Satnami tract and requesting some literate persons to read it to them."[61] The tract had found its way to sections of the group that had been targeted as its potential readers and audience. The missionary's comment also suggests that the reading of the tract as a collective rehearsal of telling of and listening to a story had become part of the fluid world of popular religious discourse.

This is not really surprising. The history constructed by *Satyanami Panth aur Shri Gosain Ghasidas* had forged a tendentious (and *outre*) but not all together distant relationship with the Satnami past. A comparison with another tract, *Satnam Panth Darshak*, also written by a missionary for the Satnamis, is revealing.[62] *Satnam Panth Darshak* rehearsed a familiar plot. Ghasidas, an ordinary man whose mind was set on truth despite his poverty, set off on a pilgrimage to Jagannath after the death of his child. When he reached Cuttack he met white missionaries who taught him about "truth." Ghasidas came back to Girod and asked his fellow caste members to give up the use of intoxicating substances and meat, to lead pure lives, and to give up idol worship in favor of a belief in one *satyanam.* These were intermediate steps. Ghasidas revealed that he was only a guard who was spreading the word of *satyanam.* He was going to be followed by white missionaries. With hats on their heads and religious books in their hands, these men would bring in a reign of faith, justice, equality, and truth. After Ghasidas's death his descendants inherited the seat of the guru, became rich, and deviated from the path of their forefather. This led to the decline and ruin of Satnampanth. It was the arrival and presence of missionaries that once again offered the path of redemption to the fallen Satnamis.[63] The rest of the account, its main body, was concerned with narrating the story of the life of Jesus and the embodiment of truth in Christ, his word, and teachings.[64]

Despite its invocation of familiar themes, *Satnam Panth Darshak* was cast in a completely different idiom from M. M. Paul's narrative. If we situate *Satnam Panth Darshak* within the matrix of Chhattisgarhi popular religious discourse, the ruse of simplicity of language, a deliberate watereddown version of Hindi, reveals itself as a flatness of tone and texture. The clarity and neatness of the narrative turn into a cut-and-dried and, indeed, lifeless picture. The intention behind the text to mediate and bring together Satnampanth and Christianity was sabotaged by its principles of construction. In sharp contrast to M. M. Paul's *Satyanami Panth aur Shri Gosain Ghasidas*, the lack of play with different rhetorical signposts and narrative techniques and the absence of tropes and traces of popular traditions within *Satnam Panth Darshak* both indexed and promoted a lack of engagement with the myths, beliefs, and practices of Satnampanth and of the Satnami converts to Christianity.

It was this engagement with the forms and idioms of popular religious discourse rooted within oral traditions that had provided evangelism with a creative force. The blind catechist Simon, for example, had rendered the story of the prodigal son in Chhattisgarhi following the conventions—the use of cymbals, a singing accompanist, and several embellishments and elaborations including the telling of tales that were not a part of the original story—of a folk oral narrative to turn it into a powerful and moving performance. Audiences made up of converts and members of different castes were moved to tears as they sat spellbound for up to three hours listening to these dramatic presentations of the Bible narratives.[65] The force of such engagement, including the use of *bhajans* of the catechist Simon alias Surdas Shimon, underlay M. M. Paul's work. Indeed, *Satyanami Panth aur Shri Gosain Ghasidas* reveals that its rhetorical devices and narrative techniques were often linked to—and provide leads toward understanding— modes of apprehension rooted within oral traditions. In the absence of direct evidence for the reading of the text, we have to be content with these clues.

At the same time, *Satyanami Panth aur Shri Gosain Ghasidas* did not merely seek to establish a social relationship of the spoken to the written word, which affirmed oral traditions. It also sought to hold up a mirror to the Satnamis in order to frame the collective self-consciousness of the group in the truth of Christ. This was a large undertaking that involved shifts in the meanings of the Satnami past. In 1936 M. M. Paul had written from Pithora,

> We preached in this area . . . and then turned specifically towards the Satnami sect. First of all we had announced that in the several villages to come together in an appointed circle and hear about the Satnam (True Name) to whom Christians are following, and we were glad to meet them in several hundreds at a time. Spent with them four hours in talking . . . After that they themselves declared that the time is coming when they would accept the only True Name and not the true-name which they are following.[66]

A year later the missionary stated his expectations: "These Satnamis are very much dissatisfied with their faith at the present moment and if even one of their leaders is converted to Christianity through the grace of our Lord thousands are expected to follow him within the Christian fold."[67] It was within this space of millenarian hopes that the missionary constructed his elaborate pun on *satya*. The evangelical effort, centered around M. M. Paul's tract, met with a degree of success. In 1937–38 the missionary reported the largest number of conversions: eighty converts were adults of local castes and another eight were young children of Christian families.[68] The new converts were largely Gandas but did include a few Satnamis.[69] Could the text have brought about these conversions? M. M. Paul's reports after 1938 find him dealing with the earlier problems of the reluctance of Satnamis to convert and of converts returning to the "Satnami fold" because of the restrictions and binds on life-cycle rituals—marriage, birth, and death—entailed by a Christian way of life. The drive of the text to secure a metamorphosis of the story of the Satnami past into Christian truth in the form of thousands of Satnamis witnessing Christ did not come about. The Satnamis did not see their reflection in the mirror held up by M. M. Paul's text.[70]

The relationship forged by the text between the spoken and the written word could, however, serve to frame the self-consciousness of Satnami converts to Christianity. In January 1989 I attended a Satnami *chauka* in a village called Narbadakhapri. Khilawan, who had invited me, pointed to two houses just outside the village and said that bad people lived there. They were, he said, relatives at one time but now had left the caste. The next morning I went and met the head of one of the households. Bhukwa was a Satnami convert to Christianity who worked as a day laborer. He told me that the other Satnamis did not know the true story of Ghasidas. I was curious. Bhukwa was a good storyteller. His account closely followed M. M. Paul's narrative. When I asked him where he had heard the account Bhukwa was visibly upset. "It is the true thing," he said, and then as final proof added that this was *likhit itihas*, written history. It turned out that his uncle, a carpenter, was literate and used to read aloud from a book that told the true story of Ghasidas. Bhukwa couldn't show me the book because his cousins had left the village. "Otherwise," he shook his head, "you could have read the real history. I wouldn't have needed to speak, you wouldn't have needed to write."

A Brief Epilogue

Even as Bhukwa's statement seemingly forecloses history, it also highlights that the interplay between meaning and power in the construction of pasts of the Satnamis is very much a part of the here and now. The Conclusion points out some of the ways in which the myths and oral testimonies discussed in this book function today. Here I briefly take up an example of how the symbols and resources of the postcolonial Indian state have been implicated in the fashioning of novel traditions, identities, and histories among Satnamis in recent years.

Some years ago, the internal conflicts between rival politicians and power brokers in the Congress (I) party led Arjun Singh, a seasoned political leader from Madhya Pradesh, to sponsor a government initiative to celebrate Guru Ghasidas as a messiah of the poor and the downtrodden. This was part of a bid to counter the influence of politicians from Chhattisgarh in the party and the province (and the region and the nation), and to use the Scheduled Castes, particularly the Satnamis, as a provincial political constituency. Guru Ghasidas was accorded the dignity of history when 18 December 1757 was declared as his date of birth to locate him in written and fixed, linear and chronological time. The naming of a university in the town of Bilaspur after the guru was a recognition of Ghasidas's immense knowledge and wisdom. But arguably the most major initiative here was the support extended by the state to a *mela* (fair) held at the village of Girod, the birthplace of Ghasidas, which has served to turn a small affair featuring a few hundred Satnamis into a mammoth event involving tens of thousands of members of the community over the past fifteen years.

These state initiatives have led to unintended consequences for religious organization among the Satnamis. The members of the community have found their own uses for the government sponsorship of Ghasidas. The written form and the printed word, marks of authority in local cultures still defined by attributes of orality, have been pressed into the service of the worship of the founding guru. Today, the recitation and repetition of these newly fashioned texts—part of a collective telling of and listening to songs and stories within idioms of popular religious discourse—is increasingly situated alongside modern modes of orality, technically sophisticated aural and visual messages, to constitute novel forms and attributes of Ghasidas. Indeed, the guru has been accorded a novel centrality in the belief structures of the Satnamis. Even as fresh legends accrue around the figure of Ghasidas, the myths about the later gurus are slowly being erased from a once widely known picture to become more esoteric forms of knowledge.

All this underlies novel processes of the constitution of truths and the fashioning of traditions among the community. We find here that recent years have witnessed an ever-widening spread of the performance of the *chauka*: on the one hand, the ritual has been steadily invested with ever-newer meanings as it has undergone innovations, modifications, and transformations at the hands of Satnami specialists of the sacred, and, on the other, its novel forms are elaborated as essential parts of a timeless tradition of the community. Similarly, there is a fashioning of fresh festivities and modes of worship, an eclectic and redefined ordering of time that simultaneously draws upon the myths and the ritual calendar of the Satnamis and on official histories and almanacs, and increasing investments in creative cultural imaginings of the *mela* at Girod—and of other initiatives—shored by the state. All these processes underlie refigurings of the sense(s) of the self and the solidarity of the community. In the midst of dominant interventions, grounded in power, that bear upon the construction of history and the organization of the sacred among the Satnamis, members of the community are fashioning new meanings of the group's pasts, boundaries, and identities.

CHAPTER EIGHT

Conclusion

In the winter of 1989 I was discussing the prevalence and ways of witches and questions of magic and sorcery with a small group of Satnamis in a village not far from the town of Bilaspur. The word spread and soon there were nearly twenty of us in a crowded courtyard. It was a passionate and invigorating interchange. The issues ranged from the reasons for the ashen complexion of *tonhis* (witches) to their propensity to drink the blood of babies (through a thread/tube that could travel for miles before attaching itself to the navel of a new born) to their apparently morbid sexuality. Many stories were told, chilling tales of fear and foreboding. There was also sympathy and relief all around that long ago my mother had escaped the wiles of witchcraft in Chhattisgarh. She was lying in a cot, a helpless babe of a few days, when black strings were wound tightly around her wrists and ankles, evidently by a *tonhi*. But just as the little hands and legs were beginning to turn blue my attentive grandmother had cut the strings, a release from the clutches of evil. My mother's paternal uncle, with whom my grandmother and her children were staying then, was an important judge in Raipur at the time. There was a larger moral here. At the end of three hours the general consensus was that people should take care, to the extent these matters are in one's own hands, not to invoke the ire of a *tonhi* since nobody, high or low, was safe from her wrath. Then a shy youth named Prakash muttered, really to himself, "But the *havaldar* (constable)? But the *tonhi*? But the *billa*

[badge of office]?" Several pairs of eyes turned toward him. The youth seemed to shrink into himself, but was gently teased and cajoled to explain. He haltingly elaborated on the cryptic clues. The only person safe from a *tonhi*, Prakash said, is a *havaldar*: it is the *billa*, the badge of official power, that makes him immune from the immense strength of witchcraft. The approval, curiosity, and expectation of all present were palpable. Prakash continued, now more confidently, "It does not matter if the constable is a heavyweight wrestler or a skeletal figure, a man with a bushy mustache or clean shaven, as long he wears the *billa* he is safe from witches. It is only when this badge is taken off that the witch can strike." Everyone seemed to agree. The discussion went on for another hour, variations on the new theme.

State and Community

This vignette underscores the immense power encoded in the signs, symbols, and metaphors of governance of the state and their critical place in structuring the perceptions, practices, and contours of communities. The encounter between the constable's badge, an embodiment of official authority, and the powers of the witch is a metaphor for the interplay and interpenetration between emblems of state(s) and forms of communities. The theme, it seems to me, has not always been adequately addressed in South Asian historiography. I will briefly take up a few representative and significant examples. The early exercises of the *Subaltern Studies* endeavor rescued subordinate communities and groups from "the enormous condescension of posterity" by casting them in the heroic role of opposing and resisting, through a variety of means, the marauding and exploitative forces of the colonial state that worked in tandem with sections of the indigenous elite.[1] In Ranajit Guha's pioneering book of 1983, the signs of dominance of the colonial state played a role in structuring the identity of the subaltern at moments of passivity. But the essence of the initiatives of these subordinate groups lay in insurgency, an autonomous and truly emancipatory expressive moment involving a prescriptive reversal aimed at the complete subversion and erasure of the insignia of subalternity.[2] Six years later Guha further elaborated his arguments and told us that the alien moment of power of this colonial state constituted a "dominance without hegemony," an autocratic regime "singularly incapable of relating to the society on which it had imposed itself."[3] And a design of history drawn from the binary division of state and community continued to be woven into the fabric of other pasts.

Dipesh Chakrabarty's important study of the jute-mill workers of Bengal gave a theoretical call for a critical understanding of the relations that went into the making of the quotidian experience of hierarchy and the importance of attending to culture and consciousness—the "unthought" of Indian Marxism—in studying working-class history in a society where the assumptions of a hegemonic bourgeois culture did not apply. Nonetheless, it ended up by exploring facets of the culture of Calcutta jute-mill workers solely in terms of the essential givenness of "strong primordial loyalties of community, language, religion, caste, and kinship," all virtually homeostatic features of a precapitalist society.[4] Gyan Pandey's sustained critique of the construction of the colonial sociology of communalism seized upon community—defined quite simply as "Indian society beyond the confines of the state"—as the sign of alterity and difference, a sign that served to interrogate dominant knowledge(s).[5] From a different perspective, Sandria Freitag examined the domain of public arenas—a coherent and consistent realm of symbolic behavior in which "community has been expressed and redefined through collective activities in public spaces"—as being in opposition to (and by implication, in its internal constitution, sealed off from) the imperial state and its institutions.[6] The opposition has once again been reiterated in Partha Chatterjee's wide-ranging and sophisticated critique of the "grand narrative of capital," a critique that draws its evidence from colonial and postcolonial India, particularly Bengal.[7] Chatterjee argues that this narrative of capital seeks to suppress "an independent narrative of community," a suppression that also lies at the heart of modern European social theory.

> If there is one great moment that turns the provincial thought of Europe to universal philosophy, the parochial history of Europe to universal history, it is the moment of capital—capital that is global in its territorial reach and universal in its conceptual domain. It is the narrative of capital that can turn the violence of mercantilist trade, war, genocide, conquest, and colonialism into a story of universal progress, development, modernization, and freedom.[8]

Here the modern state, embedded within this larger narrative of capital, "cannot recognize within its jurisdiction any form of community except the single, determinate, demographically enumerable form of the nation," while "by its very nature, the idea of community [rooted within modernity and, mercifully, not tradition] marks a limit to the realm of disciplinary power."[9] To take a final example, Dipesh Chakrabarty's recent attempt to "write difference into the history of our [Bengali/Indian] modernity in a mode that resists the assimilation of this history to the political imaginary of European-derived institutions . . . which dominate our lives," nonetheless ends up by replicating the givenness of many of the key categories and central elements that lie at the heart of the epistemic violence he seeks to challenge and interrogate.[10] Thus, in Chakrabarty's analysis the gendered domains of the public and the domestic, the concepts of personhood and the civil-political, and indeed that terribly fetishized category of the modern state are not rendered in alternative ways in the context of a colonial modernity. Rather, these distinctions and categories, derived as it were from an *ur* scheme of history, are configured as part of the natural order of modernities, all held in place by that overriding opposition between state and community.

Against the grain of such readings, my own construction of a history of the Satnamis suggests a rather more intricate relationship between the signs of the state and the constitution of community. It may even seem a pessimistic picture when placed alongside portrayals of the community, rendered in the capital case, as the protagonist of new heroic histories. In the myths of Satnampanth that symbolically constructed the Satnami community, Ghasidas's authority was recognized by the *angrez saheb* and Balakdas triumphed over the *angrez sarkar*. The two gurus forced colonial power—which was unjust and unlawful, corrupt and ignorant—to recognize their purity and the legitimacy of the community through the truth of *satnam*. This, arguably, revealed the glimmers of an alternate legality, encoded within the interiority of faith: the purity and power of the gurus and *satnam*. At the same time, the myths also seemed to reproduce the formal colonial separation between religion and politics. The gurus demarcated their separate sphere of authority from the state and kept within the bounds of colonial law. They also gave it a twist that was both in tune and out of tenor with colonial governance. The Satnami claim on upper-caste symbols was secured by its legitimation in government papers, but only after the colonial regime had been compelled to act as a properly constituted moral authority.

This complex dynamic between the symbols of state and the contours of community was also played out in key ways in the activities of the Satnami Mahasabha. The interventions of outsiders, particularly G. A. Gavai and Baba Ramchandra, helped to shape this Satnami endeavor. The Satnami gurus and *mahants* learned the rules of a new language that allowed them to enter the arenas of institutional politics defined by colonial administration, the Indian National Congress, the depressed-classes movement, and the All-India Scheduled Caste Federation. They petitioned the government, held meetings, set up a school, entered district bodies and the legislative council of the province, and the conflicts between the gurus were played out in the new arenas. This fitted well with a larger pattern where the elite of different castes and communities often organized themselves to impinge upon imperial administration and its institutions in order to claim some of the benefits and pittances on offer.[11] There was, however, much more to the picture. The authoritarian impulse of the interventions of those who stood outside the group found a niche in the structures of authority within the community. The symbolic resources offered by colonial administration became a part of a drive to reform and control the Satnamis that was cast in idioms of law and command. The focal signs of the community were situated alongside the metaphors of power of the colonial order in the construction of new legalities to produce the "true law of Ghasidas." The project of education too was inextricably bound to diverse forms of authority and offered its Satnami patrons substantive symbols of the colonial *saheb*'s power. Satnami oral narratives in presenting the past of the Mahasabha highlight the legality of the venture through a reworking of the signs of colonial power: old and new meanings of the symbols of state lie at the heart of these accounts.

All this has wider implications. The symbols, metaphors, and practices of colonial governance offered a pool of resources that were deployed in selective and contending ways by indigenous groups to define identities, constitute traditions, fashion legalities, and construct new notions of order within communities. Oppositions are neat but insidious devices. The binary division between state and community stands in the way of understanding how colonialism, built as a cultural process involving the joint energies of the colonizer and the colonized, exercised its hegemony through saturated signs that found their way within the interstices of communities. These signs could never entirely escape the significance of earlier meanings. Yet, these signs were also reworked in local arenas to generate novel visions, and were thus prevented from becoming the universal and uniform currency of capital and colonialism.

Evangelical Entanglements

The shared past of the colonial entanglement was played out in diverse and inherently contradictory ways in the evangelical encounter. I begin with the links between the mission project and colonialism. Evangelical missionaries in Chhattisgarh could be supported by colonial administrators, but they rarely intervened in the arena of institutionalized politics. Moreover, it is a pernicious naivete—shared by several historians and theorists of colonial discourse—which assumes the working of a seamless web of colonial interests with a uniform Western mentality. We need to turn instead to the contradictory location of the mission project within colonial cultures of rule. The missionaries described the converts as equal in the Kingdom of God. However, they also constructed powerful images of the non-Western Other: the stock and evocative metaphors and the routine and emotive images of missionary representations that we encountered in passing formed a part of the powerful cultural idioms of domination in which Western communities invested. Moreover, the missionaries invoked the precept of individual self-determination to argue for the religious freedom of the convert. But these converts were childlike and had to be nurtured and controled by a paternalist authority. Finally, the mission project was committed to civilizing the converts through key practices revolving around buildings, clothes, writing, and the printed word. At the same time, these were also the critical instruments through which the missionaries participated in the conscious fashioning of the boundaries, embedded in distinct life styles, of the "community" of Euro-Americans. It was arguably within the interstices of these contradictory movements that the missionary constructed a sense of belonging to a community of white settlers, reinforced the familiar symbols and signs of the cultural order of colonial rule, invested in colonial mythologies of racial supremacy, and established structures of paternalist authority. It is the cultural and discursive agendas of the mission project in Chhattisgarh that help to unravel its colonial connections and political implications.

Did the locus of the initiative in the processes of cultural encounter always lie with the white man? In their early encounters, the missionaries could be incorporated as affiliates in the domain of the authority of gurus and deities. Similarly, it was within the matrix of local cultures that the missionaries were fashioned as masters who commanded the practices initiated by the mission project. The arts and signs of civilization had contradictory consequences: they were imbricated in the everyday definition and reinforcement of missionary authority; and the converts deployed them in their challenge to the missionaries. This suggests the working of a broader process of the apprehension, appropriation, and refashioning of the "word" and the "book," of Christian divinities, saints and martyrs, of clothes and buildings, of Western notations of time and of the spatial organization of work, and of the regenerative powers of missionary medicine and Christ the Savior, within the modes of worship and practices of the communities of converts.

Ties of kinship and the paternalist economy of the villages around mission stations, it would seem, proved critical to the growth of Christian congregations and converts' communities. The missionary was the *malguzar*, the owner-proprietor, and the pastor of these villages, which obscured the division between temporal and spiritual power. The missionary along with the native leaders of the converts drew up rules to order the life of congregations: these regulations, viewed through the grid of local cultures, show continuities with rules of caste and sect—the mechanisms of incorporation and ostracism, and the concerns of purity and pollution—and the institutions of village life, which were rearranged and acquired new meanings within the relocated communities. Clearly, the missionary participated—as an active agent and a hapless victim—in the subversion of a cardinal principle of Protestant theology and in the creation of an indigenous

Christianity. The missionaries' concern with monogamy and their fear of adultery meant that the converts were forbidden secondary marriages. The evangelical benefactors indeed saw the practice as an instance of the moral sloth of the world of "wilderness" and sought to impose marriage as a sacred contract between individuals. But this was also the domain in which the converts consistently flouted missionary authority and continued to form "adulterous" secondary marriages. The converts defied the missionaries in fashioning their understanding of marriage and sexual transgression. They did not replicate the institutions and practices of a modernized social order in the image of missionary masters and had their own uses—in the construction of myths and stories, perceptions and practices—for the "truth" offered by the missionaries.

Recasting Hinduism

In tracing the network of novel and beaten tracks that made the past of the Satnamis, this book has entered into recent, key debates in South Asian history and anthropology. Are the categories of Hindu and Hinduism the creations of colonial imaginings, the products of the nineteenth century? My account has attempted to recast the debate around this question in terms of the perspectives drawn from the pasts of a group who stood on the margins of these categories, categories which in turn were elaborated within wider cultural processes defined by power. By focusing on the multiple negotiations and interrogations, reworkings and contestations that went into the production of different meanings of Hinduism (not merely of the word, but also of the social relationships made up of domination, subordination, and resistance that it describes), this history of the Satnamis has revealed the limitations of a preoccupation with the origins of the categories of Hindu and Hinduism and the dangers of reifying them as static and hypostatized entities. Rather, these categories need to be understood as descriptive and analytical shorthands that allow us to comprehend the changing patterns and lived arrangements of religious meanings and practices involving several elaborations, negotiations, and contestations of the intermeshing of divine, ritual, and social hierarchies not only in colonial but also in precolonial and postcolonial South Asia, *and* as resources that were drawn upon and deployed in selective and contending ways by various castes and communities in their articulations of sameness and difference, of religious and political identities, particularly in the nineteenth and twentieth centuries. Here the growing rigidity of concerns of purity and pollution that worked against the Chamars and thus informed the construction of Satnampanth was not conjured by the colonial regime, but had its beginnings in precolonial Chhattisgarh ruled by the Marathas. Likewise, in the nineteenth and early twentieth centuries the Satnamis fashioned a distinct identity that constructed "otherness" *within* the Hindu caste order. Finally, from the 1920s members of the group went on to variously negotiate different constructions of the Hindu order, negotiations that had contradictory and unintended consequences for Satnami articulations of community and nation. Indeed, the meanings gleaned from margins suggest the need to rethink central theories of community and caste in South Asia.

My account highlights the limits of Dumont's dominant model of the relationship between caste and sect, renunciation and asceticism by making a case for the permeable boundaries of the householder and the renouncer and for the interpenetration, in practice, of principles of caste and sect. This history of a non-twice-born group, which consistently challenged its ascribed caste status as untouchables by constituting itself as a sect, has also shown that while Ghasidas remained an ascetic householder guru, from the time of Balakdas the guru as the head of the organizational hierarchy and (after 1867) the formal owner-proprietor of Bhandar simultaneously embodied the truth of *satnam* and the symbolically constituted attributes of royalty of the raja and the dominant caste. Declan Quigley has recently argued that in the final analysis ultimate purity lies in transcending the social world of caste, an avenue available only to the "perfect renouncer and the perfect king."[12] Confounding the logical schemes established by Dumont and Quigley, the Satnami gurus did not try to become the perfect renouncer or the perfect raja and fashioned distinct perceptions and practices of kingship and asceticism, perceptions and practices in which the gurus embodied "perfect purity" precisely because they remained in the "social world."

Untouchable Pasts has also drawn upon the myths and practices of the Satnamis and their oral accounts about *gaonthia zamana* (the era of landlords) in order to recast the debate about the nature of power in caste society. We find here that an exclusive emphasis on the ritual hierarchy of purity and pollution as ultimately a matter of religious values, or a sole preoccupation with the ritual centrality of kingship, or, indeed, the judicious construction of a bipolar model where, depending on the context, the Brahman or the dominant caste can reign supreme—all efforts toward the construction of a synthetic theory of caste in South Asia—tend to obscure the intermeshing of different axes of dominance, elaborated over time, in the constitution of power in caste society. The ritual hierarchy of purity and pollution and the ritual centrality of kingship and dominant caste(s) were both symbolic schemes that elaborated modes of domination and power. Defined by meanings and practices that articulated and were articulated by relations of authority, they worked together to secure the subordination of the Satnamis and other untouchable communities in Chhattisgarh. These symbolic schemes were further intertwined with the signs and metaphors of colonial power. Clearly, this was not merely a matter of the conferral of proprietary rights by the colonial regime, which then allowed upper-caste village proprietors to initiate policies that further strengthened their hand. Rather, at work here was the central place of these village proprietors' control over writing—involving a purchase they commanded on account of their superior understanding of documents writ large with a colonial legality, instruments of guile and power and ruses for enactments of expropriation—along with their crucial links with subordinate officials of colonial administration, and the consequent larger Satnami perception that the *sarkar* had given the village proprietors the right to (and underwritten their rites of) rule over villages. All this went into the making of the *malguzar* as the raja of the village. The symbols and practices of colonial governance played a key role in the constitution of the nature of power in the caste order in Chhattisgarh. It was these different but inextricably linked idioms of authority that were also seized upon by the Satnamis to challenge their subordination.

Idioms of Resistance, Languages of Domination

The Satnami challenge to authority—a profusion of the "poetics and politics of transgression" as widespread and varied as the dissemination and use of this talisman in the arena of Cultural Studies today—raises important issues. It actually underlines the variety of means of resistance and defense forged by the group, and shows that the scholarly method of adducing parallels and similarities, characteristic of students of religions, neglects a focus on processes of symbolic construction, which involve "relations of contrast, counterpoint, inversion, and apposition."[13] It also highlights the key place of languages of domination in the constitution of resistance, and the reproduction of forms of hierarchy and authority in the domain of popular religion.

The formation of Satnampanth occurred within the wider context of the contradictory economic and cultural pulls faced by the Chamars of Chhattisgarh, which stemmed from the administrative measures of the Marathas and British superintendents in the region. The subaltern religious endeavor at once drew from popular traditions and the ritual hierarchy of purity and pollution, rejected the divine and social hierarchies that centered on the Hindu pantheon, and repositioned the signs in a new matrix. It questioned and challenged the ascribed ritual status of Chamars as low untouchables. The Chamar farm servants, cultivators, and *gaonthias* who joined the sect were said to be cleansed of their impurity and marks of ritual subordination and reconstituted as Satnamis. In the new sect, the rejection of distinctions of caste among its predominantly Chamar and a few hundred Teli and Rawat members was accompanied by prohibitions that governed the transactions with other castes. These norms crystallized under Balakdas, the second guru. Members of ritually low castes could not be initiated into Satnampanth. Satnamis had to observe rules of commensality with all other castes and were forbidden, under the sanction of excommunication, from engaging a service caste. If the Satnamis contested their untouchability, they also reproduced the significance of meaning(s) and power embedded within the ritual schemes of the caste order.

The Satnami guru replaced the gods and goddesses of the Hindu pantheon, and this rejection of the divine hierarchy within Satnampanth simultaneously reinforced the guru's power within the community. In Satnami modes of worship the centrality of the gurus was accompanied by the group's fashioning of new divinities: the pilgrimages to Girod and Bhandar, the taking of the guru's *amrit* during his *ramat*, and the worship of gurus on *dashera* and *janmashtami* were situated alongside novel representations of Mahadeo and Drupda *mata*. The Satnami life-cycle rituals, beliefs in ghosts and witches, and participation in festivals associated with the agricultural cycle, once again, combined an accommodation of village beliefs and practices with the centrality of the gurus and the distinctive practices of the community. All this worked together to challenge the tenor of upper-caste religious authority. The elaboration of the organizational hierarchy of Satnampanth constituted an alternative to the formidable network of relationships of village proprietors and dominant landholding groups with service castes. But this centrality of the gurus and the institutionalization of the Satnami organizational hierarchy also worked in tandem with the practice of *ramat* to provide the gurus and *mahants* with means of control over the community.

The solidarity of the Satnamis informed their practices within the agrarian economy in the second half of the nineteenth century. The proprietary rights conferred by the colonial government strengthened the hand of the newly styled *malguzars* and left the vast majority of cultivators, occupancy tenants, and tenants-at-will with few defenses. The Brahman and Marwari *malguzars* squeezed out the tenants through a variety of means and increased their own holdings. Satnami cultivators and *malguzars* lost out. They persisted with *lakhabata* in Satnami villages as a relatively egalitarian measure and in the famine years of the 1890s launched a tenant initiative against upper-caste *malguzars*. The combined effects of the famine and of the stationing of punitive police by the colonial administration served to quell the initiative of Satnami tenants. Other less confrontational means of survival took its place. In the first half of the twentieth century, Satnami cultivators took to the transport of grain and other commodities, engaged in subsidiary occupations, and adopted the strategy of seasonal migration in an effort to cope with adverse economic processes. The limits to the development of agricultural production in Chhattisgarh meant that Satnami cultivators had to extend their holdings in order to assure profits from agriculture. The increased occupation of land and the system of high *nazranas* made this a difficult venture for Satnami cultivators since about a third were tenants in "average circumstances" and another 20 percent were no better than agricultural laborers. The Satnamis continued to fall into debt and, as they angrily explain, lose their land.

In the nineteenth and twentieth centuries, the economic difficulties of the Satnamis were compounded by the principles of ritual subordination and forms of discrimination that pervaded everyday life. The Satnami structure of beliefs, modes of worship, and social organization—including the place of the *sathidar* and the *bhandari*—allowed the group to negotiate, cope with, and resist these relations of authority and domination. These principles and practices worked in tandem with the myths of the group to engage with and question, challenge and subvert, but also to reproduce and be contained by, relationships of power in Chhattisgarh that involved an intermeshing of the ritual hierarchy of purity and pollution, a culturally and ritually constituted centrality of kingship and landholding dominant castes, and forms of power derived from colonial administration. Finally, even as the focal signs of Satnampanth were pressed into a claim for a reformed Hindu status of the group under the aegis of the Satnami Mahasabha, the members of the community once again fashioned their own uses of Hindu emphases and symbols: their modes of worship, in the newly built temples, centered on the gurus, and they turned their appropriation of Hindu sacred texts and their being reinvested with the *janeu* and the *kanthi* into marks of difference and superiority over Brahmans and *purohits*. At the same time, these moves of the Mahasabha and the larger community came about because the very constitution and elaboration of Satnampanth had carried forward the meanings embedded within the ritual hierarchy of purity and pollution.

Gender and Power

The contradictions centering on gender also constrained the contestatory credentials of the community, and my account has worked toward integrating the critical category of gender with the analytical domains of kinship, ritual, and myth. Satnami kinship practices valued the labor of women but gave them few firm rights within the natal and affinal homes. As members of a sect, Satnami women could bypass some of the restraints of boundary maintenance that govern the economies of sexuality in the caste order, although here too the upper hand generally lay with men of other castes, and members of the Satnami organizational hierarchy used their privileges to gain access to the women of the group. The flexible marriage patterns of *churi* afforded these women a degree of space to negotiate, cope with, and now and again subvert the principles of patrilineal and patrilocal kinship. For upper-caste men the "promiscuity" of Satnami women was a ruse for their sexual exploitation. The ordering of gender in *jhanjeri chauka* seems to suggest that women were constituted as key protagonists and actors whose participation and agency was central to the maintenance of the simultaneously sexual and symbolic boundaries of the community. The ritual also poses difficult questions about interpreting the nature and implications of the constructions of women's agency and sexuality, wifehood and motherhood. These questions are closely tied to the ethics of willfully going against the grain of the accounts of the people who make our ethnographies and histories possible, and the limits of an upper-caste male's account that relies—not for want of trying but on account of the exigencies of the politics of gender in field work—on the word of Satnami men. (Instead of focusing on my encounter with the Satnamis as a central object of inquiry that could quite easily have lent itself to a self-indulgent solipsism, I have sought to weave aspects of this encounter into what strike me as appropriate moments in the larger story.) Satnami myths evidently drew a clearer connection between the sexuality of women and their agency: the mediation of feminine guile and desire led to divisions, disputes, and disorder.

It is not surprising that important interventions of Baba Ramchandra —and of the missionaries, discussed a little earlier—focused on the key areas of marriage and gender. Baba Ramchandra elaborated a new code of morality and economy for the Satnami household, which privileged motherhood and *pativrata dharma* as ideals for Satnami women and sought to exercise ritual and political power by controling the intimate but diffuse domains of production, sexuality, and nurture in the Satnami household. The code, characteristically, was to be implemented by men within Satnampanth. The Satnamis had their own uses for these interventions. In the 1930s the Satnami converts to Christianity drew upon missionary injunctions against adultery and the principles of maintenance of boundaries of groups, grounded in rules of caste and sect, to invoke a threat to the chastity of "virgin Christian sisters" and, thereby, turned the honor of women into an evocative metaphor for order within the community and a symbol that constituted its boundary. The Satnami leaders of the Mahasabha went a part of the way to sanitize the Satnami household. Then they waylaid and jettisoned the ambitious plans for the community of their upper-caste benefactor. If the Satnami challenge to varied forms of authority was premised upon structures of domination, the play of power in the community too was accompanied by the Satnamis' implicit questioning of alien idioms of control. All this was, of course, a part of a wider debate, embedded in historical practice, about the intricate texture of the relationship between meaning and power, the past and the present.

Past Matters

The myths of Satnampanth provided the group with a powerful statement of its past. The myths historicized the reconstitution of Chamars as Satnamis by locating it within a complex play between Ghasidas and *satnampurush.* Ghasidas and Balakdas, the protagonists of a heroic history, effected resolutions and displaced figures who populated the cosmic and social order in order to define the boundary and orchestrate the symbolic construction of Satnampanth. The myths and practices of the Satnamis engaged with the cultural and ritual attributes of kingship to fashion the gurus as figures who were on par with the king. A regal aspect and rituals of royalty were a concomitant and a prerogative, a defining feature, of the figure and seat of the Satnami gurus beginning with Balakdas. But the guru never became a raja. (We have already noted that the gurus demarcated their separate spheres of authority from kings and the state and have also discussed the contradictory dynamic between the gurus and the colonial regime.) The later gurus continued to embody the twin, inextricably linked, attributes of the raja and the guru. They too remained within the bounds of colonial law, but could not claim the paper from Queen Victoria giving them all the rights of upper-caste Hindus that the *sarkar* was now offering to them on a platter. Among them weakness had replaced resolve. These gurus did not command the truth of *satnam.* The uncontroled desire and untamed sexuality of the women married into Ghasidas's patrilineage orchestrated principles of disorder. The guru *gaddi* was divided.

The book has discussed the past as a disputed domain, a contested arena. This is evident in the myths of Satnampanth, which embodied aspects of the historical consciousness of the group. The missionaries, Baba Ramchandra, and the Shri Path Pradarshak Sabha, in turn, seized upon history as a negotiable resource that was reworked in their bids to transform the Satnamis. These contending histories only partly corresponded to and largely subverted the set of ordered norms that have been identified by Arjun Appadurai as organizing "the past as a scarce resource" in his influential construction of a (largely unchanging) cultural framework, which is seen to constrain the debate on the past.[14] The accounts, in various ways and to different degrees, cited textual evidence only to reiterate orality (and thereby augmented the authority of a narrative), played with the need for the ratification of a text from an external authoritative figure in the past, ignored the necessity of an authoritative document that indexed the privileges of the Satnamis alongside the claims of a maximum number of other relevant groups, and came up with novel visions of what constituted antiquity and the documented past. The Satnami past was a contentious and debated terrain. Yet the construction of the rival histories of the group reveals an abundance of resources (of innovation and play) in the ordering of this past.

Renato Rosaldo has reminded us that forms of historical consciousness vary in their degree of symbolic elaboration, their ability to pervade multiple contexts, and their capacity to capture people's imagination.[15] While Rosaldo's argument refers to these variations across societies and cultures, I think it useful to extend his emphases in a more restricted way to the cultural conceptions of history of a community. The point is less, for instance, about the nuances of time reckoning and more about how these conceptions, embodied in stories and oral narratives, are variously organized in the discussion of different aspects of the past of the group. Thus, the question of authenticity was central to all Satnami tales. Yet it was configured in several ways. This was also true of other devices of dealing with the past and the manner in which different dimensions of history were articulated in the present.

The authentic nature of Satnami myths about Ghasidas and Balakdas hinged on their being sacred narratives: their rehearsal in story, song, and dance at times replete with ritual resonances and at more mundane moments was always charged with sacral attributes because the presence of the divinity of the two gurus informed the telling of these tales in diverse contexts. And it was only after the heroic history of the first two gurus was replaced by an account featuring the successive failures of their descendants that the myths became a relatively more specialized domain of knowledge, a genealogy that documented the travails of the community and thus could not be rehearsed in the manner of narratives celebrating its triumph. Nothing succeeded like success in the capacity of Satnami myths to capture the imagination of the group. The telling power of the oral narratives of *gaonthia zamana* meant that these accounts of the difficulties faced by the community in this period formed a much more broad-based explanation for the hard times experienced by the community. Their authenticity too was premised upon a principle of presence—the importance accorded to a person's having actually seen and lived through the era of landlords—even as the interplay between an experienced past and an inherited and transmitted oral tradition underlay their enactment in the present. The shape of the stories was well known through their being told across generations and served to organize the memory of the group as a bounded community. Finally, the detailed oral testimonies—as distinct from the more fragmented memories—centering on the Mahasabha were confined to a rather smaller number of Satnamis. They recounted this past having heard about it from the older members of their families, who had generally been associated with the organizational endeavor. These tales tended to authenticate themselves through frequent allusions to figures and events drawn from the realm of the history of institutionalized politics, even as they were arranged in ways that reiterated earlier emphases and constituted new meanings and truths. Clearly, the high degree of symbolic elaboration of these different Satnami accounts of history showed variations, depending on which past was addressed.

The emphasis here on understanding myth as a form of historical consciousness, the past as a negotiable and reworkable resource and a contested terrain, and the variations in the cultural conceptions of the past of a community has involved an implicit critique of commonplace and dominant constructions of history. This criticism, of necessity, is elaborated from within the discipline. History for long has been preeminently a sign of the modern. The several traditions of classical social theory, history, and ethnography have generally been complicit (in different ways and to various degrees) in seeking to separate simple and sacral non-Western societies, rooted in ritual and myth, from complex and secular Western orders with reason and history. The legacy persists even as there has been an increasing recognition not only of the continuous making of traditions and the profoundly ideological character of modernity, but also that there are many historically specific modernities—although the latter point, ironically, often tends to be relegated to the margins in critiques that interrogate the centrality of the grand narratives of colonialism, state and nation, and challenge the universal claims of explanation and meaning of post-Enlightenment traditions. In this context, the questioning of a singular notion of history assumes significance. The plea here is not for a critique of modernity, which simply seeks to go behind it: a charming picture of an enchanted and sacred garden—for is it not by envisioning such charms that one steers clear of Hieronymus Bosch's vision of the "Garden of Earthly Delights"?—from which human beings have been banished, the immense cost of rational advance and the "disenchantment of the world." It aims for something more. In the famous European film maker Tarkovsky's last feature, *The Sacrifice*, a person looks somewhat wistfully at an old map and comments, possibly with a hint of longing, on how the world looked so different *then*: but everything about the composition of the shot suggests the futility of peering into the past to return there, the inescapability from human histories and the hold of the here and now through the mere trick of turning our backs on all that has gone into the making of the present. In tune with this testimony, my account has sought to defy easy dualisms and recognize the mixed-up nature of social life, where the worlds of the Satnamis were complex fusions of the conventionally and conveniently opposed categories of modernity and magicality, history and myth, rationality and ritual. To question a singular notion of history then is simultaneously an argument against reified, bloated, and overarching typologies whose oppositions, determinations, and teleologies reproduce themselves by obscuring the many imaginative pathways of human practice.[16] An uncritical celebration and lyrical romanticisation of a people or community—which fails to recognize the contradictions and the underside of cultural worlds and, thus, actually mocks its subjects—has little place here. This history of the Satnamis has attempted to capture some of these entangled energies and the economies of their enactment.

Appendix 1: Genealogy of Satnami Gurus, Four Generations

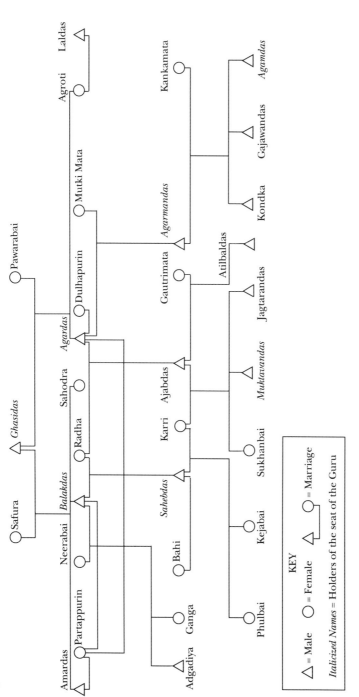

Appendix 2

Population of Satnamis, 1901–1931

	1901			1911			1921			1931		
	TOTAL	MALE	FEMALE	TOTAL	MALE	FEMALE	TOTAL	MALE	FEMALE	TOTAL	MALE	FEMALE
Raipur	224779	107913	116866	182452	88229	94223	162303	77269	85034	114461	54753	59708
Bilaspur	117476	55757	61719	100647	47839	52808	99596	47689	51907	131159	63370	67789
Durg				100742	50336	50406	99375	49503	49872	103828	50075	53753
Feudatory States	40638	20237	20401	65685	32689	32996	46320	23369	22951	1717	892	825
C.P.* & Berar	389599	187322	202277	460280	224577	235703	430361	209069	221292	351559	169258	182301

Appendix 2, cont.

Population of Chamars Including Sub-Castes, 1901–1931

	1901			1911			1921			1931		
	TOTAL	MALE	FEMALE	TOTAL	MALE	FEMALE	TOTAL	MALE	FEMALE	TOTAL	MALE	FEMALE
Raipur	245126	117945	127181	203078	98701	104377	203297	95507	107790	206417	99179	107238
Bilaspur	209517	101166	108351	214321	103768	110553	225336	110588	114748	239137	110936	128201
Durg				121382	58069	63313	104063	49978	54085	113324	54650	58674
Feudatory States	58869	29309	29560	82604	40960	41644	66320	33287	33033	89937	44126	45211
C.P.* & Berar	735262	359271	375991	901594	443059	458535	881674	432937	448737	967155	474891	492264

* Central Provinces

Source: Census volumes, 1901–1931

Glossary

amrit	nectar
angrez sarkar	British government
anuloma	hypergamy
ashwin	September–October
athgawana	committee of eight villages
avatar	incarnation
bahiya	man touched by divine madness
baiga	shaman
baikunth	heaven
banjara	gypsy, pack trader
begar	unremunerated labor
behatri	compensation for brideprice
bhad athon	eighth day of bhad (August–September)
bhajan	devotional song
bhakti	devotion/devotional worship
bhandari	Satnami village religious functionary
bhat	cooked, boiled rice
chait	March–April
chaprasi	peon
chauka	Satnami ritual
charanamrit	water of the feet of god/higher being
chaupai	small cot
chhatti	ceremony on the sixth day after the birth of a child
chhattra	ornamental canopy
chhua	touch pollution
churi	bangle, also secondary marriage
dand	punitive fine
darshan	vision/seeing
dashera	festival celebrating victory of the god-king Rama
devi	goddess
dharm	faith
diwali	festival of lights in the month of October–November
diwan	Satnami organizational functionary
ekjati	single caste
gaddi	seat/throne
gaonthia	village headman, see also *malguzar*

gaonthia zamana	era of landlords
garh	fort
gawahi	testimony
gora	white/fair
hareli/haryali	agricultural festival in July–August
holi	fesival of colors in February–March
hukum	command
jait khamb	victory pillar
janeu	sacred thread
janmashtami	festival marking the birth of god Krishna, also distinct Satnami festival
jati	caste
jat sayan	elders of a caste
jhanjeri chauka	Satnami ritual
jila saheb	district magistrate
jumma dabdar	the Bible
kan phunkne- * wala guru*	Satnami guru who addresses the ear with an incantation
kanthi	necklace of wooden beads
keli	sexual intercourse
kos	measure of distance, two miles
kotwar	village law-and-order functionary
kund	pond
lakhabata	periodic redistribution of land
lok	world
lota	round vessel
lugda	short saree
maghi puno	day/night of full moon in the month of magh (January–February)
mahant	high-ranking functionary among the Satnamis
malguzar	village proprietor
mantra	incantation
mata	mother/wife of guru
mela	village and urban fair
nagar	plough
nazrana	money paid to village proprietor to receive consent to sell land or transfer holdings of land
palki	palanquin
panch pauni	five fingers
panchamrit	mixture of five pure substances, among Satnamis—includes water in which the feet of five Satnami men have been washed

panchayat	village and/or caste council
panthi geet	songs of Satnampanth
panthi naach	dance of Satnampanth
para	neighborhood
pathoni	the bride's ritual move to her affinal home after marriage
pativrata	devoted wife
pativrata dharma	creed of fidelity and service to the husband
patrani	most prominent wife, literally queen who sits on the thigh
pendra saheb	white missionary
prachin	elders
pratiloma	hypogamy
puja	worship
puno	full moon
puranmasi	night of full moon
purohit	priest
ramat	tour of Satnami guru
rawat	village grazier
saheb	white official, master
sant	pious man
sarkar	government
sathidar	Satnami village functionary
satkhoji	seeker of truth
satnam	true and pure name
satyanam	true and pure name
shuddhikaran	purification
shwet	white/pure
subahdar	governor, Maratha office
surhuti	festival celebrating the goddess Lakshmi
tahsil	administrative unit
tahsildar	administrator of tahsil
teerth	place of pilgrimage
tilak	mark on the forehead
tonhi	witch
vansh	lineage
yagya	sacrifice
zamindar	landlord

NOTES

Chapter 1. Introduction

1. A few representative anthologies and collections within historical anthropology—itself a wide arena with diverse analytical emphases—that have variously influenced my work include, Aletta Biersack (ed.), *Clio in Oceania: Toward a Historical Anthropology* (Washington: Smithsonian Institution Press, 1991); John Comaroff and Jean Comaroff, *Ethnography and the Historical Imagination* (Boulder: Westview, 1992); Nicholas Dirks (ed.), *Colonialism and Culture* (Ann Arbor: University of Michigan Press, 1992); Emiko Ohnuki-Tierney (ed.), *Culture through Time: Anthropological Approaches* (Stanford: Stanford University Press, 1990). On histories from below in India see, Ranajit Guha (ed.), *Subaltern Studies: Writings on South Asian History and Society*, vols. 1–6 (Delhi: Oxford University Press, 1982–89); Partha Chatterjee and Gyan Pandey (eds.), *Subaltern Studies VII: Writings on South Asian History and Society* (Delhi: Oxford University Press, 1992); David Arnold and David Hardiman (eds.), *Subaltern Studies VIII: Writings on South Asian History and Society* (Delhi: Oxford University Press, 1994). The "everyday" as an analytical perspective is elaborated in Michel de Certeau, *The Practice of Everyday Life* (Berkeley and Los Angeles: University of California Press, 1984), and David Warren Sabean, *Property, Production, and Family in Neckerhausen, 1700–1870* (Cambridge: Cambridge University Press, 1990).

2. Important contributions here include Shahid Amin, *Event, Metaphor, Memory: Chauri Chaura 1922–1992* (Berkeley and Los Angeles: University of California Press, 1995); Arjun Appadurai, *Worship and Conflict under Colonial Rule: A South Indian Case* (Cambridge: Cambridge University Press, 1981); Susan Bayly, *Saints, Goddesses and Kings: Muslims and Christians in South Indian Society* (Cambridge: Cambridge University Press, 1989); Bernard Cohn, *An Anthropologist among the Historians and Other Essays* (Delhi: Oxford University Press, 1987); Nicholas B. Dirks, *The Hollow Crown: Ethnohistory of an Indian Kingdom* (Cambridge: Cambridge University Press, 1987); and Peter Van der Veer, *Gods on Earth: The Management of Religious Experience in a North Indian Pilgrimage Center* (Delhi: Oxford University Press, 1988).

3. These issues are elaborated in Saurabh Dube, "India: Historias desde abajo," *Estudios de Asia y Africa*, forthcoming 1997. A somewhat different version of this paper in English, "Histories from below in India," forms a

part of Saurabh Dube, *Historical Cultures, Ethnographic Pasts,* manuscript, n.d. Henceforth, the references will cite the version in English.

4. Michel de Certeau, *Everyday Life,* p. ix.

5. Indeed, the controversy can be traced back to the beginning of the word *Hinduism.* Thus, Sir Monier Monier-Williams, whose book *Hinduism* (1877) is widely credited to have introduced the term *Hinduism* into general English usage, had recognized that the categories of Brahmanism and Hinduism, which he used to describe the "esoteric" and "popular" dimensions of the religion of the Hindus, were "not names recognized by the natives." See, John Strawton Hawley, "Naming Hinduism," *Wilson Quarterly,* 15, 3 (1991), pp. 20–22.

6. C. J. Fuller, *The Camphor Flame: Popular Hinduism and Society in India* (Princeton: Princeton University Press, 1992), p. 10; Hawley, "Naming Hinduism," pp. 20–34; Harjot Oberoi, *The Construction of Religious Boundaries: Culture, Identity, and Diversity in the Sikh Tradition* (Chicago: University of Chicago Press, 1994), pp. 1–18; Brian K. Smith, *Reflections on Resemblance, Ritual and Religion* (New York: Oxford University Press, 1989), pp. 5–7. The point was made nearly three and a half decades ago, from the perspective of comparative religion, by Wilfred Cantwell Smith, *The Meaning and End of Religion* (New York: Mentor, 1963), p. 71. See also, Dirks, *Hollow Crown.*

7. Fuller, *Camphor Flame,* p. 10.

8. Oberoi, *Religious Boundaries,* pp. 1–17.

9. See, for instance, Partha Chatterjee, "Claims on the past: The genealogy of modern historiography in Bengal" in Arnold and Hardiman (eds), *Subaltern Studies VIII,* pp. 1–49.

10. Peter Van der Veer, *Religious Nationalism: Hindus and Muslims in India* (Berkeley and Los Angeles: University of California Press, 1994), p. 20. See also, Wendy Doniger, "Hinduism by any other name," *Wilson Quarterly,* 15, 3 (1991), pp. 35–41; Alf Hiltebeitel, "Of camphor and coconuts," *Wilson Quarterly,* 15, 3 (1991), pp. 26–28.

11. David Lorenzen, "Introduction: The historical vicissitudes of Bhakti religion," in Lorenzen (ed.), *Bhakti Religion in North India: Community Identity and Political Action* (Albany: SUNY Press, 1994), pp. 2–13; Sheldon Pollock, "Ramayana and political imagination in India," *Journal of Asian Studies,* 52 (1993), pp. 261–97; Cynthia Talbot, "Inscribing the other, inscribing the self: Hindu-Muslim identities in pre-colonial India," *Comparative Studies in Society and History,* 37 (1995), pp. 692–722; Van der Veer, *Religious Nationalism,* pp. 12–24.

12. I recognize that my understanding of Hinduism may well be considered to be too inclusive. Yet, I prefer to err in this direction than to construct a definition of such exaggerated precision as the one by Brian Smith: *"Hinduism is the religion of those humans who create, perpetuate, and transform*

traditions with legitimizing reference to the authority of the Veda." The immense ease with which this definition is put forward almost lulls us into forgetting that what is lacking here are entire arenas of human energies, imaginations, and practices in relation to the sacred and the divine in the Hindu universe. As Harjot Oberoi has pointed out with regard to Smith (and others who argue along similar lines), "By importing a Judeo-Christian and Islamic understanding of texts and scriptures into discussion of Indian religions, we could end up establishing religious identities that do not exist beyond the scholar's imagination." Indeed, Brian Smith's cavalier exorcism of all "heterodox movements" from Hinduism and his spectacular reification of the "canon" suggest that his definition has little place for people, processes, and power within social relationships that have constituted Hinduism, emphases that are central to my understanding of this category. At the same time, it needs to be clarified that in making a case for the elaborations, negotiations, and contestations of divine, ritual, and social hierarchies within Hinduism as central to a working definition of this category, I am not casting the net so wide as to include all Indic religions within its fold. Thus, in effecting and claiming a decisive break with the interlocking hierarchies within Hinduism, a religion steps outside its pale, although the continuities and the interconnections here still remain significant analytical issues, whether the religion is Buddhism or Jainism, the institution of the Khalsa Sikhs or the regime of the Singh Sabhas, or indeed the construction of an "indigenous" Christianity and Islam in South Asia. Brian Smith, *Resemblance, Ritual and Religion,* pp. 13–14 (emphasis in the original), 15–29. Oberoi, *Religious Boundaries,* pp. 8–9, 4–7.

13. I follow Fuller's argument here, but also emphasize that rather than seeing "hierarchical inequality" and the "partial continuity between humanity and divinity" as static principles, we need to focus on how they are variously elaborated over time within changing social relationships, often marked by conflict. Fuller, *Camphor Flame,* pp. 3–4.

14. Andre Wink, *Land and Sovereignty in India: Agrarian Society and Politics under the Eighteenth-Century Maratha Svarajya* (Cambridge: Cambridge University Press, 1986); Stewart Gordon, "The slow conquest," *Modern Asian Studies,* 11 (1977), pp. 1–40; "Role of resistance in the shaping of indigenous Maratha kingdoms," unpublished paper; See also C. A. Bayly, *Indian Society and the Making of the British Empire, The New Cambridge History of India* II.1 (Cambridge: Cambridge University Press, 1988).

15. Louis Dumont, "World renunciation in Indian religions," *Religion/Politics and History in India* (Paris and The Hague: Mouton, 1970), pp. 33–60.

16. Richard Burghart, "Renunciation in the religious traditions of South Asia," *Man* (n.s.), 18 (1983), pp. 635–53; Veena Das, *Critical Events:*

An Anthropological Perspective on Contemporary India (Delhi: Oxford University Press, 1995), pp. 34–40. Peter Van der Veer, *Gods on Earth*, pp. xii–xiii, 66–182; David Lorenzen, "Kabirpanth and social protest," in Karine Schomer and W. H. Mcleod (eds.), *The Sants: Studies in a Devotional Tradition of India* (Delhi: Motilal Banarsidas, 1987), pp. 281–303; On objections to the use of the term *sect*, W. H. McLeod, "On the word panth: A problem of definition and terminology," *Contributions to Indian Sociology* (n.s.), 12 (1978), pp. 287–95.

17. Louis Dumont, *Homo Hierarchicus: The Caste System and Its Implications* (London: Weidenfeld and Nicolson, 1970), p. 188. The difficulties in Dumont's use of oppositions have been discussed by Richard Burghart, "Renunciation in South Asia," pp. 636–37; Peter Van der Veer, *Gods on Earth*, pp. xii–xiii, 66–68; Veena Das, *Structure and Cognition: Aspects of Hindu Caste and Ritual* (Delhi: Oxford University Press, 1977), pp. 46–49.

18. Richard Burghart, "Renunciation in South Asia," pp. 641–50; Peter Van der Veer, *Gods on Earth*, pp. 66–182.

19. Louis Dumont, *Homo Hierarchicus*.

20. See, Nicholas B. Dirks, "The original caste: Power, history and hierarchy in South Asia," *Contributions to Indian Sociology* (n.s.), 23 (1989), p. 61; Gloria Goodwin Raheja, "Centrality, mutuality and hierarchy: Shifting aspects of inter-caste relationships in north India," *Contributions to Indian Sociology* (n.s.), 23 (1989), p. 8; Dirks, *Hollow Crown*; Gloria Goodwin Raheja, *The Poison In the Gift: Ritual Prestation and the Dominant Caste in a North Indian Village* (Chicago: University of Chicago Press, 1988); Declan Quigley, *The Interpretation of Caste* (Oxford: Clarendon Press, 1993).

21. It is equally significant that "materialist" criticisms of Dumont have tended to replicate his absolute separation of and opposition between ideology and power. While Dumont (and his supporters) broadly encompasses *artha* (economic and political power) within *dharma* (ideology and status), with the ritual hierarchy of purity and pollution fixing the extreme poles of the ranking of castes and leaving "power" only a residual role in affecting this ordering in the middle, his materialist critics have tended to emphasize that caste is essentially a matter of economic and political power, and that ideology (the ritual hierarchy of purity and pollution) is merely a gloss to basic inequities and social divisions. Both sides ignore the way power is structured into the cultural schemes of the ritual hierarchy of purity and pollution. A recent bibliographical survey of the main lines of the divide is contained in I. -B Krause, "Caste and labor relations in North West Nepal," *Ethnos*, 53 (1988), pp. 5–36.

22. This is reflected, for instance, in Raheja's attempt to develop a bipolar model, which accounts for both the ritual centrality of a dominant farming caste and the purity-impurity principle at an all-India level. She ar-

gues that areas with a strong dominant farming caste are marked by the ritual centrality of the group, while contexts where Brahmans are the dominant land holders foreground the ritual hierarchy of purity and pollution. In the final analysis, the two remain contextually separate but also broadly opposed principles. Raheja, "Centrality, mutuality and hierarchy," pp. 97–99.

23. Dirks, *Hollow Crown*.

24. Michael Moffatt, *An Untouchable Community in South India: Structure and Consensus* (Princeton: Princeton University Press, 1979); see also, Kenneth David, "Hierarchy and equivalence in Jaffna, North Sri Lanka: Normative code as mediator," in Kenneth David (ed.), *The New Wind: Changing Identities in South Asia* (The Hague: Mouton, 1977), pp. 189–92.

25. The examples here include important parts of the *nirguni* tradition, particularly the Kabirpanthis and the Raidasis. They also extend to several recent ethnographic studies of untouchable groups and communities. Thus, James M. Freeman's detailed and sensitive life history of Muli, a Bauri of Orissa, has revealed the innovative aspects of the religion of the untouchables, the ambivalence of the Bauri pimp Muli's attitude toward upper castes, and the interpenetration of apparent passivity and resistance in everyday life. R. S. Khare has discussed a range of contemporary ideological responses and strategies of the Chamars of Lucknow to discuss the untouchable in "his own terms," where the elaborations of asceticism and an egalitarian rhetoric among the Lucknow Chamars question the picture produced by Moffatt. Lynn Vincentnathan has drawn upon earlier ethnographic studies of untouchables from different parts of India and field work among the Paraiyars of Tamil Nadu in her overview of caste origin myths, eschatological beliefs, and hierarchies among the untouchables to discuss untouchable "subcultural concepts of person and society," which both resemble and differ from those of caste Hindus and are at once hierarchical and egalitarian. David Lorenzen, "Traditions of non-caste Hinduism: The Kabirpanth," *Contributions to Indian Sociology* (n.s.), 21 (1987), particularly pp. 264–66; James M. Freeman, *Untouchable: An Indian Life History* (Stanford: Stanford University Press, 1979); R. S. Khare, *The Untouchable as Himself: Ideology, Identity and Pragmatism among the Lucknow Chamars* (Cambridge: Cambridge University Press, 1984); Lynn Vincentnathan, "Untouchable concepts of person and society," *Contributions to Indian Sociology* (n.s.), 27 (1993), pp. 53–82.

26. V. N. Volosinov, *Marxism and the Philosophy of Language* (Cambridge, Mass.: Harvard University Press, 1984), p. 65.

27. See particularly, Michel de Certeau, *Everyday Life*, pp. xi–xv.

28. Sherry B. Ortner, "Resistance and the problem of ethnographic refusal," *Comparative Studies in Society and History*, 37 (1995), pp. 173–93.

29. The conduct of resistance in a religious idiom in the South Asian context has been discussed, for instance, by David Hardiman, *The Coming of the Devi: Adivasi Assertion in Western India* (Delhi: Oxford University Press, 1987); Rosalind O'Hanlon, *Caste, Conflict and Ideology: Mahatma Jotirao Phule and Low-Caste Protest in Nineteenth-Century Western India* (Cambridge: Cambridge University Press, 1985); Mark Juergensmeyer, *Religion as Social Vision: The Movement against Untouchability in Twentieth-Century Punjab* (Berkeley and Los Angeles: University of California Press, 1982); Gyan Prakash, "Becoming a Bhuinya: Oral traditions and contested domination in eastern India," in Douglas Haynes and Gyan Prakash (eds.), *Contesting Power: Resistance and Everyday Social Relations in South Asia* (Delhi: Oxford University Press, 1991).

30. See, for instance, Jonathan D. Hill (ed.), *Rethinking History and Myth: Indigenous South American Perspectives on the Past* (Urbana and Chicago: University of Illinois Press, 1988); Dirks, *Hollow Crown*, pp. 57–107.

31. I borrow the category of mythic tradition from Gananath Obeyesekere, extending it in a somewhat different manner for Satnampanth. Gananath Obeyesekere, *The Cult of the Goddess Pattini* (Chicago: University of Chicago Press, 1983).

32. Walter J. Ong, *Orality and Literacy: The Technologizing of the Word* (London: Methuen, 1982), and *"Marantha: Death and life in the text of the book," Journal of the American Academy of Religion*, 45 (1977), pp. 419–49. There are few works in South Asian historiography that discuss the relationship between orality and writing. Gyan Prakash, *Bonded Histories: Genealogies of Labor Servitude in Colonial India* (Cambridge: Cambridge University Press, 1990), pp. 38–40; On the interpenetration of written and oral narratives, Rosalind O'Hanlon, *Caste, Conflict and Ideology*, pp. 164–86.

33. These issues are elaborated in the conclusion below.

34. See, for instance, Dipesh Chakrabarty, "The difference-deferral of a colonial modernity: Public debates on domesticity in British India," in Arnold and Hardiman (eds.), *Subaltern Studies VIII*, pp. 50–88. A critique of this reading of a colonial modernity is elaborated in Dube, "Histories from below."

35. Michel Foucault, "Politics and reason," in *Politics, Philosophy, Culture: Interviews and Other Writings 1977–1984* (New York: Routledge, 1988), pp. 57–85; Michel Foucault, "Governmentality," in Graham Burcell, Colin Gordon, and Peter Miller (eds.), *The Foucault Effect: Studies in Governmentality* (Chicago: University of Chicago Press, 1992), pp. 87–104.

36. It is only recently that historians, instead of presuming that Christian converts in India made a complete break with indigenous institutions in the image of the missionaries, have begun to explore the meanings of conversion and the articulation of missionaries, converts, and Christianity

with indigenous schemes of rank, honor, caste, and sect. Susan Bayly, *Saints, Goddesses and Kings*; Dennis Hudson, "The first Protestant mission to India: Its social and religious development," *Sociological Bulletin*, 42 (1993), pp. 39–59; Rowena Robinson, "Some neglected aspects of conversions of Goa: A socio-historical perspective," *Sociological Bulletin*, 42 (1993), pp. 72–80. The evangelical encounter in the nineteenth and twentieth centuries in South Asia has remained a relatively neglected area of study. Richard Eaton's work, which explores the changing encounter between Christian conceptions of divinity and the religious system of the Nagas to explore the strategies of Protestant missionaries and the Naga conversion to Christianity, is an interesting but somewhat flawed exception. The difficulties in Eaton's work stem from the rather rigid and formal opposition that he sets up between Christianity as a religion with universal characteristics and the religion of the Nagas as rooted in a narrow domain defined by local divinities. Thus, it was only when the conceptual universe of the Nagas broadened through an exposure to broader processes—for example, World War II—that large scale conversions took place. The picture is much too neat and the opposition overarching. It contrasts, for instance, with efforts in the past two years to address the wider issues raised by the historical and ethnographic record of the evangelical encounter, including its engagement with colonial ideologies and cultures of rule. Richard Eaton, "Conversion to Christianity among the Nagas, 1876–1971," *Indian Economic and Social History Review*, 21 (1984), pp. 1–44; David Scott, "Conversion and demonism: Colonial Christian discourse on religion in Sri Lanka," *Comparative Studies in Society and History*, 34 (1992), pp. 331–65; Saurabh Dube, "Issues of Christianity in Colonial Chhattisgarh," *Sociological Bulletin*, 41 (1992), pp. 37–63; "Paternalism and freedom: The evangelical encounter in colonial Chhattisgarh, central India," *Modern Asian Studies*, 29 (1995), pp. 171–201; and (ed.) *Everyday Encounters: A Diary of an Indigenous Christianity*, manuscript, n.d.

37. Ranajit Guha (ed.), *Subaltern Studies*, vols. 1–6; Chatterjee and Pandey (eds.), *Subaltern Studies VII*; Arnold and Hardiman (eds.), *Subaltern Studies VIII*.

38. Dipesh Chakrabarty, "Post-coloniality and the artifice of history: Who speaks for 'Indian' pasts?" *Representations*, 37 (Winter 1992), pp. 1–26; Saurabh Dube, "Peasant insurgency and peasant consciousness," *Economic and Political Weekly*, 20 (1985), pp. 447–48; and Dube, "Histories from below."

39. Clearly there exist other lines and forms of criticism of *Subaltern Studies*, some of which have been made with telling effect by its critics, comrades, and contributors. The Conclusion below and my articles cited in the note above discuss some of my other difficulties with *Subaltern Studies*, particularly its more recent exercises.

40. Representative, recent writings here that have influenced my work include, Jane Collier and Sylvia Yanagisako (eds.), *Gender and Kinship: Essays toward a Unified Analysis* (Stanford: Stanford University Press, 1987); Leela Dube, "On the construction of gender: Hindu girls in patrilineal India," *Economic and Political Weekly*, 23 (1988), (ws) 11–19; Joyce Burkhalter Flueckiger, *Gender and Genre in the Folklore of Middle India* (Ithaca: Cornell University Press, 1996); Lindsey Harlan and Paul Courtright (eds.), *From the Margins of Hindu Marriage: Essays on Gender, Religion, and Culture* (New York: Oxford University Press, 1995); Gloria Goodwin Raheja and Ann Grodzins Gold, *Listen to the Heron's Words: Reimagining Gender and Kinship in North India* (Berkeley and Los Angeles: University of California Press, 1994); William Sax, *Mountain Goddess, Gender and Politics in a Himalyan Pilgrimage* (New York: Oxford University Press, 1991). See also, Mrinalini Sinha, *Colonial Masculinity: The "Manly Englishman" and the "Effeminate Bengali" in the Late Nineteenth Century* (Manchester: Manchester University Press, 1995).

41. Lloyd and Susan Rudolph, *The Modernity of Tradition* (Chicago: University of Chicago Press, 1967); Robert L. Hardgrave, *The Nadars of Tamilnad: The Political Culture of a Community in Change* (Berkeley and Los Angeles: University of California Press, 1969).

42. David Washbrook, "The development of caste organizations in South India 1880 to 1925," in C. Baker and D. Washbrook (eds.), *South India: Political Institutions and Political Change, 1880–1940* (Meerut: Macmillan, 1975), pp. 151–203.

43. O'Hanlon, *Caste, Conflict and Ideology*; Juergensmeyer, *Religion as Social Vision*; Gail Omvedt, *Cultural Revolt in a Colonial Society: The Non-Brahman Movement in Western India—1873 to 1930* (Bombay: Scientific Socialist Education Trust, 1976); Eugene Irschick, *Politics and Social Conflict in South India: The Non-Brahman Movement and Tamil Separatism 1916–1929* (Berkeley and Los Angeles: University of California Press, 1969); Eleanor Zelliot, "Learning the use of political means: The Mahars of Maharashtra," in Rajni Kothari (ed.), *Caste in Indian Politics* (New Delhi: Orient Longman, 1970), pp. 29–69. See also, Lawrence A. Babb, "The Satnamis—Political involvement of a religious movement," in Michael J. Mahar (ed.), *The Untouchables in Contemporary India* (Tucson: University of Arizona Press, 1972), pp. 143–51.

44. All translations and transcriptions from Hindi and Chhattisgarhi of oral testimonies, texts, and other written materials are mine. I thank Ishita Banerjee Dube for all the translations from the German language texts and materials.

45. I need to add here that it is the distinct analytical emphases and the interplay of a variety of different kinds of written sources and oral testimonies within this historical account that allow it to critically engage with

but to also go beyond most anthropological studies of the dynamics of untouchable groups, studies that are based primarily upon field work and are rooted in the ethnographic present. See, for instance, Bernard Cohn, "The changing status of a depressed caste," and "The Changing traditions of a low caste," in *An Anthropologist among the Historians and Other Essays* (Delhi: Oxford University Press, 1987), pp. 255–83, pp. 284–98; Owen M. Lynch, *The Politics of Untouchability: Social Mobility and Social Change in India* (New York: Columbia University Press, 1969); Freeman, *Untouchable: An Indian Life History*; Khare, *Untouchable as Himself*; Vincentnathan, "Untouchable concepts of person and society."

Chapter 2. The Making of Satnampanth, 1780–1850

1. There is an acute lack of sources to help us reconstruct the processes of continuity and change in the texture of village life, the determinate social relationships, and the cultural order in the eighteenth and early nineteenth centuries in Chhattisgarh. Most records—contained in the Board's Collection (1796–1830), IOL; the Nagpur Residency Records and NRSR, MPRO; and the Foreign Department Political Consultations, NAI—provide us at best with brief glimpses of disparate aspects of the history of Chhattisgarh. The literature on popular religion in the late eighteenth and early nineteenth centuries in central India is also very thin. The most detailed evidence for the period refers to the political institutions and administrative and revenue practices within the region. It is contained in reports of two administrators, Patrick Vans Agnew, *A Report on the Subah or Province of Chhattisgarh Written in 1820 A.D.* (Nagpur, 1922) and Richard Jenkins, *A Report on the Territories of the Raja of Nagpur 1827* (Nagpur, 1866). My account of the making of Satnampanth—a necessary exercise that draws upon available evidence—is limited by this paucity of sources.

2. The Haihaya, a dynasty that ruled Chhattisgarh, was a younger branch of the Chedi family of Tripuri. Hiralal and Nelson, *Raipur District Gazetteer*, 1909 (Bombay, 1909), p. 49.

3. This study focuses on the Chhattisgarh plain, especially present-day districts of Raipur, Bilaspur, and Durg.

4. Agnew, *Chhattisgarh*, pp. 10–11.

5. Hiralal Kavyopadhyaya, "A grammar of the dialect of Chhattisgarh in the Central Provinces" (trans. and ed. George A. Grierson), *JASB*, LIX, part I (1890), p. 1.

6. S. C. Dube, *Field Songs of Chhattisgarh* (Lucknow: Universal, 1947), pp. 2–10; Edward Jay, "Bridging the gap between castes: Ceremonial friendship in Chhattisgarh," *Contributions to Indian Sociology* (n.s.), 7 (1973),

pp. 144–58; Joyce Burkhalter Flueckiger, "Genre and community in the folklore system of Chhattisgarh," in Arjun Appadurai, Frank J. Korom, and Margaret A. Mills (eds.) *Gender, Genre, and Power in South Asian Expressive Traditions* (Philadelphia: University of Pennsylvania Press, 1991), pp. 181–200.

7. Agnew, *Chhattisgarh*, pp. 5–6.

8. Wills did not specify these "tribal" groups and clarified that his account of the social and political organization of Chhattisgarh before 1745 was based on "extraordinarily unreliable" evidence. C. U. Wills, "The territorial system of the Rajput kingdoms of mediaeval Chhattisgarh," *JASB* (n.s.), 15 (1919), p. 216.

9. Ibid., p. 199.

10. Ibid., pp. 198–99.

11. Ibid., p. 213.

12. P. F. McEldowney, "Colonial administration and social developments in the C.P. 1861–1921," unpublished Ph.D. dissertation, University of Virginia (1981), p. 493.

13. Agnew, *Chhattisgarh*, p. 3.

14. Ibid., pp. 3–4; Jenkins, *Nagpur*, p. 110.

15. See Andre Wink, *Land and Sovereignty*; Stewart Gordon, *Marathas, Marauders, and State Formation in Eighteenth-Century India* (Delhi: Oxford University Press, 1994) and "The role of indigenous resistance in shaping the Maratha kingdom," unpublished paper. For an overview of the development of the historiography of the Marathas see Stewart Gordon, *The Marathas: 1600–1818, The New Cambridge History of India* II.3 (Cambridge: Cambridge University Press, 1993), pp. 1–9.

16. B. S. Thakur, "Chhattisgarh mein Bhonsla rajya (1818–54)," unpublished Ph.D. dissertation, University of Raipur (1974), p. 57.

17. Agnew, *Chhattisgarh*, p. 17.

18. Ibid., p. 37.

19. Ibid., p. 17.

20. Thakur, "Bhonsla rajya," p. 56.

21. Gordon, "Role of resistance," pp. 10–18; Agnew, *Chhattisgarh*, p. 12.

22. Jenkins, *Nagpur*, p. 96; Agnew, *Chhattisgarh*, p. 12; Wink, *Land and Sovereignty*, p. 365.

23. "Captain J. C. Blunt's Narrative of a Journey in 1794," Revenue and Miscellaneous, no. 13, 1859, NRSR, MPRO.

24. Agnew, *Chhattisgarh*, pp. 12–13.

25. Wink, *Land and Sovereignty*, p. 341, pp. 339–75.

26. Agnew, *Chhattisgarh*, p. 4.

27. Ibid., pp. 12, 14.

28. Gordon, "Role of resistance," pp. 10–38.

29. Agnew, *Chhattisgarh*, p. 12.

30. "Memo on the connection between landlord and tenant in the Chhattisgarh division," 19 April 1869, Revenue Department, no. 5 (after) 1869 (Supplementary Index), NRSR, MPRO, pp. 2–3.

31. Agnew, *Chhattisgarh*, p. 12.

32. For example, *LRS Raipur 1869*, pp. 34, 101; Revenue Department, no. 12, 1868, NRSR, MPRO.

33. Agnew, *Chhattisgarh*, p. 3.

34. "Memo on the connection between landlord and tenant in the Chhattisgarh division," 19 April 1869, Revenue Department, no. 5 (after) 1869, NRSR, MPRO.

35. Agnew, *Chhattisgarh*, pp. 3–4.

36. Ibid.

37. Agnew, *Chhattisgarh*, p. 38; *Census of Central Provinces 1866* (Nagpur, 1867), pp. 15–16.

38. This oral tradition recorded by K. C. Dubey, an administrator-ethnographer, in 1961 stated that the village had been founded eight generations ago. I am taking a generation as about twenty years. K. C. Dubey, *Kosa: A Village Survey, Census of India, 1961*, vol. 8, Madhya Pradesh, part 6, Village Survey Monographs, no. 9 (Bhopal, 1967), p. 3.

39. *Raipur District Gazetteer* (1909), pp. 109–10; Settlement Officer, Bilaspur to Secretary, Chief Commissioner, Central Provinces, 11 April 1868, Revenue Department, no. 12, 1868, NRSR, MPRO.

40. Agnew, *Chhattisgarh*, p. 12, pp. 35–36. There is no evidence to suggest that the pattern of the settlement of castes in villages in Chhattisgarh changed significantly on account of Chamars moving into mixed-caste villages or members of other castes moving into primarily Chamar villages over the nineteenth century.

41. Ibid., p. 10, p. 36.

42. Ibid., p. 12; Mr. Sinclair to Captain Hallet, 19 April 1869, Revenue Department, no. 5 (after) 1869, NRSR, MPRO; Richard Jenkins, Resident to the Marquis of Hastings, Governor General, 31 July 1823, no. 79, 1823, Foreign Department Political Consultations, NAI.

43. Deputy Commissioner, Raipur to Commissioner, Nagpur, 3 August 1855, Revenue Department , no. 6, 1855, NRSR, MPRO.

44. Mr. Sinclair to Captain Hallet, 19 April 1869, Revenue Department, no. 5 (after) 1869, NRSR, MPRO.

45. Hiroshi Fukuzawa, "The state and caste system (jati)," in Fukuzawa, *The Medieval Deccan: Peasants, Social Systems and States: Sixteenth to Eighteenth Centuries* (Delhi: Oxford University Press, 1991), pp. 91–113.

46. Agnew, *Chhattisgarh*, p. 37; see also Gordon, "Slow conquest," p. 21.

47. Ibid., p. 6.

48. Ibid., p. 42.

49. Agnew had stated, "Distinctions not reconcilable to our notions were made in reference to the caste of the parties, as well as in determining the quality of the offense as the punishment with which it was to be visited." Ibid., p. 42.

50. Ibid., p. 37.

51. Ibid., p. 25.

52. Jenkins, *Nagpur*, pp. 69–70.

53. Agnew, *Chhattisgarh*, p. 23, p. 37, pp. 40–44.

54. Ibid., p. 43. Now disputes over property and intercaste relationships in villages were to be settled by *panchayats*, assembled according to "custom" by the *gaonthias*. When conflicting claims over such matters could not be settled within the village, the dispute was taken to the *kamavisdar*. If the *kamavisdar* considered the matter sufficiently grave, he referred it to a higher *panchayat*, which met in the "Public Kutcherry" under the superintendence of a *punjee* (according to Agnew, an ancient office that had fallen into disuse under the Marathas), who was selected every year by the *gaonthias*, cultivators, and the notables of a *pargana*. This decision was then confirmed by the superintendent. Ibid., pp. 40–44.

55. "Memo on the connection between landlord and tenant in the Chhattisgarh division," 19 April 1869, Revenue Department, no. 5 (after) 1869 (Supplementary Index), NRSR, MPRO.

56. See Irfan Habib, *The Agrarian System of Mughal India* (London: Asia Publishing House, 1963), p. 343.

57. Mamuri cited in Habib, *Agrarian System*, p. 343.

58. Ibid.

59. Ibid., p. 344.

60. Ibid.

61. Isardas cited in Habib, *Agrarian System*, p. 343.

62. Habib assumes that the Sadh manuscript, *Satnam Sahai, Pothi Giyan Bani Sadh Satnami*, was written by the founder of the Satnami sect. He does not adduce any evidence in support of his assumption. An introductory statement in English establishes that the manuscript was compiled in 1817 by the head of the Sadh sect and given to W. H. Frank. Now the difficulty with Habib's procedure is that even if it is acknowledged that the Sadhs were descendants of the Satnamis of Narnaul, the questions of changes in the sect over the next hundred and fifty years are ignored. The manuscript is in Brajbhasha and is written in both the Nagri and Arabic scripts. *Satnam Sahai, Pothi Giyan Bani Sadh Satnami*, Library of the Royal Asiatic Society, London.

63. H. H. Wilson, "A sketch of the religious sects of the Hindus," *Asiatic Researches*, XVII (1832), p. 300.

64. *Adi Upadesh* cited in Wilson, "A sketch of the Hindus," p. 300; *Satnam Sahai, Pothi Giyan Bani Sadh Satnami*, fol. 1(a).
65. Wilson, "A sketch of the Hindus," p. 301.
66. Ibid., p. 300.
67. Ibid., pp. 301–302.
68. Ibid.; *Satnam Sahai*, fol. 2(a), fol. 10(b), fol. 21(a).
69. Wilson, "A sketch of the Hindus," p. 301; *Satnam Sahai*, fol. 1(b).
70. Wilson, "A sketch of the Hindus," p. 302.
71. Ibid.
72. Ibid., p. 302; B. H. Badley, "Jagjivandas the Hindu reformer," *The Indian Antiquary*, VIII (1879), p. 289.
73. K. M. Sen, *Mediaeval Mysticism of India* (London: Luzac, 1930), p. 124.
74. Badley, "Jagjivandas," *The Indian Antiquary*, VIII (1879), p. 290.
75. Ibid., pp. 289–90.
76. *LRS Bilaspur 1868*, p. 47.
77. The early life of Ghasidas and the setting up of Satnampanth was described to me several times and without significant variations (but often in much greater detail) during field work. In the notes which follow I indicate the first detailed oral testimony on a particular issue. Oral testimony of Sawaldas, Koni, 27 November 1989.
78. *LRS Bilaspur 1868*, pp. 45–6.
79. Ibid., p. 46.
80. Ibid.
81. Ibid., pp. 46–47.
82. Russell and Hiralal, *The Tribes and Castes of Central Provinces*, 4 vols., (London: Macmillan, 1916), p. 406.
83. Ibid., p. 47.
84. Mss. MAR, D-46, IOL. The information about sects and ascetic customs in Chhattisgarh is contained in fol. 20(b). The manuscript was written in Marathi in the Mudi script by Vinayak Rao Aurangawadkar and in a large measure formed the basis for Agnew's account. I am grateful to Sumit Guha for informing me about this manuscript and translating the relevant passages.
85. It is interesting that a Satnami myth staged an encounter between Ghasidas and Agnew in which the *sahib* accepted the guru's authority. Here I do not wish to cull out elements for a linear and chronological "history" from myth, but to suggest rather that the Satnami ordering of past and power featured the British superintendent as a critical figure within the cosmic and social order whose authority had to be negotiated and displaced by Ghasidas in order to orchestrate the symbolic construction of Satnampanth. This theme is elaborated in chapter 5 below.

86. It is instructive, for instance, to compare Chisholm's account of the creation of Satnampanth outlined above with the manner in which Satnami myths rehearse the theme, discussed in chapter 5.

87. *LRS Bilaspur 1868*, p. 47; Oral testimony of Khilawan, Chhotti Koni, 18 November 1989.

88. K. M. Sen, *Mediaeval Mysticism*, p. 124.

89. This myth is elaborated in chapter 5 below.

90. *C. P. Ethnographic Survey XVII, Draft Articles on Hindustani Castes*, First Series (Nagpur, 1914), pp. 25–27; Lorenzen, "Kabirpanth and social protest," pp. 287–90.

91. *LRS Bilaspur 1868*, p. 49.

92. *C. P. Ethnographic Survey XVII, Draft Articles on Hindustani Castes*, First Series (Nagpur, 1914), pp. 26–39.

93. Oral testimony of Diwan Chand, Sendri, 26 November 1989; Oral testimony of Kotu, Birkona, 18 February 1990. The first informant is a Satnami, the second a Panka Kabirpanthi.

94. See, for instance, Richard Burghart, "The disappearance and re-appearance of Janakpur," *Kailash*, 6 (1978), 257–84; Charlotte Vaudeville, "Braj, lost and found," *Indo-Iranian Journal*, 18 (1976), 195–213.

95. Lorenzen, "Kabirpanth and social protest," pp. 300–301. On the "reproduction" of a sect see Burghart, "The founding of the Ramanandi sect," *Ethnohistory*, 25, 2 (1978), pp. 121–39.

96. Oral testimony of Khilawan, Chhotti Koni, 18 November 1989; Oral testimony of Diwan Chand, Sendri, 26 November 1989. Here the point repeatedly reiterated in various oral testimonies was that the modular form of Satnampanth separated the Satnamis from (Kanaujia) Chamars and did not permit distinctions of caste among its members, and that this characteristic set it apart from Kabirpanth. This was true of the past and the present. As regards my further questions about whether there could have been certain distinctions retained among the different castes that had joined Satnampanth (and if in some situations the Satnamis did marry Kanaujia Chamars) in earlier times or in other parts of Chhattisgarh, I was told by my informants that even if there were exceptions like these, they knew nothing about them. Once when I persisted with this line of questioning, I was firmly told that my queries should be directed to Brahmans and Chamars (or those castes that had joined and not joined Satnampanth). See also the discussion in chapter 3 below.

97. *Raipur District Gazetteer* (1909), pp. 80–81.

98. Moffatt has elaborated how the association with "death pollution" is central to the definition of lowness of untouchable groups. Moffatt, *Untouchable Community*, pp. 111–17.

99. *C. P. Ethnographic Survey*, p. 48.

100. *LRS Bilaspur 1868*, pp. 45–46; Oral testimony of Pyarelal, Koni, 20 November 1989.

101. *C. P. Ethnographic Survey*, p. 48.

102. Lawrence Babb, *The Divine Hierarchy: Popular Hinduism in Central India* (New York and London: Columbia University Press, 1975), pp. 51–53; Edward Harper, "Ritual pollution as an integrator of caste and religion," *Journal of Asian Studies*, 23 (1964), pp. 181–83.

103. *C. P. Ethnographic Survey*, p. 48.

104. Harper, "Ritual pollution," pp. 151–97; Babb, *Divine Hierarchy*, pp. 31–67, 177–97, 215–46.

105. *C. P. Ethnographic Survey*, p. 48; *LRS Bilaspur 1868*, p. 47; Oral testimony of Pyarelal, Koni, 6 December 1989.

106. *LRS Bilaspur 1868*, p. 48.

107. Oral testimony of Sonuram, Koni, 6 December 1989.

108. To the extent that there is a universality about such a process of symbolic construction, Satnampanth constituted a "bricolage." This concept of Levi Strauss has been used by historians and anthropologists to describe processes of symbolic construction in varied historical contexts. See, Claude Levi Strauss, *The Savage Mind* (London: Weidenfeld and Nicolson, 1966); Jean Comaroff, *Body of Power, Spirit of Resistance: The Culture and History of a South African People* (Chicago: University of Chicago Press, 1985); David Warren Sabean, *Power in the Blood: Popular Culture and Village Discourse in Early Modern Germany* (Cambridge: Cambridge University Press, 1984), pp. 90–91; Sumit Sarkar, "The kalki avatar of Bikrampur: A village scandal in early twentieth-century Bengal" in Guha (ed.), *Subaltern Studies VI*, p. 48.

Chapter 3. Malguzars, Gurus, and Missionaries, 1850–1900

1. McEldowney, "Colonial administration," p. 248.

2. Crispin Bates has argued that the administrators in the Central Provinces, imbued with "classical economic theory," elaborated a developmental ideology and policy that sought to increase both the revenue from land and the prosperity of the region. At the same time, the financial constraints of the administration meant that the British could do little more than manipulate the local agrarian structure through the use of revenue and settlement policies. Crispin Bates, "Regional dependence and rural development in central India, 1820–1930," unpublished Ph.D. dissertation, University of Cambridge (1984), pp. 90–92.

3. McEldowney, "Colonial administration," pp. 251–52.

4. Bates, "Regional dependence," p. 92.

5. McEldowney, "Colonial administration," pp. 252–55.

6. Bates, "Regional dependence," p. 95.

7. R. Temple, *Report on the Administration of the Central Province up to August 1862* (Nagpur, 1862), p. 3. Another administrator had been even more forceful, arguing that the object of the settlement was to "improve the condition of the head of the villages, re-establish old families, encourage them to take an interest in local improvements and associate them with ourselves in the repression of crime, show them practically the value of their estates and give them inducements for improving the capabilities of the lands they hold." Nagpur Commissioner, 12 May 1860, in J. F. Dyer, *Introduction to the Revenue and Settlement System of the Central Provinces* (Nagpur, 1956), p. 37.

8. This correspondence is contained in "Investigation of property rights in Raipur district and conferral of the same," Revenue Department, no. 21, 1863, NRSR; "Connection between landlord and tenant in the Chhattisgarh Division," Revenue Department, no. 5 (after)1869 (Supplementary Index), NRSR; "Periodical redistribution of land in Chhattisgarh," Revenue Department, no. 12, 1868, NRSR, MPRO.

9. Apart from these categories a cultivator whose claim to the proprietorship of his holding was superior to the *gaonthia* of the village—that is, it went back further in time—was declared a *malik makbuza* (plot proprietor). *LRS Bilaspur 1868*, pp. 155–58.

10. It also needs pointing out here that Chhattisgarh had a large number of *zamindaris* (landed estates under petty chieftains) that had a semi-independent status. In 1864, on the report of Sir Richard Temple, the *zamindars* (petty chieftains) were declared British subjects and were put under the charge of the Deputy Commissioner of the *zamindari* system. The first regular settlement of the *zamindaris* was carried out toward the end of the 1910s. The rights of the *zamindars* and the tenants were clearly defined so that the cultivators were protected from arbitrary eviction, while the *zamindars* continued to derive customary revenue from forests, excise, and *takoli* (tribute). Ibid., pp. 114–17, 110–11. The themes addressed in this book are located mainly in the *khalsa* (land under the direct supervision of the Crown) in Chhattisgarh.

11. For example, on the wide variations in "rents" for similar qualities of soil on account of British attempts to devise an assessment from the old plough tax, see Crispin Bates, "Regional dependence," p. 102.

12. Ibid., p. 99.

13. Commissioner, Chhattisgarh Division to Chief Commissioner, C. P., 6 February 1868, Revenue Department, no. 12, 1868, NRSR, MPRO.

14. *Census of the C. P. 1866* (Nagpur, 1867), pp. 15–16.

15. *LRS Raipur 1869*, p. 32.

16. *Census of India 1891*, XI, I (Calcutta, 1893), p. 74.

17. *LRS Bilaspur 1868*, p. 57.
18. Bates, "Regional dependence," Appendix 3, p. 265.
19. *LRS Bilaspur 1868*, p. 58.
20. Ibid., p. 156.
21. We find here that there was a high concentration of Satnamis and Chamars in Simga *tahsil* (28.8 percent) and Mungeli *tahsil* (36.4 percent). South and east of these areas their number declined to roughly 20 percent in Raipur and Seorinarayan *tahsils* and about 16 percent in Durg and Bilaspur *tahsils*. The southern *tahsil* of Dhamtari showed the lowest of 7.5 percent. *LRS Bilaspur 1886–90*, p. 27; *LRS Durg 1896–1902*, pp. 33–4; *LRS Raipur 1910–11*, p. 13.
22. Memo by Extra Assistant Commissioner, Raipur, 10 July 1870, General Department Compilation, no. 412, 1872, MPRO.
23. McEldowney, "Colonial administration," pp. 232–36.
24. "Migration here was none to speak of . . . a few individual cases of permanent migration may have possibly occurred but they are not worth anything." Commissioner, Chhattisgarh Division to the Secretary to the Chief Commissioner, Central Provinces, 19 September 1870, General Department Compilation, no. 412, 1872, MPRO.
25. Memo by Extra Assistant Commissioner, Raipur, 10 July 1870, General Department Compilation, no. 412, 1872, MPRO.
26. Deputy Commissioner, Raipur to Commissioner, Chhattisgarh Division, 29 July 1870, General Department Compilation, no. 412, 1872, MPRO.
27. Commissioner, Chhattisgarh Division to Chief Commissioner, Central Provinces, 6 February 1868, Revenue Department, no. 12, 1868, NRSR, MPRO.
28. Deputy Commissioner, Raipur to Commissioner, Chhattisgarh Division, 29 July 1870; Memo by Extra Assistant Commissioner, Raipur, 10 July 1870; Commissioner, Chhattisgarh Division to Chief Commissioner, Central Provinces, 6 February 1868, General Department Compilation, no. 412, 1870, MPRO; Settlement Officer, Raipur to Captain Hallett, 19 April 1869, Revenue Department, no. 5 (after) 1869, NRSR, MPRO.
29. Commissioner, Chhattisgarh Division to Chief Commissioner, Central Provinces, 19 September 1870, General Department Compilation, no. 412, 1872, MPRO.
30. This account has drawn upon the comprehensive discussion of changes in land policy and legislation from the late 1860s to 1890s in McEldowney, "Colonial administration," pp. 261–77.
31. McEldowney, "Colonial administration," pp. 308–15.
32. Bates, "Regional dependence," Appendix 3, p. 265.
33. Deputy Commissioner, Bilaspur to Commissioner, Chhattisgarh

Division, 29 September 1899, Revenue and Agriculture, no. 54–59, 1899, MPRO.

34. Bates, "Regional dependence," pp. 142, 204–205.

35. J. B. Fuller, *Enquiry into the Condition of the Lower Classes in C.P.* (London, 1885), pp. 16–17.

36. "Disabilities suffered by Chamars and Satnamis—about 1875," (handwritten note), FS, MPDP, EAL; the themes are repeated in less detail in von Th. Tanner, *Im Lande der Hindus oder Kulturschilderungen aus Indien* (St. Louis: The German Evangelical Synod of North America, 1894), pp. 32–34.

37. These issues tie up with Satnami oral accounts about the forms of discrimination faced by the group in the twentieth century, discussed in the next chapter.

38. *LRS Bilaspur 1868*, pp. 158–59; Deputy Commissioner, Raipur to Commissioner, Chhattisgarh Division, 29 July 1870; Memo by Extra Assistant Commissioner, Raipur, 10 July 1870, General Department Compilation, no. 412, 1872, MPRO; Mr. Sinclair to Captain Hallet, 19 April 1869, Revenue Department, no. 5 (after) 1869, NRSR, MPRO.

39. Commissioner, Chhattisgarh Division to Secretary to Chief Commissioner, Central Provinces, 6 February 1868, Revenue Department, no. 12, 1868, NRSR, MPRO.

40. *LRS Raipur 1885–89*, p. 34.

41. *LRS Raipur 1869*, p. 101.

42. Settlement Officer, Raipur to Secretary to Chief Commissioner, Central Provinces, 11 April 1868, Revenue Department, no. 12, 1868, NRSR, MPRO.

43. C. B. Lucie-Smith to Chief Commissioner, Central Provinces, 30 September 1880, cited in Bates, "Regional dependence," p. 98; *LRS Durg 1896–1902*, p. 45.

44. Ibid., p. 65.

45. Ibid., p. 44.

46. Blenkinsop, Settlement Officer, Raipur, 8 February 1901, cited in McEldowney, "Colonial administration," p. 528.

47. *LRS Durg 1896–1902*, p. 44.

48. *Report on the Police Administration of the Central Provinces for 1892* (Nagpur, 1893), p. 3; *Report on the Police Administration of the Central Provinces for 1896* (Nagpur, 1897), p. 3; *Report on the Police Administration of the Central Provinces for 1898* (Nagpur, 1899), p. 3.

49. *Census of the Central Provinces 1881*, II (Bombay, 1883), p. 37.

50. *C. P. Ethnographic Survey, Draft Articles on Hindustani Castes*, First Series (Nagpur, 1914), pp. 56–57.

51. *LRS Durg 1896–1902*, pp. 45, 62.

52. This account has been constructed by placing the brief references in archival material and administrators' reports alongside missionary accounts and Satnami oral testimonies. The missionary records include three manuscript reports in Hindi that were written by native workers of the American Evangelical Mission in the early twentieth century. I draw upon these reports and oral accounts in this section when the information fits with material from the nineteenth century. Moreover, information in these reports points to the institutions and practices that had developed over the nineteenth century and stood clearly defined in the early twentieth century.

53. Jai Singh, "Satnami Dharma ke Vishay mein Note" (manuscript note on Satnami religious practices), 1924, p. 2, FS, MPDP, EAL.

54. *LRS Bilaspur 1868*, p. 48.

55. Jai Singh, "Satnami Dharma," p. 2; *C.P. Ethnographic Survey*, p. 51.

56. Oral testimony of Sawaldas, Sakri, 12 December 1989.

57. *Der Friedensbote*, 79, 20 (1928), pp. 310–11.

58. Deputy Superintendent Police, Raipur to Deputy Commissioner, Raipur, July 1870, General Department Compilation, no. 412, 1872, MPRO.

59. Untitled and unsigned note in Hindi on Satnami religious practices, possibly written in the 1910s, 8 pages, p. 4, FS, MPDP, EAL.

60. *C. P. Ethnographic Survey*, p. 51; *LRS Bilaspur 1868*, p. 47.

61. *Census of the Central Provinces 1881*, II, p. 38.

62. P. N. Bose, "Chhattisgar: Notes on its tribes, sects and castes," *Journal of the Asiatic Society of Bengal*, 59, part 1, 3 and 4 (1891), pp. 293–94.

63. *Census of India 1901*, XIII, I (Nagpur, 1902), p. 87.

64. Jai Singh, "Satnami Dharma," p. 3, FS, MPDP, EAL.

65. *Der Friedensbote*, 79, 20 (1928), p. 310.

66. At the same time, chapter 5 below discusses that the guru never did become a raja.

67. J. J. Lohr, *Bilder aus Chhattisgarh und den Central Provinzen Ostindiens* (place of publication not given, 1899).

68. *C.P. Ethnographic Survey*, p. 52.

69. See chapter 5 below.

70. Oral testimony of Kanhaiyalal Kosariya, Bhopal, June 1988.

71. *Census of the Central Provinces 1881*, II, p. 36.

72. P. N. Bose, "Chhattisgar: tribes, sects, castes," pp. 293–94.

73. Jai Singh, "Satnami Dharma," p. 5, FS, MPDP, EAL.

74. *Report of the Ethnological Committee* (Nagpur, 1867), p. 104; *LRS Bilaspur 1868*, pp. 50–51; Oral testimony of Girja, Birkona, 25 February 1990; Oral testimony of Manru, Birkona, 18 January 1990; *Census of the Central Provinces 1881*, II, pp. 22–23; Lorenzen "Kabirpanth and social protest," pp. 299–301.

75. This contrast cropped up frequently in discussions with Panka

and Suryavanshi (Chamar) Kabirpanthis in Birkona in January–February 1990.

76. *C. P. Ethnographic Survey*, pp. 54–55.

77. Oral testimony of Kanhaiyalal Kosariya, Bhopal, June 1988; Oral testimony of Pyarelal, Koni, 21 November 1989.

78. The report on the census of 1881, while recognizing the difficulties of separating different castes from Chamars among the Satnamis, mentioned that the roughly two thousand non-Chamar members of the sect belonged to all castes "from Brahman downwards," *Census of the Central Provinces 1881*, p. 34; *LRS Bilaspur 1868*, p. 47; *C. P. Ethnographic Survey*, p. 50; Oral testimony of Pyarelal, Koni, 21 November 1989. The picture of the beliefs and practices of Satnamis that follows was, in fact, corroborated during my field work between November 1989 and April 1990. I have referred to the first detailed oral testimony on the specific points not mentioned in archival material.

79. Jai Singh, "Satnami Dharma," p. 4, FS, MPDP, EAL.

80. Ibid.

81. Untitled and unsigned note on Satnamis, p. 3, FS, MPDP, EAL.

82. *Census of the Central Provinces 1881*, p. 39

83. Untitled and unsigned note on Satnamis, pp. 3–6, FS, MPDP, EAL.

84. See chapter 5 below.

85. Oral testimony of Suritram, Sakri, 11 December 1989.

86. Untitled and unsigned note on Satnamis, p. 2, FS, MPDP, EAL.

87. *LRS Bilaspur 1868*, p. 43.

88. It is interesting, for instance, that when a large number of Satnamis who broke the injunction on tobacco came to be classified as a subgroup, *chungias*, within the sect in the 1860s, they claimed that Ghasidas in a vision had commanded them to resume smoking. *LRS Bilaspur 1868*, p. 48.

89. I am aware that the discussion that follows of the Satnami construction and worship of gods and goddesses and of their participation in festivals in village life is inadequate; but in constructing my account here I have accepted the limits set by a larger paucity of evidence on these issues rather than engaging in speculation based upon present-day Satnami practices in these arenas, the more so because my informants were barely forthcoming on the pasts of these practices.

90. Jai Singh, "Satnami Dharma," p. 7, FS, MPDP, EAL.

91. Ibid., p. 6. For a rich discussion of the worship of Draupadi in other contexts, see Alf Hiltebeitel, *The Cult of Draupadi*, vol. 1, *Mythologies: From Ginjee to Kurukshetra* (Chicago: University of Chicago Press, 1988) and *The Cult of Draupadi*, vol. 2, *On Hindu Ritual and the Goddess* (Chicago: University of Chicago Press, 1991).

92. See Fuller, *Camphor Flame*, pp. 114–27.

93. Jai Singh, "Satnami Dharma," p. 6, FS, MPDP, EAL.

94. *C. P. Ethnographic Survey*, pp. 55–56. M. P. Davis, "Notes on Satnamis" (handwritten manuscript, which was perhaps intended to be turned into a book, 1933), FS, MPDP, EAL.

95. Oral testimony of Suritram, Sakri, 8 December 1989.

96. Jai Singh, "Satnami Dharma," pp. 6–7, FS, MPDP, EAL. On the *baiga* in Chhattisgarh see Lawrence Babb, *Divine Hierarchy*, pp. 197–214.

97. Jai Singh, "Satnami Dharma," p. 7, FS, MPDP, EAL.

98. Oral testimony of Khilawan, Koni, 22 November 1989.

99. Jai Singh, "Satnami Dharma," pp. 7–8, FS; Untitled and unsigned note on Satnamis, pp. 3–4, FS, MPDP, EAL.

100. M. P. Davis, "Notes on Satnamis," FS, MPDP, EAL.

101. Jai Singh, "Satnami Dharma," pp. 4–5, FS, MPDP, EAL.

102. Ibid. Jai Singh, the author of this brief statement, was a Satnami convert to Christianity. Note the shift from "they" to "we" in his account.

103. *Census of the Central Provinces 1881*, II, p. 38.

104. *C. P. Ethnographic Survey*, p. 53; Davis, "Note on Satnamis," p. 7, FS, MPDP, EAL; *Census of the Central Provinces 1881*, II, p. 38; Oral testimony of Jambai, Chhoti Koni, 11 November 1989. In the context of the widely held perception that Satnami gurus had sexual access to the wives of all members of the group, the visits of the newlyweds to Bhandar were often understood by other castes as signifying that the guru had the first right to a married woman's body. *Census of the Central Provinces 1881*, II, p. 38; *Census of India 1901*, XIII, II, pp. 86–87. Further evidence that can sustain wider commentary on this question is not really forthcoming, but see the related discussion in chapter 4 below.

105. Account of death rituals among the Satnamis (untitled and unsigned note in Hindi, possibly written in the 1910s), FS, MPDP, EAL.

106. It is worth noting here that the five Satnami men, whose feet were washed in water which then became a constituent of the *panchamrit*, did not always belong to the village of the dying person. Nor do we have any evidence that these men were necessarily agnatic kin and not affines. Finally, it is interesting that Satnami death rituals were directed at fulfilling obligations towards the *bhancha* (sister's son). Otherwise, it may well have been possible to take up another line of inquiry, cast along the principles of village exogamy, where women who are married into the village are outsiders, and men constitute the true (gendered) boundary of the community through a fusion of kinship and village solidarities. These issues are discussed in the context of Satnami myths in chapter 5 below. For recent, sensitive discussions of related themes see Flueckiger, *Gender and Genre*; Raheja and Gold, *Heron's Words*; and Sax, *Mountain Goddess*. See also, Thomas

Trautmann, *Dravidian Kinship* (Cambridge: Cambridge University Press, 1981).

107. Typescript, "Autobiography of Oscar Lohr" (manuscript written in German in 1902 and translated into English in 1971), p. 2, EAL. For details of Lohr's early life and the setting up of the interdenominational German Evangelical Mission Society in New Jersey in 1865 see Dube, "Paternalism and freedom," pp. 174–76. This section draws heavily upon this article, and I am grateful for permission from *Modern Asian Studies* to reprint relevant portions.

108. Ibid., p. 3.

109. Ibid., pp. 3–4.

110. *Der Friedensbote*, 79, 20 (1928), pp. 309–15, EAL.

111. Thus the missionary Notrott in the manuscript of the first history of the mission at Bisrampur. The manuscript was written in 1892; Notrott revised and typed the history in 1936. Both copies are in German. Notrott, "Typescript history of mission," p. 5, EAL.

112. See, for instance, Gwyn Prins, *The Hidden Hippopotamus: Reappraisals in African History* (Cambridge: Cambridge University Press, 1980).

113. Theodore C. Seybold, *God's Guiding Hand: A History of the Central India Mission 1868–1967* (Philadelphia: United Church Board for World Ministeries of the United Church of Christ), pp. 21–22; *Der Friedensbote*, 79, 21 (1928), pp. 325–31, EAL.

114. In December 1869 a cautious but modestly satisfied Lohr had reported to the Home Board: "I haven't baptized anyone but inspite of it I am happier than I was a year back. We have applications from a few Satnamis. But in reality there are more converts this year and it is I who hasn't baptized them. I have become more careful and I don't want to please myself by gathering a group of nominal Christians. Besides what is required is a deeper understanding of Christian truth and a thorough grounding in the same than what the sons of wilderness can grasp in three or four months. Finally, decisiveness about what one feels and holding one's ground in the face of persecution and enmity is required from the heathens. This can be expected when the value of Christian religion is understood which is too much to expect from this folk in a few months, given the limitedness of their understanding and their materialist instincts." *DDM*, 6, 4 (April 1870), p. 1, EAL.

115. I discovered during field work in 1995 that one of these Satnamis, Anjori Paulus, was actually a Gond, but since he had married a Satnami woman he was initiated and incorporated into Satnampanth.

116. Report of the Chuttesgurh Mission, June 1870–July 1871, pp. 5–6, ARM, EAL.

117. Ibid., p. 5.

118. *DDM*, 8, 4 (April 1872), p. 25, EAL.

119. Report of the Chuttesgurh Mission, June 1871–July 1872, pp. 8–9, ARM, EAL.

120. Ibid., p. 9. The missionaries, much more than colonial officials, understood the difference between Satnamis and Chamars. At the same time, this did not prevent them from referring to Satnamis as Chamars in their reports.

121. *DDM*, 8, 4 (April 1872), pp. 25–6; *DDM*, 9, 2 (February 1873), p. 10; *DDM*, 9, 11 (November 1873), p. 83, EAL. By 1883 the number of converts at Bisrampur, for instance, had grown to 175 and there were other relatives of these families who were waiting for baptism. The baptismal register for the village shows that this process of slow growth went on till 1890 when the number of converts came to stand at 258. The famine years around the turn of the century were to see a dramatic increase in conversions and, very soon, what a missionary called "backsliding from Christianity." Report of the Chuttesgurh Mission, 1883, p. 17, ARM, EAL; Bisrampur Baptismal Register, 1870–90, EAL.

122. This picture is confirmed by the Annual Reports of the Chuttesgurh Mission, 1870–83 (Bound Volumes), ARM, EAL. It is also reinforced by the missionary reports from Bisrampur and other mission stations published in *DDM*, 1870–90, EAL.

123. *DDM*, 9, 7 (July 1873), p. 48.

124. *DDM*, 10, 8 (August 1874), p. 57.

125. Jean Comaroff and John Comaroff, "Christianity and colonialism in South Africa," *American Ethnologist*, 13 (1986), pp. 1–22.

126. *DDM*, 6, 4 (April 1870), p. 3; *DDM*, 8, 11 (November 1872), p. 82; *DDM*, 13, 2 (February 1877), p. 11; *DDM*, 10, 10 (October 1874), p. 74; *DDM*, 11, 2 (February 1875), p. 13; Annual Report of the Chuttesgurh Mission, 1874–75, pp. 10–14, ARM, EAL.

127. *DDM*, 8, 7 (July 1872), p. 50; *DDM*, 8, 11 (November 1872), p. 85; *DDM*, 9, 8 (August 1873), p. 58; J. J. Lohr, *Bilder aus Chhattisgarh*.

128. *C. P. Ethnographic Survey*, p. 57.

129. The Satnami converts' challenge to missionary authority and their uses of Christianity are discussed in Dube, "Paternalism and Freedom."

130. *Bisrampur Kalasiya ki Vishesh Agyayen* (Special Rules of the Congregation at Bisrampur), (Bisrampur, 1890).

131. Ibid., pp. 2–3.

132. Ibid., pp. 5–6; *DDM*, 9, 8 (August 1873), pp. 57–58; Annual Report of the Chuttesgurh Mission, 1876–77, pp. 2–3. Apart from the reports included in the notes the arguments of the last three paragraphs are based upon the information contained in several issues of *DDM* between 1870–1900.

133. In 1866 the report of the Ethnological Committee had first suggested in passing that Ghasidas's teaching may have derived from higher,
Western sources. *Report of the Ethnological Committee*, p. 103.

134. Von Th. Tanner, *Im Lande der Hindus*, pp. 35–36.

135. The number of Chamars in Raipur and Bilaspur districts, for instance, had declined by about 100,000 between 1891 and 1901. *Census of
India 1891*, XI, I, p. 74; *Census of India 1901*, XIII, II, pp. 234–35.

136. The famines of 1896 and 1897 and 1889–1900, apart from feed-
ing into the antagonism and conflict between Satnami *malguzars*, had another specific consequence in the boost it gave to the migration of labor
from Chhattisgarh. The famine of 1868–69 had not led to any migration
from the region. But during the famine at the turn of the century Craddock
wrote: "Of late years emigration to Assam has sprung up and developed
considerably under the stimulus of recruiting agencies." Bilaspur was one of
the chief centers of operation, which involved both licensed contractors
and garden *sardars*. Most of the laborers recruited in 1897 were not registered but Craddock estimated the number at 25,000. In 1889–1900, "some
3,500 laborers were registered and a considerable number were despatched
by [unlicensed] contractors." R. H. Craddock, *Report on the Famine in the
Central Province in 1896 and 1897*, vol. 1 (Nagpur, 1898), p. 46.

137. Seybold, *God's Guiding Hand*, pp. 41–46; *DDM* (n.s.), 18, 10 (October, 1901), pp. 78–79; *DDM* (n.s.), 25, 7 (September 1908), pp. 51–53.
The preoccupation of missionaries with actual relief work during the famine years meant that their reports had little to say about the encounter of
the new converts with Christian beliefs, practices, and institutions in this
period. And then these converts left and rejoined Satnampanth.

Chapter 4. Satnamis in Village Life, 1900–1950

1. There is "no reason to believe that there has since [the late nineteenth century] been any great change in the proportion in which main
castes occur." "Raipur Maturity Report," CPG SSD, no. 22-23, 1927, MPSRR.

2. "Final Report of the Durg Khalsa," CPG SSD, no. 4-6, 1933; "Assessment cum Takoli Report of Barbaspur in Bemetara Tahsil," CPG SSD,
no. 4-42, 1933; "Forecast Report of Durg," CPG SSD, no. 22-11, 1929;
"Raipur Maturity Report," CPG SSD, no. 22-3, 1927; "Combined Rent Rate
and Assessment Report of Latha Group in Baloda Bazar Tahsil," CPG SSD,
no. 4-5, 1929, MPSRR; *LRS Bilaspur 1927–32*, p. 24. We need to remember
that these statistics derive from rather rough and ready surveys that could
miss out on the considerable complexity of the agrarian structure. The reports from the archives cited in this section were all quite brief.

3. "Raipur Maturity Report," CPG SSD, no. 22-3, 1927, MPSRR.

4. Officiating Deputy Commissioner, Durg to Settlement Commissioner, Nagpur, 3 May 1927, CPG SSD, no. 22-2, 1927, MPSRR.

5. "Note on Durg Settlement Report," CPG SSD, no. 4-6, 1933, MPSRR.

6. "Forecast Report of Durg," CPG SSD, no. 22-11, 1929; "Raipur Maturity Report," CPG SSD, no. 22-3, 1927, MPSRR. A note written in 1933 established the official position on the course of prices, "even in this period of depression . . . the price of rice and wheat is 376 percent higher than at the first settlement [1868–69]." "Note on Durg Settlement Report," CPG SSD, no. 4-6, 1933, MPSRR.

7. *LRS Bilaspur 1927–1932*, p. 1; "Combined Rent Rate and Assessment Report of Latha Group in Baloda Bazar Tahsil," CPG SSD, no. 4-5, 1929; "Forecast Report of Durg," CPG SSD, no. 22-11, 1929, MPSRR.

8. Commissioner, Chhattisgarh Division to Secretary, AD, Nagpur, 28 March 1927, CPG AD, no. 1(a)-38, 1927, MPSRR.

9. "Forecast Report of Durg," CPG SSD, no. 22-11, 1929; "Forecast Report of Raipur and Durg Zamindaris," CPG SSD, no. 4-18, 1922; "Raipur Maturity Report," CPG SSD, no. 22-3, 1927, MPSRR. At times the figures were truly staggering. An officer rapidly touring Bilaspur district found that 621 acres of land with a rental assessment of 545 rupees had been sold for 37,826 rupees: here the *nazrana* was 61 times the rental assessment and the proprietors had received 122 years revenue in advance. Commissioner, Raipur to Secretary, AD, Nagpur, 28 March 1927, CPG AD, no. 1(a)-38, 1927, MPSRR.

10. Commissioner, Raipur to Secretary, AD, Nagpur, 28 March 1927, CPG AD, no. 1(a)-38, 1927, MPSRR.

11. R. P. Deshmukh, Malguzar, Baghera to Secretary, SSD, Nagpur, 6 November 1928, CPG SSD, no. 22-3, 1927, MPSRR.

12. Commissioner, Raipur to Secretary, AD, Nagpur, 28 March 1927, CPG AD, no. 1(a)-38, 1927, MPSRR.

13. J. C. McDougall, "Economic survey of a typical village in the central provinces and Berar," CPG AD, no. 1-22, 1927, MPSRR.

14. The survey admitted that this average was somewhat misleading since a large number of these holdings were very small in size and were held by agricultural laborers. The average size of the holdings of pucca (proper) cultivators who "engaged purely in agriculture and in nothing else"—itself a somewhat inaccurate definition since, as we shall see, a large number of cultivators, particularly Satnami tenants undertook subsidiary occupations—had come down from twenty-seven acres in 1868 to about seventeen acres in 1927. It needs to be added here that Sargaon was a representative but prosperous village. In certain other areas the average size of holdings could be as low as 7.04 acres. Ibid., pp. 22–24.

15. Ibid., p. 24.
16. Ibid., p. 25.
17. Ibid.
18. Ibid., p. 57.
19. Ibid.
20. Ibid., p. 56.
21. Ibid., p. 58; Bates, "Regional dependence," pp. 202–203.
22. J. C. McDougall, "Economic Survey," p. 77, CPG AD, no. 1-22, 1927, MPSRR.
23. Bates, "Regional dependence," p. 203.
24. *LRS Bilaspur 1927–32*, p. 8.
25. Ibid.; Bates, "Regional dependence," p. 203.
26. *LRS Bilaspur 1927–32*, p. 8.
27. Bates, "Regional dependence," p. 205.
28. "Forecast Report of Durg," CPG SSD, no. 22-11, 1929, MPSRR.
29. Ibid.; "Raipur Maturity Report," CPG SSD, no. 22-3, 1927, MPSRR; Russell and Hiralal, *Tribes and Castes*, p. 420.
30. "Forecast Report of Durg," CPG SSD, no. 22-11, 1929, MPSRR.
31. *CPPBECR*, vol. 4, pp. 910–11; "Raipur Maturity Report," CPG SSD, no. 22-3, 1927; "Forecast Report of Durg District," CPG SSD, no. 22-11, 1929, MPSRR.
32. It was this temporary character of migration that, in fact, distinguished it from migration to the Assam tea gardens, which was considered a permanent step: people in Chhattisgarh spoke of their relatives and neighbors who had gone to the tea gardens "as if they had passed beyond their kin." Deputy Commissioner, Raipur to Commissioner, Chhattisgarh Division, 13 January 1932, CPG CI, no. 11-1, 1932, MPSRR.
33. Officiating Commissioner, Nagpur to Secretary, Industry Department, Nagpur, 25 November 1922, CPG CI, no. 26-62, 1922, MPSRR.
34. Ibid.
35. I have been unable to cull evidence for the effects these spells outside Chhattisgarh had on the Satnamis.
36. "Raipur Maturity Report," CPG SSD, no. 22-3, 1927, MPSRR.
37. Ibid.
38. This dispute is discussed in Saurabh Dube, "Telling tales and trying truths: Transgressions, entitlements and legalities in late colonial central India," *Studies in History* 12 (1996), 171–201. King Emperor vs. Santram, Sessions Trial, no. 1, 1939, Bilaspur, DSC, RR, Raipur.
39. "Meri Daura Report [My Tour Report]" (Hindi manuscript), 2A, SW, BRP, NMML. See also the Introduction above and chapters 5 and 6 below.
40. Ibid., fols. 3–5. My translation.

41. Ibid., fol. 2.
42. There were a number of Satnamis who did not wish to be named as the narrators of these accounts of *gaonthia zamana*. In the notes, therefore, I use pseudonyms for informants and villages. Oral testimony of Pyare, Koni, 7 December 1989.
43. Oral testimony of Uttara, Birkona, 21 January 1990.
44. Oral testimony of Umesh, Chhotti Koni, 25 November 1989.
45. *LRS Bilaspur 1927–32*, p. 32.
46. Oral testimony of Pitambar, Khulna, 27 February 1990.
47. Oral testimony of Manu, Narbadakhapri, 1 December 1989.
48. *LRS Bilaspur 1927–32*, p. 32.
49. Chandu, Koni, 5 December 1989.
50. Oral testimony of Magnu, Birkona, 19 January 1990.
51. *LRS Bilaspur 1927–32*, p. 32.
52. Oral testimony of Jaggu, Khubra, 26 January 1990.
53. Oral testimony of Chotelal, Koni, 24 November 1989.
54. Oral testimony of Khem, Sendri, 10 December 1989.
55. Oral testimony of Samelal, Sendri, 3 December 1989. In 1921 the literacy figures for Chamars—there are no separate figures for Satnamis—in the Central Provinces reveal that out of a total of 881,674 only 3,706 or 00.42 percent were literate and a mere 152 or 00.017 percent were literate in English. *Census of India 1921*, XI, II (Allahabad, 1923), p. 75.
56. Oral testimony of Udayram, Birkona, 19 January 1990.
57. Oral testimony of Shyamlal, Koni, 8 April 1990.
58. Oral testimony of Kallu, Chhotti Koni, 10 December 1990.
59. A number of these sanctions were played out in the dispute between a group of Satnamis and dominant members of the village community in Darri in the Bilaspur district in the late 1930s. See Dube, "Telling tales and trying truths."
60. Oral testimony of Khilawan, Koni, 1 December 1989.
61. As the Introduction has discussed, this crucial place of aspects of colonial governance in the constitution of power within the caste order is left out by the main theories of caste in South Asia.
62. The two paragraphs that follow are based on several discussions I had with members of the different castes—among them Brahmans (including *purohits*), members of service castes, Rajputs, and Satnamis—between February and April 1990.
63. This is not to deny important differences in the various exchange relations between dominant castes and *purohits* and service castes in late colonial Chhattisgarh. The problems with clubbing together different forms of prestations and exchanges and an emphasis on the giving of *dana* as the constituting element and basic structural principle of the ritual

centrality of the farming caste—where *dana* by the *jajmans* (patrons of the sacrifice) of the dominant castes to *purohits* and members of service castes serves to enhance the former's power through a transferal of inauspiciousness to the latter—have been very well developed recently by Jens Lerche. My point here is merely that the relationships with service castes played a key role in serving to define kingly authority at the level of the village. Jens Lerche, "Dominant castes, rajas, Brahmins and inter-caste exchange relations in coastal Orissa: Behind the facade of the '*jajmani* system,'" *Contributions to Indian Sociology* (n.s.), 27 (1993), pp. 237–66.

64. Oral testimony of Briju, Koni, 1 December 1989.

65. The concerns of *chhua* and the discriminatory practices it entails—including the Satnami exclusion from the web of relationships with service castes—continue to be a part of village life in Chhattisgarh today.

66. Oral testimony of Ramlal, Koni, 1 December 1989.

67. Oral testimony of Dukhwa, Narbadakhapri, 21 January 1990.

68. Oral testimony of Sukaloo, Jharonda, 22 January 1990.

69. Oral testimony of Dharmu, Pendri, 3 April 1990.

70. Thus, *contra* Gloria Raheja the ritual hierarchy of purity and pollution and the ritual centrality of kingship and dominant caste(s) do not emerge here as contextually separate and broadly opposed principles. See Raheja, "Centrality, mutuality and hierarchy" and the discussion in the Introduction above.

71. Dumont, *Homo Hierarchicus*; Dirks, "The original caste" and *The Hollow Crown*; Raheja, *Poison in the Gift*; Quigley, *Interpretation of Caste*. See the discussion of these issues in the Introduction above.

72. *C.P. Ethnographic Survey* (Nagpur, 1914), pp. 55–56.

73. Oral testimony of Asaram, Sakri, 22 January 1990.

74. Oral testimony of Behram, Jharonda, 28 November 1989.

75. Oral testimony of Khilawan, Koni, 17 December 1989.

76. Oral testimony of Gunaram, Sendri, 3 December 1989.

77. Ibid.

78. Oral testimony of Dhanu, Kharra, 26 November 1989.

79. Oral testimony of Khilawan, Koni, 29 November 1989.

80. Saurabh Dube, "Colonial law and village disputes: Two cases from Chhattisgarh" in N. Jayaram and Satish Saberwal (eds.), *Social Conflict: Oxford Readings in Sociology and Social Anthropology* (Delhi: Oxford University Press, 1996), pp. 434–44.

81. Oral testimony of Khilawan, Koni, 29 November 1989.

82. Dube, "Colonial law and village disputes," pp. 426–34.

83. This dispute is discussed in Dube, "Telling tales and trying truths." King Emperor vs. Balli and 13 others, Sessions Trial, no. 34, 1940, Bilaspur, DSC RR, Raipur.

84. Oral testimony of Uttara, Koni, 11 April 1990.

85. Leela Dube, "Construction of gender;" Flueckiger, *Gender and Genre*, Harlan and Courtright (eds.), *Margins of Hindu Marriage*; Raheja and Gold, *Heron's Words*; Sax, *Mountain Goddess*. It should be evident that my discussion here owes much to the work of Gloria Goodwin Raheja.

86. See also Sylvia J. Vatuk, "Gifts and affines," *Contributions to Indian Sociology* (n.s.), 5 (1975), 155–96; and Leela Dube, *Women and Kinship: Comparative Perspectives on Gender in South and South-East Asia* (Tokyo: United Nations University Press, 1997).

87. Gloria Goodwin Raheja, "'Crying when she is born, and crying when she goes away': Marriage and the idiom of the gift in Pahansu song performance," in Harlan and Courtright (eds.), *Margins of Hindu Marriage*, pp. 22–25. For an argument stressing the divergent devolutions of property in north India see Stanley J. Tambiah, "Dowry and bridewealth and the property rights of women in South Asia," in Jack Goody and Stanley J. Tambiah, *Bridewealth and Dowry* (Cambridge: Cambridge University Press, 1973).

88. Pierre Bourdieu, *Outline of a Theory of Practice* (Cambridge: Cambridge University Press, 1977), p. 36.

89. Ibid., p. 35.

90. Discussions of Bourdieu's writings have become academic industry, but for a valuable critique that ties up with some of the concerns developed in this book, particularly the difficulties that surround the analytical opposition between state and community, see Michael Herzfeld, *Anthropology through the Looking-Glass: Critical Ethnography in the Margins of Europe* (Cambridge: Cambridge University Press, 1987).

91. Bourdieu, *Theory of Practice*, p. 38. I have modified and extended Bourdieu's analogy here.

92. Raheja and Gold, *Heron's Words*, p. 32.

93. Ibid., pp. 73–120 and passim; Leela Dube, "Construction of gender;" Sax, *Mountain Goddess*.

94. Raheja, "Crying when she is born," p. 26; Flueckiger, *Gender and Genre*, pp. 77–103.

95. I borrow the category of historical field work from Shahid Amin, modifying it for my purposes. During field work, my discussions with informants kept in view issues suggested by the archive, but even as I pursued more conventional anthropological questions these were cast in a dialogue with the "historical imagination." Similarly, my reading of official records and nonofficial material was informed by an ethnographic sensibility. Such modes of reading, research, and writing underlie this book, including my discussions of gender among the Satnamis. Now, Gloria Raheja and Ann Gold have argued that repositioning the concerns of *Subaltern Studies*

scholars within an ethnographic enquiry into gender, kinship, and power makes it possible "to ask questions concerning contextual shifts in meaning and value, sometimes indexed only by an ironic tone, a gesture, a pattern of rhyme in a wedding song. Sociality often finds its meaning in such evanescent subtlety, the embellishments and improvisations that provide the ground for creativity and resistance and that can only rarely be recovered from the historical archive." It is true that Raheja and Gold's sensitive ethnographic enquiry leads them to "grasp the relation between hegemonic discourses on kinship and gender, on the one hand, and women's subjectivity and agency, on the other," within the context of lives they came to share, in ways that far exceed the paucity of the historical archive here. Yet, an ethnographic history that sets up a dialogue between archival and field work and reads the historical record against the grain through ethnographic filters contains the possibility of an alternate (if less detailed) take regarding the discontinuities of subaltern voices, and the interpenetration of the hegemonic and the subversive in subaltern visions, including the ways in which these discontinuities and interpenetrations are played out in the (simultaneously "structural" and "existential") domains of gender and kinship. Amin, *Event, Metaphor, Memory*; Raheja and Gold, *Heron's Words*, pp. 14–17.

96. Chapters 5 and 6 below take up issues of gender and kinship in the contexts of the analytical domain of myth and the agendas of community and nation, respectively.

97. *C.P. Ethnographic Survey*, pp. 52–53.

98. Oral testimony of Bhagwan, Vishapur, 11 January 1990.

99. Through a certain stretch of the imagination we can see possible links between *jhanjeri chauka* and practices of *tantra* and/or polyandry. Extreme paucity of evidence, however, makes it very difficult to establish the roots and development of the ritual. Instead of constructing a speculative history, posing as disinterested science, I focus here on the questions of meaning and power relating to gender within *jhanjeri chauka* from available accounts.

100. On barrenness and the metaphors of the field and the seed see Leela Dube, "Seed and earth: The symbolism of biological reproduction and sexual relations of production," in Leela Dube, Eleanor Leacock, Shirley Ardener (eds.) *Visibility and Power: Essays on Women in Society in Development* (Delhi: Oxford University Press, 1986), pp. xi–xliv; pp. 22–53.

101. Of course, it possibly also helps matters that the epic *Mahabharata* "offers us, in three generations, positive images of women who have had several husbands, the first generation [Ambika, Ambalika and Vyasa] through *niyoga* [practice allowing a widow to have sexual relations with her deceased husband's brother in order to bear children], the second

[Kunti, Madri, and the five gods] through a pseudo-*niyoga*, and the third [Draupadi and the five Pandavas] through simple polyandry." Wendy Doniger, "Begetting on margin: Adultery and surrogate pseudomarriage in Hinduism," in Lindsey Harlan and Paul Courtright (eds.), *Margins of Hindu Marriage*, p. 176.

102. Oral testimony of Mogra, Bhopal, June 1985. This testimony was recorded by S. C. Dube after Mogra had begun to treat him as her brother within the networks of fictive kinship. Not only was it virtually impossible for me as a younger male to get much information on the subject from Satnami women and men, even after Leela Dube, a senior woman anthropologist who had carried out research on Gond women in Chhattisgarh in the 1950s, joined me in the field for three weeks of field work together, the information on sexual exploitation of Satnami women was barely forthcoming.

103. Baba Ramchandra, "Meri Daura Report," 2A, SW, BRP, NMML. Baba Ramchandra, "Satnami Panchkanya Dehati ki Jeevni" (Hindi manuscript), no. 4, fols. 6–8, 2A, SW III, BRP, NMML. See also chapter 6 below.

104. Ibid.

105. The following two paragraphs are based on discussions with Satnami men and women and members of other castes in the field between November 1989 and April 1990.

106. The high incidence of *churi* among the Satnamis is admitted by the group in its self-representations and was also written about by administrators. At the turn of the century the census reported, the Satnamis are "distinguished by their carelessness of the fidelity of their wives, which they justify by saying, 'If my cow wanders and comes home again, shall I not let her enter the stall again.'" *Census of India 1901*, XIII, I, p. 87. Twenty years earlier the census had commented on the "good many" Satnami women who would go to jail for bigamy if the Penal Code were strictly administered in Chhattisgarh. *Census of the Central Provinces 1881*, II, p. 39.

107. Leela Dube, "Caste and women" in M. N. Srinivas (ed.) *Caste: Its Twentieth Century Avatar* (New Delhi: Viking Penguin, 1996); F. A. Marglin, *Wives of the God King: The Rituals of the Devadasis of Puri* (Delhi: Oxford University Press, 1985), pp. 46–64.

108. Maya Unnithan-Kumar, "Gender and 'tribal' identity in western India," *Economic and Political Weekly*, (1991), pp. (ws.) 37. For an argument that the institution of brideprice increases a wife's bargaining power, see Pauline Kolenda, *Regional Differences in Family Structure in India* (Jaipur: Rawat, 1987), pp. 108–11.

109. Unnithan-Kumar, "Gender and identity," p. 38.

110. The details of the devolution of property among the Satnamis are discussed in K. C. Dubey, *Kosa: A village Survey*, pp. 41–42.

111. This is not to suggest that women of those castes who do not have secondary marriages, widow remarriages, and levirate are passive and inert victims of patriliny. I am merely arguing here that *churi* among the Satnamis imparts a specific character and distinct flavor to the forms of maneuver and the shape of relative autonomy within wider patrilineal structures for the women of the group.

112. Simon Schama, *The Embarrassment of Riches: An Interpretation of Dutch Culture in the Golden Age* (New York: Alfred A. Knopf, 1988), p. 4.

113. The King vs. Samelal Santokhi, Sessions Trial, no. 42, 1947, Bilaspur, DSC RR, Raipur.

114. Oral testimony of Bhukhan, Kormi, 24 February 1990.

115. Deposition of Witness Uderam, PW 4, Sessions Trial, no. 42, 1947, Bilaspur.

116. Deposition of Witness Uderam, PW 4, Sessions Trial, no. 42, 1947, Bilaspur.

117. Lainmati or Laini was thirteen years old in 1947 and, I was told, died a few years ago. Oral testimony of Bhuru, Kormi, 26 February 1990.

118. Samelal was not listed as an independent cultivator in the village settlement records of 1928–1929 and his father Santokhi owned only 6.03 acres of land. Settlement Records, Bandobast, no. 74, Patwari Halka, no. 67, Collectorate Record Room, Bilaspur.

119. Deposition of Witness Uderam, PW 4, Sessions Trial, no. 42, 1947, Bilaspur.

120. Deposition of Witness Chintadass, PW 1, Sessions Trial, no. 42, 1947, Bilaspur.

121. Ibid.

122. According to the *malguzar* of the village, "Puna and Samelal had come [from Calcutta] with money. Puna had bought land after her return from Calcutta. The price was paid by her." Deposition of witness Malikram, PW 3, Sessions Trial, no. 42, 1947, Bilaspur.

123. Samelal had stated, "The field was bought with the money which both of us had earned in Calcutta." Examination of the accused Samelal, Sessions Trial, no. 42, 1947, Bilaspur.

124. Deposition of witness Uderam, PW 4, Sessions Trial, no. 42, 1947, Bilaspur.

125. Ibid.

126. Ibid.

127. Ibid.

128. Judgement, Sessions Trial, no. 42, 1947, Bilaspur.

129. Deposition of witness Ratanlal, PW 9, Sessions Trial, no. 42, 1947, Bilaspur.

130. Ibid.

131. Oral testimony of Bhuru, Kormi, 26 February 1990.

Chapter 5. A Contested Past: The Myths of Satnampanth

1. Baba Ramchandra did not say very much more about his wife except that he left her well provided for when he decided to come back to India. Kapil Kumar, "Rural women in Oudh 1917–47: Baba Ramchandra and the women's question," in Kumkum Sangari and Sudesh Vaid (eds.), *Recasting Women: Essays in Colonial History* (New Delhi: Kali for Women, 1988), p. 340.

2. See Kapil Kumar, *Peasants in Revolt: Tenants, Landlords, Congress and the Raj in Oudh 1886–1922* (New Delhi: Manohar, 1984), and "Using the Ramcharitmanas as a radical text: Baba Ramchandra in Oudh 1920–50," in Sudhir Chandra (ed.), *Social Transformations and Creative Imagination* (Delhi: Allied, 1984); Gyan Pandey, "Peasant revolt and Indian nationalism: Peasant movement in Awadh 1919–22," in Guha (ed.), *Subaltern Studies I*, pp. 143–97; M. H. Siddiqi, *Agrarian Unrest in North India: The United Provinces 1918–22* (New Delhi: Manohar, 1978).

3. The specific term used by Ramchandra was *poonjipatiyon ki Congress*, a Congress of capitalists. Ramchandra was disenchanted with the Congress because, as he saw it, his discussions with Jawaharlal Nehru failed. Moreover, peasants from Bihar and Ajmer were insulted—including not being allowed to enter the arena of meetings—which resulted in a battle ending in a victory for the peasants. No.1, fol. 8, 2C, SW, BRP, NMML.

4. The first substantial part of the *Vanshavali* is in 5, II, SW, BRP, NMML; I came across the second part of the manuscript in 2B, III, BRP, NMML. The *Vanshavali* is incomplete.

5. Santdas Sant (Baba Ramchandra), (*Sankshipt* [condensed]) *Satnam Sagar, Bhag I Itihas* (Raipur, 1929). See also chapter 7 below.

6. It is perhaps significant that what Ong calls the modern "discovery" of oral cultures came about with Milman Parry's thesis that virtually every distinctive characteristic of Homeric poetry was enforced on it by oral methods of composition. Ong, *Orality and Literacy*, pp. 20–27.

7. Jonathan D. Schaeffer, "The use and misuse of Giambattista Vico: Rhetoric, orality and theories of discourse," in H. Aram Veeser (ed.), *The New Historicism* (New York and London: Routledge, 1989), pp. 89–101.

8. Juan M. Ossio, "Myth and history: The seventeenth-century chronicle of Guaman Poma de Ayala," in Ravindra Jain (ed.), *Text and Context: The Social Anthropology of Tradition* (Philadelphia: Institute for the Study of Human Issues, 1977), pp. 51–93.

9. *Vanshavali*, fol. 2, 5, II, SW, BRP, NMML.

10. Santdas [Baba Ramchandra], *Satnam Sagar* (Raipur, 1929).

11. This is not to suggest, of course, that each oral rendering of these myths that I heard and recorded during field work corresponded in every detail to the way they were written in the *Vanshavali*. Rather, it is to argue that the main elements of the myths about Ghasidas and Balakdas were known to the older Satnamis because, as they claimed, the tales had been told across generations. Even the more obscure details within the myths often surfaced in one retelling or another. Some of these retellings were brief and others detailed, many relatively straightforward and a few extraordinarily embellished—depending upon the circumstances of my meeting with the narrator and his/her knowledge and passion—as parts of inherited and ongoing oral traditions. In this account, I rehearse the myths as recorded in the *Vanshavali*, but also indicate the key points where the tales I heard during field work differed significantly from their written version in the text.

12. Interview with Sunderlal Tripathi, Bhopal, June 1987.

13. Oral testimony of Mahant Sonwani, Girodpuri, 1 March 1989.

14. Most Satnami oral accounts that I heard and recorded during field work, discussed in chapter 2 above, recalled an anecdote or two about Ghasidas's early life, before taking up the critical encounter with his agricultural master.

15. *Vanshavali*, fol. 1.

16. Ibid., fols. 1–2. Satnami oral accounts often do not mention that *satnampurush* tied the two pieces of coconut to Ghasidas's clothes; but, as we shall see, this act was critical for the version rehearsed before and/or by Baba Ramchandra.

17. Ibid., fol. 2.

18. Ibid., fol. 3. In contemporary oral accounts of the Satnamis, the death of Ghasidas's children is generally presented as an outcome of their eating fish they had caught in a pond, despite the warning issued by *satnampurush* who spoke to them through the medium of the dead fish. At the same time, in these oral testimonies, quite like the account rehearsed in the *Vanshavali*, the sudden death of his children paves the way for Ghasidas's mood of renunciation and his retirement to the forest of Sonakhan.

19. Ibid., fols. 3–5.

20. Obeyesekere, *Pattini*, pp. 306–12.

21. *Vanshavali*, fol. 6.

22. Obeyesekere, *Pattini*, pp. 292–93.

23. *Vanshavali*, fol. 7. The *Vanshavali* does not tell us anything more about the moneylender or the Gond raja. It is possible that the raja was Veer

Narayan Singh who, in colonial eyes, was a recalcitrant *zamindar.* Jenkins, *Nagpur,* pp. 134–35.

24. Ibid., fols. 7–8.

25. It has been suggested to me that a simpler and more convincing intepretation of this myth consists of arguing that, by sending betel leaves and coconuts to the Gond king, Ghasidas was acting as a superior distributor of *prasad,* and by not sending money he was avoiding putting himself in the position of an inferior donor of tribute. But it must be kept in mind here that in Satnami myths Ghasidas is consistently described as a guru who commanded coconuts and betel leaves but no money, the signifiers of different spheres of authority. I am grateful to this reader, who must remain anonymous, for these and other suggestions.

26. Ibid., fol. 8.

27. Ranajit Guha has discussed modes of transport as symbols of upper-caste domination and their appropriation as an act of inversion. Ranajit Guha, *Elementary Aspects of Peasant Insurgency in Colonial India* (Delhi: Oxford University Press, 1983), pp. 66–68.

28. The next two paragraphs are based on *Vanshavali,* fols. 9–10.

29. Kapil Kumar has discussed how Baba Ramchandra himself addressed peasant meetings sitting on a cot tied up high between the branches of trees. The incident of Ghasidas perched on a tree could have been an addition made either by Ramchandra or his Satnami informants after hearing about it from him. At the same time, the fact of Ghasidas's *darshan,* of the transmission of his authority through sight, has an important place within the myths of Satnampanth. Kapil Kumar, *Peasants in Revolt,* pp. 89–90.

30. The place of *darshan* of a guru, a two-way process that constitutes a spectacle, occupies a central place within *bhakti* and *sant* traditions. For an interesting discussion of the transmission of a guru's authority through sight see Lawrence Babb, *Redemptive Encounters: Three Modern Styles in the Hindu Tradition* (Delhi: Oxford University Press, 1987), pp. 78–79.

31. On writing as a form of power in the colonial Indian context see, for instance, Ranajit Guha, *Elementary Aspects,* pp. 51–55.

32. On the relationship of a woman with her husband's elder brother in the Chhattisgarh region, see Flueckiger, *Gender and Genre,* p. 91.

33. *Vanshavali,* fols. 7–8.

34. The concept of sanskritization was first developed by M. N. Srinivas. See Srinivas, *Religion and Society among the Coorgs of South India* (Oxford: Oxford University Press, 1952); *Social Change in Modern India* (Berkeley and Los Angeles: University of California Press, 1966), pp. 1–45. The concept has been extended to the Satnamis by McEldowney, "Colonial administration," pp. 499–500.

35. The concept of sanskritization has been used, debated, and criticized seemingly endlessly over the years. David Hardiman has engaged with and provided an effective recent critique of the category. My criticisms of the concept take up and carry forward Hardiman's arguments: Sanskritization underestimates conflict generated by the appropriation of upper-caste symbols by low castes. The theory lacks a convincing historical dimension, and the way out of the impasse does lie in relating values to power. At the same time, I also stress that such appropriation of upper-caste symbols tends to reproduce the significance of dominant meanings since it often functions within hegemonic limits. Hardiman, *Coming of the Devi*, pp. 157–65.

36. Veena Das makes a similar point in "Subaltern as perspective" in Guha (ed.), *Subaltern Studies VI*, pp. 318–19.

37. *Vanshavali*, fols. 18–20.

38. Interview with Kanhaiyalal Kosariya, Bhopal, 3–4 June 1987.

39. *Vanshavali*, fols. 28–29.

40. Ibid., fols. 29–30.

41. *Vanshavali*, fols. 13–14, 21–22.

42. Ibid., fols. 23–24.

43. Ibid., fols. 15–16.

44. Ibid., fols. 31–34. This is the point at which the first part of the *Vanshavali* ends. The next part was written on sheets of a smaller size and carried new folio numbers.

45. *Vanshavali*, fol. 1, 2B, III, SW, BRP, NMML.

46. The myths about the later gurus that follow constitute a more specialized domain of knowledge than those about Ghasidas and Balakdas. A few of my informants, notably those who belonged to the families of *mahants* (or those who were otherwise close to the extended guru family), knew the stories about the later gurus in rudimentary forms, but they could never match the immense detail of the *Vanshavali* here. These informants often mentioned that the myths about the later gurus that I was seeking were much better known to people—here specific individuals were generally identified and named before me—of their grandfather's and father's generation who had died, sometimes many years ago. There is also a larger point here. Mythic dramas rehearsing stories of success and heroic histories of Ghasidas and Balakdas had a much greater capacity to capture the imagination of the Satnamis than the more fragmentary tales recounting the failures of the later gurus. See the Conclusion below.

47. See Raheja and Gold, *Heron's Words*.

48. Ibid.

49. See Bourdieu, *Theory of Practice*.

50. A discussion of these themes in the context of disputes among

kin in village life is contained in Dube, "Telling tales and trying truths," pp. 174–91; and Dube, "Village disputes and colonial law," pp. 426–34.

51. *Vanshavali,* fols. 11, 23, 5, II, SW, BRP, NMML.
52. *Vanshavali,* fol. 1, 2B, III, SW, BRP, NMML.
53. Ibid.
54. Ibid., fol. 2.
55. Ibid.
56. Ibid., fols. 3–4.
57. Ibid., fol. 4.
58. Ibid., fol. 5.

Chapter 6. Reform and Authority: The Satnami Mahasabha, 1925–1950

1. The illiteracy of the Satnamis also meant that it was the intervention of the figure of the outsider, of writing within an oral tradition, which generated most of the sources of the Satnami Mahasabha. Although certain petitions, tracts, and letters mention the year and place they were written/published, a substantial body of the papers are in the form of fragments from personal notebooks that do not refer to the moment they were constituted. Moreover, it is only on rare occasions that administrators' reports and newspapers at the provincial level register the voices and efforts of a local initiative. The nature of the sources permits only a rough chronology for the Satnami Mahasabha and its activities. At the same time, the sources—in Hindi, Chhattisgarhi, and Awadhi, scripted in Devanagri—and Satnami oral narratives about the leaders of the Mahasabha, situated alongside archival, missionary, and newspaper reports and oral testimonies, lend themselves to a reading of the cultural process and the play of authority and power that underlay the Satnami organizational endeavor.

2. See Rafiuddin Ahmed, *The Bengal Muslims: A Quest for Identity* (Delhi: Oxford University Press, 1981); N. G. Barrier (ed.), *The Census in British India: New Perspectives* (New Delhi: Manohar, 1981); Paul Brass, *Language, Religion and Politics in North India* (New York: Cambridge University Press, 1974); Sandria B. Freitag, *Collective Action and Community: Public Arenas and the Emergence of Communalism in North India* (Delhi: Oxford University Press, 1990); Peter Hardy, *Muslims of British India* (Cambridge: Cambridge University Press, 1972); Kenneth W. Jones, *Arya Dharma: Hindu Consciousness in Nineteenth-Century Punjab* (Berkeley and Los Angeles: University of California Press, 1976); J. T. F. Jordens, *Dayanand Saraswati: His Life and Ideas* (Delhi: Oxford University Press, 1978); David Lelyveld, *Aligarh's First Generation: Muslim Solidarity in British India* (Princeton: Princeton University

Press, 1978); Barbara Metcalf, *Islamic Revival in British India: Deoband 1860–1900* (Princeton: Princeton University Press, 1982); Oberoi, *Construction of Religious Boundaries*; Gyanendra Pandey, *The Construction of Communalism in Colonial North India* (Delhi: Oxford University Press, 1990).

3. See Pandey, *Construction of Communalism*; and Chatterjee, "Claims on the past."

4. See, for instance, Partha Chatterjee, *The Nation and Its Fragments: Colonial and Postcolonial Histories* (Delhi: Oxford University Press, 1994); Rosalind O'Hanlon, "Issues of widowhood: Gender and resistance in colonial western India," in Douglas Haynes and Gyan Prakash (eds.), *Contesting Power: Resistance and Everyday Social Relations in South Asia* (Delhi: Oxford University Press, 1991); and the studies of caste initiatives discussed in the Introduction above.

5. See, for instance, Ranajit Guha (ed.), *Subaltern Studies*, vols. 1–6 (Delhi, 1982–89); Chatterjee and Pandey (eds.), *Subaltern Studies VII*; Arnold and Hardiman (eds.), *Subaltern Studies VIII*; Pandey, *Construction of Communalism*; and Hardiman, *Coming of the Devi*.

6. Pandey, *Construction of Communalism*, p. 211.

7. Chatterjee, *Nation and Its Fragments*, p. 238.

8. Pandey, *Construction of Communalism*, p. 231–32.

9. Chatterjee, *Nation and Its Fragments*, p. 237.

10. Ibid.

11. See the Conclusion below.

12. Chatterjee, *Nation and Its Fragments*, p. 237.

13. D. E. U. Baker, *Changing Political Leadership in an Indian Province: The Central Provinces and Berar 1919–39* (Delhi: Oxford University Press, 1979).

14. *The Hitavada*, 1 May 1920; *The Hitavada*, 29 April 1926.

15. Thus, Kalicharan Ganujee, president of the C.P. Depressed Classes Association at Gondia declared in 1926 that he was a supporter of the Congress creed; and when Anjordas of the Satnami Mahasabha stood as an independent in the C.P. Legislative Council elections of 1926 he was supported by the Swarajists in Chhattisgarh. *The Hitavada*, 23 October 1920; *The Hitavada*, 1 November 1925; *The Hitavada*, 15 April 1926; *The Hitavada*, 3 January 1926; *The Hitavada*, 29 April 1926; *The Hitavada*, 4 November 1926; CPG GAD, no. 24-21, MPSRR.

16. Baker, *Changing Political Leadership*, pp. 17, 100, 115–17.

17. We do not know whether these steps of Naindas and Anjordas were influenced by the activities of the All India Cow Protection Conference. The Conference had met at Nagpur in the last week of December 1920 and asked for a ban on the slaughter of cows. *The Hitavada*, 8 January 1921; *The Hitavada*, 22 January 1921.

18. Oral testimony of Mahant Ramsanehi, Sendri, 27 November 1989; Oral testimony of Mahant Sawaldas Mahilang, Girod, 2 March 1990.

19. Interview with Bhuvanlal Mishra, Raipur, 4 September 1988; Letters from different castes—Mehra Samaj, Chauhan Mandli, Panka Mandli, Kandra Mandli, Ganda Mandli, Baya Mandli, Bajaniya Mandli—to Rajiv Lochan Temple Committee (no date), Sunderlal Sharma Papers, Rajim.

20. G. A. Gavai, Secretary of the Depressed Classes Association to Pandit Sunderlal Sharma, 24 October 1925, Sunderlal Sharma Papers, Rajim.

21. Oral testimony of Mahant Ramsanehi, Sendri, 29 November 1989; Oral testimony of Mahant Sawaldas Mahilang, Girod, 2 March 1990.

22. Deputy Commissioner, Durg to Commissioner, Chhattisgarh Division, 28 June 1926, CPG GAD, no. 24-26, 1926, MPSRR. The activities of the divisional, district, and local chapters of the Depressed Classes Association were mainly supported by substantial members of the constituent communities. *The Hitavada*, 5 June 1927.

23. No.1, fol. 8, 2C, SW, BRP, NMML.

24. Ibid.

25. Petition from the Satnami Mahasabha, 27 January 1926, CPG GAD, no. 24-26, 1926, MPSRR. The petition was signed by G. A. Gavai, Ratiram, Anjordas, and Naindas on behalf of the Satnami Mahasabha.

26. Ibid.

27. Of the different headings under which the notations on the file were organized, only numbers (1), (3), and (6) were considered important for investigation by the Governor. Note of Governor, 27 January 1926, CPG GAD, no. 24-26, 1926, MPSRR.

28. Note of Chief Secretary, 2 February 1926, CPG GAD, no. 24-26, 1926, MPSRR.

29. Deputy Commissioner, Bilaspur to the Secretary to Government, CP, GAD, 29 April 1926; Deputy Commissioner, Raipur to the Secretary to Government, CPG GAD, 11 May 1926, CPG GAD, no. 24-26, 1926, MPSRR.

30. Note by the Deputy Inspector General Police, Eastern Range, CP, 24 May 1926, CPG GAD, no. 24-26, 1926, MPSRR.

31. Inspector General Police, C.P. to the Secretary to Government, C.P., GAD, 27 May 1926, CPG GAD, no. 24-26, 1926, MPSRR.

32. Commissioner, Chhattisgarh Division to the Director of Public Instruction, Nagpur, 4 August 1926, CPG GAD, no. 24-26, 1926, MPSRR.

33. Ibid.

34. Deputy Commissioner, Durg to Commissioner, Chhattisgarh Division, 28 June, 1926; Deputy Commissioner, Raipur to Commissioner, Chhattisgarh Division, 23 July, 1926; Deputy Commissioner, Bilaspur to Commissioner, Chhattisgarh Division, 29 June 1926, CPG GAD, no. 24-26, 1926, MPSRR.

35. Circular No. C-105/130(A)-IV, Chief Secretary to the Government, C.P. to Mr. Ratiram Malguzar, President of the Satnami Mahasabha of Chhattisgarh Division, 7 October 1926, CPG GAD, no. 24-26, 1926, MPSRR.

36. In 1928 the Kanaujia Chamars of Chhattisgarh appealed to the "benign government" to remove the "vulgar" word *Chamar* and to refer to the community as Kanaujias. The effort was a part of a larger drive of reform that briefly involved the Kanaujia Chamars in giving up the occupations of midwifery and of skinning and removing dead animals in villages. A year later there was an appeal to record the followers of Ravidas among the Chamars as Rabidasis and not as Chamars or Satnamis. The appeal was revived in 1936 and 1939 when the Rabidasi Chamars—who had evidently won the demand that they be called Rabidasis without, however, losing the attendant signifier of Chamar—asked the government to record them as Suryavanshi Ramanandis. The government rejected the petition from the Kanaujia Chamars and the second round of appeals of the Rabidasi Chamars. CPG GAD, no. 24-27, 1928, MPSRR; CPG GAD, no. 11-1, 1939, MPSRR; *The Hitavada*, 20 January, 1927.

37. *The Hitavada*, 23 December, 1926.

38. Oral testimony of Suritram, Sakri, 7 December 1989.

39. Oral testimony of Kamaundram, Devarmal, 23 March 1990.

40. Oral testimony of Mahant Sawaldas Mahilang, Girod, 3 March 1990.

41. The leaflet signed by Anjordas and Bisaldas was printed at the District Council Press, Raipur on 24 January 1929. No. 5, II, SW, BRP; no. 5, fol. 14, II, BRP, NMML.

42. No. 5, fol. 14, II, BRP, NMML.

43. No. 5, II, BRP, NMML.

44. Oral testimony of Bisahu, Jarhabhata, 25 February 1990.

45. No. 5, II, BRP, NMML.

46. Ibid.

47. Ibid.

48. The critical place of education in an untouchable initiative emerges, for instance, in the report of the Ad Dharm Mandal reproduced in Juergensmeyer, *Religion as Social Vision*, pp. 300–305.

49. Oral testimony of Mahant Ramsanehi, Sendri, 2 December 1989. The missionary Seybold had commented, "Even the low caste people, as the Chamars, are now beginning to send their boys to the middle schools in towns, and an Ashram, that is a sort of boarding house, was recently opened in Raipur for Chamar boys coming from villages." Seybold, Annual Report, Raipur, 1928, ARM, EAL.

50. "Meri Daura Report," 19(II), II, fol. 2, BRP, NMML; Anjordas, Raipur to Sunderlal Sharma, Rajim, 16 January 1928, Sunderlal Sharma Papers, Rajim.

51. Oral testimony of Mahant Sawaldas Mahilang, Girodpuri, 2 March 1990.

52. No. 1, fol. 7, 2C, SW, BRP, NMML. The educational venture received the support of the Raipur District Council. Raipur District Council, Minutes of Meeting, 1 November 1926, Proceedings of Raipur District Council (15 July 1922 to 30 January 1927), Panchayat Office, Raipur.

53. What we know about the formation of the school comes from a resolution drafted in the late 1920s by Baba Ramchandra and signed by Agamdas, Naindas, Anjordas, Anmoldas, Baba Ramchandra, Sarsu, and Balaram. No. 5, II, BRP, NMML.

54. Ibid.

55. Ibid.

56. Ibid.

57. Ramchandra continued, "If I get a proper answer to these questions then it is all right because Satnamis who have made contributions have asked me for explanations. I should get the reply soon. If there is no reply the matter shall be placed before the important members of the big committee. Whatever decision is taken there everyone will have to follow the proceedings. Understand this completely and then give me an answer. Each would bear the consequences of his action. It is not my fault." The letter dated 27 April 1929 was signed "one desiring your benefit, Baba Ramchandra, Organising President." No. 5, II, BRP, NMML.

58. These problems of financial and organizational mismanagement, in fact, seem to have been fairly standard within educational institutions set up by early caste associations and in initiatives of social reform. See O'Hanlon, *Caste, Conflict and Ideology,* pp. 281–82; Jordens, *Dayanand Saraswati,* pp. 65–66.

59. M. P. Davis, "The Satnami Tragedy," *The Evangelical Herald,* St. Louis, Mo., 8 June 1933.

60. Ibid.

61. No. 5, II, SW, BRP, NMML.

62. Ibid.

63. No. 5, fol. 14, II, SW, BRP, NMML.

64. Ibid.

65. Ibid.

66. No. 5, fol. 47, II, BRP, NMML.

67. No. 5, fol. 62, II, BRP, NMML.

68. Ibid.

69. Oral testimony of Diwan Chand, Sendri, 25 November 1989.

70. "Satnami Tragedy" (handwritten and typed manuscript) p. 4, FS, MPDP, EAL.

71. Oral testimony of Bhandari, Ledri, 19 December 1989.

72. Oral testimony of Mahant Ramsanehi, Sendri, 3 December 1989; Oral testimony of Mahant Sawaldas Mahilang, Girod, 3 March 1990; Oral testimony of Bisahu, Jarhabhata, 25 February 1990.

73. Oral testimony of Mahant Ramsanehi, Sendri, 27 November and 1 December 1989; Oral testimony of Bisahu, Jarhabhata, 25 February 1990; Oral testimony of Suritram, Sakri, 7 December 1989.

74. Apart from the people named in the last two notes the setting up and constitution of the *athgawana* was also confirmed by a large number of other Satnamis.

75. The new categories were mentioned by M. M. Paul as a part of the established Satnami organizational order in 1936 in *Satyanami Panth aur Shri Ghasidas Girodvasi* (Raipur, 1936), p. 2.

76. K. C. Dubey, *Kosa: A Village Survey*, p. 144..

77. Baba Ramchandra, "Satnami Panchkanya Dehati ki Jeevni," no. 4, fol. 3, 2A, SW III, BRP, NMML.

78. Baba Ramchandra continued, "Big people, do not hesitate in reforming your caste by reaching the echoes of this voice of the Panchkanyas from one ear to another. Guru, Mahatma, Bhandari, Sathidars, and Sants take this book for your children and use the ways set out in it to improve your household. Otherwise, after the moment is past you will repent. Arise, arise." Ibid.

79. Ibid., fol. 1.

80. Ibid., fols. 5–8.

81. On the purity of the *kanya*, the auspiciousness of the married woman, and her opposition with widow/prostitute see Leela Dube, "On the construction of gender." It is, of course, true that the auspicious-inauspicious distinction varies with contexts. In marriage, for instance, upper-caste brides used to take the *suhag* (vermilion) from a prostitute or, in Chhattisgarh, from a *dhobin*. The prostitute and *dhobin*—since she could remarry—were considered *sada-suhagan* (eternal brides). Marglin has also argued that the auspicious-inauspicious distinction, unlike concerns of purity and pollution, is nonhierarchical. Marglin, *Wives of the God King*. See also Leela Dube and Saurabh Dube, "Women in India, Hinduism and the category of 'politics'," *Journal of Social Studies*, 37 (1987), pp. 72–80.

82. For a discussion of similar themes in other contexts, see Das, *Critical Events* and Dube, "Paternalism and freedom." See also John D. Kelly, *A Politics of Virtue: Hinduism, Sexuality, and Countercolonial Discourse in Fiji* (Chicago: University of Chicago Press, 1991).

83. "Satnami Panchkanya Dehati," fols. 14–15. Kapil Kumar has discussed how Baba Ramchandra used the *Ramcharitmanas* as a radical text for political mobilization and a critique of colonial rule during the Awadh Kisan Sabha movement. The text could equally be deployed toward more

conservative ends. Kapil Kumar, "Using the Ramcharitmanas as a radical text."

84. "Satnami Panchkanya Dehati," fols. 12–13.

85. Ibid., fols. 17–18.

86. Ibid., fols. 21–23.

87. Ibid., fols. 24–28.

88. Oral testimony of Pitambar recorded by S. C. Dube, Bhopal, June 1985.

89. Lata Mani and Rosalind O'Hanlon have discussed how women increasingly came to be the key sign in the nineteenth-century debates about the status of Hindu tradition and the legitimacy of colonial power. These debates did not offer women a voice as subjects and denied them agency. O'Hanlon also points out that issues concerning women in projects of social reform could extend the control of men over women within the community. Lata Mani, "Contentious traditions: The debate on *sati* in colonial India," in Kumkum Sangari and Sudesh Vaid (eds.), *Recasting Women: Essays in Colonial History* (New Delhi: Kali for Women, 1989), pp. 86–126; O'Hanlon, "Issues of widowhood," pp. 71–72.

90. Michel Foucault, *Power/Knowledge: Selected Interviews and Other Writings, 1972–77* (New York: Pantheon, 1980), p. 198.

91. Comaroff, *Body of Power*, p. 260. My argument follows very different lines from that of Kapil Kumar who sees Baba Ramchandra as a radical social reformer, ahead of his times, who raised the status of rural women in Awadh by encouraging monogamy—*pativrata dharma*, a "humane household"—and women's participation in political forums. Kapil Kumar, it seems to me, ignores the mechanisms of restraint inherent in Baba Ramchandra's strategies. In his earnest desire to establish Baba Ramchandra as an early protagonist of the history of feminism, for instance, Kapil Kumar glosses over Ramchandra's descriptions of his sexual exploits in Fiji, which are clear illustrations of voyeuristic male fantasy. Kapil Kumar, "Rural women in Oudh," p. 346.

92. M. P. Davis, "The Satnami tragedy," *The Evangelical Herald*, St. Louis, Mo., 8 June 1933.

93. *The Hitavada*, 17 February 1927.

94. Oral testimony of Mahant Sawaldas Mahilang, Girod, 2 March 1990.

95. Oral testimony of Bhandari, Ledri, 19 December 1989.

96. M. P. Davis, "The Satnami tragedy," *The Evangelical Herald*, St. Louis, Mo., 8 June 1933.

97. Baker, *Changing Political Leadership*, pp. 135–36.

98. Oral testimony of Bhandari, Ledri, 19 December 1989.

99. Prabhudas Munshi, "Mauza Kukda ka Satnami Mandir" (manuscript in Hindi), 1934, FS, MPDP, EAL.

100. W. Baur, "Side-lights on a Satnami mela," Second Quarterly Report, Bisrampur, 1938, QRM, EAL.

101. Ibid., p. 1.

102. Ibid., p. 2.

103. Ibid.; E. M. Gordon, *Indian Folktales: Being Sidelights on Village Life in Bilaspore, Central Provinces* (London: Elliot Stock, 1908), pp. 20–21.

104. "Side-lights on a Satnami mela," pp. 3–4.

105. Ibid., p. 4.

106. "Charakpur ka Satnami Mandir" (manuscript report in Hindi), 1938, FS, MPDP, EAL.

107. Ibid.

108. Oral testimony of Mahant Ramsanehi, Sendri, 27 November 1989.

109. Ibid.

110. Oral testimony of Diwan Chand, Sendri, 25 November 1989.

111. M. P. Davis, "A modern Satnami tragedy" (typescript), 1942, p. 1, FS, MPDP, EAL.

112. Ibid., p. 2.

113. "Satnami samaj sudhar [Social reform of the Satnamis]" in M. P. Davis, "A modern Satnami tragedy," p. 4.

114. See chapter 7 below.

115. Deputy Commissioner, Raipur to the Commissioner, Chhattisgarh Division, 10 February 1938, CPG GAD, no. 24-52, 1938, MPSRR.

116. Commissioner, Chhattisgarh Division to the Undersecretary to Government, GAD, 13 June 1938, CPG GAD, no. 24-52, 1938, MPSRR.

117. Bishelal Mandal, Secretary, Shri Path Pradarshak Sabha to the Minister for Education, C.P. and Berar, 19 July 1938, CPG GAD, no. 24-52, 1938, MPSRR.

118. Ibid.

119. Ibid.

120. Ibid.

121. Ibid.

122. "Notice to Satnamis," 25 January 1938, appended to Davis, "A Modern Satnami Tragedy," FS, MPDP, EAL.

123. "Janta ko Itla," 1940, appended to Davis, "A Modern Satnami Tragedy," FS, MPDP, EAL.

124. Oral testimony of Mahant Sawaldas Mahilang, Girod, 3 March 1990.

125. M. P. Davis, "Notes on Satnamis," p.7, FS, MPDP, EAL; Interview with Vijay Guru, Bhopal, June 1987.

126. K. L. Hamilton to IG, Police, CP, 13 September, 1930, CPG Political and Military Department, CDM/187, 1930; Note by Deputy Superinten-

dent Police, 24 September 1930, CPG Political and Military Department, CDM/175, 1930, MPSRR; Baker, *Changing Political Leadership*, p. 135, p. 140; Oral testimony of Mahant Sawaldas Mahilang, Girod, 3 March 1990; Interview with Vijay Guru, Bhopal, June 1987.

127. *The Hitavada*, 14 July 1937.

128. Deputy Commissioner, Raipur to Commissioner, Chhattisgarh Division, 5 November 1946, CPG Political and Military Department Confidential, no. 144, 1947, MPSRR.

129. Dhananjay Keer, *Dr. Ambedkar: Life and Mission* (Bombay: Popular Prakashan, 1962), p. 351.

130. Juergensmeyer, *Religion as Social Vision*, pp. 161–62.

131. Deputy Commissioner, Raipur to Commissioner, Chhattisgarh Division, 5 November 1946, CPG Political and Military Department, Confidential, no. 144, 1947, MPSRR.

132. Copy of letter dated 27 February 1926 from M. D. Amade, General Secretary, SCF Nagpur to Khemji Bhiwande, Raipur, CPG Political and Military Department, Confidential, no. 144, 1947, MPSRR.

133. Deputy Superintendent Police, Raipur to District Magistrate, Raipur, 6 November 1947, CPG Political and Military Department, Confidential, no. 108, 1947, MPSRR.

134. Memo of Deputy Superintendent Police, Raipur, 31 October 1947, CPG Political and Military Department, Confidential, no. 108, 1947, MPSRR. The activities of Ambedkar at this time are discussed in Keer, *Dr. Ambedkar: Life and Mission*, pp. 398–402; B. G. Kunte (ed.), *Source Material on Dr. Babasaheb Ambedkar and the Movement of Untouchables* I (Bombay: Popular Prakashan, 1982), p. 381.

135. Memo of Deputy Superintendent Police, Raipur, 31 October 1947, CPG Political and Military Department, Confidential, no. 108, 1947, MPSRR.

136. Extracts of letter from P. N. Rajbhog to Dada Saheb Gaekwad, 25 October 1947, CPG Political and Military Department, Confidential, no. 108, 1947, MPSRR.

137. A copy of the leaflet is contained in CPG Political and Military Department, Confidential, no. 108, 1947, MPSRR.

Chapter 7. Contending Histories: Old Stories and New Pasts

1. Santdas Sant (Baba Ramchandra), *Satnam Sagar* (Raipur, 1929).

2. M. M. Paul, *Satyanami Panth aur Shri Gosain Ghasidas Girodvasi* (Raipur, 1936).

3. Santdas Sant, *Satnam Sagar.*

4. Ibid., pp. 1–2.

5. Ibid., pp. 5–6.

6. Ibid., pp. 7–9. I am grateful to professors Sumati Mutatkar and Leela Dube for pointing out the origins of these concepts.

7. Ibid., pp. 9–13.

8. Ibid., pp. 13–14.

9. Ibid., pp. 14–16.

10. Ibid., p. 14.

11. Ibid., pp. 16–17.

12. Ibid., p. 17.

13. Ibid., pp. 18–23.

14. Ibid., p. 24.

15. Ibid., pp. 24–25.

16. Ibid., pp. 25–26.

17. Ibid., p. 26.

18. Ibid., pp. 26–27.

19. Ibid., pp. 27–29.

20. Oral testimony of Mahant Sawaldas Mahilang, Girod, 3 March 1990.

21. Oral testimony of Pyarelal, Koni, 11 April 1990.

22. Oral testimony of Mahant Sawaldas Mahilang, Girod, 3 March 1990; Oral testimony of Vijay Guru, Bhopal, June 1987, and Girod, 2 March 1990. The point was made by several other Satnamis when I discussed with them the questions of *chauka* and Hindu sacred texts within Satnampanth.

23. Oral testimony of Santokhi, Koni, 12 April 1990.

24. Satnam Pracharak [Propagation] Committee, *"Shri Satnam ka Vachan* [The Word of Satnam]" (published leaflet), 15 July 1937, FS, MPDP, EAL.

25. The different ways in which notions of freedom and independence, with their roots in contemporary nationalist discourse, came to inform and structure the perceptions and practices of communities and groups in the domains of the familiar and the everyday in village life in the period are discussed in Shahid Amin, "Gandhi as mahatma: Gorakhpur district, eastern UP, 1921–22" in Guha (ed.), *Subaltern Studies III*, pp. 1–61; Dube, "Paternalism and Freedom" and "Village Disputes and colonial law."

26. Shri Path Pradarshak Sabha, *"Satnamiyon se do do baaten* [Two words with Satnamis]" (published leaflet), n.d., FS, MPDP, EAL.

27. From M. D. Singh, Secretary, Shri Path Pradarshak Sabha, Tumgaon to the Secretary, Legislative Assembly, CP, 12 December 1936, CPG GAD, no. 24-52, 1938, MPSRR.

28. It would seem that a Pandit Ramcharan provided the Sabha with the references to the laws of Manu. I am grateful to Professor Arindam

Chakravarty for translating from the Sanskrit the relevant passages from the *Manu Samhita.* I do not cite them here.

29. S. J. Tambiah, "From varna to caste through mixed unions" in Tambiah, *Culture, Thought, and Social Action: An Anthropological Perspective* (Cambridge, Mass., and London: Harvard University Press, 1985), p. 221.

30. Ibid., pp. 221–29.

31. See here Leela Dube, "Seed and Earth."

32. From M. D. Singh, Secretary, Shri Path Pradarshak Sabha, Tumgaon to the Secretary, Legislative Assembly, CP, 12 December 1936, CPG GAD, no. 24-52, 1938, MPSRR.

33. I have been unable to trace the *Bahakta Birdavali* of Satnam Press, Banaras.

34. Shri Path Pradarshak Sabha, "*Satnamiyon se do do baaten* [Two words with Satnamis]" (published leaflet), n.d., FS, MPDP, EAL.

35. From M. D. Singh, Secretary, Shri Path Pradarshak Sabha, Tumgaon to the Secretary, Legislative Assembly, CP, 12 December 1936, CPG GAD, no. 24-52, 1938, MPSRR.

36. F. A. Goetsch, Second Quarterly Report, Bisrampur, 1926, pp. 1–3, QRM, EAL.

37. This case is discussed at length in Dube, "Paternalism and freedom."

38. Seybold, *God's Guiding Hand,* pp. 75–77, 89–93.

39. In this endeavor, the different missionary organizations—of the Methodists, the Disciples of Christ, and the American and General Conference Mennonites—that had begun work in Chhattisgarh from around the turn of the century joined hands with the American Evangelical Mission, the new name for the German Evangelical Mission Society. Ibid., pp. 75–77; J. A. Lapp, *The Mennonite Church in India* (Scottdale: Herald Press, 1972), pp. 174–78; James C. Juhnke, *A People of Mission: A History of General Conference Mennonite Overseas Mission* (Newton: Faith and Life Press, 1979), pp. 40–41.

40. Seybold, *God's Guiding Hand,* pp. 86–87. See also, S. C. Dube, *The Kamar* (Lucknow: Universal, 1951).

41. Interview with Bhuvanlal Mishra, Raipur, 5 September 1988.

42. Lachi, Isaipara to Sunderlal Sharma, Rajim, 16 June 1928, Sunderlal Sharma Papers, Rajim.

43. M. M. Paul, *Satyanami Panth aur Shri Gosain Ghasidas Girodvasi,* p. i.

44. Ibid.

45. Ibid. On the conflation of the identities of *satnampurush* and Ghasidas in the Satnami oral tradition, see Dube, "Myths, symbols and community: Satnampanth of Chhattisgarh," in Partha Chatterjee and Gyan Pandey (eds.), *Subaltern Studies VII,* pp. 139–40.

46. Ibid., pp. 1–2.
47. Ibid., p. 2.
48. Ibid., pp. 2–4.
49. Ibid., pp. 4–5.
50. Ibid., pp. 6–7.
51. Ibid., pp. 7–9.
52. Ibid., p. 9.
53. Ibid., p. 10.
54. Ibid.
55. Ibid., p. 17.
56. Ibid., pp. 17–18.
57. Ibid., p. 19.
58. Ibid., pp. 19–23.
59. M. M. Paul, Annual Report, Pithora, 1935–36, p. 2 ; M. M. Paul, Annual Report, Pithora, 1938–39, p. 3, ARM, EAL.
60. The number of tracts sold in the years that followed tended to remain constant. M. M. Paul, Annual Reports, Pithora 1939–40, p. 11; 1940–41, p. 5; 1942, p. 5, ARM, EAL.
61. M. M. Paul, Annual Report, Pithora 1938–39, p. 3, ARM, EAL.
62. *Satnam Panth Darshak* (Allahabad, 1933).
63. Ibid., pp. 1–3.
64. Ibid., pp. 3–10.
65. The missionary, M. P. Davis, added: "It would be impossible to give you a complete idea of the beauty and power of his lyrical presentations. Even the most perfect and complete translation would convey but a fraction of it. Their full significance can only be apprehended by one who understands the Chhattisgarhi language and feels the spirit behind the presentations." Davis, "The Gospel in a Chhattisgarhi garb," Typescript, 1929, p. 4, MPDP, EAL. Joseph D. Graber, Dhamtari to W. M. Anderson, General Secretary, The Mission to Lepers, 27 December 1930, Dhamtari files, Leprosy Mission Archives, London; C. D. Esch, Superintendent, Shantipur Leper Home to W. M. Anderson, General Secretary, The Mission to Lepers, 5 January 1927, Dhamtari files, Leprosy Mission Archives, London.
66. M. M. Paul, Annual Report, Pithora, 1935–36, p. 1, ARM, EAL.
67. M. M. Paul, Annual Report, Pithora, 1936–37, p. 2, ARM, EAL.
68. M. M. Paul, Annual Report, Pithora, 1937–38, p. 2, ARM, EAL.
69. "A study of Christian descendants from Chamars and Satnamis" (hand-written and typed note), 1943, p. 3, FS, MPDP, EAL.
70. On the social relationship between the spoken and the written word framing the self-consciousness of the community, see, for instance, Michael Taussig, *Shamanism, Colonialism and the Wild Man: A Study in Terror and Healing* (Chicago: University of Chicago Press, 1987), pp. 33–35.

Chapter 8. Conclusion

1. Guha (ed.), *Subaltern Studies I–VI*.
2. Guha, *Elementary Aspects*.
3. Ranajit Guha, "Dominance without hegemony and its historiography" in Guha (ed.), *Subaltern Studies VI*, pp. 210–309; and "Discipline and mobilize" in Chatterjee and Pandey (eds.), *Subaltern Studies VII*, p. 69.
4. Dipesh Chakrabarty, *Rethinking Working-Class History: Bengal 1890–1940* (Delhi: Oxford University Press, 1989), pp. xii, 69, and passim.
5. Gyanendra Pandey, *Construction of Communalism*, p. 109, and passim.
6. Sandria B. Freitag, *Collective Action and Community*, p. 6, and passim.
7. Chatterjee, *Nation and Its Fragments*.
8. Ibid., p. 237.
9. Ibid., pp. 237–38.
10. Chakrabarty, "Colonial modernity," p. 84.
11. See, for instance, the literature on caste associations and movements, discussed in the Introduction and chapter 6.
12. Quigley, *Interpretation of Caste*, p. 169.
13. See J. P. S. Uberoi, "Five Symbols of Sikh Identity" in T. N. Madan (ed.), *Religion in India: Oxford Readings in Sociology and Social Anthropology* (Delhi: Oxford University Press, 1991), p. 326.
14. Arjun Appadurai, "The past as a scarce resource," *Man* (n.s.), 16, (1981), pp. 187–211.
15. Renato Rosaldo, *Ilongot Headhunting 1883–1974: A Study in Society and History* (Stanford: Stanford University Press, 1980).
16. This discussion owes much to Comaroff and Comaroff, *Ethnography and the Historical Imagination*.

BIBLIOGRAPHY

Oral Testimonies

Instead of listing the numerous oral informants whose testimonies have been rehearsed in this book, I provide a very brief note on my field work in Chhattisgarh between November 1989 and April 1990. I was based a few miles outside Bilaspur city and travelled to villages situated at a distance of two to forty kilometres from there. The main reason behind the selection of the region was the presence of a mix of Suryavanshi (Kanaujia Chamar) and Satnami villages in the area. It soon turned out that the two groups constitute strictly endogamous subcastes. During field work I collected—wrote and (tape) recorded—Satnami myths and the remembered history of the Satnami Mahasabha and *gaonthia zamana* embodied in the oral accounts of older Satnami men and women and *mahants* and *bhandaris*, attended Satnami life-cycle rituals and ceremonies, and observed and discussed their everyday transactions with other castes within the village. I also met Kabirpanthis of different castes and Suryavanshi (Chamar) families and sought their responses on questions I had put to the Satnamis. In March and April 1990 I discussed in detail the norms and processes centering on disputes and their settlement in village life: the discussions with members of different castes—including Brahmans, Rawats, Satnamis, and Gonds—raised several issues of inter- and intracaste transactions and allowed myself to reflect upon the material I had already collected. Finally, I attended a large Satnami *mela* (fair), a four-day affair, at Girod in early March 1990, which provided me with valuable oral testimonies. In the field I used a tape recorder only after the villagers had become familiar with me and did not object to the machine, otherwise I relied on notes, which were rewritten in my field journal. The journal and a set of cards indexed the tapes, which were transcribed later.

In addition, I had earlier carried out more structured interviews with older upper-caste nationalists, the present-day Satnami guru, and other politicians and leaders of the community, and later, while conducting field work on another project—on the "Evangelical Encounter in Central India"—between November 1994 and January 1995 and in March 1996, whenever possible, I took up some of the key questions discussed in this book.

Unpublished Records

Government Records

Madhya Pradesh Record Office, Nagpur

Nagpur Residency Records.
Nagpur Residency and Secretariat Records.
General Department Compilations.
Revenue Department Records.

Madhya Pradesh Secretariat Record Room, Bhopal

Central Provinces Government Survey and Settlement Department Records.
Central Provinces Government General Administration Department Records.
Central Provinces Government Agriculture Department Records.
Central Provinces Government Commerce and Industry Department Records.
Central Provinces Government Political and Military Department Records.
Central Provinces Government Political and Military Department, Confindetial Records.
Central Provinces Government Revenue Department Records.

Bilaspur Collectorate Record Room, Bilaspur

Bilaspur District Village Settlement Records.

Raipur District and Sessions Court Record Room, Raipur

Bilaspur District Sessions Trial Cases.

National Archives of India, New Delhi

Foreign Department Political Consultations.

Private Papers

Baba Ramchandra Papers, First Installment, Nehru Memorial Museum and Library, New Delhi.
Sunderlal Sharma Papers held by Bhuvanlal Mishra, Rajim.

M. P. Davis Papers, Eden Archives and Library, Webster Groves.

Other Collections

Eden Archives and Library, Webster Groves, Missouri

Annual Reports of missionaries by name of station and missionary, 1868–1883 (bound volumes), 1883–1956.
Quarterly Reports of missionaries by name of station and missionary, 1905–1956.
Baptismal Register, Bisrampur, 1870–1895.
Manuscript histories of the mission and mission stations.
Manuscript biographies and autobiographies of missionaries.

Library of the Royal Asiatic Society, London

Manuscript of *Satnam Sahai Pothi Giyan Bani Sadh Satnami*.

Leprosy Mission Archives, London

Dhamtari files.

Official Government Publications

Census of Central Provinces 1866, Nagpur, 1867.
Census of Central Provinces 1881, Bombay, 1883.
Census of India 1891, vol. XI, Calcutta, 1893.
Census of India 1901, vol. XIII, Nagpur, 1902.
Census of India 1911, vol.X, Calcutta, 1912.
Census of India 1931, vol. XII, Nagpur, 1933.

Central Provinces Gazetteer, Charles Grant (Bombay, 1870).
Central Provinces District Gazetteers, Bilaspur District, A. E. Nelson (Allahabad, 1910).
Central Provinces District Gazetteers, Raipur District, A. E. Nelson (Bombay, 1909).
Madhya Pradesh District Gazetteers, Bilaspur, P. N. Shrivastava (Indore, 1978).
Madhya Pradesh District Gazetteers, Raipur, Rajendra Verma (Bhopal, 1978).

Report on the Land Revenue Settlement of the Belaspore District, 1868, J. W. Chisholm (Nagpur, 1869).

Report on the Land Revenue Settlement of the Raepore District, 1869, J. F. K. Hewitt (Nagpur, 1896).
Report on the Land Revenue Settlement of Bilaspur District, 1886 to 1890, Parshotum Das (Nagpur, 1892).
Report on the Land Revenue Settlement of the Raipur District, 1885 to 1889, L. S. Carey (Bombay, 1891).
Report on the Land Revenue Settlement of Durg Tahsil, 1896 to 1902, E. R. K. Blenkinshop (Nagpur, 1903).
Report on the Land Revenue Settlement of Bilaspur (Khalsa), 1904–1912, J. E. Hance (Nagpur, 1914).
Final Report on the Revision of the Land Revenue Settlement of Raipur District (Khalsa), 1926 to 1931, C. D. Deshmukh (Nagpur, 1932).
Final Report on the Resettlement of the Khalsa of the Bilaspur District, 1927–1932, Chhotelal Verma (Nagpur, 1932).

Agnew, Patrick Vans, *A Report on the Subah or Province of Chhattisgarh Written in 1820 AD* (Nagpur, 1922).
Central Provinces Ethnographic Survey XVII, Draft Articles on Hindustani Castes, First Series (Nagpur, 1914).
Central Provinces Provincial Banking Enquiry Committee Report, 4 vols. (Nagpur, 1930).
Craddock, R. H., *Report on the Famine in the Central Province in 1896 and 1897,* vol. I (Nagpur, 1898).
Dubey, K. C., *Kosa: A Village Survey, Census of India 1961,* vol. 8 Madhya Pradesh, Part 6, Village Survey Monographs no. 9 (Bhopal, 1967).
Dyer, J. F., *Introduction to the Revenue and Settlement System of the Central Provinces* (Nagpur, 1956).
Fuller, J. B., *Enquiry into the Condition of the Lower Classes in C.P.* (London, 1885).
Report of the Ethnological Committee, 1866–1867 (Nagpur, 1867).
Report of the Administration of the Central Provinces. Annual Series.
Report on the Police Administration of the Central Provinces. Annual Series.

Newspapers and Journals

The Hitavada
Der Deutsche Missionsfreund (1866–1905).
Der Friedensbote (select issues).
Evangelical Herald, St. Louis, Mo. (select issues).

Vernacular Tracts

Bisrampur Kalasiya ki Vishesh Agyayen (Bisrampur, 1890).
Paul, M. M., *Satyanami Panth aur Ghasidas Girodvasi* (Raipur, 1936).
Santdas, *Sankshipt Satnam Sagar, Bhag 1, Itihas* (Raipur, 1929).
Satnam Panth Darshak (Allahabad, 1933).

Books and Articles

Ahmed, Rafiuddin. *The Bengal Muslims: A Quest for Identity* (Delhi: Oxford University Press, 1981).

Amin, Shahid. Gandhi as Mahatma: Gorakhpur District, Eastern U.P., 1921–22, in Ranajit Guha (ed.), *Subaltern Studies III: Writings on South Asian History and Society* (Delhi: Oxford University Press, 1984), 1–55.

———. *Event, Metaphor, Memory: Chauri Chaura 1922–1992* (Berkeley and Los Angeles: University of California Press, 1995).

Appadurai, Arjun. The past as a scarce resource. *Man* (n.s.), 16 (1981), 187–211.

———. *Worship and Conflict under Colonial Rule: A South Indian Case* (Cambridge: Cambridge University Press, 1981).

Arnold, David, and David Hardiman (eds.). *Subaltern Studies VIII: Writings on South Asian History and Society* (Delhi: Oxford University Press, 1994).

Babb, Lawrence. The Satnamis—Political involvement of a religious movement, in Michael J. Mahar (ed.), *The Untouchables in Contemporary India* (Tuscon: University of Arizona Press, 1972), pp. 143–51.

———. *The Divine Hierarchy: Popular Hinduism in Central India* (New York and London: Columbia University Press, 1975).

———. *Redemptive Encounters: Three Modern Styles in the Hindu Tradition* (Delhi: Oxford University Press, 1987).

Badley, B. H., Jagjivandas the Hindu reformer. *The Indian Antiquary*, 8 (1879), 289–92.

Baker, D. E. U. *Changing Political Leadership in an Indian Province: The Central Provinces and Berar 1919–1939* (Delhi: Oxford University Press, 1979).

Barrier, N. G. (ed.). *The Census in British India: New Perspectives* (New Delhi: Manohar, 1981).

Bayly, C. A. *Indian Society and the Making of the British Empire: The New Cambridge History of India* II. 1(Cambridge: Cambridge University Press, 1988).

Bayly, Susan. *Saints, Goddesses and Kings: Muslims and Christians in South Indian Society 1700–1900* (Cambridge: Cambridge University Press, 1989).

Biersack, Aletta. *Clio in Oceania: Toward a Historical Anthropology* (Washington: Smithsonian Institution Press, 1991).

Bose, P. N., Chhattisgar: Notes on its tribes, sects and castes. *Journal of the Asiatic Society of Bengal*, 59 (1891), 269–300.

Bourdieu, Pierre. *Outline of a Theory of Practice*. Trans. Richard Nice (Cambridge: Cambridge University Press, 1977).

Brass, Paul. *Language, Religion and Politics in North India* (New York: Cambridge University Press, 1974).

Burghart, Richard. The founding of the Ramanandi sect. *Ethnohistory*, 25 (1978), 121–39.

———. The disappearance and reappearance of Janakpur. *Kailash*, 6 (1978), 257–84.

———. Renunciation in the religious traditions of south Asia. *Man* (n.s.), 18 (1983), 635–53.

Certeau, Michel de. *The Practice of Everyday Life*. Trans. Steven Rendall (Berkeley and Los Angeles: University of California Press, 1984).

Chakrabarty, Dipesh. *Rethinking Working-Class History: Bengal 1890–1940* (Delhi: Oxford University Press, 1989).

———. Post-coloniality and the artifice of history: Who speaks for "Indian" pasts?. *Representations*, 37 Winter (1992), 1–26.

———. The difference-deferral of a colonial modernity: Public debates on domesticity in British India, in David Arnold and David Hardiman (eds.), *Subaltern Studies VIII: Writings on South Asian History and Society* (Delhi: Oxford University Press, 1994), 50–88.

Chatterjee, Partha. *The Nation and Its Fragments: Colonial and Postcolonial Histories* (Delhi: Oxford University Press, 1994).

———. Claims on the Past: The genealogy of modern historiography in Bengal, in David Arnold and David Hardiman (eds.), *Subaltern Studies VIII: Writings on South Asian History and Society* (Delhi: Oxford University Press, 1994), 1–49.

Chatterjee, Partha, and Gyan Pandey (eds.). *Subaltern Studies VII: Writings on South Asian History and Society* (Delhi: Oxford University Press, 1992).

Cohn, Bernard. The changing status of a depressed caste, in *An Anthropologist among the Historians and Other Essays* (Delhi: Oxford University Press, 1987), 255–83.

———. The changing traditions of a low caste, in *An Anthropologist among the Historians and Other Essays* (Delhi: Oxford University Press, 1987), 284–98.

———. *An Anthropologist among the Historians and Other Essays* (Delhi: Oxford University Press, 1987).

Collier, Jane, and Sylvia Yanagisako (eds.). *Gender and Kinship: Essays toward a Unified Analysis* (Stanford: Stanford University Press, 1987).

Comaroff, Jean. *Body of Power, Spirit of Resistance: The Culture and History of a South African People* (Chicago: University of Chicago Press, 1985).

Comaroff, Jean, and John Comaroff. Christianity and colonialism. *American Ethnologist*, 13 (1986), 1–22.

Comaroff, John, and Jean Comaroff. *Ethnography and the Historical Imagination* (Boulder: Westview, 1992).

Das, Veena. *Structure and Cognition: Aspects of Hindu Caste and Ritual* (Delhi: Oxford University Press, 1977).

———. Subaltern as perspective, in Ranajit Guha (ed.), *Subaltern Studies VI: Writings on South Asian History and Society* (Delhi: Oxford University Press, 1989), 310–24.

———. *Critical Events: An Anthropological Perspective on Contemporary India* (Delhi: Oxford University Press, 1995).

David, Kenneth. Hierarchy and equivalence in Jaffna, North Sri Lanka: Normative code as mediator, in Kenneth David (ed.), *The New Wind: Changing Identities in South Asia* (The Hague: Mouton, 1977), 179–226.

Dirks, Nicholas B. *The Hollow Crown: Ethnohistory of an Indian Kingdom* (Cambridge: Cambridge University Press, 1987).

———. The original caste: Power, history and hierarchy in South Asia. *Contributions to Indian Sociology* (n.s.), 23 (1989), 59–77.

———. (ed.). *Colonialism and Culture* (Ann Arbor: University of Michigan Press, 1992).

Doniger, Wendy. Hinduism by any other name. *Wilson Quarterly*, 15, 3 (1991), 35–41.

———. Begetting on margin: Adultery and surrogate pseudomarriage in Hinduism, in Lindsey Harlan and Paul Courtright (eds.), *From the Margins of Hindu Marriage: Essays on Gender, Religion, and Culture* (New York: Oxford University Press, 1975), 160–83.

Dube, Leela. Seed and earth: The symbolism of biological reproduction and sexual relations of production, in Leela Dube, Eleanor Leacock, and Shirley Ardener (eds.), *Visibility and Power: Essays on Women in Society and Development* (Delhi: Oxford University Press, 1986), 22–53.

———. On the construction of gender: Hindu girls in patrilineal India. *Economic and Political Weekly*, 23 (1988), (ws) 11–19.

———. Caste and women, in M. N. Srinivas (ed.), *Caste: Its Twentieth-Century Avatar* (New Delhi: Viking Penguin, 1996).

———. *Women and Kinship: Comparative Perspectives on Gender in South and South-East Asia* (Tokyo: United Nations University Press, 1997)

Dube, Leela, and Saurabh Dube. Women, religion and the category of "politics." *Journal of Social Studies*, 37 (1987), 72–80.

Dube, Saurabh. Peasant insurgency and peasant consciousness. *Economic and Political Weekly*, 20 (1985), 446–48.

———. Myths, symbols and community: Satnampanth of Chhattisgarh, in Partha Chatterjee and Gyan Pandey (eds.), *Subaltern Studies VII: Writings on South Asian History and Society* (Delhi: Oxford University Press, 1992), 121–56.

———. Issues of Christianity in Colonial Chhattisgarh. *Sociological Bulletin*, 41 (1992), 37–63.

———. Idioms of authority and engendered agendas: The Satnami Mahasabha, Chhattisgarh, 1925–50. *The Indian Economic and Social History Review*, 30 (1993), 383–411.

———. Paternalism and freedom: The evangelical encounter in colonial Chhattisgarh, central India. *Modern Asian Studies*, 29 (1995), 171–201.

———. Colonial law and village disputes: Two cases from Chhattisgarh, in N. Jayaram and Satish Saberwal (eds.), *Social Conflict: Oxford Readings in Sociology and Social Anthropology* (Delhi: Oxford University Press, 1996), 423–44.

———. Telling tales and trying truths: Transgressions, entitlements and legalities in late colonial central India. *Studies in History*, 12 (1996), 171–201.

———. India: Historias desde abajo. *Estudios de Asia y Africa*, 32 (1997), forthcoming.

———. Histories from below in India, in Saurabh Dube, *Historical Cultures, Ethnographic Pasts*, manuscript, n.d.

———. (ed.). *Everyday Encounters: A Diary of an Indigenous Christianity*, manuscript, n.d.

Dube, S. C. *Field Songs of Chhattisgarh* (Lucknow: Universal, 1947).

———. *The Kamar* (Lucknow: Universal, 1951).

Dumont, Louis. *Homo Hierarchicus: The Caste System and Its Implications* (London: Weidenfeld and Nicolson, 1970).

———. World renunciation in Indian religions, in *Religion/Politics and History in India: Collected Papers in Indian Sociology* (Paris and The Hague: Mouton, 1970), 33–60.

Eaton, Richard. Conversion to Christianity among the Nagas, 1876–1971. *Indian Economic and Social History Review*, 21 (1984), 1–44.

Flueckiger, Joyce Burkhalter. Genre and community in the folklore system of Chhattisgarh, in Arjun Appadurai, Frank J. Korom, and Margaret A. Mills (eds.), *Gender, Genre, and Power in South Asian Expressive Traditions* (Philadelphia: University of Pennsylvania Press, 1991), 181–200.

———. *Gender and Genre in the Folklore of Middle India* (Ithaca: Cornell University Press, 1996).

Foucault, Michel. *Power/Knowledge: Selected Interviews and Other Writings,* 1972–77. Trans. Colin Gordon et al. (New York: Pantheon, 1980).

————. Politics and reason, in M. Foucault, *Politics, Philosophy, Culture: Interviews and Other Writings 1977–1984.* Trans. Alan Sheridan et al. (New York: Routledge, 1988), 57–85.

————. Governmentality, in Graham Burcell, Colin Gordon, and Peter Mills (eds.), *The Foucault Effect: Studies in Governmentality* (Chicago: University of Chicago Press, 1992), 87–104.

Freeman, James M. *Untouchable: An Indian Life History* (Stanford: Stanford University Press, 1979).

Freitag, Sandria B. *Collective Action and Community: Public Arenas and the Emergence of Communalism in North India* (Delhi: Oxford University Press, 1990).

Fukuzawa, Hiroshi. The state and the caste system (jati), in Fukuzawa, *The Medieval Deccan: Peasants, Social Systems and States: Sixteenth to Eighteenth Centuries* (Delhi: Oxford University Press, 1991), 91–113.

Fuller, C. J. *The Camphor Flame: Popular Hinduism and Society in India* (Princeton: Princeton University Press, 1992).

Gordon, E. M. *Indian Folk-tales: Being Sidelights on Village Life in Bilaspore, Central Provinces* (London: Elliot Stock, 1908).

Gordon, Stewart. The slow conquest: Administrative integration of Malwa into the Maratha empire, 1720–1760. *Modern Asian Studies,* 11 (1977), 1–40.

————. *Marathas, Marauders, and State Formation in Eighteenth-Century India* (Delhi: Oxford University Press, 1994).

————. *The Marathas: 1600–1818: The New Cambridge History of India* II.3 (Cambridge: Cambridge University Press, 1993).

————. Role of resistance in the shaping of indigenous Maratha kingdoms, unpublished paper, n.d.

Guha, Ranajit. *Elementary Aspects of Peasant Insurgency in Colonial India* (Delhi: Oxford University Press, 1983).

————. Dominance without hegemony and its historiography, in Guha (ed.), *Subaltern Studies VI: Writings on South Asian History and Society* (Delhi: Oxford University Press, 1989), 210–309.

————. Discipline and mobilize, in Partha Chatterjee and Gyan Pandey (eds.), *Subaltern Studies VII: Writings on South Asian History and Society* (Delhi: Oxford University Press, 1992), 69–120.

————. (ed.). *Subaltern Studies: Writings on South Asian History and Society,* vols. I–VI (Delhi: Oxford University Press, 1982–89).

Habib, Irfan. *The Agrarian System of Mughal India* (London: Asia Publishing House, 1963).

Hardgrave, Robert L. *The Nadars of Tamilnad: The Political Culture of a Community in Change* (Berkeley and Los Angeles: University of California Press, 1969).

Hardiman, David. *The Coming of the Devi: Adivasi Assertion in Western India* (Delhi: Oxford University Press, 1987).

Hardy, Peter. *The Muslims of British India* (Cambridge: Cambridge University Press, 1972).

Harlan, Lindsey, and Paul B. Courtright (eds.). *From the Margins of Hindu Marriage: Essays on Gender, Religion, and Culture* (New York: Oxford University Press, 1995).

Harper, E. B. Ritual pollution as an integrator of caste and religion. *Journal of Asian Studies*, 23 (1964), 151–97.

Hawley, J. S. Naming Hinduism. *Wilson Quarterly*, 15, 3 (1991), 20–34.

Haynes, Douglas, and Gyan Prakash (eds.). *Contesting Power: Resistance and Everyday Social Relations in South Asia* (Delhi: Oxford University Press, 1991).

Herzfeld, Michael. *Anthropology Through the Looking Glass: Critical Ethnography in the Margins of Europe* (Cambridge: Cambridge University Press, 1987)

Hill, Jonathan (ed.). *Rethinking History and Myth: Indigenous South American Perspectives on the Past* (Urbana and Chicago: University of Illinois Press, 1988).

Hiltebeitel, Alf. *The Cult of Draupadi*, vol. 1, *Mythologies: From Ginjee to Kurukshetra* (Chicago: University of Chicago Press, 1988).

———. *The Cult of Draupadi*, vol. 2, *On Hindu Ritual and the Goddess* (Chicago: University of Chicago Press, 1991).

———. Of camphor and coconuts. *Wilson Quarterly*, 15, 3 (1991), 26–28.

Hudson, Dennis. The first Protestant mission to India: Its social and religious development. *Sociological Bulletin*, 42 (1993), 37–63.

Irschick, Eugene. *Politics and Social Conflict in South India: The Non-Brahman Movement and Tamil Separatism 1916–1929* (Berkeley and Los Angeles: University of California Press, 1969).

Jay, Edward. Bridging the gap between castes: Ceremonial friendship in Chhattisgarh. *Contributions to Indian Sociology* (n.s.), 7 (1973), 144–58.

Jones, Kenneth W. *Arya Dharma: Hindu Consciousness in Nineteenth-Century Punjab* (Berkeley and Los Angeles: University of California Press, 1976).

Jordens, J. T. F. *Dayananda Saraswati: His Life and Times* (Delhi: Oxford University Press, 1978).

Juergensmeyer, Mark. *Religion as Social Vision: The Movement against Untouchability in Twentieth-Century Punjab* (Berkeley and Los Angeles: University of California Press, 1982).

Juhnke, J. C. *A People of Mission: A History of General Conference Mennonite Overseas Mission* (Newton: Faith and Life Press, 1979).

Kavyopadhyaya, Hiralal. A grammar of the dialect of Chhattisgarh in the Central Provinces (trans. and ed. George A. Grierson), *Journal of the Asiatic Society of Bengal*, LIX, part 1 (1890), 101–53.

Keer, Dhananjay. *Dr. Ambedkar: Life and Mission* (Bombay: Popular Prakashan, 1962).

Kelly, John D. *A Politics of Virtue: Hinduism, Sexuality, and Countercolonial Discourse in Fiji* (Chicago: University of Chicago Press, 1991).

Khare, R. S. *The Untouchable as Himself: Ideology, Identity, and Pragmatism among the Lucknow Chamars* (Cambridge: Cambridge University Press, 1984).

Kolenda, Pauline. *Regional Differences in Family Structure in India* (Jaipur: Rawat, 1987).

Krause, I.-B. Caste and labour relations in North West Nepal. *Ethnos*, 53 (1988), 5–36.

Kumar, Kapil. *Peasants in Revolt: Tenants, Landlords, Congress and the Raj in Oudh 1886–1922* (New Delhi: Manohar, 1984).

———. Using the Ramacharitamanas as a radical text: Baba Ramchandra in Oudh, 1920–50, in Sudhir Chandra (ed.), *Social Transformations and Creative Imagination* (Delhi: Allied, 1984), 311–34.

———. Rural women in Oudh 1917–1947: Baba Ramchandra and the Women's Question, in Kumkum Sangari and Sudesh Vaid (eds.), *Recasting Women: Essays in Colonial History* (New Delhi: Kali for Women, 1989), 337–69.

Kunte, B. G. (ed.). *Source Material on Dr. Babasaheb Ambedkar and the Movement of Untouchables*, vol. I (Bombay: Popular Prakashan, 1982).

Lapp, J. A. *The Mennonite Church in India* (Scottdale: Herald Press, 1972).

Lelyveld, David. *Aligarh's First Generation: Muslim Solidarity in British India* (Princeton: Princeton University Press, 1978).

Lerche, Jens. Dominant castes, rajas, Brahmins and inter–caste exchange relations in coastal Orissa: Behind the facade of the *"jajmani* system," *Contributions to Indian Sociology* (n.s.), 27 (1993), 237–66.

Levi-Strauss, Claude. *The Savage Mind* (London: Weidenfeld and Nicolson, 1966).

Lohr, J. J. *Bilder aus Chhattisgarh und den Central Provinzen Ostindiens* (place of publication not given, 1899).

Lorenzen, David. Kabirpanth and social protest, in Karin Schomer and W. H. McLeod (eds.), *The Sants: Studies in a Devotional Tradition of India* (Delhi: Motilal Banarsidas, 1987), 281–303.

———. Traditions of non-caste Hinduism: The Kabirpanth. *Contributions to Indian Sociology* (n.s.), 21 (1987), 263–83.

———. Introduction: The historical vicissitudes of Bhakti religion, in David Lorenzen (ed.), *Bhakti Religion in North India: Community Identity and Political Action* (Albany: SUNY Press, 1994), 1–32.

Lynch, Owen M. *The Politics of Untouchability* (New York: Columbia University Press, 1969).

Mani, Lata. Contentious traditions: The debate on sati in colonial India, in Kumkum Sangari and Sudesh Vaid (eds.), *Recasting Women: Essays in Colonial History* (New Delhi: Kali for Women, 1989), 88–126.

Marglin, F. A. *Wives of the God King: The Rituals of the Devadasis of Puri* (Delhi: Oxford University Press, 1985).

McLeod, W. H., On the word panth: A problem of definition and terminology. *Contributions to Indian Sociology* (n.s.), 12 (1978), 287–95.

Metcalf, Barbara. *Islamic Revival in British India: Deoband 1860–1900* (Princeton: Princeton University Press, 1982).

Moffatt, Michael. *An Untouchable Community in South India: Structure and Consensus* (Princeton: Princeton University Press, 1979).

Oberoi, Harjot. *The Construction of Religious Boundaries: Culture, Identity, and Diversity in the Sikh Tradition* (Chicago: University of Chicago Press, 1994).

Obeyesekere, Gananath. *The Cult of the Goddess Pattini* (Chicago: University of Chicago Press, 1983).

O'Hanlon, Rosalind. *Caste, Conflict and Ideology: Mahatma Jotirao Phule and Low-Caste Protest in Nineteenth-Century Western India* (Cambridge: Cambridge University Press, 1985).

———. Issues of widowhood: Gender and resistance in colonial western India, in Douglas Haynes and Gyan Prakash (eds.), *Contesting Power: Resistance and Everyday Social Relations in South Asia* (Delhi: Oxford University Press, 1991), 62–108.

Ohnuki-Tierney, Emiko (ed.). *Culture through Time: Anthropological Approaches* (Stanford: Stanford University Press, 1990).

Omvedt, Gail. *Cultural Revolt in a Colonial Society: The Non-Brahman Movement in Western India 1870–1930* (Bombay: Scientific Socialist Education Trust, 1976).

Ong, Walter J. *Marantha*: Death and life in the text of the book. *Journal of the American Academy of Religion*, 45 (1977), 419–49.

———. *Orality and Literacy: The Technologizing of the Word* (London and New York: Methuen, 1982).

Ortner, Sherry B. Resistance and the problem of ethnographic refusal. *Comparitive Studies in Society and History*, 37 (1995), 173–93.

Ossio, Juan. Myth and History: The seventeenth-century chronicle of Guaman Poma de Ayala, in Ravindra K. Jain (ed.), *Text and Context: The Social Anthropology of Tradition* (Philadelphia: ISHI, 1977), 51–93.

Pandey, Gyan. Peasant revolt and Indian nationalism: The peasant movement in Awadh, 1919–22, in Ranajit Guha (ed.), *Subaltern Studies I: Writings on South Asian History and Society* (Delhi: Oxford University Press, 1982), 143–97.

———. *The Construction of Communalism in Colonial North India* (Delhi: Oxford University Press, 1990).

Pollock, Sheldon. Ramayana and political imagination in India. *Journal of Asian Studies*, 52 (1993), 261–97.

Prakash, Gyan. *Bonded Histories: Genealogies of Labour Servitude in Colonial India* (Cambridge: Cambridge University Press, 1990).

———. Becoming a Bhuinya: Oral traditions and contested domination in eastern India, in Douglas Haynes and Gyan Prakash (eds.), *Contesting Power: Resistance and Everyday Social Relations in South Asia* (Delhi: Oxford University Press, 1991), 145–74.

Prins, Gwyn. *The Hidden Hippopotamus: Reappraisals in African History* (Cambridge: Cambridge University Press, 1980).

Quigley, Declan. *The Interpretation of Caste* (Oxford: Clarendon Press, 1993).

Raheja, Gloria Goodwin. *The Poison in the Gift: Ritual, Prestation, and the Dominant Caste in a North Indian Village* (Chicago: University of Chicago Press, 1988).

———. Centrality, mutuality and hierarchy: Shifting aspects of inter-caste relationships in north India. *Contributions to Indian Sociology* (n.s.), 23 (1989), 79–101.

———. "Crying when she is born, and crying when she goes away": Marriage and the idiom of the gift in Pahansu song performance, in Lindsey Harlan and Paul Courtright (eds.), *From the Margins of Hindu Marriage: Essays on Gender, Religion, and Culture* (New York: Oxford University Press, 1995), 19–59.

Raheja, Gloria Goodwin, and Ann Gold. *Listen to the Heron's Words: Reimagining Gender and Kinship in North India* (Berkeley and Los Angeles: University of California Press, 1994).

Robinson, Rowena. Some neglected aspects of conversions of Goa: A sociohistorical perspective. *Sociological Bulletin*, 42 (1993), 65–83.

Rosaldo, Renato. *Ilongot Headhunting 1883–1974: A Study in Society and History* (Stanford: Stanford University Press, 1980).

Rudolph, Lloyd, and Susan Rudolph. *The Modernity of Tradition* (Chicago: Chicago University Press, 1967).

Rusell, R. V., and R. B. Hiralal. *The Tribes and Castes of the Central Provinces of India*, 4 vols. (London: Macmillan, 1916).

Sabean, David Warren. *Power in the Blood: Popular Culture and Village Discourse in Early Modern Germany* (Cambridge: Cambridge University Press, 1984).

————. *Property, Production, and Family in Neckerhausen, 1700–1870* (Cambridge: Cambridge University Press, 1990).

Sarkar, Sumit. The kalki avatar of Bikrampur: A village scandal in early twentieth-century Bengal, in Ranajit Guha (ed.), *Subaltern Studies VI: Writings on South Asian History and Society* (Delhi: Oxford University Press, 1989), 1–53.

Sax, William S. *Mountain Goddess: Gender and Politics in a Himalyan Pilgrimage* (New York: Oxford University Press, 1991).

Schaeffer, Jonathan D. The use and misuse of Giambattista Vico: Rhetoric, orality, and theories of discourse, in H. Aram Veeser (ed.), *The New Historicism* (New York and London: Routledge, 1989), 89–101.

Schama, Simon. *The Embarrasment of Riches: An Interpretation of Dutch Culture in the Golden Age* (New York: Alfred A. Knopf, 1988).

Scott, David. Conversion and demonism: Colonial Christian discourse on religion in Sri Lanka. *Comparative Studies in Society and History*, 34 (1992), 331–65.

Sen, K. M. *Mediaeval Mysticism of India* (London: Luzac, 1930).

Seybold, Theodore C. *God's Guiding Hand: A History of the Central Indian Mission 1868–1967* (Philadelphia: United Church Board for World Ministeries of the United Church of Christ, 1971).

Siddiqi, M. H. *Agrarian Unrest in North India: The United Provinces, 1918–22* (New Delhi: Manohar, 1978).

Sinha, Mrinalini. *Colonial Masculinity: The "Manly Englishman" and the "Effeminate Bengali" in the Late Nineteenth Century* (Manchester: Manchester University Press, 1995).

Smith, Brian K. *Reflections on Resemblance, Ritual and Religion* (New York, 1989).

Smith, Wilfred Cantwell. *The Meaning and End of Religion* (New York, 1964).

Srinivas, M. N. *Social Change in Modern India* (Berkeley and Los Angeles: University of California Press, 1966).

————. *Religion and Society among the Coorgs of South India* (Oxford: Oxford University Press, 1962).

Talbot, Cynthia. Inscribing the other, inscribing the self: Hindu-Muslim identities in pre-colonial India. *Comparative Studies in Society and History*, 37 (1995), 692–722.

Tambiah, Stanley J. Dowry and bridewealth and the property rights of women in South Asia, in Jack Goody and Stanley J. Tambiah, *Bridewealth and Dowry* (Cambridge: Cambridge University Press, 1973), 59–169.

————. From varna to caste through mixed unions, in Tambiah, *Culture, Thought, and Social Action: An Anthropological Perspective* (Cambridge, Mass., and London: Harvard University Press, 1985), 212–51.

Tanner, von Th. *Im Lande der Hindus oder Kulturschilderungen aus Indien* (St. Louis: The German Evangelical Synod of North America, 1894).

Taussig, Michael. *Shamanism, Colonialism, and the Wild Man: A Study in Terror and Healing* (Chicago: University of Chicago Press, 1987).

Trautmann, Thomas. *Dravidian Kinship* (Cambridge: Cambridge University Press, 1981).

Uberoi, J. P. S. Five Symbols of Sikh Identity, in T. N. Madan (ed.), *Religion in India: Oxford Readings in Sociology and Social Anthropology* (Delhi: Oxford University Press, 1991).

Unnithan-Kumar, Maya. Gender and "tribal" identity in western India. *Economic and Political Weekly*, 26 (1991), (ws) 36–39.

Van der Veer, Peter. *Gods on Earth: The Management of Religious Experience in a North Indian Pilgrimage Centre* (Delhi: Oxford University Press, 1988).

———. *Religious Nationalism: Hindus and Muslims in India* (Berkeley and Los Angeles: University of California Press, 1994).

Vatuk, Sylvia. Gifts and affines. *Contributions to Indian Sociology* (n.s.), 5 (1975), 155–96.

Vaudeville, Charlotte. Braj, lost and found. *Indo-Iranian Journal*, 18 (1976), 195–213.

Vincentnathan, Lynn. Untouchable concepts of person and society. *Contributions to Indian Sociology* (n.s.), 27 (1993), 53–82.

Volosinov, V. N. *Marxism and the Philosophy of Language*. Trans. Ladislav Matejka and I. R. Titunik (Cambridge, Mass.: Harvard University Press, 1984).

Washbrook, David. The development of caste organisations in south India, in Christopher Baker and David Washbrook (eds.), *South India: Political Institutions and Political Change, 1880–1940* (Meerut: Macmillan, 1975), 151–203.

Wills, C. U. The territorial system of the Rajput kingdoms of mediaeval Chhattisgarh. *Journal of the Asiatic Society of Bengal* (n.s.), 15 (1919), 197–260.

Wink, Andre. *Land and Sovereignty in India: Agrarian Society and Politics under the Eighteenth-Century Maratha Svarajya* (Cambridge: Cambridge University Press, 1986).

Zelliot, Eleanor. Learning the use of political means: The Mahars of Maharashtra, in Rajni Kothari (ed.), *Caste in Indian Politics* (New Delhi: Orient Longman, 1970), 29–69.

Unpublished Ph.D. Dissertations

Bates, Crispin. Regional dependence and rural development in central India 1820–1930, University of Cambridge, 1984.

McEldowney, P. F. Colonial Administration and social development in the C.P. 1861–1921, University of Virginia, 1980.

Thakur, B. S. Chhattisgarh mein Bhonsla rajya (1818–1854), University of Raipur, 1974.

INDEX